Thinking Through the Past

Thinking Through the Past

A Critical Thinking Approach to U.S. History

Volume II: Since 1865

FIFTH EDITION

John Hollitz

College of Southern Nevada

CENGAGE
Learning·

Australia • Brazil • Japan • Korea • Mexico • Singapore • Spain • United Kingdom • United States

CENGAGE
Learning·

Thinking Through the Past:
A Critical Thinking Approach to
U.S. History, Volume II
Fifth Edition
John Hollitz

Product Director: Suzanne Jeans

Product Manager: Ann West

Content Developer: Megan
  Chrisman

Product Assistant: Liz Fraser

Marketing Brand Manager: Melissa
  Larmon

Rights Acquisitions Specialist:
  Jennifer Meyer Dare

Manufacturing Planner: Sandee
  Milewski

Art and Design Direction,
  Production Management, and
  Composition: PreMediaGlobal

Cover Image: Smithsonian
  American Art Museum,
  Washington, DC / Art Resource,
  NY

For product information and technology assistance,
contact us at **Cengage Learning Customer & Sales**
Support, 1-800-354-9706

For permission to use material from this text or product,
submit all requests online at **www.cengage.com/permissions.**
Further permissions questions can be emailed to
permissionrequest@cengage.com.

Library of Congress Control Number: 2013952528

Student Edition:

ISBN-13: 978-1-285-42744-7

ISBN-10: 1-285-42744-0

Cengage Learning
200 First Stamford Place, 4th Floor
Stamford, CT 06902
USA

Cengage Learning is a leading provider of customized learning solutions with office locations around the globe, including Singapore, the United Kingdom, Australia, Mexico, Brazil and Japan.

Locate your local office at **international.cengage.com/region.**

Cengage Learning products are represented in Canada by Nelson Education, Ltd.

For your course and learning solutions, visit **www.cengage.com.**

Purchase any of our products at your local college store or at our preferred online store **www.cengagebrain.com.**

Instructors: Please visit **login.cengage.com** and log in to access instructor-specific resources.

Printed in the United States of America
1 2 3 4 5 6 7 17 16 15 14 13

Contents

3

Evaluating Primary Sources: "Saving" the Indians in the Late Nineteenth Century   49

4

Evaluating a Historical Argument:
American Manhood and Philippine Annexation 77

5

The Problem of Historical Motivation:
The Bungalow as the "Progressive" House 108

6

Ideology and History: Advertising in the 1920s   136

7

History "From the Top Down": Eleanor Roosevelt, First Lady   163

8

History "From the Bottom Up": The Detroit Race Riot and Los Angeles Zoot Suit Riots of 1943   191

9

Popular Culture as History: The Cold War Comes Home   221

10

History and Popular Memory: The Civil Rights Movement   247

11

Causation and the Lessons of History: Explaining America's Longest War   281

12

Gender, Ideology, and Historical Change: Explaining the Women's Movement   307

13

Why Historical Interpretation Matters:
The Battle over Immigration   343

Preface

The encouraging response to the fourth edition from students and instructors has prompted me to create a fifth edition of *Thinking Through the Past*. As before, this book is inspired by the idea that interpretation is at the heart of history. That is why learning about the past involves more than mastering facts and dates, and why historians often disagree. As teachers, we know the limitations of the deadly dates-and-facts approach to the past. We also know that encouraging students to think critically about historical sources and historians' arguments is a good way to create excitement about history and to impart understanding of what historians do. The purpose of *Thinking Through the Past,* therefore, is to introduce students to the examination and analysis of historical sources.

FORMAT

To encourage students to think critically about American history, *Thinking Through the Past* brings together primary and secondary sources. It gives students the opportunity to analyze primary sources *and* historians' arguments, and to use one to understand and evaluate the other. By evaluating and drawing conclusions from the sources, students will use the methods and develop some of the skills of critical thinking as they apply to history. Students will also learn about a variety of historical topics that parallel those in U.S. history courses. Unlike most anthologies or collections of primary sources, this book advances not only chronologically, but also pedagogically through different skill levels. It provides students the opportunity to work with primary sources in the early chapters before they evaluate secondary sources in later chapters or compare historians' arguments in the final chapters. Students are also able to build on the skills acquired in previous chapters by considering such questions as motivation, causation, and the role of ideas and economic interests in history.

At the same time, this book introduces a variety of approaches to the past. Topics in *Thinking Through the Past* include social, political, cultural, intellectual, economic, diplomatic, and military history. The chapters look at history "from the top down" and "from the bottom up." Thus students have the opportunity to evaluate history drawn from slave quarters as well as from state houses. In the process, they are exposed to the enormous range of sources that historians use to construct arguments. The primary sources in these volumes include portraits, photographs, maps, letters, fiction, music lyrics, laws, oral histories, speeches, movie posters, magazine and newspaper articles, cartoons, and architectural plans.

The chapters present the primary and secondary sources so students can pursue their own investigations of the material. Each chapter is divided into five parts: a brief introduction, which sets forth the problem in the chapter; the Setting, which provides background information pertaining to the topic; the Investigation, which asks students to answer a short set of questions revolving around the problem discussed in the introduction; the Sources, which in most chapters provide a secondary source and a set of primary sources related to the chapter's main problem; and, finally, a brief Conclusion, which offers a reminder of the chapter's main pedagogical goal and looks forward to the next chapter's problem.

CHANGES TO THE FIFTH EDITION

In the fifth edition, there are significantly revised chapters in both volumes on provocative topics that have been on the cutting edge of recent historical scholarship. These topics are intended to stimulate student interest in American history. In Volume I, chapters on the Constitution, the American West, and Andrew Jackson have been revised with the addition of new source material. As before, changes reflect more recent historical scholarship and have been designed with accessibility in mind. New primary source material in Chapter 8 reflects contemporary historical scholarship on the nineteenth-century American frontier, while Chapter 9 presents a new biographical assessment of young Andrew Jackson that introduces students to a "gambler" and "carouser" who matures into a "formidable leader of men." In Volume II, a significantly revised chapter on racial and ethnic unrest on the home front during World War II is intended to provide students with a broader historical context and to excite a broader mix of contemporary students. Overall, the volumes have been revised with an eye toward making the book a more engaging learning tool. To this end, many other chapters contain new sources that provide additional insights for students as they conduct their historical investigations.

ACKNOWLEDGMENTS

Many people contributed to this book, starting with my own students. Without them, of course, it never would have been created.

I owe many thanks to the people who assisted in various ways with the revisions for this edition. At the College of Southern Nevada, Inter-Library Loan librarian Marion Martin, as always, provided cheerful and invaluable assistance. Numerous colleagues around the country, including many instructors who have used the text over several editions, offered useful suggestions regarding revisions and chapter drafts. I am honored by their commitment to *Thinking Through the Past* and thank them for helping to make it a better book.

In particular, I'd like to thank the following individuals who reviewed the fifth edition: Guy Aronoff, Humboldt State University; Terrell Goddard, Northwest Vista College; Li Hongshan, Kent State University at Tuscarawas; Abigail Markwyn, Carroll University; Linda Mollno, Cal Poly Pomona; Craig Perrier, Fairfax County Public Schools; Emily Rader, El Camino College; Alicia Rodriquez, California State University, Bakersfield; Megan Seaholm, University of Texas at Austin; Rebecca Shrum, Indiana University Purdue University Indianapolis; Garth Swanson, Genesee Community College; and Wendy Wall, Binghamton University. The reviewers of the fourth edition were: Andy Ginette, University of Southern Indiana; Terrell Goddard, Northwest Vista College; Charlotte Haller, Worcester State College; Jeffrey Johnson, Augustana College; Jennifer Mata, University of Texas Pan American; Sean O'Neill, Grand Valley State University; Phillip Payne, St. Bonaventure University; and Timothy Thurber, Virginia Commonwealth University. The reviewers of the third edition were Michael D. Wilson, Vanguard University; David A. Canton, Georgia Southern University; Paivi Hoikkala, California State Polytechnic University at Pomona; Kathleen Kennedy, Western Washington University; Monroe H. Little, Jr., Indiana University-Purdue University at Indianapolis; Cathleen Schultz, University of St. Francis; Paul C. Rosier, Villanova University; Marsha L. Weisiger, New Mexico State University; and Katherine A. S. Sibley, St. Joseph's University.

I owe thanks to many others as well for their contribution to the previous editions. Alan Balboni, DeAnna Beachley, Michael Green, Charles Okeke, the late Gary Elliott, colleagues at the Community College of Southern Nevada, offered sources, reviewed portions of the manuscript, shared insights, or simply offered encouragement. Richard Cooper and Brad Nystrom at California State University, Sacramento, listened patiently and offered helpful suggestions at the initial stages of this project. As usual, however, my biggest debt is to Patty. For her enduring support and abiding love, this book is once again dedicated to her.

J. H.

Thinking Through the Past

Introduction

"History," said Henry Ford, "is more or less bunk." That view is still shared by many people. Protests about the subject are familiar. Studying history won't help you land a job. And, besides, what matters is not the past but the present.

Such protests are not necessarily wrong. Learning about ancient Greece, the French Revolution, or the Vietnam War will hardly guarantee employment, even though many employers evaluate job candidates on critical thinking skills that the study of history requires. Likewise, who can deny the importance of the present compared to the past? In many ways, the present and future are more important than the past. Pericles, Robespierre, and Lyndon Johnson are dead; presumably, anyone reading this is not.

Still, the logic behind the history-as-bunk view is flawed because all of us rely upon the past to understand the present, as did even Henry Ford. Besides building the Model T, he also built Greenfield Village outside Detroit because he wanted to re-create a nineteenth-century town. It was the kind of place the automotive genius grew up in and the kind of place he believed represented the ideal American society: small-town, white, native-born, and Protestant. Greenfield Village was Ford's answer to changes in the early twentieth century that were profoundly disturbing to him and to many other Americans of his generation: growing cities, the influx of non-Protestant immigrants, changing sexual morality, new roles and new fashions for women, and greater freedom for young people.

Ford's interest in the past, symbolized by Greenfield Village, reflects a double irony. It was the automobile that helped to make possible many of the changes, like those in sexual morality, that Ford detested. The other irony is that Ford used history—what he himself called "bunk"—to try to better the world. Without realizing it, he became a historian by turning to the past to explain to himself and others what he disliked about the present. Never mind that Ford blamed immigrants, especially Jews, for the changes he decried in crude, hate-filled tirades. The point is that Ford's view of America was rooted in a vision of the past, and his explanation for America's ills was based on historical analysis, however unprofessional and unsophisticated.

All of us use historical analysis all the time, even if, like Ford, we think we don't. In fact, we all share a fundamental assumption about learning from the past: One of the best ways to learn about something, to learn how it came to be, is to study its past. That assumption is so much a part of us that we are rarely conscious of it.

1

Think about the most recent time you met someone for the first time. As a way to get to know this new acquaintance you began to ask questions about his or her past. When you asked, "Where did you grow up?" or "How long have you lived in Chicago?" you were relying on information about the past to learn about the present. You were, in other words, thinking as a historian. You assumed that a cause-and-effect relationship existed between this person's past and his or her present personality, interests, and beliefs. Like a historian, you began to frame questions and to look for answers that would help to establish causal links.

Because we all use history to make sense of our world, it follows that we should become more skilled in the art of making sense of the past. Ford did it crudely, and ended up promoting the very things he despised. But how exactly do you begin to think more like a historian? For too many students, this challenge summons up images of studying for history exams: cramming names, dates, and facts, and hoping to retain some portion of this information long enough to get a passing grade. History seems like a confusing grab bag of facts and events. The historian's job, in this view, is to memorize as much "stuff" as possible. In this "flash-card" approach, history is reduced to an exercise in the pursuit of trivia, and thinking like a historian is nothing but an exercise in mnemonics—a system of improving the memory.

There is no question that the dates, events, and facts of history are important. Without basic factual knowledge historians could no more practice their craft than biologists, chemists, or astrophysicists could practice theirs. But history is not a static recollection of facts. Events in the past happened only once, but the historians who study those events are always changing their minds about them. Like all humans, historians have prejudices, biases, and beliefs. They are also influenced by events in their own times. In other words, they look at the past through lenses that filter and even distort. Events in the past may have happened only once, but what historians think about them, the meaning they give to those events, is constantly changing. Moreover, because their lenses perceive events differently, historians often disagree about the past. The supposedly "static" discipline of history is actually dynamic and charged with tension.

That brings us to the question of what historians really do. Briefly, historians ask questions about past events or developments and try to explain them. Just as much as biology, chemistry, or astrophysics, therefore, history is a problem-solving discipline. Historians, like scientists, sift evidence to answer questions. Like scientists, whose explanations for things often conflict, historians can ask the same questions, look at the same facts, and come up with different explanations because they look at the past in different ways. Or they may have entirely different questions in mind and so come away with very different "pasts." Thus history is a process of constant revision. As historians like to put it, every generation writes its own history.

But why bother to study and interpret the past in our own way if someone else will only revise it again in the future? The answer is sobering: If we don't

write our own history, someone else will write it for us. Who today would accept as historical truth the notion that the Indians were cruel savages whose
extermination was necessary to fulfill an Anglo-Saxon destiny to conquer the
continent for democracy and civilization? Who today would accept the "truth"
that slaves were racially inferior and happy with their lot on Southern plantations? If we accept these views of Indians and black slaves, we are allowing
nineteenth-century historians to determine our view of the past.

Instead, by reconstructing the past as best we can, we can better understand
our own times. Like the amnesia victim, without memory we face a bewildering world. As we recapture our collective past, the present becomes more
intelligible. Subject to new experiences, a later generation will view the past
differently. Realizing that future generations will revise history does not give us
a license to play fast and loose with the facts of history. Rather each generation
faces the choice of giving meaning to those facts or experiencing the confusion
of historical amnesia.

Finding meaning in the facts of the past, then, is the central challenge of history. It requires us to ask questions and construct explanations—mental activities far different and far more exciting than merely memorizing names, dates,
and facts. More important, it enables us to approach history as critical thinkers. The more skilled we become at historical reasoning, the better we will
understand our world and ourselves. Helping you to develop skill in historical
analysis is the purpose of this volume.

The method of this book reflects its purpose. The first chapter discusses textbooks. History texts have a very practical purpose. By bringing order to the
past, they give many students a useful and reassuring "handle" on history. But
they are not the Ten Commandments, because, like all works of history, they
also contain interpretations. To most readers these interpretations are hard to
spot. Chapter 1 examines what a number of college textbooks in American history say and don't say about the role of African Americans during Reconstruction, the period immediately after the Civil War. By examining selections from
several texts and asking how and why they differ, we can see that texts are not
as objective as readers often believe.

If textbooks are not carved in stone, how can historians know anything? To
answer this question, we turn next to the raw material of history. Chapter 2, on
the living and working conditions of wage earners in industrializing America,
examines the primary sources historians use to reconstruct and interpret the
past. What are these sources? What do historians do with them? What can historians determine from them?

With a basic understanding of the nature and usefulness of primary
sources, we proceed to Chapter 3 for a closer evaluation. This chapter on
late-nineteenth-century efforts to reform the Indians shows how careful historians must be in using primary sources. Does a source speak with one
voice or with many? How can historians disagree about the meaning of the
same historical facts? By carefully evaluating primary sources in this chapter,

you can draw your own conclusions about the nature of these Indian reform efforts. You can also better understand how historians often derive different conclusions from the same body of material.

Chapter 3 is good preparation for the evaluation in Chapter 4 of one historian's argument about the decision to annex the Philippines after the Spanish-American War. In this chapter you can begin to use primary sources to reach a conclusion about a historian's argument. In as much as historians still disagree about the American decision to establish an overseas empire, the essay and the primary sources in this chapter provide another opportunity to see how subjective historical interpretation can be.

One of the most important sources of disagreement among historians is the question of motivation. What drove people to do what they did in the past? The good historian, like the detective in a murder mystery, eventually asks that question. Chapter 5 illustrates the importance of motivation by examining what was behind the promotion of a new housing style in the early twentieth century known as the bungalow. That topic also demonstrates that historians often look in some unlikely places to understand the past.

Motives in history are, of course, related to ideas, the subject of Chapter 6. What power do ideas exert in history? What is their relationship, for example, to the motives examined in the previous chapter? In Chapter 6 we try to answer these questions by examining the role of ideology in advertising during the 1920s.

Chapter 7 turns from the influence of ideas in the past to the influence of a single individual. In this chapter we examine the activities of Eleanor Roosevelt as First Lady. Few First Ladies were more admired, or hated. What can historians learn about an era by focusing on one prominent individual like Eleanor Roosevelt? In the past, many historians believed that history was nothing more than the biography of great people. How much can students of history learn about the past by looking at it this way, that is, "from the top down"? How much do they miss by doing so? Such questions are, of course, related to the topics of previous chapters: historical evidence, motivation, and the influence of ideas.

The next chapter examines history from the opposite perspective—"from the bottom up." What can historians learn by looking at the people at the bottom of a society? What challenges face historians who try? During World War II, a good place for looking at history this way is in the slums of Detroit and barrios of Los Angeles, two of America's greatest war-production centers. Chapter 8 examines the race riots that occurred there in 1943. We will see who the rioters were and why their lives are important to historians.

Having considered the questions of motivation and ideas in history and examined the past from different perspectives, in Chapter 9 we look at the impact of anticommunist hysteria on postwar popular culture. Aside from the question of causation, this chapter considers the problems historians face when they try to trace the influence of one large force in history. As we shall see, this often requires historians to synthesize, that is, to combine small pieces into a large picture.

Chapter 9 examines the influences shaping popular culture. The next chapter, on the civil rights movement, looks at the way popular culture can influence our views of the past. As with many episodes from the recent American past, popular memories of this movement have been shaped by images conveyed by the media. Those images, however, may distort our view of the past. Often, historians attempt to make more accurate assessments of an event by relying on the accounts of those involved in them. Doing so usually requires that researchers synthesize many *individual* memories into an accurate and coherent *collective* memory. And, as we shall see, using the accounts of many people who participated in such a broad movement again illustrates that the past looks different depending on whether it is presented from the "bottom up" or the "top down."

Many of the preceding chapters have used a single historical essay and an accompanying set of primary sources to examine problems of evidence, motivation, ideology, causation, grand forces, and writing of history from both the "top down" and the "bottom up." The next chapter offers an opportunity to pull together the lessons of previous chapters. Chapter 11 compares what two historians have written about a single topic, the war in Vietnam. We will consider the way the United States fought this war, historians' explanations for the way it turned out, and the lessons they draw from the experience. This requires that we examine the actions of a small but influential set of individuals as well as the attitudes of many ordinary Americans. Thus, explaining America's biggest military loss enables us to consider, in a single topic, such questions as motivation, the role of grand historical forces, and the role of the individual in history.

The goal of Chapter 12 is similar to that of Chapter 11: a synthesis, or pulling together, of lessons learned in preceding chapters. Here, however, the emphasis is on the problems of historical evidence, causation, and the role of ideology. Chapter 12 contains two essays on the rise of the women's movement in the 1960s and 1970s and a small collection of primary sources. It asks you to compare and analyze conflicting arguments, using not only primary sources but also insights drawn from previous chapters.

All of the chapters in this volume have a common purpose: to encourage you to think more like a historian and to sharpen your critical thinking skills. Chapter 13 returns to a point emphasized throughout this volume: The pursuit of the past cannot occur apart from a consideration of historical interpretation, and differences in historical interpretation matter not just to historians but to everyone. This final chapter examines differing interpretations about the impact of contemporary immigration. It contains two explanations of large-scale immigration today and primary documents that illuminate both interpretations. In addition, it underscores the way our view of the past can be used to justify policies and practices in a later time.

By the end of this volume, you will have sharpened your ability to think about the past. You will think more critically about the use of historical evidence and about such historical problems as motivation, causation, and interpretation. Moreover, by exploring several styles of historical writing and various avenues to the past—from approaches that emphasize politics or economics to those that highlight social developments or military strategy—you will come to understand better not only the historian's craft, but also the importance of the past. In short, you will think more like a historian.

Chapter
1

Historians and Textbooks: The "Story" of Reconstruction

The textbook selections in this chapter illustrate different assumptions about the meaning of post–Civil War Reconstruction history.

Sources

1. Reconstruction (1906), THOMAS W. WILSON
2. The Negro in Reconstruction (1922), CARTER WOODSON
3. The Ordeal of Reconstruction (1966), THOMAS A. BAILEY
4. Reconstruction: An Unfinished Revolution (2001), MARY BETH NORTON ET AL.

*I*n one of the most memorable scenes in movie history, Rhett Butler tells Scarlett O'Hara that he's leaving her. When Scarlett asks what she will do, Rhett answers, "Frankly, my dear, I don't give a damn." It was the climax of *Gone with the Wind,* starring Clark Gable as Rhett and Vivian Leigh as Scarlett. The David O. Selznick film, based on a best-selling novel set in the South during the Civil War and Reconstruction, was the biggest picture of 1939.

The film's success should have surprised no one. It had all the right elements: strong-willed characters, tempestuous romance, a deathbed scene that left audiences in tears, and courageous people struggling to rebuild lives and fortunes destroyed by war. Yet *Gone with the Wind* also offered an enduring image of life in the Old South and of Reconstruction's "dark days." On the O'Hara plantation, "chivalrous" whites and their loyal ex-slaves confronted "cruel and vicious" Yankee carpetbaggers in cahoots with "traitorous" scalawags. It was a theme that made sense to mostly white movie audiences in 1939. As early as 1915, D. W. Griffith's silent film *The Birth of a Nation* had told the story of the Ku Klux Klan's violent but "valiant" efforts to throw off "carpetbag" rule. Like Griffith's tale, *Gone with the Wind* found a sympathetic audience because it reflected their racial prejudices. As historical drama, it also fit comfortably with what they had learned in school, specifically, with interpretations imparted from history textbooks.

As we shall see in this chapter, however, those interpretations would change over time. In this chapter, you can consider what some twentieth-century historians have taught Americans about Reconstruction. In the process, you will have the opportunity to see that these books do not always necessarily contain the same past and that they, like such powerful movies as *The Birth of a Nation* and *Gone with the Wind,* reflect the biases of their producers. When done, you can judge how well *Gone with the Wind*'s picture of Reconstruction corresponds with those presented in textbooks today.

SETTING

Moviegoers in 1939 may have remembered producer David O. Selznick's name splashed across the screen. Far fewer recalled the author of their American history textbook. More likely than not it was David S. Muzzey, whose *American History* (1911) and *History of the American People* (1927) were bestsellers by the 1930s. Among the most enduring American history textbooks, these books probably taught several generations of Americans more about their nation's past than any other book. If audiences had learned anything about Reconstruction before *Gone with the Wind*'s opening credits, it was probably Muzzey who had taught them.

Muzzey had plenty to say about Reconstruction, and in no uncertain terms. The Republican governments established under congressional Reconstruction he judged to be "sorry affairs." The government "of the negro [sic] and his unscrupulous carpetbagger and scalawag patrons was an orgy of extravagance, fraud, and disgusting incompetence." Muzzey, a New Englander, was sympathetic to the efforts of Southerners to "redeem" their states from "negro [sic] and carpetbagger rule." Although he called white Southerners' use of violence against black voters "exasperating," their response was understandable. "Congress," he asserted, "did [Southern states] an unpardonable injury by hastening to reconstruct them on the basis of negro [sic] suffrage."[1] In short, his view of Reconstruction was that of the white Redeemers themselves.

Muzzey, of course, did not invent this "Redeemer" view of Reconstruction. How, then, had he come to these conclusions? It is impossible to be certain about the intellectual influences on this Columbia University professor. Yet we do know that two other Columbia historians had already written sympathetically about the white South's plight under congressional Reconstruction. Ex-confederate John W. Burgess was an advocate of "Nordic" racial supremacy and the "white man's burden." In *Reconstruction and the Constitution* (1902), he declared that blacks failed to subject "passion to reason." Reconstruction thus put "barbarism in power over civilization."[2] William A. Dunning, a Northerner, agreed. His Reconstruction history was peopled with corrupt carpetbaggers and blacks pursuing "vicious" policies. White Southerners had little choice but to fight back. "All the forces [in the South] that made for civilization," Dunning asserted, "were dominated by a mass of barbarous freedmen."[3]

Burgess and Dunning played a crucial role in transmitting a Southern view of Reconstruction into classrooms nationwide. At Columbia they trained several generations of historians, who wrote more books and trained still other historians. By the time *Gone with the Wind* captivated many moviegoers, the struggle for the hearts and minds of high school and college students was already over. Although a few black historians dissented, most notably W. E. B. Du Bois, the South had triumphed in the historical battle over the theory of Reconstruction. Rather than a new view of the past, *Gone with the Wind* offered white audiences a reassuring version of the past that had been embedded in the popular mind for several decades. In 1939, Hollywood ensured that it would endure for several more. Only in the second half of the last century would historians seriously challenge the established view of this era with new interpretations that turned Dunning's view on its head.

INVESTIGATION

This chapter contains four selections from American history textbooks published in the twentieth and twenty-first centuries. The first was published in 1906 and the last in 2001. Your primary assignment is to determine how these accounts of Reconstruction differ from one another and which one is most accurate. As you read them, keep in mind the questions that the authors attempt to answer about Reconstruction. These questions, mostly unstated, are not necessarily the same. Also, be careful to note the most important facts of Reconstruction that each presents and the meaning each assigns to them. To see more clearly how these textbook selections differ from one another, it would be helpful to write down brief answers to the following questions as you read each account:

1. **Does the author present the Republican governments in the Southern states as effective or ineffective? How are they described?** Is the view of the "carpetbaggers" and "scalawags" positive, negative, or neutral?

2. **What is the author's view of blacks?** Is the author's analysis of Reconstruction based on racial assumptions about the character of the freedmen? Are blacks passive or active participants in shaping Reconstruction and their own lives?

3. **What is the author's view of the overturning of Reconstruction?** Is the seizure of power by white Southerners a welcome or regrettable development? What is the author's view of such terrorist organizations as the Ku Klux Klan?

Before you begin, read your own textbook's discussion of Reconstruction. When you are finished, you should be able to explain how these selections differ, which one is closest to the interpretation in your own text, and which one is most plausible.

S O U R C E S

Reconstruction (1906)

THOMAS W. WILSON

Adventurers swarmed out of the North to cozen, beguile, and use . . . them [negroes]. These men, mere "carpet baggers" for the most part, who brought nothing with them, and had nothing to bring, but a change of clothing and their wits, became the new masters of the blacks. They gained the confidence of the negroes, obtained for themselves the more lucrative offices, and lived upon the public treasury, public contracts, and their easy control of affairs. For the negroes there was nothing but occasional allotments of abandoned or forfeited land, the pay of petty offices, a *per diem* allowance as members of the conventions and the state legislatures which their new masters made business for, or the wages of servants in the various offices of administration. Their ignorance and credulity made them easy dupes. . . .

Source: Woodrow Wilson, *A History of the American People* (New York: Harper and Bros., 1906), V: pp. 46, 47, 49, 58, 59, 60, 62, 98, 99.

. . . In Mississippi, before the work of the carpet baggers was done, six hundred and forty thousand acres of land had been forfeited for taxes, twenty per cent, of the total acreage of the State. The state tax levy for 1871 was four times as great as the levy for 1869 had been; that for 1873 eight times as great; that for 1874 fourteen times. The impoverished planters could not carry the intolerable burden of taxes, and gave their lands up to be sold by the sheriff. There were few who could buy. The lands lay waste and neglected or were parcelled out at nominal rates among the negroes. . . .

Taxes, of course, did not suffice. Enormous debts were piled up to satisfy the adventurers. . . . Treasuries were swept clean. . . .

. . . The white men of the South were aroused by the mere instinct of self-preservation to rid themselves, by fair means or foul, of the intolerable burden of governments sustained by the votes of ignorant negroes and conducted in the interest of adventurers: governments whose incredible debts were incurred that thieves might be enriched, whose increasing loans and taxes went to no public use but into the pockets of party managers and corrupt contractors. . . .

They took the law into their own hands, and began to attempt by intimidation what they were not allowed to attempt by the ballot or by any ordered course of public action. They began to do by secret concert and association what they could not do in avowed parties. Almost by accident a way was found to succeed which led insensibly farther and farther afield into the ways of violence and outlawry. In May, 1866, a little group of young men in the Tennessee village of Pulaski, finding time hang heavy on their hands after the excitements of the field, so lately abandoned, formed a secret club for the mere pleasure of association, for private amusement—for anything that might promise to break the monotony of the too quiet place. . . .

. . . Year by year the organization spread, from county to county, from State to State. Every country-side wished to have its own Ku Klux, founded in secrecy and mystery like the mother "Den" at Pulaski, until at last there had sprung into existence a great *Ku Klux Klan*, an "Invisible Empire of the South," bound together in loose organization to protect the southern country from some of the ugliest hazards of a time of revolution. . . .

It was impossible to keep such a power in hand. Sober men governed the counsels and moderated the plans of those roving knights errant; but it was lawless work at best. They had set themselves, after the first year or two of mere mischievous frolic had passed, to right a disordered society through the power of fear. Men of hot passions who could not always be restrained carried their plans into effect. . . .

The reconstruction of the southern States had been the undoing of the Republican party. The course of carpet bag rule did not run smooth. Every election fixed the attention of the country upon some serious question of fraud or violence in the States where northern adventurers and negro majorities were in control. . . . Before [Ulysses S. Grant's] term was out the white voters of the South had rallied strong enough in every State except South Carolina, Florida, and Louisiana to take their governments out of the hands of the men who were preying upon them.

The Negro in Reconstruction (1922)
CARTER WOODSON

Reconstruction began in the schoolhouses not in the State houses, as uninformed persons often say. . . . As the Union armies gradually invaded that area the soldiers opened schools for Negroes. Regular teachers came from relief societies and the Freedmen's Bureau. These enlightened a fair percentage of the Negroes by 1870. The illiteracy of the Negroes was reduced to 79.9 by that time. When about the same time these freedmen had a chance to participate in the rehabilitation of State governments in the South, they gave that section the first free public school system, the first democratic education it ever had. . . .

The [majority of] other States in the South, from 1868 to about 1872, became subjected to what is commonly known as "Negro carpet-bag rule."

To call this Negro rule, however, is very much of a mistake. As a matter of fact, most of the local offices in these commonwealths were held by the white men, and those Negroes who did attain some of the higher offices were usually about as competent as the average whites thereto elected. Only twenty-three Negroes served in Congress from 1868 to 1895. The Negroes had political equality in the Southern States only a few years, and with some exceptions their tenure in Congress was very short. . . .

The charge that all Negro officers were illiterate, ignorant of the science of government, cannot be sustained. In the first place, the education of the Negro by Union soldiers in the South began in spots as early as 1861. Many of the Negro leaders who had been educated in the North or abroad returned to the South after the war. Negro illiteracy had been reduced to 79.9 by 1870, just about the time the freedmen were actually participating in the reconstruction. The masses of Negroes did not take a part in the government in the beginning of the reconstruction.

It is true that many of them were not prepared to vote, and decidedly disqualified for the positions which they held. In some of the legislatures, as in Louisiana and South Carolina, more than half of the Negro members could scarcely read or write. They, therefore, had to vote according to emotions or the dictates of the demagogues. This, of course, has been true of legislatures composed entirely of whites. In the local and State administrative offices,

Source: Carter G. Woodson and Charles H. Wesley, *The Negro in Our History,* (Washington, D.C.: Associated Publishers Inc., 1962; originally published in 1922), pp. 382, 388, 401–410, 431–414.

however, where there were frequent chances for corruption, very few ignorant Negroes ever served. . . .

Most of the local, State and Federal offices, however, were held not by Negroes but by southern white men, and by others who came from the North and profited by the prostration of the South. They were in many respects selfish men, but not always utterly lacking in principle. The northern whites, of course, had little sympathy for the South. They depended for their constituency upon the Negroes, who could not be expected to placate the ex-slaveholders. Being adventurers and interested in their own affairs, the carpet-baggers became unusually corrupt in certain States. They administered affairs selfishly. Most Negro officers who served in the South came out of office with an honorable record. . . .

Reconstruction history, however, was distorted by J. W. Burgess, a slaveholder of Giles County, Tennessee, who was educated in the North and finally attained distinction as a teacher and writer at Columbia University; and by W. A. Dunning, the son of an industrialist of Plainfield, New Jersey, who became the disciple of Burgess. The two trained or influenced in the same biased way the sons and sympathizers of former slaveholders who prostituted modern historiography to perpetuate the same distortion. These pseudo-historians refused to use the evidence of those who opposed slavery, discredited the testimony of those who favored Congressional Reconstruction, and ignored the observations of travellers from the North and from Europe. These makers of history to order were more partial than required by the law of slavery, for they rejected the evidence from Negro sources and thus denied the Negro not only the opportunity to testify against the white man but even to testify in favor of himself. . . .

Wherever they could, the native whites instituted government by investigation to expose all shortcomings of Negro officials. The general charge was that they were corrupt. The very persons who complained of the corruption in the Negro carpet-bag governments and who effected the reorganization of the State governments in the South when the Negroes were overthrown, however, became just as corrupt as the governing class under the preceding régime. In almost every restored State government in the South, and especially in Mississippi, the white officers in control of the funds defaulted. These persons who had been so long out of office came back so eager to get the most out of it that they filled their own pockets from the coffers of the public. No exposure followed. . . .

The attack on the policies of the carpet-bag governments, moreover, had the desired effect among the poor and ignorant whites. Reared under the degrading influences of slavery, they could not tolerate the blacks as citizens. The Negroes thereafter were harassed and harried by disturbing elements of anarchy, out of which soon emerged an oath-bound order called the Ku Klux Klan, established to terrorize the Negroes with lawlessness and violence.

The Ordeal of Reconstruction (1966)
THOMAS A. BAILEY

Enfranchised Freedmen

The sudden thrusting of the ballot unto the hands of the ex-slaves, between 1867 and 1870, set the stage for stark tragedy. As might have been foreseen, it was a blunder hardly less serious than thrusting overnight freedom upon them. Wholesale liberation was probably unavoidable, given the feverish conditions created by war. But wholesale suffrage was avoidable, except insofar as the Radicals found it necessary for their own ends, both selfish and idealistic.

The bewildered Negroes were poorly prepared for their new responsibilities as citizens and voters. Democracy is a delicate mechanism, which requires education and information. Yet about nine-tenths of the 700,000 adult Negro males were illiterate. When registering, many did not know their ages; and boys of sixteen signed the rolls. Some of these voters could not even give their last name, if indeed they had any. Bob, Quash, Christmas, Scipio, Nebuchadnezzar would take any surname that popped into their heads, often that of "massa." Sometimes they chose more wisely than they knew. On the voting lists of Charleston, South Carolina, there were forty-six George Washingtons and sixty-three Abraham Lincolns.

The tale would be amusing were it not so pathetic and tragic. After the Negroes were told to come in for registration, many appeared with boxes or baskets, thinking that registration was some new kind of food or drink. Others would mark their ballots and then carefully deposit them in mail boxes.

While these pitiable practices were going on, thousands of the ablest Southern whites were being denied the vote, either by act of Congress or by the new state constitutions. . . .

Enthroned Ignorance

Some of the new Southern legislatures created in 1867–1870, not unlike some Northern legislatures, presented bizarre scenes. They were dominated by newly arrived carpetbaggers, despised scalawags, and pliant Negroes. Some of the ex-bondsmen were remarkably well educated, but many others were illiterate. In a few of the states the colored legislators constituted a strong minority. In once-haughty South Carolina, the tally stood at 88 Negroes to 67 whites; and ex-slaves held offices ranging from speaker to doorkeeper. Negroes who had been raising cotton under the lash of the

Source: Thomas Bailey, *The American Pageant,* 3rd edition. Copyright © 1966 by D. C. Heath and Company. By permission of Houghton Mifflin Company.

overseer were now raising points of order under the gavel of the speaker. As a Negro song ran:

De bottom rail's on de top
And we's gwine to keep it dar.

Greatly to their credit, these Negro-white legislatures passed much desirable legislation and introduced many overdue reforms. In some states a better tax system was created, state charities were established, public works were launched, property rights were guaranteed to women, and free public schools were encouraged—for Negroes as well as whites. Some of these reforms were so welcome that they were retained, along with the more enlightened state constitutions, when the Southern whites finally strong-armed their way back into control.

But the good legislation, unhappily, was often obscured by a carnival of corruption and misrule. Graft and theft ran wild, especially in states like South Carolina and Louisiana, where designing whites used naive Negroes as cats-paws. The worst black-and-tan legislatures purchased, under "legislative supplies," such items as hams, perfumes, suspenders, bonnets, corsets, champagne, and a coffin. One "thrifty" carpetbag governor in a single year "saved" $100,000 from a salary of $8000.

The public debt of the Southern states doubled and trebled, as irresponsible carpetbag legislatures voted appropriations and bond issues with lighthearted abandon. Burdensome taxes were passed in Mississippi, where some 6,000,000 acres were sold for delinquent taxes. The disfranchised and propertied whites had to stagger along under a tax burden that sometimes rose ten or fifteenfold. . . .

One should also note that during this hectic era corruption was also rampant in the North, among Republicans as well as Democrats. The notorious Tweed Ring of New York City probably stole more millions, though with greater sophistication, than the worst of the carpetbag legislatures combined. And when the Southern whites regained the whip hand, graft by no means disappeared under Democratic auspices.

The Rule of Night Riders

Goaded to desperation, once-decent Southern whites resorted to savage measures against Negro-carpetbag control. A number of secret organizations blossomed forth, the most notorious of which was the Ku Klux Klan, founded in Tennessee in 1866. Besheeted night riders, their horses' hoofs muffled, would hammer on the cabin door of a politically ambitious Negro. In ghoulish tones one thirsty horseman would demand a bucket of water, pour it into a rubber attachment under pretense of drinking, smack his lips, and declare that this was the first water he had tasted since he was killed at the battle of Shiloh. If fright did not produce the desired effect, force was employed.

Such tomfoolery and terror proved partially effective. Many Negroes and carpetbaggers, quick to take a hint, were scared away from the polls. But those stubborn souls who persisted in their forward ways were flogged, mutilated, or even murdered. In one Louisiana parish in 1868, the whites in two days killed or wounded two hundred victims; a pile of twenty-five bodies was found half-buried in the woods. By such atrocious practices was the Negro "kept in his place."

Reconstruction: An Unfinished Revolution (2001)
MARY BETH NORTON ET AL.

Reconstruction Politics in the South

From the start, Reconstruction encountered the resistance of white southerners. In the black codes and in private attitudes, many whites stubbornly opposed emancipation, and the former planter class proved especially unbending. In 1866 a Georgia newspaper frankly observed that "most of the white citizens believe that the institution of slavery was right, and . . . they will believe that the condition, which comes nearest to slavery, that can now be established will be the best."

White Resistance   Fearing loss of control over their slaves, some planters attempted to postpone freedom by denying or misrepresenting events. Former slaves reported that their owners "didn't tell them it was freedom" or "wouldn't let [them] go." Agents of the Freedmen's Bureau reported that "the old system of slavery [is] working with even more rigor than formerly at a few miles distant from any point where U.S. troops are stationed." To hold onto their workers, some landowners claimed control over black children and used guardianship and apprentice laws to bind black families to the plantation.

Whites also blocked blacks from acquiring land. A few planters divided up plots among their slaves, but most condemned the idea of making blacks landowners. A Georgia woman whose family was known for its support of religious education for slaves was outraged that two property owners planned to "rent their lands to the Negroes!" Such action was, she declared, "injurious to the best interest of the community."

Adamant resistance by propertied whites soon manifested itself in other ways, including violence. In one North Carolina town a local magistrate clubbed a black man on a public street, and bands of "Regulators" terrorized blacks in parts of that state and in Kentucky. Such incidents were predictable in a defeated society in which many planters believed, as a South Carolinian put it, that blacks "can't be governed except with the whip."

After President Johnson encouraged the South to resist congressional Reconstruction, white conservatives worked hard to capture the new state governments. Many whites also boycotted the polls in an attempt to defeat Congress's plans; by sitting out the elections, whites might block the new constitutions, which had to be approved by a majority of registered voters. This tactic was tried in North Carolina and succeeded in Alabama, forcing Congress to base ratification of the Fourteenth Amendment and of new state constitutions on a majority of "votes cast" (the provision of the Fourth Reconstruction Act).

Black Voters and Emergence of a Southern Republican Party   Very few black men stayed away from the polls. Enthusiastically and hopefully, they voted Republican. Most agreed with one man who felt he should "stick to the end with the party that freed me." Illiteracy did not prohibit blacks (or uneducated whites) from making intelligent choices. Although Mississippi's William Henry could read only "a little," he testified that he and his friends had no difficulty selecting the Republican ballot. "We stood around and watched," he explained. "We saw D. Sledge vote; he owned half the county. We knowed he voted Democratic so we voted the other ticket so it would be Republican." Women, who could not vote, encouraged their husbands and sons, and preachers exhorted their congregations to use the franchise. With such group spirit, zeal for voting spread through the entire black community.

Thanks to a large black turnout and the restrictions on prominent Confederates, a new southern Republican Party came to power in the constitutional conventions of 1868–1870. Republican delegates consisted of a sizable contingent of blacks (265 out of the total of just over 1,000 delegates throughout the South), some northerners who had moved to the South, and native southern whites who favored change. Together these Republicans brought the South into line with progressive reforms adopted earlier in the rest of the nation. The new constitutions were more democratic. They eliminated property qualifications for voting and holding office, and they turned many appointed offices into elective posts. They provided for public schools and institutions to care for the mentally ill, the blind, the deaf, the destitute, and the orphaned. . . .

The Myth of "Negro Rule"   Within a few years, as centrists in both parties met with failure, white hostility to congressional Reconstruction began to dominate. Some conservatives had always desired to fight Reconstruction through pressure and racist propaganda. They put economic and social pressure on blacks: one black Republican reported that "my neighbors will not employ me, nor sell me a farthing's worth of anything." Charging that the South had been turned over to ignorant blacks, conservatives deplored "black domination," which became a rallying cry for a return to white supremacy.

Such attacks were inflammatory propaganda, and part of the growing myth of "Negro rule," which would serve as a central theme in battles over the memory of Reconstruction. African Americans participated in politics but hardly dominated or controlled events. They were a majority in only two out of ten state constitutional writing conventions (transplanted northerners were a majority in one). In the state legislatures, only in the lower house in South Carolina did blacks ever constitute a majority; among officeholders, their numbers generally were far fewer than their proportion in the population. Sixteen blacks won seats in Congress before Reconstruction was over, but none was ever elected governor. Only eighteen served in a high state office such as lieutenant governor, treasurer, superintendent of education, or secretary of state. In all, some four hundred blacks served in political office during the Reconstruction era. Although they never dominated the process, they established a rich tradition of government service and civic activism. Elected officials, such as Robert Smalls in South Carolina, labored tirelessly for cheaper land prices, better healthcare, access to schools, and the enforcement of civil rights for their people. The black politicians of Reconstruction are lost in the mists, the forgotten heroes of this seedtime of America's long civil rights movement.

Carpetbaggers and Scalawags   Conservatives also assailed the allies of black Republicans. Their propaganda denounced whites from the North as "carpetbaggers," greedy crooks planning to pour stolen tax revenues into their sturdy luggage made of carpet material. Immigrants from the North, who held the largest share of Republican offices, were all tarred with this brush.

In fact, most northerners who settled in the South had come seeking business opportunities or a warmer climate and never entered politics. Those who did enter politics generally wanted to democratize the South and to introduce northern ways, such as industry, public education, and the spirit of enterprise. Carpetbaggers' ideals were tested by hard times and ostracism by white southerners.

In addition to tagging northern interlopers as carpetbaggers, Conservatives invented the term "scalawag" to discredit any native white southerner who cooperated with the Republicans. A substantial number of southerners did so, including some wealthy and prominent men. Most scalawags, however, were yeoman farmers, men from mountain areas and nonslaveholding districts who had been restive under the Confederacy. They saw that they could benefit from the education and opportunities promoted by Republicans. Banding together with freedmen, they pursued common class interests and hoped to make headway against the power of long-dominant planters. Cooperation even convinced a few scalawags that "there is but little if any difference in the talents of the two races," as one observed, and that all should have "an equal start." Yet this black-white coalition was vulnerable to the race issue, and most scalawags did not support racial equality. Republican tax policies also cut into upcountry yeoman support because reliance on the property tax hit many small landholders hard.

Tax Policy and Corruption as Political Wedges   Taxation was a major problem for the Reconstruction governments. Republicans wanted to maintain prewar services, repair the war's destruction, stimulate industry, and support important new ventures such as public schools. But the Civil War had destroyed much of the South's tax base. One category of valuable property—slaves—had disappeared entirely. And hundreds of thousands of citizens had lost much of the rest of their property—money, livestock, fences, and buildings—to the war. Thus an increase in taxes was necessary even to maintain traditional services, and new ventures required still higher taxes. Inevitably, Republican tax policies aroused strong opposition, especially among the yeomen.

Corruption was another serious charge levied against the Republicans. Unfortunately, it often was true. Many carpetbaggers and black politicians engaged in fraudulent schemes, sold their votes, or padded expenses, taking part in what scholars recognize was a nationwide surge of corruption in an age ruled by "spoilsmen." Corruption carried no party label, but the Democrats successfully pinned the blame on unqualified blacks and greedy carpetbaggers among southern Republicans.

Ku Klux Klan   All these problems hurt the Republicans, whose leaders also allowed factionalism along racial and class lines to undermine party unity. But in many southern states the deathblow came through violence. The Ku Klux Klan, a secret veterans' club that began in Tennessee in 1866, spread through the South and rapidly evolved into a terrorist organization. Violence against African Americans occurred from the first days of Reconstruction but became far more organized and purposeful after 1867. Klansmen rode to frustrate Reconstruction and keep the freedmen in subjection. Nighttime harassment, whippings, beatings, and murder became common, and terrorism dominated some counties and regions. . . .

Klan violence injured Republicans across the South. No fewer than one-tenth of the black leaders who had been delegates to the 1867–1868 state constitutional conventions were attacked, seven fatally. In one judicial district of North Carolina the Ku Klux Klan was responsible for twelve murders, over seven hundred beatings, and other acts of violence, including rape and arson. A single attack on Alabama Republicans in the town of Eutaw left four blacks dead and fifty-four wounded. In South Carolina five hundred masked Klansmen lynched eight black prisoners at the Union County jail, and in nearby York County the Klan committed at least eleven murders and hundreds of whippings. According to historian Eric Foner, the Klan "made it virtually impossible for Republicans to campaign or vote in large parts of Georgia."

Failure of Reconstruction   Thus a combination of difficult fiscal problems, Republican mistakes, racial hostility, and terror brought down the Republican regimes. In most southern states, "Radical Reconstruction" lasted only a few years. The most enduring failure of Reconstruction, however, was not political; it was social and economic. Reconstruction failed to alter the

South's social structure or its distribution of wealth and power. Without land of their own, freed men and women were dependent on white landowners who could and did use their economic power to compromise blacks' political freedom. Armed only with the ballot, freed men in the South had little chance to effect major changes.

CONCLUSION

These discussions of Reconstruction should make it clear that history textbooks contain interpretations. They are no different from other historical writing in that regard. Modern texts are also written by people with biases and opinions, although their interpretations may be as difficult to spot today as Muzzey's were for his students. In part that's because historians often do not reveal their most important assumptions, as the selection from *The American Pageant*, another best-selling American history textbook, demonstrates. The original author, Stanford University historian Thomas A. Bailey, approached his task in much the same spirit as Muzzey; he wrote history as a lively story, with the accomplishments of prominent people giving direction to the narrative. Behind this approach was the unspoken assumption that the lives of people at the bottom of the society mattered less than the bold actions of diplomats, generals, and politicians. Moreover, Bailey wrote and revised earlier editions of *The American Pageant* before civil rights protests had overthrown legal racial segregation. The 1966 edition excerpted in this chapter appeared after historians began to mount a successful assault on the Dunning view of Reconstruction, but before textbooks fully reflected the outcome of this battle. On the other hand, Mary Beth Norton and the other authors of *A People and a Nation* are of the generation of scholars who came of age in the 1960s. Not only do many of these historians incorporate ordinary people into their accounts, but their racial assumptions also differ markedly from those of most historians earlier in the twentieth century.

It is usually easier to spot interpretations in older textbooks because their authors do not share our premises. The first textbook selection, written with an unquestioned assumption of black inferiority, is a good example. Its author, Thomas W. Wilson, was probably as unfamiliar to you as were William Dunning and David Muzzey. He is better known today as Woodrow Wilson, the Princeton historian and Southerner who later became the twenty-eighth president of the United States and, as president, introduced racial segregation to the federal government. If Wilson's text reflects the racist assumptions at the heart of the triumphant Southern view of Reconstruction, the second selection reveals that not all historians accepted this dominant view, even in the early twentieth century. Its author, Carter Woodson, was a Virginia-born African American who earned a Ph.D. from Harvard University in 1912. Like the work of fellow Harvard-trained black historian W. E. B. Du Bois, Woodson's *The Negro* in *Our History* and his other Negro history textbooks were largely ignored by white historians and students. In its own way, of course, Woodson's text also demonstrates the importance of racial assumptions in shaping inter- pretations about Reconstruction. It also illustrates that historians are more than mouthpieces for the dominant views of their day.

Together, all of these texts remind us that Americans' social views have not remained frozen since the early twentieth century. And although the questions historians ask are not entirely dependent on whatever social views happen to be popular, historians are surely influenced by their times. However, these selections also make clear that historians do not simply mirror what happened in the past but instead give meaning to the "facts" of history. To do that, they study primary sources—the materials left to us by people in the past. We turn to them next.

FURTHER READING

W. E. B. Du Bois, *Black Reconstruction* (New York: Russell and Russell, 1935).

Frances FitzGerald, *America Revised: History Schoolbooks in the Twentieth Century* (New York: Random House, 1979).

Michael W. Fitzgerald, *Splendid Failure: Postwar Reconstruction in the American South* (Chicago: Ivan R. Dee, 2007).

Eric Foner, A *Short History of Reconstruction, 1863–1977* (New York: Harper and Row, 1990).

Nicolas Lemann, *Redemption: The Last Battle of the Civil War* (New York: Farrar, Straus, and Giroux, 2006).

James W. Loewen, *Lies My Teacher Told Me: Everything Your American History Textbook Got Wrong* (New York: The New Press, 1995).

NOTES

1. David Saville Muzzey, *History of the American People* (New York: Ginn and Com- pany, 1935), pp. 408, 410.
2. John W. Burgess, *Reconstruction and the Constitution, 1866–1876* (New York: Da Capo Press, 1970; reprint of 1902 edition), p. viii.
3. William A. Dunning, *Reconstruction, Political and Economic* (New York: Harper and Brothers, 1907), p. 212.

Chapter

2

Using Primary Sources: Industrialization and the Condition of Labor

This chapter introduces primary sources. The documents presented give information on nineteenth-century working conditions.

Sources

1. Testimony of Workingmen (1879)
2. "Earnings, Expenses and Conditions of Workingmen and Their Families" (1884)
3. "Human Power. . . Is What We Are Losing" (1910), CRYSTAL EASTMAN
4. Why We Struck at Pullman (1895)
5. Colored Workmen and a Strike (1887)
6. "I Struck Because I Had to" (1902)
7. Women Make Demands (1869)
8. Summary of Conditions Among Women Workers Found by the Massachusetts Bureau of Labor (1887)
9. A Union Official Discusses the Impact of Women Workers (1897)
10. Work in a Garment Factory (1902)
11. Gainful Workers by Age, 1870–1920
12. Breaker Boys (1906), JOHN SPARGO

*I*n 1873 a financial panic sparked a severe depression. Four years later, business was still stagnant, and, with unemployment at perhaps one million, working people grew restless. In Pennsylvania's coal mining regions, the militia was called on repeatedly to keep order. Then, in 1877, wage cuts and layoffs on the railroads exploded into a paralyzing railroad strike. After the violent confrontation was over, many people lay dead, millions of dollars of property had been destroyed, and dazed Americans stared at the specter of class warfare.

In 1878 Congress appointed a committee to investigate the causes of the "General Depression in Labor and Business." One of the witnesses called to testify was the Yale University professor William Graham Sumner. Sumner was a proponent of what would be known as Social Darwinism, a theory that applied Darwin's theories of evolution to society in an attempt to justify uncontrolled economic competition. Sumner later shared his views about the "survival of the fittest" through books and a stream of popular magazine articles. Now, he responded to Congress with answers that many middle-class Americans found reassuring. When asked by one congressman what effect the spread of machinery had on workers, Sumner admitted that they suffered a loss of income and "a loss of comfort." Asked if there was any way to help, Sumner responded, "not at all." And when pressed to admit that there was "distress among the laboring classes," Sumner shot back, "I do not admit any such thing. I cannot see any evidence of it."[1]

If anything, Sumner was a man of the Gilded Age. His father was frugal and hardworking, though unsuccessful. Sumner, in the words of one student of the era, had imbibed a "deep-grained prejudice in favor of the business-like virtues."[2] He was not alone. Many of Sumner's contemporaries accepted unquestioningly the assumption that individuals were solely responsible for their financial success or failure. Many of them also could not see, or were untroubled by, any suffering that industrialization may have caused. Yet it would be foolish for us to reason this way. Instead, we can rely on a wide variety of primary sources—the historical evidence and artifacts that survive from the past—to understand the ways industrialization influenced the lives of workers. Without them, historians are at the mercy of other people's interpretations of the past. With them, they can make direct contact with the past. In this chapter, therefore, we turn to these sources to examine the same question about the "laboring classes" posed to William Graham Sumner in 1878.

SETTING

Historians who study workers in the late nineteenth century have a wealth of primary sources. They include "literary" or *written* sources, *statistical* sources relating to such information as wages and the cost of living, and such *nonwritten* sources as sketches and photographs. Many of these sources are available because a variety of bureaus, commissions, and committees in the late nine-teenth century began to investigate the effects of industrial growth on labor. By the 1880s, for instance, a number of states had set up bureaus of labor statistics to assess the living and working conditions of wage earners. In 1884, Congress established the Bureau of Labor, which two years later began to issue annual reports related to the conditions of workers. At about the same time, the U.S. Senate issued a five-volume *Report upon the Relations Between Capital and Labor*. In addition, in 1901 and 1902, its Industrial Commission produced a massive report on the effects of industrial growth. Meanwhile, other investigators also began to produce valuable sources. Often armed with only pens and cameras, such reformers as Jacob Riis, Lewis Hine, John Spargo, and Upton Sinclair recorded the conditions in the industrial workplace at the turn of the century. *The Atlantic Monthly, Independent, Outlook*, and other popular magazines also published articles on the living and working conditions of laborers. Added to these sources are newspaper accounts, diaries, songs, and documents from such organizations as charities, labor unions, corporations, and business associations. In short, the sources reflecting the condition of labor in industrial America are as varied as they are numerous.

INVESTIGATION

The main problem we investigate in this chapter is the question posed to William Graham Sumner in the congressional investigation in 1878: Was there "distress" among the "laboring classes" as the United States industrialized in the late nineteenth century? That question is a very broad one, and, given the abundance of primary sources, it might seem easy to answer. Yet it is not. First, by 1900, there were more than 13 million nonagricultural wage earners in the United States, and their working conditions varied greatly. Second, we must define *distress* and determine whether our definition is the same as that of industrial wage earners themselves. We need to know the "objective" conditions as defined by wages, hours of labor, and cost of living, as well as what people at the time thought about them. That might depend, in turn, on workers' expectations. The question Sumner answered with such certainty is thus more complicated than it first appears. A good answer must be based on a careful consideration of the evidence. It should also address the following questions:

1. **Overall, do conditions appear to be improving or getting worse?** What important qualifications must be made to any generalizations about the conditions of workers? Does the race, class, or gender of the workers affect their conditions?

2. **What do workers think about their conditions?** Which sources are especially valuable in understanding what it was like to be a wage earner in the late nineteenth century? Are some of the sources more biased than others?

3. **Many late nineteenth-century commentators like William Graham Sumner argued that "in the cold light of reason" employers could not be accused of treating workers as a mere commodity. They also asserted that it was not the role of government to improve the condition of the working classes. Based on the evidence in this chapter, do you agree?** What does the "cold light" of your reason applied to this evidence suggest to you about the validity of Sumner's assertions?

Before you begin, read the sections in your textbook on the condition of labor in the late nineteenth century and its response to industrial growth. See if you can detect a point of view regarding the living and working conditions of industrial workers.

SOURCES

1　In 1878, the Massachusetts Bureau of the Statistics of Labor sent a questionnaire to working men and women throughout the state to solicit their opinions about their own work. According to the report, many of the respondents "expressed themselves at length upon some phase of the labor question."[3] Does this report show that workers were content or unhappy with their jobs? What were their primary complaints?

Testimony of Workingmen (1879)

Hours of Labor

From a Carpet-Mill Operative　　I am satisfied with sixty hours a week: it is plenty time for any man, although there are some employed in the same place over that time, and get nothing extra for it. I know of one young man under age who was absent two Saturday afternoons, and his overseer gave him his bill on Monday morning when he went in. If there is any inspector of the ten-hour law, he would do well to call round, and see for himself.

From a Shoemaker　　I think there ought to be an eight-hour law all over the country. There is not enough work to last the year round, and work over eight hours a day, or forty-eight hours a week. There can be only about so much work to do any way: and, when that is done, business has got to stop, or keep dragging the year round, so that a man has to work for almost any price offered; when, if there was an eight-hour law, things would be more

Source: John A. Garraty, *The Transformation of American Society, 1870–1890* (Columbia: University of South Carolina Press, 1968). Reprinted by permission of the University of South Carolina Press.

even, and a man could get what his labor was worth, according to the price of living, and there would be plenty of work for all, and business would be good the year round. . . .

Overwork

From a Harness-Maker   In answer to the question, "Do you consider yourself overworked?" I answered, "Yes"; and it is my honest and firm conviction that I am, by at least two hours a day. With the great increase in machinery within the last fifteen or twenty years, I think, in justice, there ought to be some reduction in the hours of labor. Unless the hours of labor are shortened in proportion to the increase of machinery, I consider machinery an injury rather than a benefit to humanity. I tell you that ten hours a day, hard, steady work, is more than any man can stand for any length of time without injuring his health, and therefore shortening his life. For my own part, although my work is not very laborious, when I stop work in the evening, I feel completely played out. I would like to study some; but I am too fatigued. In fact it is as much as I can do to look over the evening paper; and I am almost certain that this is the condition of a majority of workingmen. . . .

From a Quarryman   In filling this blank, there are a good many questions which I did not answer relative to men with families; but, however, I would say, on behalf of married men in this locality, that they are poorly situated, working hard eleven and a half hours a day for $1.25 in summer, and 80 cents a day in winter, and obliged to purchase merchandise in company stores, and pay enormous rents for tenements. Merchandise being thirty per cent above market price, and being paid monthly, they are obliged to purchase at supply store; if not, they will be discharged, and starvation is the result. It is ridiculous in a free country that the laws are not more stringent, whereby the capitalist cannot rule and ruin his white slaves. I would draw your attention carefully to this matter, and I lay before you all truth, not hearsay, but from experience, I am a single man, and I would not be so if times were better than they are now. . . .

From a Machinist   In reply to your question concerning overwork, I wish to say, that, in employment requiring close application of mind or body, to be successful, the diligent and conscientious workman often, I might say always, finds his energy exhausted long before his ten hours are up. Then he is obliged to keep up an appearance to get the pay for his day's work, which he might do in eight hours as well as ten. If we are to have our pay by the hour, I should not advocate the eight-hour system. I think the employer would be the gainer, and the employé the loser. In the shop I work a little less than ten hours. To do that I have to leave home at 5:30 A.M., and arrive home again at 7 P.M.; so you see it makes a pretty long day. I travel not less than thirty-four miles daily, and pay $28.50 per quarter for car-fare. If I want to have a garden, I must do the work nights, or hire it done. I do not think I should be able to follow up work in this way until the age of sixty-five. Hope to find some way to avoid some of the long hours and some of the heavy work before then. I do not mean to complain; but it does seem as if the burdens and the pleasures of this world were very unequally divided. It is a hard matter to say what is right in every case. If my answers and statements should be of any service in improving the condition, prospects, or possibilities of the toiling thousands in our State, I shall be well paid for the same. . . .

The Use of Machinery

From a Boot and Shoe Cutter   Tax machinery. Bring it in common with hand labor, so a man can have twelve months' work in a year, instead of six or eight months. Protect hand labor, same as we protect trade from Europe, by tax or tariff. . . .

From a Machinist   Machinery and the swarms of cheap foreign labor are fast rendering trades useless, and compelling the better class of mechanics to change their occupation, or go to farming. . . .

Habits of Industry

From a Shoe-Cutter   There is no way I think I could be paid more fairly than I now am. I do not consider that my employers profit unfairly by my labor. My labor is in the market for sale. My employers buy it just as they buy a side of leather, and expect, and I think are willing to pay, a fair market price for it. The miller who makes a grade of flour up to the very highest point in excellence will command the highest price for it in the market. The workingman who makes his labor of the most value will generally command the highest market price for it, and sharp business men are quick to discover its value. I consider all legislation in regard to any thing connected with labor as injurious. All trades-unions and combinations I also consider as injurious to the mass of working-people. A few profit by these associations, and the many pay the bills. If working-people would drop the use of beer, tobacco, and every thing else that is not of real benefit, and let such men as _____ and a host of others earn their own living, they would have far more money for the general expenses of a family than they now have. I live in a village of about two thousand inhabitants; and I do not know of a family in destitute circumstances which has let alone vicious expenditures, and been industrious. It is the idle, unthrifty, beer-drinking, don't-care sort of people, who are out at the elbows, and waiting for some sort of legislation to help them. The sooner working-people get rid of the idea that somebody or something is going to help them, the better it will be for them. In this country, as a general thing, every man has an equal chance to rise. In our village there are a number of successful business men, and all began in the world without any thing but their hands and a will to succeed. The best way for working-people to get help is to help themselves. . . .

2   In 1884, the Illinois Bureau of Labor Statistics conducted an investigation of the standard of living of Illinois workers and their families. One result was a tabulation of the amount of money that 2,139 families in a number of communities actually earned and spent. As the bureau's report put it, "this minute catalogue of the details governing the life of each family portrays more vividly than any mere array of figures the common current of daily life among the people."[4] As you study these summaries, pay attention to the standard of living of families in this sample. Note the characteristics of the families who earned the most money or had the highest standard of living and of those who earned the least or had the lowest standard of living.

"Earnings, Expenses and Conditions of Workingmen and Their Families" (1884)

No. 35   LABORER   *Italian*

EARNINGS—Of father $270

CONDITION—Family numbers 5—parents and three children, all boys, aged one, three and five. Live in one room, for which they pay $4 per month rent. A very dirty and unhealthy place, everything perfectly filthy. There are about fifteen other families living in the same house. They buy the cheapest kind of meat from the neighboring slaughter houses and the children pick up fuel on the streets and rotten eatables from the commission houses. Children do not attend school. They are all ignorant in the full sense of the word. Father could not write his name.

FOOD—*Breakfast*—Coffee and bread.
        Dinner—Soups.
        Supper—Coffee and bread.

COST OF LIVING—
    Rent $ 48
    Fuel   5
    Meat and groceries   100
    Clothing, boots and shoes and dry goods   15
    Sickness   5
        Total $173

Source: Illinois Bureau of Labor Statistics, "Earnings, Expenses and Conditions of Workingmen and Their Families," *Third Biennial Report* (Springfield, Ill., 1884), pp. 164, 267–271, 357–362, 365, 369–370, 373, 375, 383–385, 390–393, 395, 401–402, 404, 406–407, 410.

No. 46   LABORER   *American*

EARNINGS—Of father	$360	
Of wife	100	
Total		$460

CONDITION—Family numbers 7—parents and five children, aged from six months to eight years. They live in a house which they rent, and pay rental of $10 per month. Two of the children attend school. House is situated in good, respectable neighborhood. The furniture and carpets are poor in quality, but substantial. The father is not a member of a labor organization, but subscribes for the labor papers. Their living expenses exceed their income.

FOOD—*Breakfast*—Salt meat, bread, butter and coffee.
     Dinner—Bread, meat and vegetables.
     Supper—Bread, coffee, etc.

COST OF LIVING—

Rent	$120	
Fuel, meat and groceries	225	
Clothing, boots, and shoes and dry goods	85	
Books, papers, etc.	2	
Sundries	75	
Total		$507

No. 47   LABORER   *Irish*

EARNINGS—Of father $343

CONDITION—Family numbers 5—parents and three children, two girls, aged seven and five, and boy, aged eight. They occupy a rented house of 4 rooms, and pay a rental, monthly of $7. Two of the children attend school. Father complains of the wages he receives, being but $1.10 per day, and says it is extremely difficult for him to support his family upon that amount. His work consists in cleaning yards, basements, out-buildings, etc., and is, in fact, a regular scavenger. He also complains of the work as being very unhealthy, but it seems he can procure no other work.

FOOD—*Breakfast*—Black coffee, bread and potatoes.
     Dinner—Corned beef, cabbage and potatoes.
     Supper—Bread, coffee and potatoes.

Cost of Living

Rent	$84
Fuel	15
Meat and groceries	180
Clothing, boots and shoes and dry goods	40
Sundries	20
Total	$339

No. 51   MACHINIST   *American*

EARNINGS—Of father	$540
Of mother	255
Of son, aged sixteen	255
Total	$1,050

CONDITION—Family numbers 10—parents and eight children, five girls and three boys, aged from two to sixteen. Four of the children attend school. Father works only 30 weeks in the year, receives $3 per day for his services. They live in a comfortably furnished house, of 7 rooms, have a piano, take an interest in society and domestic affairs, are intelligent, but do not dress very well. Their expenditures are equal, but do not exceed their income. Father belongs to trades union, and is interested and benefited by and in it.

FOOD—*Breakfast*—Bread, meat and coffee.
        Dinner—Bread, meat, vegetables and tea.
        Supper—Bread, meat, vegetables and coffee.

Cost of Living—

Rent	$300
Fuel	50
Meat	100
Groceries	200
Clothing	160
Boots and shoes	50
Dry goods	25
Books, papers, etc.	15
Trades unions	10
Sickness	50
Sundries	90
Total	$1,050

No. 105   BRAKEMAN   *Irish*

EARNINGS—Of father $360

CONDITION—Family numbers 10—parents and eight children, six girls and
two boys, aged one year to fifteen. Four of them attend public school.
Family occupy a house of 3 rooms, for which they pay $5 per month
rental. The house presents a most wretched appearance. Clothes ragged,
children half dressed and dirty. They all sleep in one room regardless
of sex. The house is devoid of furniture, and the entire concern is as
wretched as could well be imagined. Father is shiftless and does not
keep any one place for any length of time. Wife is without ambition or
industry.

FOOD—*Breakfast*—Bread, coffee and syrup.
    Dinner—Potatoes, soup and bread, occasionally meat.
    Supper—Bread, syrup and coffee.

COST OF LIVING—

Rent	$ 60	
Fuel	25	
Meat	20	
Groceries	360	
Clothing	50	
Boots and shoes	15	
Dry goods	30	
Books, papers, etc.	20	
Sickness	5	
Total		$585

No. 112   COAL MINER   *American*

EARNINGS—Of father $250

CONDITION—Family numbers 7—husband, wife, and five children, three
girls and two boys, aged from three to nineteen years. Three of them go
to the public school. Family live in 2 rooms tenement, in healthy locality,
for which they pay $6 per month rent. The house is scantily furnished,
without carpets, but is kept neat and clean. They are compelled to live
very economically, and every cent they earn is used to the best advantage.
Father had only thirty weeks work during the past year. He belongs to
trades union. The figures for cost of living are actual and there is no doubt
the family lived on the amount specified.

FOOD—*Breakfast*—Bread, coffee and salt meat.
    Dinner—Meat, bread, coffee and butter.
    Supper—Sausage, bread and coffee.

COST OF LIVING—

Rent	$72
Fuel	20
Meat	20
Groceries	60
Clothing	28
Boots and shoes	15
Dry goods	20
Trades union	3
Sickness	10
Sundries	5
Total	$252

No. 130	COAL MINER	*Irish*

EARNINGS—

Of father	$420
Of son, twenty-one years of age	420
Of son, eighteen years of age	420
Of son, sixteen years of age	150
Total	$1,410

CONDITION—Family numbers 6—parents and four children, three boys and one girl. The girl attends school, and the three boys are working in the mine. Father owns a house of six rooms, which is clean and very comfortably furnished. Family temperate, and members of a church, which they attend with regularity. They have an acre of ground, which they work in summer, and raise vegetables for their consumption. They have their house about paid for, payments being made in installments of $240 per year. Father belongs to mutual assessment association and to trades union.

FOOD—*Breakfast*—Steak, bread, butter, potatoes, bacon and coffee.
    Dinner—Bread, butter, meat, cheese, pie and tea.
    Supper—Meat, potatoes, bread, butter, puddings, pie and coffee.

COST OF LIVING—

Rent	$240
Fuel	10
Meat	200
Groceries	700
Clothing	80
Boots, shoes and dry goods	70
Books, papers, etc.	15
Life insurance	18
Trades unions	3
Sickness	4
Sundries	75
Total	$1,415

No. 131   COAL MINER   *German*

EARNINGS—Of father $200

CONDITION—Family numbers 6—parents and four children, two boys and two girls, aged two, four, nine and eleven years. Two of them attend school. Family occupy a house containing 3 rooms, for which they pay $60 per annum. Father works all he can, and only receives $1 per day for his labor. He has only been in this country two and one half years and is anxious to get back to Germany. The house is miserably furnished, and is a wretched affair in itself. They have a few broken chairs and benches and a bedstead. Father is a shoemaker by trade, and does some cobbling which helps a little toward supporting his family. He receives the lowest wages in the shaft.

FOOD—*Breakfast*—Bread and coffee.
　　　Dinner—Bread, meat and coffee.
　　　Supper—Bread, meat, potatoes and coffee.

COST OF LIVING—

Rent	$60	
Meat	36	
Groceries	84	
Clothing	12	
Boots and shoes and dry goods	15	
Sickness	1	
Sundries	20	
Total		$228

No. 137   IRON AND STEEL WORKER   *English*

EARNINGS—Of father	$1,420	
Of son, aged fourteen	300	
Total		$1,720

CONDITION—Family numbers 6—parents and four children; two boys and two girls, aged from seven to sixteen years. Three of them attend school, and the other works in the shop with his father. Family occupy their own house, containing 9 well-furnished rooms, in a pleasant and healthy locality. They have a good vegetable and flower garden. They live well, but not extravagantly, and are saving about a thousand dollars per year. Father receives an average of $7 per day of twelve hours, for his labor, and works about thirty-four weeks of the year. Belongs to trades union, but carries no life insurance. Had but little sickness during the year.

FOOD—*Breakfast*—Bread, butter, meat, eggs, and sometimes oysters.
　　　Dinner—Potatoes, bread, butter, meat, pie, cake or pudding.
　　　Supper—Bread, butter, meat, rice or sauce, and tea or coffee.

COST OF LIVING—

Fuel	$ 55
Meat	100
Groceries	300
Clothing	75
Boots and shoes	50
Dry goods	50
Books, papers, etc.	10
Trades unions	6
Sickness	12
Sundries	50
Total	$708

No. 159	ROLLER BAR MILL	*American*

EARNINGS—Of father $2,200

CONDITION—Family numbers 5—parents and three children, two boys and one girl, aged four, six and eight years. Do not attend school. Family occupy house containing 3 rooms, well furnished in healthy locality, but the surroundings are not of the best. Family ordinarily intelligent. Father works eleven hours per day for 37 weeks in the year, and receives $10 per day for his labor; he saves about $1,400 per year, which he deposits in the bank. Family live well, but not extravagantly.

FOOD—*Breakfast*—Bread, meat, eggs, and coffee.
        Dinner—Bread, meat, vegetables, fruits and coffee.
        Supper—Bread, fruits, coffee and meat.

COST OF LIVING—

Rent	$120
Fuel	40
Groceries	200
Clothing	55
Boots and shoes	35
Dry goods	60
Books, papers, etc.	8
Sickness	50
Sundries	75
Total	$768

3   In the first years of the twentieth century, a philanthropic foundation funded a sweeping study of conditions in Pittsburgh, Pennsylvania, the center of the nation's iron and steel industry. The result was one of the early twentieth century's best documented descriptions of life in industrial America. Lawyer and socialist Crystal Eastman wrote the survey's volume on industrial accidents.

"Human Power. . . Is What We Are Losing" (1910)
CRYSTAL EASTMAN

In a year when industrial activity was at its height—that is, from July 1, 1906, to June 30, 1907—526 men were killed by work-accidents in Allegheny County, Pennsylvania. During three months, April, May and June, of the same year, the hospitals of the county received over 509 men injured in such accidents. It is impossible to state the total number of injuries during that quarter, because there is no available record except of cases received at the hospitals. But even were an accurate estimate of the number of injuries in a year possible, it would be of little value. A scratched finger and a lost leg can not be added together if you look for a useful truth in the sum. It is better, therefore, not to try to estimate the total number of injuries in a year, but to concentrate our attention on the permanent loss of health and power involved in the injuries we are sure of. In 294 of the 509 non-fatal accident cases of which we have record (those received at the hospitals during the three selected months), it was possible to learn the nature and extent of the injury. One hundred and twenty-seven of the men escaped without permanent injury. Ninety-one sustained what is here called a slight permanent injury; for instance, a lame leg, arm, foot hand, or back, not serious enough to disable a man, the loss of a finger, slight impairment of sight or hearing, and the like. Seventy-six men (25.5 per cent) suffered a serious permanent injury. Lest there should be doubt as to what is meant here by "serious," it will be better to state exactly what these injuries were. Seven men lost a leg, sixteen men were hopelessly crippled in one or both legs, one lost a foot, two lost half a foot, five lost an arm, three lost a hand, ten lost two or more fingers, two were left with crippled left arms, three with crippled right arms, and two with two useless arms. Eleven lost an eye, and three others had the sight of both eyes damaged. Two men have crippled backs, two received internal injuries, one is partially paralyzed, one feebleminded, and two are stricken with the weakness of old age while still in their prime. Finally three men suffer from a combination of permanent injuries. One of these has a rupture and a crippled foot; another a crippled left leg, and the right foot gone; the third has lost an arm and leg.

Source: Crystal Eastman, *The Pittsburgh Survey: Work-Accidents and the Law* (New York: Charities Publication Committee, 1910), pp. 11–14.

Estimating the hospital cases for a year on the same basis we have the Pittsburgh District annually sending out from its mills, railroad yards, factories, and mines, 45 one-legged men; 100 hopeless cripples walking with crutch or cane for the rest of their lives; 45 men with a twisted, useless arm; 30 men with an empty sleeve; 20 men with but one hand; 60 with half a hand gone; 70 one-eyed men—500 such wrecks in all. Such is the trail of lasting miseries work-accidents leave behind. . . .

There is no bright side to this situation. By industrial accidents, Allegheny County loses more than 500 workmen every year, of whom nearly half are American born, 70 per cent are workmen of skill and training, and 60 per cent have not reached the prime of their working life. Youth, skill, strength—in a word, human power—is what we are losing.

Workers Respond

Workers did not react passively to the conditions they confronted in the late nineteenth century. What do the following sources reveal about the conditions workers faced and what they thought about those conditions? What challenges did workers confront in attempting to improve their conditions?

4   In 1894, workers at George Pullman's "model" company town went on strike after a series of wage cuts. The strike would spread from Pullman, where workers manufactured the Pullman railroad sleeper cars, to the nation's rail system, leaving much of it shut down. This is a statement of a Pullman striker at the Chicago Convention of the American Railway Union, which represented unskilled railroad workers involved in the strike.

Why We Struck at Pullman (1895)

We struck at Pullman because we were without hope. We joined the American Railway Union because it gave us a glimmer of hope. Twenty thousand souls, men, women, and little ones, have their eyes turned toward the convention today, straining eagerly through dark despondency for a glimmer of the heaven-sent message you alone can give us on this earth.

In stating to this body our grievances it is hard to tell where to begin. . . . Five reductions in wages, work, and in conditions of employment swept through the shops at Pullman between May and December 1893. The last was the most severe, amounting to nearly 30 percent and our rents had not fallen. . . .

Source: Joshua Freeman et al., *Who Built America? Working People and the Nation's Economy, Politics, Culture, and Society* (New York: Pantheon Books, 1992), 11: p. 140; originally from U.S. Strike Commission, *Report on the Chicago Strike of June–July 1894* (1895).

No man or woman of us all can ever hope to own one inch of George Pullman's land. Why even the streets are his. . . .

Pullman, both the man and the town, is an ulcer on the body politic. He owns the houses, the schoolhouses, the churches of God. . . . The revenue he derives from these, the wages he pays out with one hand—the Pullman Palace Car Company, he takes back with the other—the Pullman Land Association. He is able by this to bid under any contract car shop in the country. His competitors in business, to meet this, must reduce the wages of their men. . . . And thus the merry war—the dance of skeletons bathed in human tears—goes on, and it will go on, brothers, forever, unless you, the American Railway Union, stop it; end it; crush it out.

 This letter was written by an African American iron worker at the Black Diamond Steel Works.

Colored Workmen and a Strike (1887)

To the Editor:

As a strike is now in progress at the Black Diamond Steel Works, where many of our race are employed, the colored people hereabouts feel a deep interest in its final outcome. As yet few colored men have taken part in it, it having been thus far thought unwise to do so. It is true our white brothers, who joined the Knights of Labor and organized the strike without conferring with, or in any way consulting us, now invite us to join with them and help them to obtain the desired increase in wages and control by the Knights of Labor of the works. But as we were not taken into their schemes at its inception, and as it was thought by them that no trouble would be experienced in obtaining what they wanted without our assistance, we question very much the sincerity and honesty of this invitation. Our experience as a race with these organizations has, on the whole, not been such as to give us either great satisfaction or confidence in white men's fidelity. For so often after we have joined them, and the desired object has been attained, we have discovered that sinister and selfish motives were the whole and only cause that led them to seek us as members.

A few years ago a number of colored men working at this mill were induced to join the Amalgamated Association, thereby relinquishing the positions which they held at these works. They were sent to Beaver Falls, Pa., to work in a mill there controlled by said Association, and the men there, brothers too, mark you, refused to work with them because they were black. It is true Mr. Jaret, then chairman of that Association, sat down upon those skunks, but when that mill closed down, and those men went out from there

Source: Philip S. Foner and Ronald L. Lewis, eds., *Black Workers: A Documentary History from Colonial Times to the Present* (Philadelphia: Temple University Press, 1989), pp. 220–221; originally from *New York Freeman,* August 13, 1887.

to seek employment in other mills governed by the Amalgamated, while the men did not openly refuse to work with them, they managed always to find some pretext or excuse to keep from employing them.

Now, Mr. Editor, I am not opposed to organized labor. God forbid that I should be when its members are honest, just and true! But when I join any society, I want to have pretty strong assurance that I will be treated fairly. I do not want to join any organization the members of which will refuse to work by my side because the color of my skin happens to be of a darker hue than their own. Now what the white men in these organizations should and must do, if they want colored men to join with and confide in them, is to give them a square deal—give them a genuine white man's chance—and my word for it they will flock into them like bees into a hive. If they will take Mr. B. F. Stewart's advice! "take the colored man by the hand and convince him by actual fact that you will be true to him and not a traitor to your pledge," he will be found with them ever and always; for there are not under heaven men in whose breasts beat truer hearts than in the breast of the Negro.

John Lucus Dennis
Colored Puddler at Black Diamond
Steel Works, Pittsburgh, Pa., Aug. 8.

6   In 1902, the United Mine Workers union went out on strike against Pennsylvania coal mine operators. The strike ended after President Theodore Roosevelt threatened to intervene with federal troops and in a later settlement the miners won higher wages and a shorter day. In this source, one coal miner discusses his life and offers it as an example to explain the strike.

"I Struck Because I Had to" (1902)

I am thirty-five years old, married, the father of four children, and have lived in the coal region all my life. Twenty-three of these years have been spent working in and around the mines. . . .

Three of my brothers are miners; none of us had any opportunities to acquire an education. We were sent to school (such a school as there was in those days) until we were about twelve years of age, and then we were put into the screen room of a breaker to pick slate. From there we went inside the mines as driver boys. As we grew stronger we were taken on as laborers, where we served until able to call ourselves miners. We were given work in the breasts and gangways. There were five of us boys. One lies in the cemetery—fifty tons of top rock dropped on him. He was killed three weeks after he got his job as a miner—a month before he was to be married.

Source: Independent 54 (June 12, 1902), pp. 1407–1410.

In the fifteen years I have worked as a miner I have earned the average rate of wages any of us coal heavers get. To-day I am little better off than when I started to do for myself. I have $100 on hand; I am not in debt; I hope to be able to weather the strike without going hungry.

I am only one of the hundreds you see on the street every day. The muscles on my arms are no harder, the callous on my palms no deeper than my neighbors' whose entire life has been spent in the coal region. By years I am only thirty-five. But look at the marks on my body; look at the lines of worriment on my forehead; see the gray hairs on my head and in my mustache; take my general appearance, and you'll think I'm ten years older.

You need not wonder why. Day in and day out, from Monday morning to Saturday evening, between the rising and the setting of the sun, I am in the underground workings of the coal mines. From the seams water trickles into the ditches along the gangways; if not water, it is the gas which hurls us to eternity and the props and timbers to a chaos.

Our daily life is not a pleasant one. When we put on our oil soaked suit in the morning we can't guess all the dangers which threaten our lives. We walk sometimes miles to the place—to the man way or traveling way, or to the mouth of the shaft on top of the slope. And then we enter the darkened chambers of the mines. On our right and on our left we see the logs that keep up the top and support the sides which may crush us into shapeless masses, as they have done to many of our comrades.

We get old quickly. Powder, smoke, after-damp, bad air—all combine to bring furrows to our faces and asthma to our lungs.

I did not strike because I wanted to; I struck because I had to. A miner— the same as any other workman—must earn fair living wages, or he can't live. And it is not how much you get that counts. It is how much what you get will buy. I have gone through it all, and I think my case is a good sample.

I was married in 1890, when I was 23 years old. . . . The woman I married is like myself. She was born beneath the shadow of a dirt bank; her chances for school weren't any better than mine; but she did have to learn how to keep house on a certain amount of money. After we paid the preacher for tying the knot we had just $185 in cash, good health and the good wishes of many friends to start us off.

Our cash was exhausted in buying furniture for housekeeping. In 1890 work was not so plentiful, and by the time our first baby came there was room for much doubt as to how we would pull out. Low wages, and not much over half time in those years, made us hustle. In 1890–91, from June to May, I earned $368.72. That represented eleven months' work, or an average of $33.52 per month. Our rent was $10 per month; store not less than $20. And then I had my oil suits and gum boots to pay for. The result was that after the first year and a half of our married life we were in debt. Not much, of course, and not as much as many of my neighbors, men of larger families, and some who made less money, or in whose case there had been sickness or accident or death. These are all things which a miner must provide for.

I have had fairly good work since I was married. I made the average of what we contract miners are paid; but, as I said before, I am not much better off than when I started.

In 1896 my wife was sick eleven weeks. The doctor came to my house almost every day. He charged me $20 for his services. There was medicine to buy. I paid the drug store $18 in that time. Her mother nursed her, and we kept a girl in the kitchen at $1.50 a week, which cost me $15 for ten weeks, besides the additional living expenses.

In 1897, just a year afterward, I had a severer trial. And mind, in those years, we were only working about half time. But in the fall of that year one of my brothers struck a gas feeder. There was a terrible explosion. He was hurled downward in the breast and covered with the rush of coal and rock. I was working only three breasts away from him and for a moment was unable to realize what had occurred. Myself and a hundred others were soon at work, however, and in a short while we found him, horribly burned over his whole body, his laborer dead alongside of him.

He was my brother. He was single and had been boarding. He had no home of his own. I didn't want him taken to the hospital, so I directed the driver of the ambulance to take him to my house. Besides being burned, his right arm and left leg were broken, and he was hurt internally. The doctors—there were two at the house when we got there—said he would die. But he didn't. He is living and a miner today. But he lay in bed just fourteen weeks, and was unable to work for seven weeks after he got out of bed. He had no money when he was hurt except the amount represented by his pay. All of the expenses for doctors, medicine, extra help and his living were borne by me, except $25, which another brother gave me. The last one had none to give. Poor work, low wages and a sickly woman for a wife had kept him scratching for his own family.

Women at Work

By 1900, five million of the twenty-five million Americans in the work force were women, most of whom worked at wages far below those of male workers. Note what the following sources reveal about the conditions confronting many female wage earners. How do they compare to conditions confronting male workers?

7   In 1869, a group of women petitioned the Massachusetts legislature to have the state help finance homes for them. Their demands were discussed in a meeting held in Boston. This account is from the *Working-man's Advocate,* an influential labor paper.

Women Make Demands (1869)

A convention of Boston work women was held in that city on the 21st ult. at which some extraordinary developments were made. We append some of the discussions:

Opening Address by Miss Phelps

Miss Phelps said: the subject of this meeting is to bring out the purpose of the petition just read, and the facts whereon it is based. We do not think the men of Massachusetts know how the women live. We do not think if they did they would allow such a state of things to exist. Some of us who signed the petition have had to work for less than twenty-five cents a day, and we know that many others have had to do the same. True, many get good wages comparatively for women. There are girls that get from $1 to $1.50 per day, either because they are superior laborers or have had unusual opportunities. But many of these poor girls among whom it has been my fortune to live and work, are not skilled laborers. They are incapable of going into business for themselves, or carrying on for themselves, and incapable of combination; they are uneducated, and have no resource but the system that employs them. There are before me now women who I know to be working at the present time for less than twenty-five cents a day. Some of the work they do at these rates from the charitable institutions of the city. These institutions give out work to the women with the professed object of helping them, at which they can scarcely earn enough to keep them from starving; work at which two persons, with their utmost exertions cannot earn more than forty-five cents a day. These things, I repeat, should be known to the public. . . .

Source: Rosalyn Baxandall et al., *America's Working Women: A Documentary History–1600 to the Present* (New York: Vintage Books, 1976), pp. 105–106; originally from *Workingman's Advocate* 5, No. 41 (May 8, 1869), p. 3.

8   Summary of Conditions Among Women Workers Found by the Massachusetts Bureau of Labor (1887)

Feather-sorters, fur-workers, cotton-sorters, all workers on any material that gives off dust are subject to lung and bronchial troubles. In soap-factories the girls' hands are eaten by the caustic soda, and by the end of the day the fingers are often raw and bleeding. In making buttons, pins, and other manufactures . . . there is always liability of getting the fingers jammed or caught. For the first three times the wounds are dressed without charge. After that the person injured must pay expenses. . . .

In food preparation girls who clean and pack fish get blistered hands and fingers from the saltpetre. . . . Others in "working stalls" stand in cold water all day. . . .

In match-factories . . . necrosis often attacks the worker, and the jaw is eaten away. . . .

Source: Barbara M. Wertheimer, *We Were There: The Story of Working Women in America* (New York: Pantheon Books, 1977), pp. 212–213.

9   By the turn of the twentieth century, the American Federation of Labor was the dominant labor union in the country. Its aim was to win gains for skilled workers, who were overwhelmingly white, native-born males. In this source, one AF of L official discusses the union's policy toward women workers.

A Union Official Discusses the Impact of Women Workers (1897)

The invasion of the crafts by women has been developing for years amid irritation and injury to the workman. The right of the woman to win honest bread is accorded on all sides, but with craftsmen it is an open question whether this manifestation is of a healthy social growth or not.

The rapid displacement of men by women in the factory and workshop has to be met sooner or later, and the question is forcing itself upon the leaders and thinkers among the labor organizations of the land.

Is it a pleasing indication of progress to see the father, the brother and the son displaced as the bread winner by the mother, sister and daughter?

Is not this evolutionary backslide, which certainly modernizes the present wage system in vogue, a menace to prosperity—a foe to our civilized pretensions? . . .

The growing demand for female labor is not founded upon philanthropy, as those who encourage it would have sentimentalists believe; it does not spring from the milk of human kindness. It is an insidious assault upon the home; it is the knife of the assassin, aimed at the family circle—the divine injunction. It debars the man through financial embarrassment from family responsibility, and physically, mentally and socially excludes the woman equally from nature's dearest impulse. Is this the demand of civilized progress; is it the desire of Christian dogma? . . .

Capital thrives not upon the peaceful, united, contented family circle; rather are its palaces, pleasures and vices fostered and increased upon the disruption, ruin or abolition of the home, because with its decay and ever glaring privation, manhood loses its dignity, its backbone, its aspirations. . . .

To combat these impertinent inclinations, dangerous to the few, the old and well-tried policy of divide and conquer is invoked, and to our own shame, it must be said, one too often renders blind aid to capital in its warfare upon us. The employer in the magnanimity of his generosity will give

Source: Edward O'Donnell, "Women as Bread Winners—the Error of the Wage," *American Federationist* 4, No. 8 (October 1897). As edited in Eileen Boris and Nelson Lichtenstein, eds., *Major Problems in the History of American Worker: Documents and Essays* (Lexington, Mass.: D.C. Heath, 1991), pp. 232–234.

employment to the daughter, while her two brothers are weary because of their daily tramp in quest of work. The father, who has a fair, steady job, sees not the infamous policy back of the flattering propositions. Somebody else's daughter is called in in the same manner, by and by, and very soon the shop or factory are full of women, while their fathers have the option of working for the same wages or a few cents more, or take their places in the large army of unemployed. . . .

College professors and graduates tell us that this is the natural sequence of industrial development, an integral part of economic claim.

Never was a greater fallacy uttered of more poisonous import. It is false and wholly illogical. The great demand for women and their preference over men does not spring from a desire to elevate humanity; at any rate that is not its trend.

The wholesale employment of women in the various handicrafts must gradually unsex them, as it most assuredly is demoralizing them, or stripping them of that modest demeanor that lends a charm to their kind, while it numerically strengthens the multitudinous army of loafers, paupers, tramps and policemen, for no man who desires honest employment, and can secure it, cares to throw his life away upon such a wretched occupation as the latter.

The employment of women in the mechanical departments is encouraged because of its cheapness and easy manipulation, regardless of the consequent perils; and for no other reason. The generous sentiment enveloping this inducement is of criminal design, since it comes from a thirst to build riches upon the dismemberment of the family or the hearthstone cruelly dishonored. . . .

But somebody will say, would you have women pursue lives of shame rather than work? Certainly not; it is to the alarming introduction of women into the mechanical industries, hitherto enjoyed by the sterner sex, at a wage uncommandable by them, that leads so many into that deplorable pursuit.

 A garment worker wrote this description for *The Independent* magazine.

Work in a Garment Factory (1902)

At seven o'clock we all sit down to our machines and the boss brings each one the pile of work that he or she is to finish during the day. . . . This pile

Source: Joshua Freeman et al., *Who Built America? Working People and the Nation's Economy, Politics, Culture, and Society* (New York: Pantheon Books, 1992), 11: p. 173; originally from *The Independent* (1902).

is put down beside the machine and as soon as a skirt is done it is laid on the other side of the machine. Sometimes the work is not all finished by six o'clock and then the one who is behind must work overtime. . . . The machines go like mad all day, because the faster you work the more money you get. Sometimes in my haste I get my finger caught and the needle goes right through it. . . . The machines are all run by foot power, and at the end of the day one feels so weak that there is a great temptation to lie right down and sleep. But you must go out and get air, and have some pleasure. . . .

Children at Work

Industrial growth in the late nineteenth century had an impact on working children. Note what these sources reveal about the numbers of children working full time and about the conditions under which they labored.

Gainful Workers by Age, 1870–1920

(In thousands of persons 10 years old and over)

		Age (in years)				
Year	Total Workers	10 to 15	16 to 44	45 to 64	65 and over	Unknown
1930	48,830	667	33,492	12,422	2,205	44
1920	42,434	1,417	29,339	9,914	1,691	73
1910	37,371	1,622	26,620	7,606	1,440	83
1900	29,073	1,750	20,223	5,804	1,202	94
1890	23,318	1,504	16,162	4,547	1,009	97
1880	17,392	1,118		16,274		
1870	12,925	765		12,160		

Source: Historical Statistics of the United States: Colonial Times to 1957 (Washington, D.C.: Bureau of the Census, 1960), p. 72.

Spargo was the author of *The Bitter Cry of the Children*, a major exposé of child labor.

Breaker Boys (1906)
JOHN SPARGO

According to the census of 1900, there were 25,000 boys under sixteen years of age employed in and around the mines and quarries of the United States. In the state of Pennsylvania alone,—the state which enslaves more children than any other,—there are thousands of little "breaker boys" employed, many of them not more than nine or ten years old. The law forbids the employment of children under fourteen, and the records of the mines generally show that the law is "obeyed." Yet in May, 1905, an investigation by the National Child Labor Committee showed that in one small borough of 7000 population, among the boys employed in breakers 35 were nine years old, 40 were ten, 45 were eleven, and 45 were twelve—over 150 boys illegally employed in one section of boy labor in one small town! During the anthracite coal strike of 1902, I attended the Labor Day demonstration at Pittston and witnessed the parade of another at Wilkesbarre. In each case there were hundreds of boys marching, all of them wearing their "working buttons," testifying to the fact that they were *bona fide* workers. Scores of them were less than ten years of age, others were eleven or twelve.

Work in the coal breakers is exceedingly hard and dangerous. Crouched over the chutes, the boys sit hour after hour, picking out the pieces of slate and other refuse from the coal as it rushes past to the washers. From the cramped position they have to assume, most of them become more or less deformed and bent-backed like old men. When a boy has been working for some time and begins to get round-shouldered, his fellows say that "He's got his boy to carry round wherever he goes." The coal is hard, and accidents to the hands, such as cut, broken, or crushed fingers, are common among the boys. Sometimes there is a worse accident: a terrified shriek is heard, and a boy is mangled and torn in the machinery, or disappears in the chute to be picked out later smothered and dead. Clouds of dust fill the breakers and are inhaled by the boys, laying the foundations for asthma and miners' consumption. I once stood in a breaker for half an hour and tried to do the work a twelve-year-old boy was doing day after day, for ten hours at a stretch, for sixty cents a day. The gloom of the breaker appalled me. Outside the sun shone brightly, the air was pellucid, and the birds sang in chorus with the trees and the rivers. Within the breaker there was

Source: John Spargo, *The Bitter Cry of the Children* (New York: The Macmillan Company, 1906).

blackness, clouds of deadly dust enfolded everything, the harsh, grinding roar of the machinery and the ceaseless rushing of coal through the chutes filled the ears. I tried to pick out the pieces of slate from the hurrying stream of coal, often missing them; my hands were bruised and cut in a few minutes; I was covered from head to foot with coal dust, and for many hours afterwards I was expectorating some of the small particles of anthracite I had swallowed.

I could not do that work and live, but there were boys of ten and twelve years of age doing it for fifty and sixty cents a day. Some of them had never been inside of a school; few of them could read a child's primer. True, some of them attended the night schools, but after working ten hours in the breaker the educational results from attending school were practically *nil*. "We goes fer a good time, an' we keeps de guys wots dere hoppin' all de time," said little Owen Jones, whose work I had been trying to do. How strange that barbaric patois sounded to me as I remembered the rich, musical language I had so often heard other little Owen Joneses speak in faraway Wales. As I stood in that breaker I thought of the reply of the small boy to Robert Owen. Visiting an English coal-mine one day, Owen asked a twelve-year-old lad if he knew God. The boy stared vacantly at his questioner: "God?" he said, "God? No, I don't. He must work in some other mine." It was hard to realize amid the danger and din and blackness of that Pennsylvania breaker that such a thing as belief in a great All-good God existed.

CONCLUSION

When he was a graduate student, the future historian and president Woodrow Wilson protested that he had to learn "one or two hundred dates and one or two thousand minute particulars" about "nobody knows who." He took comfort in knowing that he would easily forget this "mass of information."[5] The sources in this chapter represent another set of "minute particulars." From them we can learn any number of forgettable facts, from the annual wages of laborers to the number of children working full-time in 1880. By themselves these facts are not useful; contrary to the cliché, they do not "speak for themselves." Rather, they have meaning and interest only when historians select order, and arrange them. Some historians, for instance, might be guided by a desire to understand or explain the growth of unions in the late nineteenth century. Others might work with these and other sources to explain how industrial growth influenced family or gender relations.

Historians' concerns, and therefore what the "thousand minute particulars" tell us, are also influenced by contemporary concerns. Americans still debate the proper role of the government in their society, the regulation of business, the value of labor unions, the usefulness of "schemes" for helping people, and the desirability of letting people rise or fall on their own. Just as such debates help to frame the questions historians ask about the past, answers to these questions lend historical perspective to the debates. The questions in this chapter are thus part of the ongoing dialogue between the past and present. And if you compare your answers to this chapter's questions to those of your classmates, you will see that all of you did not come to the same conclusions. Historians do not always agree about the answers to their inquiries either. In fact, debate is at the heart of their discipline.

These sources further demonstrate that historians must do more than just select certain facts; they must also know what people in the past perceived and believed. In this case, we need to understand workers' circumstances as well as what they thought about those circumstances. In fact, as we shall see in Chapter 3, primary sources are often more valuable to historians for the opinions and biases they reflect than for the facts that they contain.

FURTHER READING

Margaret F. Byington, *Homestead: The Households of a Mill Town* (1910; repr., Pittsburgh, Pa.: University Center for International Studies, 1974).

Lizabeth A. Cohen, "Embellishing a Life of Labor: An Interpretation of the Material Culture of American Working-Class Homes, 1885–1915," in *Common Places: Readings in American Vernacular Culture*, ed. Dell Upton and John Michael Vlach (Athens: University of Georgia Press, 1986).

Melvyn Dubofsky, *Industrialism and the American Worker, 1865–1920* (Arlington Heights, Ill.: AHM Publishing Corp., 1975).

Joshua Freeman et al., *Who Built America? Working People and the Nation's Economy, Politics, Culture, and Society*, Vol. II (New York: Pantheon Books, 1992).

Upton Sinclair, *The Jungle* (New York: Modern Library 2002; originally published in 1906).

John Spargo, *The Bitter Cry of the Children* (London: Macmillan and Co., 1906).

NOTES

1. *Investigation by a Select Committee of the House of Representatives Relative to the Causes of the General Depression in Labor and Business*, 45th Cong., 3rd sess., Misc. House Doc. No. 29 (Washington, D.C.: U.S. Government Printing Office, 1879), pp. 310–321.

2. Robert Green McCloskey, *American Conservatism in the Age of Enterprise* (Cambridge: Harvard University Press, 1951), p. 32.

3. *Massachusetts Bureau of the Statistics of Labor Reports* (1878, 1881), in *The Transformation of American Society, 1870–1890*, ed. John A. Garraty (Columbia: University of South Carolina Press, 1968), p. 88.

4. *Illinois Bureau of Labor Statistics Report* (1884), in *The Transformation of American Society, 1870–1890*, ed. John A. Garraty (Columbia: University of South Carolina Press, 1968), p. 120.

5. Quoted in James A. Henretta, *The Origins of American Capitalism* (Boston: Northeastern University Press, 1991), pp. xv, xvi.

Chapter

3

Evaluating Primary Sources: "Saving" the Indians in the Late Nineteenth Century

The primary sources in this chapter were produced by late nineteenth-century Indian reformers and by Native Americans. They illustrate the biases often found in primary source material.

Sources

1. "Land and Law as Agents in Educating Indians" (1885)
2. The Dawes Act (1887)
3. A Cheyenne Tells His Son About the Land (ca. 1876)
4. Cheyennes Try Farming (ca. 1877)
5. A Sioux Recalls Severalty (ca. 1900)
6. Supervised Indian Land Holdings by State, 1881–1933
7. A Proposal for Indian Education (1888)
8. Instructions to Indian Agents and Superintendents of Indian Schools (1889)
9. The Education of Indian Students at Carlisle (1891)
10. Luther Standing Bear Recalls Carlisle (1933)
11. Wohaw's Self-Portrait (1877)
12. Taking an Indian Child to School (1891)
13. A Crow Medicine Woman on Teaching the Young (1932)
14. Percentage of Population Over Ten Illiterate, 1900–1930

*T*he guests of the rambling hotel had chosen a perfect spot to gather in October 1883. While strolling along Lake Mohonk, less than a hundred miles north of New York City, they could take in autumn's splendor in a landscape punctuated by cliffs, boulders, and caverns. The main attraction, though, was the hotel itself. Built of wood and rock, the multistoried Mohonk House arose at the end of the lake in a forest of chimneys, turrets, and gables. In proper Victorian style, gingerbread frills adorned the exterior, while inside an air of quiet gentility prevailed. The hotel's Quaker proprietors prohibited strong drink, card playing, and dancing, but these guests did not seem to mind. They could relax in a large parlor tastefully filled with wicker chairs, writing desks, books, and flowers freshly cut from the hotel's gardens. Besides, they had come to Lake Mohonk for work, not play. And their work, they knew, was of utmost importance.

Here on the fringe of New York's peaceful Catskills a hundred or so people gathered for four days to discuss and—they hoped—influence the fate of the Native Americans. The Lake Mohonk Conference of the Friends of the Indian, the first of many such meetings held each October at the resort, attracted delegates from the country's leading Indian reform organizations as well as members of Congress and federal officials. Mostly Easterners, the conferees had been stirred into action by distressing reports out of the West. From the Great Plains to the Pacific, Indians and their reservation lands were under a massive assault. After years of white–Indian warfare that raged from the Dakotas to California, reformers grew more determined by the 1880s to save America's 250,000 or so indigenous inhabitants from total destruction. This gathering at Lake Mohonk marked a growing unity among them.

The objects of the reformers' concern, of course, were far removed from this tranquil setting. And although some of these "friends" of the Indians could claim firsthand knowledge of the Western tribes, Native American representatives were not present at Lake Mohonk. Their absence, however, did not seem to trouble the conferees, who were imbued with a sense of high moral purpose and a conviction that they knew what was best for the Indians. Nor were these reformers disturbed that their campaign to "save" the Indian—and Native Americans' responses to it—reflected conflicting cultural assumptions. In ways that *neither* group could clearly perceive, competing values lay at the heart of late nineteenth-century Indian reform. What people in the past missed, however, modern students of history *can* see. The historical sources left by reformers and Native Americans alike may give us a better understanding of America's solution to the "Indian problem" than possessed even by people at the time.

SETTING

Like the organized efforts to save the Indians of the West, the assault on them began at the Civil War's end. After 1865, the spread of the iron rail opened up large portions of the country to white settlers. At the same time, the government and the military could again turn their attention to the Indians. In the years after Appomattox, the federal government renewed a campaign, begun as early as the late eighteenth century, to confine Indians to separate land. The result, after 1865, was a concerted effort by the military to place Indians in the West on reservations. The nomadic tribes of the Great Plains became the military's primary target. By the 1870s, scores of battles had bloodied the prairie from Texas to Montana. After the war, soldiers and hunters also launched a relentless campaign of slaughter against millions of buffalo, pushing the animal to the brink of extinction by the early 1880s. Bloodshed, however, was not confined to the plains. From the verdant Northwest to the sun-bleached southwestern deserts, tribes were assaulted and gradually stripped of their lands as prior treaties were renegotiated in favor of encroaching settlers. Wherever they lived, Indians discovered the same thing: resistance to military force only inflamed whites. Even events in remote northern California could stoke anti-Indian sentiment in the rest of the nation. There, in 1873, the Modoc Indians fled their reservation and fought off the Army for seven months before surrendering. Three years later, hatred of the Indian reached a fever pitch when Americans in the midst of their nation's centennial celebration received news of the Sioux Indians' shocking annihilation of Colonel George Custer and his Seventh Cavalry detachment at Little Big Horn in Montana.

In the years following Custer's "Last Stand," however, intense white animosity toward the Indians began to wane as their resistance was gradually broken. In addition, several events covered widely in the Eastern press contributed to a more favorable view of Native Americans by the late 1870s. In 1877, Chief Joseph led the Nez Perces on a dramatic 1,500-mile trek through Idaho, Wyoming, and Montana while heroically fighting off Army troops. By the time Chief Joseph and his harried band surrendered, their determined effort to secure the return of the Nez Perces' northwest homeland had won the sympathy of many Americans. So too did the struggle of Nebraska's Ponca Indians about the same time to get back *their* land, which had been inadvertently included in a Sioux reservation by an earlier treaty. When the Sioux attempted to force the Poncas off their land in the 1870s, the government intervened and shipped the Poncas against their will to the Indian Territory of present-day Oklahoma, where many died of disease. Then, when Chief Standing Bear led a Ponca band back to its homeland in 1879, the Army moved in to stop them. Meanwhile, popular sentiments had also been aroused by the flight of Cheyennes from the Indian Territory to their traditional tribal lands in Montana. Led by Dull Knife and Little Wolf, the band eluded troops across Kansas and Nebraska, only to be cut down by soldiers after attempting to break out of their eventual confinement at Fort Robinson, Nebraska, in 1878.

Such determined efforts to return to lost homes drew a sympathetic white response and swelled the ranks of Indian reformers by 1880. In 1879, the Philadelphia-based Woman's National Indian Association and the Boston Indian Citizenship Committee were formed in the wake of the Ponca affair. Three years later, the Indian Rights Association was organized in Philadelphia, and the year after that representatives of these and other Indian-reform groups came together on the shores of Lake Mohonk to discuss the Indians' future. Indeed, not since the end of the Civil War had prospects looked better for the advocates of reform. They would be boosted further when New England–born Helen Hunt Jackson decided to write a book after attending a lecture by Ponca chief Standing Bear on the tribe's heartbreaking loss of its ancestral land. Published in 1881, *A Century of Dishonor* provided an account of the government's "shameful record of broken treaties and unfulfilled promises" regarding the Indians.[1] Jackson, who sent copies of the book to every member of Congress, helped win even greater support for resolving once and for all the country's long-standing "Indian problem."

Increasingly organized, and armed with Jackson's exposé, reformers set their sights on government policy toward the Indian. It was an issue with which these mostly well-to-do Protestants were already familiar. In 1869, the Grant administration brought religious denominations into the administration of Indian policy through the Board of Indian Commissioners, established to help oversee a scandal-ridden Office of Indian Affairs. The commissioners—one of whom owned the Mohonk House and many of whom represented Protestant religious groups—for a time administered Indian policy and disbursed reservation funds. Meanwhile, various missionary organizations took over the appointment of reservation agents. Like other reformers who initially supported the reservation system, the commissioners had put great faith in its power to reform the Indian. By the late 1870s, however, Protestant reformers came to view the reservation itself as the chief obstacle in the way of Native American progress. There they saw a still-corrupt federal Indian service, increasing Native American dependence on government largesse, and stubborn resistance to a new way of life. The solution to the "Indian problem," they concluded, required breaking up the reservations. And that was not all. This radical change in policy had to be accompanied by a program to educate Indian children. By the time of the first Lake Mohonk conference, these determined reformers were devoting their efforts almost exclusively to promoting these goals. Before the end of the decade, their labors would begin to bear fruit.

INVESTIGATION

This chapter contains a variety of primary sources relating to late nineteenth-century Indian reform. Produced both by white reformers and by Native Americans, the sources are as useful for the opinions and biases that they reveal as for the facts that they contain. As you analyze them, your main job is to evaluate the Indian reform program and its impact on Native Americans. In other words, you must determine in what ways late nineteenth-century reformers' efforts to "save" the Indian succeeded or failed and the reasons why their fruits proved bitter or sweet to Native Americans themselves. A good analysis of this reform movement will address these questions:

1. **What did white reformers hope to achieve with the breakup of the reservations and with schools for Indian children?** What problems were these reforms designed to solve? Were their goals and remedies appropriate?

2. **What were the reformers' attitudes toward the Indians and their culture?** How did their views or beliefs influence their proposals?

3. **What impact did the reformers' solutions to the "Indian problem" have on the Indians and their culture?** How did the Native Americans' views or beliefs influence their response to these reforms?

4. **What were the most important factors influencing the nature and impact of Indian reform?** What factors or circumstances would have changed the outcome?

As you evaluate the sources in this chapter, look not only for the stated beliefs but also the unstated assumptions of white reformers and Native Americans. Before you begin, read the sections in your textbook on the opening of the West and white–Indian relations after the Civil War as well as any discussion of the Indian reform movement. Pay particular attention to your text's interpretation of the last development, for you may want to use the evidence in this chapter to assess it.

SOURCES

Reformers and the Reservation

This section contains a selection by a prominent Indian reformer on the need to abandon the reservation system (Source 1) and an excerpt from the General Allotment Law of 1887, commonly known as the Dawes Act (Source 2). As you evaluate these sources, look for evidence of the way reformers defined the "Indian problem," their views about the reservation, and their attitudes toward the Indians. Also consider the ways in which the Dawes Act reflected these views.

 Merrill E. Gates was one of the most prominent late nineteenth-century Indian reformers. The president of Rutgers College and, later, Amherst College, Gates was appointed by President

Chester A. Arthur to the Board of Indian Commissioners in 1884. For many years, he also presided over the Lake Mohonk conferences. In 1885, he presented a paper to the Board of Indian Commissioners that advanced his solution to the Indian problem. What are his views on the nature of Indian society?

"Land and Law as Agents in Educating Indians" (1885)

Two peculiarities which mark the Indian **life,** if retained, will render his progress slow, uncertain and difficult. These are:

1. The tribal organization.
2. The Indian reservation.

I am satisfied that no man can carefully study the Indian question without the deepening conviction that these institutions must go if we would save the Indian from himself. . . .

A false sentimental view of the tribal organization commonly presents itself to those who look at this question casually. It takes form in such objections as this:

> The Indians have a perfect right to bring up their children in the old devotion to the tribe and the chief. To require anything else of them is unreasonable. These are their ancestral institutions. We have no right to meddle with them.

The correction for this false view seems to me to come from the study of the tribe and its actual effects upon the family and upon the manhood of the individual.

The highest right of man is the right to be a man, with all that this involves. The tendency of the tribal organization is constantly to interfere with and frustrate the attainment of his highest manhood. The question whether parents have a right to educate their children to regard the tribal organization as supreme, brings us at once to the consideration of the family.

And here I find the key to the Indian problem. More than any other idea, this consideration of the family and its proper sphere in the civilizing of races and in the development of the individual, serves to unlock the difficulties which surround legislation for the Indian.

The family is God's unit of society. On the integrity of the family depends that of the State. There is no civilization deserving of the name where the family is not the unit of civil government. . . .

The tribal organization, with its tenure of land in common, with its constant divisions of goods and rations per capita without regard to service

Source: Merrill E. Gates, "Land and Law as Agents in Educating Indians," in Francis Paul Prucha, ed., *Americanizing the American Indians: Writings by the "Friends of the Indian," 1880–1900* (Cambridge, Mass.: Harvard University Press, 1973), pp. 48–52; originally from *Seventeenth Annual Report of the Board of Indian Commissioners* (1885).

rendered, cuts the nerve of all that manful effort which political economy teaches us proceeds from the desire for wealth. True ideas of property with all the civilizing influences that such ideas excite are formed only as the tribal relation is outgrown. . . .

But the tribal system paralyzes at once the desire for property and the family life that ennobles that desire. Where the annuities and rations that support a tribe are distributed to the industrious and the lazy alike, while almost all property is held in common, there cannot be any true stimulus to industry. . . .

As the allegiance to tribe and chieftain is weakened, its place should be taken by the sanctities of family life and an allegiance to the laws which grow naturally out of the family! Lessons in law for the Indian should begin with the developing and the preservation, by law, of those relations of property and of social intercourse which spring out of and protect the family. First of all, he must have land in severalty.

Land in severalty, on which to make a home for his family. This land the Government should, where necessary, for a few years hold in trust for him or his heirs, inalienable and unchargeable. But it shall be his. It shall be patented to him as an individual. He shall hold it by what the Indians who have been hunted from reservation to reservation pathetically call, in their requests for justice, "a paper-talk from Washington, which tells the Indian what land is his so that a white man cannot get it away from him." "There is no way of reaching the Indian so good as to show him that he is working for a home. Experience shows that there is no incentive so strong as the confidence that by long, untiring labor, a man may secure a home for himself and his family." The Indians are no exception to this rule. There is in this consciousness of a family-hearth, of land and a home in prospect as permanently their own, an educating force which at once begins to lift these savages out of barbarism and sends them up the steep toward civilization, as rapidly as easy divorce laws are sending some sections of our country down the slope toward barbaric heathenism. . . .

We must as rapidly as possible break up the tribal organization and give them law, with the family and land in severalty as its central idea. We must not only give them law, we must force law upon them. We must not only offer them education, we must force education upon them. Education will come to them by complying with the forms and the requirements of the law.

---

2   The passage of the General Allotment Law, or Dawes Act, in 1887 represented a major victory for reformers. Sponsored by Massachusetts Republican Senator Henry L. Dawes, the act allotted reservation lands in severalty (that is, with individual ownership rights) to Indians. How do the specific provisions of this law reflect widespread assumptions about the Indians and their culture?

The Dawes Act (1887)

An act to provide for the allotment of lands in severalty to Indians on the various reservations, and to extend the protection of the laws of the United States and the Territories over the Indians, and for other purposes.

Be it enacted by the Senate and House of Representatives of the United States of America in Congress assembled, That in all cases where any tribe or band of Indians has been, or shall hereafter be, located upon any reservation created for their use, either by treaty stipulation or by virtue of an act of Congress or executive order setting apart the same for their use, the President of the United States be, and he hereby is, authorized, whenever in his opinion any reservation or any part thereof of such Indians is advantageous for agricultural and grazing purposes, to cause said reservation, or any part thereof, to be surveyed, or resurveyed if necessary, and to allot the lands in said reservation in severalty to any Indian located thereon in quantities as follows:

To each head of a family, one-quarter of a section;

To each single person over eighteen years of age, one-eighth of a section;

To each orphan child under eighteen years of age, one-eighth of a section; and

To each other single person under eighteen years now living, or who may be born prior to the date of the order of the President directing an allotment of the lands embraced in any reservation, one-sixteenth of a section: *Provided,* That in case there is not sufficient land in any of said reservations to allot lands to each individual of the classes above named in quantities as above provided, the lands embraced in such reservation or reservations shall be allotted to each individual of each of said classes pro rata in accordance with the provisions of this act: *And provided further,* That where the treaty or act of Congress setting apart such reservation provides for the allotment of lands in severalty in quantities in excess of those herein provided, the President, in making allotments upon such reservation, shall allot the lands to each individual Indian belonging thereon in quantity as specified in such treaty or act: *And provided further,* That when the lands allotted are only valuable for grazing purposes, an additional allotment of such grazing lands, in quantities as above provided, shall be made to each individual.

Sec. 2.   That all allotments set apart under the provisions of this act shall be selected by the Indians, heads of families selecting for their minor children, and the agents shall select for each orphan child, and in such manner as to embrace the improvements of the Indians making the selection. Where the improvements of two or more Indians have been made on the same legal subdivision of land, unless they shall otherwise agree,

Source: United States Statutes at Large, 24 (1887): pp. 388–391.

a provisional line may be run dividing said lands between them, and the amount to which each is entitled shall be equalized in the assignment of the remainder of the land to which they are entitled under this act: Provided, That if any one entitled to an allotment shall fail to make a selection within four years after the President shall direct that allotments may be made on a particular reservation, the Secretary of the Interior may direct the agent of such tribe or band, if such there be, and if there be no agent, then a special agent appointed for that purpose, to make a selection for such Indian, which election shall be allotted as in cases where selections are made by the Indians, and patents shall issue in like manner. . . .

Sec. 5. That upon the approval of the allotments provided for in this act by the Secretary of the Interior, he shall cause patents to issue therefor in the name of the allottees, which patents shall be of the legal effect, and declare that the United States does and will hold the land thus allotted, for the period of twenty-five years, in trust for the sole use and benefit of the Indian to whom such allotment shall have been made, or, in case of his decease, of his heirs according to the laws of the State or Territory where such land is located, and that at the expiration of said period the United States will convey the same by patent to said Indian, or his heirs as aforesaid, in fee, discharged of said trust and free of all charge or incumbrance whatsoever. . . .

Sec. 6. That upon the completion of said allotments and the patenting of the lands to said allottees, each and every member of the respective bands or tribes of Indians to whom allotments have been made shall have the benefit of and be subject to the laws, both civil and criminal, of the State or Territory in which they may reside; and no Territory shall pass or enforce any law denying any such Indian within its jurisdiction the equal protection of the law. And every Indian both within the territorial limits of the United States to whom allotments shall have been made under the provisions of this act, or under any law or treaty, and every Indian **born** within the territorial limits of the United States who has voluntarily taken up, within said limits, his residence separate and apart from any tribe of Indians therein, and has adopted the habits of civilized life, is hereby declared to be a citizen of the United States, and is entitled to all the rights, privileges, and immunities of such citizens, whether said Indian has been or not, by birth or otherwise, a member of any tribe of Indians within the territorial limits of the United States without in any manner, impairing or otherwise affecting the right of any such Indian to tribal or other property. . . .

Sec. 8. That the provision of this act shall not extend to the territory occupied by the Cherokees, Creeks, Choctaws, Chickasaws, Seminoles, and Osage, Miamies and Peorias, and Sacs and Foxes, in the Indian Territory, nor to any of the reservations of the Seneca Nation of New York Indians in the State of New York, nor to that strip of territory in the State of Nebraska adjoining the Sioux Nation on the south added by executive order.

Native Americans and Severalty

This section contains sources that reflect Native Americans' views. In sources 3, 4, and 5, Native Americans speak for themselves revealing their attitudes about the land and their experience with severalty and farming of reservation lands. As you examine these sources, consider what they reveal about the Dawes Act as a solution to the Indian problem.

3   Wooden Leg was a Northern Cheyenne who fought George Custer and his forces at Little Big Horn, Montana, in 1876. In the early twentieth century, he recounted his early life to a white physician who was practicing among the Cheyennes. In the following passage, he recalls his father's views about the land. What do Wooden Leg's recollections suggest about the forces working against the reformers' plans for the Indians?

A Cheyenne Tells His Son About the Land (ca. 1876)

After we had been driven from the Black Hills and that country was given to the white people my father would not stay on any reservation. He said it was no use trying to make farms as the white people did. In the first place, that was not the Indian way of living. All of our teachings and beliefs were that land was not made to be owned in separate pieces by persons and that the plowing up and destruction of vegetation placed by the Great Medicine and the planting of other vegetation according to the ideas of men was an interference with the plans of the Above. In the second place, it seemed that if the white people could take away from us the Black Hills after that country had been given to us and accepted by us as ours forever, they might take away from us any other lands we should occupy whenever they might want these other lands. In the third place, the last great treaty had allowed us to use all of the country between the Black Hills and the Bighorn river and mountains as hunting grounds so long as we did not resist the traveling of white people through it on their way to or from their lands beyond its borders. My father decided to act upon this agreement to us. He decided we should spend all of our time in the hunting region. We could do this, gaining our own living in this way, or we could be supported by rations given to us at the agency. He chose to stay away from all white people. His family all agreed with him.

Source: Thomas B. Marquis, *Wooden Leg: A Warrior Who Fought Custer* (Lincoln: University of Nebraska Press, 1965), pp. 155–156.

4   John Stands-in-Timber was a Northern Cheyenne who related his tribe's experience with farming in the late 1870s. What do his recollections reveal about the difficulties of transforming the Indian into a yeoman farmer?

Cheyennes Try Farming (ca. 1877)

The government started the Indians raising gardens as soon as they surrendered. Some had gardens of corn and other crops. . . . They had forgotten how, though they all used to garden in the old days before they hunted buffalo. Now they were learning about new crops as well, things they had never seen before. The Dull Knife people got to Oklahoma in 1877 about the time the watermelons ripened, and when the Southern Cheyennes gave them some they cut them up and boiled them like squash. They did not know you could eat them raw. But later when they planted their own they put sugar with the seeds. They said it would make them sweeter when they grew.

When they reached Tongue River every man was supposed to have a garden of his own. A government farmer went around to teach them. And many of them worked hard, even carrying buckets of water from the river by hand. One man, Black White Man, wanted to raise cotton. He had seen it in Oklahoma. He plowed a piece of ground and smoothed it up, and when it was ready he took his wife's quilt and made little pieces from the inside and planted them with a garden hoe. When his wife missed the quilt, she got after him. He was afraid to tell her, but finally he said, "I got it and took out the cotton and planted it. We will have more quilts than we need, as soon as it grows."

When they first learned to plow in Oklahoma the farmer told them to get ready and come to a certain place and he would show them. They did not understand. They thought "Get ready" meant fancy costumes and not their new pants and shirts. So everybody had feathers on their heads and necklaces and leggings and fancy moccasins. It looked like a dance, not a farming lesson. And all the women and children went along to see them.

The farmer told one man to grab the handles while he started ahead with the team. But the plow jumped out of the ground and turned over, and the Indian fell down. But he tried again, and by the time they got back around he was doing pretty well. Then they all tried. At last they came to one man who had been watching closely. When he started off the dirt rolled right over and he went clear around that way, and the criers started announcing, "Ha-aah! See that man!" The women made war cries and everybody hollered just as if he had counted coup.*

*To ceremoniously recount one's exploits in battle.

Source: John Stands-in-Timber and Margo Liberty, *Cheyenne Memories* (New Haven, Conn.: Yale University Press, 1967), pp. 276–278.

Another time when they practiced plowing down there, one man plowed up a bull snake and the next man plowed up a rattlesnake, and after that they were all afraid to go.

In Montana they began to help each other. The government issued plows to quite a few men, and in Birney the Fox Military Society used to plow together as soon as the frost was out. They would all gather at the farthest place up the river and work together until that was done, and then move to the next. They had seven or eight plows and it went faster that way. Besides, it was more fun. . . .

Ella C. Deloria, a Yankton Sioux, recalled the impact of the division of reservation lands into individual allotments. What does her account reveal about the Dawes Act's impact on traditional patterns of life?

A Sioux Recalls Severalty (ca. 1900)

At length there came the time when individual allotments of land were made. Families were encouraged to live out on them and start to be farmers forthwith. Equipment for this, as well as some essential furniture, was given the most docile ones by way of inducement. But again, it wasn't easy to make the spiritual and social adjustment. The people were too used to living in large family groups, cooperatively and happily. Now, here they were in little father-mother-child units (with an occasional grandparent, to be sure), often miles from their other relatives, trying to farm an arid land—the very same land from which, later on, white farmers of Old World tradition and training could not exact even a subsistence living. Enduring frightful loneliness and working at unfamiliar tasks just to put himself ahead financially were outside the average Dakota's ken. For him there were other values. The people naturally loved to foregather; and now the merest excuse for doing so became doubly precious. For any sort of gathering it was the easiest thing to abandon the small garden, leave the stock to fend for themselves, and go away for one to four weeks. On returning, they might find the place a wreck. That was too bad; but to miss getting together with other Dakotas was far worse. . . .

The man was the tragic figure. Frustrated, with his age old occupation suddenly gone, he was left in a daze, unable to overcome the strange and passively powerful inertia that stayed him from doing anything else. And so he sat by the hour, indifferent and inactive, watching—perhaps envying—his wife, as she went right on working at the same essential role of woman

Source: Ella C. Deloria, *Speaking of Indians* (Vermillion, S.Dak.: Dakota Press, 1979), pp. 60, 62–63.

that had been hers since time immemorial. In such a mental state, what did he care that unsympathetic onlookers called him "lazy Indian" and accused him of driving his wife, like a slave, while "he took his ease"! As though he enjoyed it! If, as he sat there, someone had called, "Hey! There's a herd of buffalo beyond that hill! Come quick!" he would have sprung into life instantly again. But, alas, no such thing would ever happen now. All he could do, or thought he could do, on his "farm" was to water the horses mechanically, bring in fuel and water, cut a little hay, tend a little garden. He did it listlessly, almost glad when the garden died on his hands for lack of rain. His heart was not in what he was doing anyway—until something human came up: a gathering of the people, where he could be with many relatives again; or a death, when he must go to help with the mourning; or a cow to be butchered, reminiscent of the hunt; or time to go to the agency for the biweekly issue of rations. That he must not miss. For him and his family, that was what still gave meaning to life.

6 The table on the next page relates to land holding among Indians subject to the Dawes Act in the late nineteenth and early twentieth centuries. What does it reveal about one impact of severalty on Native Americans? Do previous sources provide any explanations for the pattern revealed in this table?

Supervised Indian Land Holdings by State, 1881–1933

	1881	1890	1900	1911[a]	1933
Idaho	2,748,981	2,273,421	1,364,500	770,706	803,239
Kansas	137,747	102,026	28,279	273,408	34,821
Michigan	66,332	27,319	8,317	153,910	20,233
Minnesota	5,026,447	2,254,781	1,566,707	1,480,647	549,320
Montana	29,356,800	10,591,360	9,500,700	6,263,151	6,055,009
Nebraska	436,252	136,947	74,592	344,375	69,280
North Dakota		5,861,120	3,701,724	2,786,162	1,034,123
South Dakota	36,616,448	11,661,360	8,991,791	7,221,939	5,544,424
Washington	7,779,348	4,045,248	2,333,574	2,948,708	2,712,915
Wisconsin	526,026	512,129	381,061	590,094	395,919
Total	82,694,381	37,465,711	27,951,245	22,833,100[a]	17,219,283
Oklahoma	41,100,915	39,156,040	27,397,237	22,736,473[a]	2,919,886
Arizona	3,092,720	6,603,191	15,150,757	17,358,741	18,657,984
California	415,841	494,045	406,396	437,629	625,354
Colorado	12,467,200	1,094,400	483,750	556,621	443,751
Nevada	885,015	959,135	954,135	696,749	866,176
New Mexico	7,228,731	10,002,525	1,667,485	4,520,652	6,188,964
Oregon	3,853,800	2,075,240	1,300,225	1,719,561	1,718,510
Utah	2,039,040	3,972,480	2,039,040	219,101	1,571,020
Wyoming	2,342,400	2,342,400	1,810,000	318,543	2,249,576
Total U.S.	156,120,043	104,314,349	78,372,185	71,464,393[a]	52,651,393

[a]Totals include all allotted land.

Source: Indians, Bureaucrats, and Land: The Dawes Act and the Decline of Indian Farming, by Leonard A. Carlson. Data from "Statistical Supplement to the Annual Report of the Commissioner of Indian Affairs, for the Fiscal Year ended June 30, 1940," p. 37.

Reformers and Indian Education

Reformers did not believe that the Indian problem could be solved only by breaking up the reservation. Instead, education had to supplement severalty. After the breakup of the reservations, therefore, the education of Native American children was the chief interest of most "friends of the Indian" in the late nineteenth century. This section contains sources that reflect their concerns. As you examine them, note the reformers' goals and methods. Also consider what these sources reveal about the reformers' values—and what they thought about the Indians' values.

7   The Reverend Lyman Abbott, one of the most committed Indian reformers, advanced a plan for a universal system of education for Indian children at the Lake Mohonk Conference in 1888. On what grounds does Abbott argue that education must accompany severalty?

A Proposal for Indian Education (1888)

The Indian problem is three problems—land, law, and education. The country has entered upon the solution of the land problem. It has resolved to break up the reservation system, allot to the Indians in severalty so much land as they can profitably occupy, purchase the rest at a fair valuation, throw it open to actual settlers, and consecrate the entire continent to civilization, with no black spot upon it devoted to barbarism. Upon that experiment the country has entered, and it will not turn back. The law problem, also, has been put in the way of solution. It is safe to assume that it will not be long before the existing courts are open to the Indians; and it is reasonable to hope that special courts will be provided for their special protection, in accordance with the general plan outlined by the law committee of the Lake Mohonk Conference. But nothing has yet been done toward the solution of the educational problem. A great deal has been done toward the education of individual Indians, something, perhaps, toward the education of single tribes, but no plan has been agreed upon; and it is hardly too much to say that no plan has even been proposed for solving the educational problem of the Indian race,—for converting them from groups of tramps, beggars, thieves, and sometimes robbers and murderers, into communities of intelligent, industrious, and self-supporting citizens. But this

Source: Francis Paul Prucha, ed., *Americanizing the American Indians: Writings by the "Friends of the Indian," 1880–1900* (Cambridge, Mass.: Harvard University Press, 1973), pp. 208–210, 212; originally from *Proceedings of the Sixth Annual Meeting of the Lake Mohonk Conference of Friends of the Indian* (1888).

is by far the most important problem of the three. Put an ignorant and imbruted savage on land of his own, and he remains a pauper, if he does not become a vagrant and a thief. Open to him the courts of justice, and make him amenable to the laws of the land, and give him neither knowledge nor a moral education, and he will come before those courts only as a criminal; but inspire in him the ambition of industry, and equip him with the capacity of self-support, and he will acquire in time the needful land and find a way to protect his personal rights. These reforms must move on together. Certain it is that without the legal and the educational reform the land reform will be death to the Indian, and burden, if not disaster, to the white race. My object in this paper is simply to set before the Lake Mohonk Conference the outlines of a possible educational system, in the hope that the principles here announced, and the methods here suggested, may at least be found worthy of discussion, out of which may be evolved a plan worthy to be presented to the country for its adoption.

At present we have no system of Indian education. Some Christian and philanthropic individuals and societies are attempting, in various fragmentary ways, to do a work of education in special localities. The Government is doing some educational work under teachers whom it has appointed and whom it supports; but the efficacy of these governmental efforts depends largely upon the ability and character of the agent of the reservation on which the school is situated. . . .

Nor is this the only vice of the present essentially vicious no-system of Indian education. A minority of Indian children are taught more or less feebly the rudiments of civilization, some in boarding schools, some in day schools, some on the reservation, some off it, some under one, others under another sectarian influence. When a little smattering of education has been given them, they drift back, or are sent back to the reservation, to forget what they have learned,—to take off the beaver and put on the feathers, to lay aside the hoe and take up the hatchet, and resume the war paint which they had washed from their faces at the schoolhouse door. That so many Indians are able to resist the evil influences of their savage environments, and interpenetrate their tribe with any civilizing influences whatever, affords a singular testimony to the stability of character which goes along with a saturnine disposition. What the country should do, what the friends of Indian emancipation—rather let me say of justice, humanity, and equal rights—should do, is to substitute for this chaotic congeries of fragmentary efforts, a system which shall secure within a generation the education of all Indian children within the borders of the United States in the essentials of American civilization. Certain propositions looking to this ultimate result I desire to put before the Lake Mohonk Conference for its discussion.

1. The United States Government must undertake to provide this education, not to supplement provision made by others. . . .

2. The education thus to be afforded must not merely be offered as a gift; it must be imposed by superior authority as a requirement. In other words, the education of Indian children must be made compulsory. It is a great mistake to suppose that the red man is hungering for the white man's culture, eager to take it if it is offered to him. The ignorant are never hungry for education, nor the vicious for morality, nor barbarism for civilization; educators have to create the appetite as well as to furnish the food. The right of Government to interfere between parent and child must indeed be exercised with the greatest caution; the parental right is the most sacred of all rights; but a barbaric father has no right to keep his child in barbarism, nor an ignorant father to keep his child in ignorance.

---

8   Soon after he was appointed Commissioner of Indian Affairs in 1889, Thomas J. Morgan issued instructions to Indian agents in charge of reservation schools. What did he see as the main goal of Indian education? How did he propose to achieve it?

Instructions to Indian Agents and Superintendents of Indian Schools (1889)

The great purpose which the Government has in view in providing an ample system of common school education for all Indian youth of school age, is the preparation of them for American citizenship. The Indians are destined to become absorbed into the national life, not as Indians, but as Americans. They are to share with their fellow-citizens in all the rights and privileges and are likewise to be called upon to bear fully their share of all the duties and responsibilities involved in American citizenship.

It is in the highest degree important, therefore, that special attention should be paid, particularly in the higher grades of the schools, to the instruction of Indian youth in the elements of American history, acquainting them especially with the leading facts in the lives of the most notable and worthy historical characters. While in such study the wrongs of their ancestors cannot be ignored, the injustice which their race has suffered can be contrasted with the larger future open to them, and their duties and opportunities rather than their wrongs will most profitably engage their attention.

Source: Francis Paul Prucha, ed., *Americanizing the American Indians: Writings by the "Friends of the Indian," 1880–1900* (Cambridge, Mass.: Harvard University Press, 1973), pp. 257–259; originally from "Instructions to Indian Agents in Regard to Inculcation of Patriotism in Indian Schools," in *House Executive Document* No. 1, part 5, vol. II, 51st Cong., 2nd sess, serial 2841, p. clxvii.

Pupils should also be made acquainted with the elementary principles of the Government under which they live, and with their duties and privileges as citizens. To this end, regular instructions should be given them in the form of familiar talks, or by means of the use of some elementary text-book in civics. Debating societies should be organized in which may be learned the practical rules of procedure which govern public assemblies. Some simple manual of rules of order should be put into the hands of the more advanced students, and they should be carefully instructed in its use.

On the campus of all the more important schools there should be erected a flagstaff, from which should float constantly, in suitable weather, the American flag. In all schools of whatever size and character, supported wholly or in part by the Government, the "Stars and Stripes" should be a familiar object, and students should be taught to reverence the flag as a symbol of their nation's power and protection.

Patriotic songs should be taught to the pupils, and they should sing them frequently until they acquire complete familiarity with them. Patriotic selections should be committed and recited publicly, and should constitute a portion of the reading exercises.

National holidays—Washington's birthday, Decoration Day, Fourth of July, Thanksgiving, and Christmas—should be observed with appropriate exercises in all Indian schools. It will also be well to observe the anniversary of the day upon which the "Dawes bill" for giving to Indians allotments of land in severalty became a law, viz, February 8, 1887, and to use that occasion to impress upon Indian youth the enlarged scope and opportunity given them by this law and the new obligations which it imposes.

In all proper ways, teachers in Indian schools should endeavor to appeal to the highest elements of manhood and womanhood in their pupils, exciting in them an ambition after excellence in character and dignity of surroundings, and they should carefully avoid any unnecessary reference to the fact that they are Indians.

They should point out to their pupils the provisions which the Government has made for their education, and the opportunities which it affords them for earning a livelihood, and for achieving for themselves honorable places in life, and should endeavor to awaken reverence for the nation's power, gratitude for its beneficence, pride in its history, and a laudable ambition to contribute to its prosperity.

Agents and school superintendents are specially charged with the duty of putting these suggestions into practical operation.

Captain Richard Henry Pratt was an Army officer who fought the Indians on the Southern plains and then devoted many years to Indian education. After supervising an experiment in the education of Indian prisoners at Fort Marion, Florida, Pratt established a school for Native American students in some old army barracks at Carlisle, Pennsylvania, in 1879 and served as its superintendent until 1904. A vocational training school, Carlisle was considered a model institution by many Indian reformers. What parallels does Pratt see between Indians and African Americans? What is his argument for educating Indian students off the reservation?

The Education of Indian Students at Carlisle (1891)

A great general has said that the only good Indian is a dead one, and that high sanction of his destruction has been an enormous factor in promoting Indian massacres. In a sense, I agree with the sentiment, but only in this: that all the Indian there is in the race should be dead. Kill the Indian in him, and save the man. . . .

"Put yourself in his place" is as good a guide to a proper conception of the Indian and his cause as it is to help us to right conclusions in our relations with other men. For many years we greatly oppressed the black man, but the germ of human liberty remained among us and grew, until, in spite of our irregularities, there came from the lowest savagery into intelligent manhood and freedom among us more than seven millions of our population, who are to-day an element of industrial value with which we could not well dispense. However great this victory has been for us, we have not yet fully learned our lesson nor completed our work; nor will we have done so until there is throughout all of our communities the most unequivocal and complete acceptance of our own doctrines, both national and religious. . . .

Inscrutable are the ways of Providence. Horrible as were the experiences of its introduction, and of slavery itself, there was concealed in them the greatest blessing that ever came to the Negro race,—seven millions of blacks from cannibalism in darkest Africa to citizenship in free and enlightened America; not full, not complete citizenship, but possible—probable–citizenship, and on the highway and near to it.

There is a great lesson in this. The schools did not make them citizens, the schools did not teach them the language, nor make them industrious and self-supporting. Denied the right of schools, they became English-speaking and industrious through the influences of association. Scattered here and there, under the care and authority of individuals of the higher race, they learned self-support and something of citizenship, and so reached their

Source: Francis Paul Prucha, ed., Americanizing the American Indians: Writings by the "Friends of the Indian," 1880–1900 (Cambridge, Mass.: Harvard University Press, 1973), pp. 260–261, 262, 263–264, 269; originally from Proceedings of the Ninth Annual Meeting of the Lake Mohonk Conference of Friends of the Indian (1891).

present place. No other influence or force would have so speedily accomplished such a result. Left in Africa, surrounded by their fellow-savages, our seven millions of industrious black fellow-citizens would still be savages. Transferred into these new surroundings and experiences, behold the result. They became English-speaking and civilized, because forced into association with English-speaking and civilized people; became healthy and multiplied, because they were property; and industrious, because industry, which brings contentment and health, was a necessary quality to increase their value.

The Indians under our care remained savage, because forced back upon themselves and away from association with English-speaking and civilized people, and because of our savage example and treatment of them. . . .

This ponderous Indian question relates to less than two hundred and fifty thousand people, numerically less than double the population of this city. They are divided into about seventy tribes and languages. Their plane of life has always been above that of the African in his native state. That they have not become civilized and incorporated in the nation is entirely our fault. We have never made any attempt to civilize them with the idea of taking them into the nation, and all of our policies have been against citizenizing and absorbing them. Although some of the policies now prominent are advertised to carry them into citizenship and consequent association and competition with other masses of the nation, they are not, in reality, calculated to do this.

We are after the facts. Let us take the Land in Severalty Bill. Land in severalty, as administered, is in the way of the individualizing and civilization of the Indians, and is a means of holding the tribes together. Land in severalty is given to individuals adjoining each other on their present reservations. And experience shows that in some cases, after the allotments have been made, the Indians have entered into a compact among themselves to continue to hold their lands in common as a reservation. The inducement of the bill is in this direction. The Indians are not only invited to remain separate tribes and communities, but are practically compelled to remain so. The Indian must either cling to his tribe and its locality, or take great chances of losing his rights and property.

The day on which the Land in Severalty Bill was signed was announced to be the emancipation day for the Indians. The fallacy of that idea is so entirely demonstrated that the emancipation assumption is now withdrawn.

We shall have to go elsewhere, and seek for other means besides land in severalty to release these people from their tribal relations and to bring them individually into the capacity and freedom of citizens. . . .

As we have taken into our national family seven millions of Negroes, and as we receive foreigners at the rate of more than five hundred thousand a year, and assimilate them, it would seem that the time may have arrived when we can very properly make at least the attempt to assimilate our two hundred and fifty thousand Indians. . . .

The school at Carlisle is an attempt on the part of the government to do this. Carlisle has always planted treason to the tribe and loyalty to the nation at large. It has preached against colonizing Indians, and in favor of individualizing them. It has demanded for them the same multiplicity of chances which all others in the country enjoy. Carlisle fills young Indians with the spirit of loyalty to the stars and stripes, and then moves them out into our communities to show by their conduct and ability that the Indian is no different from the white or the colored, that he has the inalienable right to liberty and opportunity that the white and the negro have. Carlisle does not dictate to him what line of life he should fill, so it is an honest one. It says to him that, if he gets his living by the sweat of his brow, and demonstrates to the nation that he is a man, he does more good for his race than hundreds of his fellows who cling to their tribal communistic surroundings. . . .

Indians and the White Man's Education

Sources 10–13 in this section were written or created by Native Americans and reflect the Native American experience at Indian schools. As you examine all the sources in this section, consider what they reveal about Indian culture, the Indians' views about their own education, and the effectiveness of reformers' educational efforts.

10 In 1879, when he was eleven years old, Plenty Kill, the son of Standing Bear, left his South Dakota home with other Sioux boys and girls to enroll at Captain Richard Pratt's new school for Indians at Carlisle, Pennsylvania, where he received a new name: Luther Standing Bear. Later, he recalled his experiences as a student at Carlisle. What does this account reveal about Pratt's methods and their impact?

Luther Standing Bear Recalls Carlisle (1933)

At the age of eleven years, ancestral life for me and my people was most abruptly ended without regard for our wishes, comforts, or rights in the matter. At once I was thrust into an alien world, into an environment as

Source: Reprinted from *Land of the Spotted Eagle* by Luther Standing Bear by permission of the University of Nebraska Press. Copyright © 1933, by Luther Standing Bear. Renewal copyright © 1960, by May M. Jones.

different from the one into which I had been born as it is possible to imagine, to remake myself, if I could, into the likeness of the invader.

By 1879, my people were no longer free, but were subjects confined on reservations under the rule of agents. One day there came to the agency a party of white people from the East. Their presence aroused considerable excitement when it became known that these people were school teachers who wanted some Indian boys and girls to take away with them to train as were white boys and girls. . . .

At last at Carlisle the transforming, the "civilizing" process began. It began with clothes. Never, no matter what our philosophy or spiritual quality, could we be civilized while wearing the moccasin and blanket. The task before us was not only that of accepting new ideas and adopting new manners, but actual physical changes and discomfort had to be borne uncomplainingly until the body adjusted itself to new tastes and habits. Our accustomed dress was taken and replaced with clothing that felt cumbersome and awkward. Against trousers and handkerchiefs we had a distinct feeling—they were unsanitary and the trousers kept us from breathing well. High collars, stiff-bosomed shirts, and suspenders fully three inches in width were uncomfortable, while leather boots caused actual suffering. We longed to go barefoot, but were told that the dew on the grass would give us colds. That was a new warning for us, for our mothers had never told us to beware of colds, and I remember as a child coming into the tipi with moccasins full of snow. Unconcernedly I would take them off my feet, pour out the snow, and put them on my feet again without any thought of sickness, for in that time colds, catarrh, bronchitis, and la *grippe* were unknown. But we were soon to know them. Then, red flannel undergarments were given us for winter wear, and for me, at least, discomfort grew into actual torture. I used to endure it as long as possible, then run upstairs and quickly take off the flannel garments and hide them. When inspection time came, I ran and put them on again, for I knew that if I were found disobeying the orders of the school I should be punished. My niece once asked me what it was that I disliked the most during those first bewildering days, and I said, "red flannel." Not knowing what I meant, she laughed, but I still remember those horrid, sticky garments which we had to wear next to the skin, and I still squirm and itch when I think of them. Of course, our hair was cut, and then there was much disapproval. But that was part of the transformation process and in some mysterious way long hair stood in the path of our development. For all the grumbling among the bigger boys, we soon had our heads shaven. How strange I felt! Involuntarily, time and time again, my hands went to my head, and that night it was a long time before I went to sleep. If we did not learn much at first, it will not be wondered at,

I think. Everything was queer, and it took a few months to get adjusted to the new surroundings.

Almost immediately our names were changed to those in common use in the English language. Instead of translating our names into English and calling Zinkcaziwin, Yellow Bird, and Wanbli K'leska, Spotted Eagle, which in itself would have been educational, we were just John, Henry, or Maggie, as the case might be. I was told to take a pointer and select a name for myself from the list written on the blackboard. I did, and since one was just as good as another, and as I could not distinguish any difference in them, I placed the pointer on the name Luther. I then learned to call myself by that name and got used to hearing others call me by it, too. By that time we had been forbidden to speak our mother tongue, which is the rule in all boarding-schools. This rule is uncalled for, and today is not only robbing the Indian, but America of a rich heritage. The language of a people is part of their history. Today we should be perpetuating history instead of destroying it, and this can only be effectively done by allowing and encouraging the young to keep it alive. A language unused, embalmed, and reposing only in a book, is a dead language. Only the people themselves, and never the scholars, can nourish it into life.

Of all the changes we were forced to make, that of diet was doubtless the most injurious, for it was immediate and drastic. White bread we had for the first meal and thereafter, as well as coffee and sugar. Had we been allowed our own simple diet of meat, either boiled with soup or dried, and fruit, with perhaps a few vegetables, we should have thrived. But the change in clothing, housing, food, and confinement combined with lonesomeness was too much, and in three years nearly one half of the children from the Plains were dead and through with all earthly schools. In the graveyard at Carlisle most of the graves are those of little ones.

---

11   Wohaw, a Kiowa Indian, was imprisoned along with other warriors of the Southern plains tribes at Fort Marion, Florida. There he and many of the other prisoners produced numerous drawings that depicted their earlier lives. After his release in 1878, Wohaw continued to draw scenes that reflected the experience of many Plains Indians who, like himself, had been educated by whites. As you examine this drawing, notice the way Wohaw represented his two worlds. (The small structure next to his left foot represents a church. The offering of a pipe was a sign of respect, while the smoke from the animals was an indication of power.) In which direction is Wohaw being pulled?

Wohaw's Self-Portrait (1877)

WOHAW

Missouri Historical Society, St. Louis. Art Acc.# 1882.18.32.

12   According to a Bureau of Indian Affairs clerk at the Crow reservation, this drawing was made by Carlisle school boys. His notes on the drawing read: "Major Wyman, U.S. Ind[ian] Agent at Crow Agency Mont. with his chief of Police 'Boy that Grabs' trying to get Indian children for the school. A Crow Indian squaw leading her little girl by the hand to deliver her to the Capt. of Police."[2] What is the view here of the cigar-smoking agent? What do the gesture and facial expression of the mother indicate about her attitude toward the captain of police?

Taking an Indian Child to School (1891)

1930.51. Drawing by Boys from Carlisle Indian School. Crow, 1981. Charles H. Barstow Collection, Special Collections Library, Montana State University-Billings.

---

13 Pretty-shield, a Crow medicine woman, reflected in the early twentieth century on relations between adults and children in the old days. What does her account reveal about the impact of white culture on those relations? On the lives of Indian adults and children?

A Crow Medicine Woman on Teaching the Young (1932)

"We were a happy people when I came onto this world, Sign-talker. There was plenty to eat, and we could laugh. Now all this is changed. But I will try to begin with the first things I remember.

"About the time when I came to live on this world my aunt, Strikes-with-an-axe, lost two little girls. They had been killed by the Lacota; and so had her man. This aunt, who was my mother's sister, mourned for a long time, growing thinner, and weaker, until my mother gave me to her, to heal her heart. This aunt, Strikes-with-an-axe, was a River Crow. You know that because of a quarrel, just before my time [about 1832], the Crows divided into two tribes, the Mountain Crows, and the River Crows? Well, I was born a Mountain Crow, and this aunt was a River Crow.

"I can remember going away to live with my aunt, and the River Crows, although I could not have been three years old. This separation from my mother and my sisters was in fact not a very real one, because all the Crows came together often. These meetings gave me opportunities to see my family, so that I was happy, perhaps happier than I should have been at home. My aunt's lodge was large, and she lived alone, until I came to stay with her. She needed me, even though I was at first too young to help her.

"I well remember the first time that the Crow clans gathered after I had left my mother to live with my aunt. It was in the springtime. A crier, on a beautiful bay horse, rode through the big village telling the people to get ready to move to the mountains. His words set thoughts of again seeing my mother and sisters and brothers dancing in my young head. I felt very happy. Almost at once my aunt began to pack up; and then she took down her lodge.

"How I loved to move, especially when the clans were going to meet at some selected place, always a beautiful one." She turned to look out of the window at the wide plains, screened by the giant cottonwoods that surround Crow Agency, her eyes wistful.

"A crier would ride through the village telling the people to be ready to move in the morning. In every lodge the children's eyes would begin to shine. Men would sit up to listen, women would go to their doors to hear where the next village would be set up, and then there would be glad talking until it was time to go to sleep. Long before the sun came the fires would be going in every lodge, the horses, hundreds of them, would come thundering in, and then everybody was very busy. Down would come the lodges, packs would be made, travois loaded. Ho! Away we would go, following the men, to some new camping ground, with our children playing around us. It was good hard work to get things packed up, and moving; and it was hard, fast work to get them in shape again, after we camped. But in between these times we rested on our traveling horses. Yes, and we women visited while we traveled. There was plenty of room on the plains then, so that many could ride abreast if they wished to. There was always danger of attack by our enemies, so that far ahead, on both sides, and behind us, there were our wolves who guarded us against surprise as we traveled. The men were ever watching these wolves, and we women constantly watched the men.

"I have been dreaming," she said, smiling, "not telling stories. I will try to stay awake after this."

Just here a boy of about sixteen years entered the room with an air of assurance. Decked out in the latest style of the "movie" cowboy, ten-gallon hat, leather cuffs and all, he approached Pretty-shield, spoke a few words to her in Crow, and then stood waiting while the old woman dug down into a hidden pouch for a silver dollar, which she gave him without a word.

"My grandson," said Pretty-shield, when the boy had gone. "I have told you that I have raised two families of grandchildren. This one is of the first lot. They never get over *needing* me, though," she smiled, her kind face again merry.

"I wonder how my grandchildren will turn out," she said, half to herself, a dazed look coming into her eyes. "They have only me, an old woman, to

Source: Pages 20–24 from *Pretty Shield: Medicine Woman of the Crows* by Frank Linderman. Copyright 1932 by Frank B. Linderman, renewed © 1960 by Norma Waller, Verne Linderman, and Wilda Linderman. Reprinted by permission of HarperCollins Publishers and Heirs of Frank Bird Linderman.

guide them, and plenty of others to lead them into bad ways. The young do not listen to the old ones now, as they used to when I was young. I worry about this, sometimes. I may have to leave my grandchildren any day now."

"Did you ever whip your own children?" I asked.

"No, Sign-talker, you know that my people never did such things. We talked to our children, told them things they needed to know, but we never struck a child, never."

She stopped short, her lips pressed tightly together. "Lately I *did* strike a child," she said, grimly. "There seemed to be nothing else to do. Times and children have changed so. One of my grand-daughters ran off to a dance with a bad young man after I had told her that she must not go. I went after her. It was a long way, too, but I got her, and in time. I brought her home to my place, and used a saddle-strap on her. I struck hard, Sign-talker. I hope it helped her, and yet I felt ashamed of striking my grandchild. I am trying to live a life that I do not understand.

"Young people know nothing about our old customs, and even if they wished to learn there is nobody now to teach them."

 As you examine this table, compare the illiteracy levels and trends for different population groups in the early twentieth century. Do Sources 7–13 offer explanations for the level and trend of Indian illiteracy?

Percentage of Population Over Ten Illiterate, 1900–1930

Class	1900	1910	1920	1930
All classes	10.7	7.7	6.0	4.3
Indian	56.2	45.3	34.9	25.7
White	6.2	5.0	4.0	3.0
Native	4.6	3.0	2.0	1.6
Foreign-born	12.9	12.7	13.1	10.8
Negro	44.5	30.4	22.9	16.3
All others	26.6	13.1	14.5	12.3

Source: Indians, Bureaucrats, and Land: The Dawes Act and the Decline of Indian Farming, by Leonard A. Carlson. Data from The Indian Population of the United States and Alaska, 1930, p. 143.

CONCLUSION

The sources in this chapter demonstrate that historians' primary material is often biased, reflecting not only objective conditions but also what people thought about them. The sources also make clear that these biases and views are as important as historical facts. In this case, historians can learn a great deal about white–Indian relations because their sources reflect the beliefs and perceptions of both Indian reformers and Native Americans.

Historians whose primary sources reflect only a narrow range of views risk writing history biased by unrepresentative sources. As we saw in Chapter 1, our conclusions about Reconstruction changed dramatically as historians considered the views of people other than white, male Redeemers. Likewise, who today would think that the writings of big business defenders like William Graham Sumner presented an accurate or complete view of industrial growth's impact on American workers? So, too, the writings of white Indian reformers might well tell us much more about the reformers than the people they sought to change.

Similarly, historians' writings—called secondary sources—contain different views of the past, even when they rely on the same primary sources. Thus, historians' debates often hinge less on matters of fact than on their own assumptions and values. Early twentieth-century historians holding the dominant racial views of that day, for instance, might well consider the sources in this chapter and reach conclusions about Indian reform similar to those held by the white reformers, themselves. By shaping the questions that they ask, historians' assumptions and values often determine the facts they choose to emphasize. Remembering that will make it easier in the following chapters to evaluate both primary and secondary sources and to use one kind of historical source to appraise the other.

FURTHER READING

David Wallace Adams, *Education for Extinction: American Indians and the Boarding School Experience, 1875–1928* (Lawrence: University of Kansas Press, 1995).

Susan Bettelyoun and Josephine Waggoner, *With My Own Eyes: A Lakota Woman Tells Her People's History* (Lincoln: University of Nebraska Press, 1998).

Frederick E. Hoxie, *A Final Promise: The Campaign to Assimilate the Indians, 1880–1920* (Lincoln: University of Nebraska Press, 1984).

Arnold Krupat, ed., *Native American Autobiography: An Anthology* (Madison: University of Wisconsin Press, 1994).

Janet A. McDonnell, *The Dispossession of the American Indian, 1887–1934* (Bloomington: Indiana University Press, 1991).

Luther Standing Bear, *My People the Sioux* (Lincoln: University of Nebraska Press, 2006).

Robert M. Utley, *The Indian Frontier of the American West, 1846–1890* (Albuquerque: University of New Mexico Press, 1983).

NOTES

1. Helen Hunt Jackson, *A Century of Dishonor* (New York: Harper & Row, Publishers, 1881), p. 339.
2. Quoted in Evan M. Maurer et al., *Visions of the People: A Pictorial History of Plains Indian Life* (Minneapolis: The Minneapolis Institute of Arts, 1992), p. 284.

Chapter

4

Evaluating a Historical Argument: American Manhood and Philippine Annexation

This chapter presents one secondary source, an argument concerning the American decision to annex the Philippines after the Spanish-American War, and primary sources that can be used to evaluate that argument.

Secondary Source

1. Male Degeneracy and the Allure of the Philippines (1998), KRISTIN L. HOGANSON

Primary Sources

2. "Recommended by Hoar" (1899)
3. "The Anti-Expansion Ticket for 1900" (1899)
4. "The White Man's Burden" (1899)
5. "The Filipino's First Bath" (1899)
6. "The Strenuous Life" (1899), THEODORE ROOSEVELT
7. William McKinley on Annexation (1899)
8. "In Support of an American Empire" (1900), ALBERT J. BEVERIDGE
9. Selections from the Treaty Debate (1899)
10. Value of Manufactured Exports, 1880–1900
11. Value of U.S. Exports by Country of Destination, 1880–1900

*I*n early 1899, many Americans could agree with Secretary of State John Hay that the just-concluded conflict with Spain was "a splendid little war." The previous summer, the United States had defeated Spain in a matter of months. Fewer than four hundred American troops died in combat in the Spanish-American War. The American experience in the Philippines seemed especially splendid. In May 1898, Commodore George Dewey's fleet steamed into Manila Bay and sunk the entire Spanish fleet without suffering a single casualty. American troops now occupied Manila and it appeared likely that the former Spanish colony in the Far East—recently ceded to the United States by a defeated Spain—would become a permanent American overseas possession.

Before the war, most Americans cared little about this distant place across the Pacific. In fact, most probably would have had difficulty locating it on the map. Few knew much more about it when the war ended. But with American forces in possession of the country's principal city, many influential Americans began calling for the United States to keep the entire Philippines—a sprawling chain of some seven thousand islands. The matter would be settled in February 1899, when the Senate voted on the treaty signed with Spain two months earlier. After a fierce debate in and outside the halls of Congress, the Senate made its decision: The United States would annex the Philippines and, in effect, turn it into an American colony in the Far East.

Few Americans foresaw the consequences of this decision, even though some Filipinos had already turned their guns from the Spanish to the American occupation forces. For the next two years, the United States would be tied down in a bloody conflict with Filipino nationalists that was marred by atrocities on both sides. Certainly, there was nothing splendid about American operations in the Philippines, which claimed more lives than had the Spanish-American War itself. By 1902, more than 126,000 American troops had been committed to the Philippines and more than 4,200 had died. Meanwhile, perhaps as many as 200,000 civilians had perished. Although President Theodore Roosevelt declared the fighting over in the summer of 1902, Filipino Muslim fighters actually continued their armed opposition to American occupation for more than a decade. Their resistance was finally quelled, but American military forces would still be in the Philippines four decades later when invading Japanese troops drove them out and took over the islands at the start of World War II. In fact, only after this war would the Philippines finally achieve independence. Long before the Stars and Stripes were finally lowered, historians sought explanations for the American decision to establish an overseas empire at the end of the nineteenth century. At the beginning of another century, that search goes on. As the United States continues to assert its power around the globe, few topics from the turn of a previous century could be more timely.

SETTING

Historians have been drawn to the decision to annex the Philippines for several important reasons. When the United States took control of the country, it broke with its own revolutionary past and anti-colonial ideals. The decision for empire also provides a powerful case study—for some, a cautionary tale—regarding the unintended consequences of intervening in foreign lands. In this case, of course, that consequence was a prolonged, bloody military struggle far from American shores. Finally, Philippine annexation occurred just as the United States had arrived as a great power, a status it holds more than a century later. To many historians, then, American imperialism at the turn of the twentieth century represents an important key for understanding the rise of the United States as a global power.

If historians do not dispute the importance of Philippine annexation, they do not necessarily agree about the reasons for it. Often, their explanations reflect conflicting views about the most important influences on foreign policy. Some scholars argue that democratic or popular influences play an important role in shaping policy; others contend that elites dominate decision making. Still others insist that American foreign policy has been shaped primarily by powerful ideas and cultural forces. For the better part of a century, explanations for Philippine annexation have reflected these competing views about influence. The result has been a fierce debate among historians not only about the forces propelling American imperialism at the turn of the twentieth century, but also about the nature of foreign policy in a democratic society.

One argument, an extension of President William McKinley's own explanation at the time, emphasized a humanitarian impulse behind American overseas expansion at the end of the nineteenth century. In this view, the decision to go to war with Spain so as to liberate Cuba from the oppressive Spanish rule naturally spilled over to a desire to keep the Philippines once the war was over. Annexation would "uplift" the Filipinos and prevent another oppressive power from seizing an independent but weak Philippines. Proponents of this view maintain that the American empire was thus "accidental" in nature. An unthinking response to events in Cuba and the Philippines, it was carried out without forethought or assessments about American strategic or economic interests. In other words, the decision for empire was an "aberration" that was unrelated to the needs of America's expanding industrial economy.

That view did not long go unchallenged. In fact, early in the twentieth century many historians believed that the search for overseas markets explained both the war with Spain and the subsequent decision for empire. In the 1930s, for example, historian Charles Beard argued that McKinley's decision for war reflected his close ties to expansionist business leaders. This interpretation was especially popular during the Great Depression, when economic issues were on the minds of many people. Americans generally held business responsible for the country's economic ills, and "war profiteers" were under investigation by the U.S. Senate for their role in World War I. At the same time, historian Julius Pratt argued that another influential, elite group was more responsible for American imperialism than profit-minded businessmen. In *Expansionists of 1898* (1936), Pratt concluded that many prominent business leaders actually opposed going to war with Spain. Vocal and well-placed officials such as Assistant Secretary of the Navy Theodore Roosevelt, Navy Captain Alfred Thayer Mahan, and Senator Henry Cabot Lodge pushed McKinley to war with Spain. Only when these expansionists pressed for retaining the Philippines, Pratt concluded, did the business community finally join the annexationist chorus.

Later, many historians rejected arguments about the responsibility of these elite groups for American overseas expansion. Reminded by World War II of the powerful effects of mass hysteria, in the postwar years they emphasized the emotional or irrational nature of American overseas expansion at the end of the nineteenth century. In their view, McKinley and the Congress were swept toward war and colonialism by a public whipped to a frenzy by so-called yellow journalism—the sensationalist coverage of Spanish oppression in Cuba. The decision for war, then, was an "unthinking" response by political leaders to popular passion. As historian Ernest May argued in *Imperial Democracy* (1961), William McKinley was simply unable to withstand the tide of public opinion and "led his country unwillingly toward a war that he did not want."[1] A little later, historian Richard Hofstadter extended this thesis when he concluded that Americans were suffering from a collective "psychic crisis" in the 1890s brought on by economic depression and social turmoil related to industrialization. Increasingly frightened about their own prospects at home, Hofstadter concluded, Americans were especially susceptible to manipulation by the yellow press, which offered them the prospect of overseas conquests as a cure for their own frustrations. As in the humanitarian-impulse interpretation, America's unthinking decisions for war and empire were aberrations that had more to do with popular influence on the government than with concerns for overseas markets.

It was not long before some historians questioned these conclusions too. By the 1960s, the Vietnam War had created doubts among many Americans about popular influence on government policy and the motives of elite policy makers. At the same time, William Appleman Williams and other "New Left"* historians began to emphasize the economic influences on American foreign policy and the expansionist nature of capitalism. These historians downplayed the role of the yellow press and public opinion. They pointed instead to the desire of American leaders to find commercial outlets abroad. In *The New Empire* (1963), for instance, Walter LaFeber argued that American leaders realized the economic benefits of overseas expansion and led the nation to war with Spain to build a commercial empire. Historian Thomas McCormick agreed in *China Market* (1967), which concluded that the acquisition of the Philippines was essential to realizing profits in China—potentially a huge market for American goods in the Far East.

*The label was applied to distinguish these historians from the "Old Left" of the 1930s.

In the last decades of the twentieth century, many historians stressed the important role of culture in shaping the past, even in the field of foreign relations. These historians emphasized the ideological, rather than purely economic, motives behind American overseas expansion, in particular the belief in the duty of the "Anglo-Saxon race" to uplift "uncivilized" peoples. In *Spreading the American Dream* (1982), for instance, Emily Rosenberg argued that assumptions about the superiority of Anglo-Saxons and of American political, religious, and economic institutions propelled American expansion at the turn of the century. In *Ideology and U.S. Foreign Policy* (1987), historian Michael Hunt likewise argued that an ideological stew containing generous portions of chauvinism and racism led many Americans to assume that they could simply remake other societies.

This emphasis on the cultural roots of expansionism has given rise even more recently to a renewed focus on changes in late nineteenth-century American society, especially those affecting Americans' own views about themselves and their nation. In *The United States and Imperialism* (2001), for instance, historian Frank Ninkovich argues that agrarian unrest, immigration, and labor unrest helped to create a national "identity crisis" in the late nineteenth century. To many influential Americans, the cure was for the United States to become a leading player in a new "global community" by adhering to a European "standard of civilization"—one that emphasized the need to "civilize" the "backward" areas of the world. Other recent historians such as Paul A. Kramer and Kristin Hoganson have focused on the way ideas about race or gender influenced American expansion and, in particular, the American colonial experience in the Philippines. Often writing from a transnational perspective, recent historians like Kramer and Matthew Freye Jacobson have traced the ways that American colonialism, in turn, influenced ideas about race and society at home. By emphasizing mass psychology, the role of elites, and the idea of cultural uplift, such explanations are in some ways an extension of older arguments about American expansion. They serve as reminders that historians build on the work of those who came before them and that their interpretations are not necessarily mutually exclusive. By pointing to developments far from the steamy jungles of the Philippines to explain the presence of American troops there, they also remind us that studying American involvement in other countries promises to tell us much about our own.

INVESTIGATION

Unlike the previous chapters, this one presents a secondary source—the work of a historian—as well as the usual set of primary sources. You will be able to use the evidence from the primary sources to evaluate the argument in the secondary source. The main question presented by the secondary and primary sources is why the United States annexed the Philippines following the Spanish-American War. Like many contemporary historians, the author of the secondary source traces the roots of American expansionism at the turn of the twentieth century to an aspect of American culture—in this case, late nineteenth-century conceptions about masculinity. First determine the argument presented in this source, paying attention to the evidence it presents to support it. Then assess what light the primary sources shed on the argument offered in the secondary source. A good analysis of the American decision for annexation will address the following questions:

1. **According to the essay (Source 1), how did concerns about American masculinity influence the decision to annex the Philippines?** What developments in American society reinforced these concerns by the time Americans debated the fate of the Philippines? According to the essay, were annexationists' concerns about masculinity an important independent factor in the American decision to hold the Philippines or important only because they reinforced the influence of other factors?

2. **Do the primary sources indicate that views about gender played a role in the debate over the Philippines?** Is there evidence that annexationists' fears about masculinity were connected to other concerns or desires?

3. **Do you agree with the author's explanation for the American annexation of the Philippines?** Compared to other factors, how important were the gender concerns that she identifies? Were there more important issues in the minds of expansionists?

4. **Based on the sources in this chapter, what explanation would you offer to account for the American decision to take the Philippines?** What is the most important evidence to support it?

Before you begin, read the sections in your textbook on American overseas expansion in the late nineteenth century and on the Spanish-American War. Note what factors or forces it points to in explaining this expansion and, in particular, American annexation of the Philippines. When you are finished with this assignment, you will be able to compare your text's conclusions with the interpretation offered in Source 1 of this chapter.

SECONDARY SOURCE

In this selection, historian Kristin Hoganson argues that while a number of influences were evident in the American decision to annex the Philippines, they were related to overriding fears about declining masculinity. Note how she connects fears about masculinity to other concerns or desires on the part of annexationists. How, in the minds of expansionists, would annexing the Philippines help restore American masculinity, according to Hoganson?

1 Male Degeneracy and the Allure of the Philippines (1998)

KRISTIN L. HOGANSON

Begun as a chivalrous crusade to redeem American honor and liberate the Cubans from Spanish oppression, the Spanish-American War ended as a self-aggrandizing war, a war that resulted not only in the temporary occupation of Cuba but also in the annexation of Puerto Rico and Guam. Most ironic of all, it ended in a bloody colonial war in the Philippines that involved over 126,000 American soldiers, more than 4,000 of whom lost their lives. For years, historians have grappled with the question, Why did the United States finish one war, waged in the name of liberty, only to start another, waged in behalf of empire?

The United States initially became involved in the Philippines as part of the war effort against Spain. After Commodore Dewey sank the Spanish fleet in Manila Bay, President McKinley sent reinforcements, who took the city of Manila from the Spaniards in an attack on August 13, 1898. (During the hostilities the Filipino nationalists who ringed the city established a foothold in some of its suburbs.) The peace treaty with Spain, signed on December 10, ceded the Philippines along with Guam and Puerto Rico to the United States. The treaty, known as the Treaty of Paris, then went to the U.S. Senate for ratification. But the Filipinos who had been fighting for independence from Spain did not want to be ceded. On February 4, 1899, shortly before the Senate voted on the treaty, fighting broke out between Filipino troops and American soldiers when a private from Nebraska fired at Filipinos who refused to obey his command to halt. The Senate went ahead and narrowly ratified the treaty ending the war with Spain on February 6, leaving the nation to confront an even greater issue: whether to wage a war against the Filipino nationalists.

Economic motives certainly played a significant role in the decision to fight for the control of the Philippines, which were located close to the hotly contested and potentially lucrative China market. Those who believed the nation needed strategic bases to secure its share of eastern profits regarded

Source: Kristin L. Hoganson, *Fighting for American Manhood: How Gender Politics Provoked the Spanish-American and Philippine-American Wars*, pp. 133–134, 138–140, 142–143, 149–150, 153–154, 176–177, 178–179. Copyright © 1998. Reprinted by permission of the publisher, Yale University Press.

the Philippines as a stepping-stone. Yet a troubling question remains: What led Americans to set their democratic scruples aside and wage a trans-Pacific war of conquest? To answer this question, a number of historians have turned to the racial assumptions of the time. Imperialists generally thought the Filipinos *unfit* for self-government. They viewed them as even less adept than the Cubans, who at least had enjoyed a favorable image as heroic fighters prior to the Spanish-American War. . . .

Unlike the anti-imperialists, who drew on negative stereotypes of the Filipinos to argue that the United States should not admit the islands into the Republic, imperialists employed images of savage, childish, and feminine Filipinos to argue that the United States had humanitarian obligations in the Philippines. Claiming that the seemingly unmanly Filipinos were unfit to govern themselves, imperialists held that the United States had a duty to do it for them. Yet given the brutality of the war (an estimated sixteen to twenty thousand Filipino soldiers and two hundred thousand civilians died in the conflict) such humanitarian assertions seem more a justification of imperialist policies than a reflection of a guiding spirit of altruism. But if assessments of the Filipinos served primarily to make U.S. policies seem more palatable, we are left with the original question: Why did the United States wage a lengthy war for control of the Philippines? What explains the imperialist impulse?

To more fully understand the imperialist impulse, meaning the desire to take and govern the Philippines, it is necessary to turn the spotlight from perceptions of the Filipinos to American self-perceptions. Imperialists' comments on American men and American democracy indicate that they wanted to govern the Philippines not only because they doubted the Filipinos' governing capacity, but, just as important, because they doubted their own. In addition to being motivated by markets (and the military bases that seemed necessary to secure them), imperialists were driven by another fundamentally self-interested motive: the conviction that holding colonies would keep American men and their political system from degenerating.

Although a number of Americans believed that, by creating a new cohort of veterans, the Spanish-American War had ensured the well-being of the nation's political system for another generation, some men continued to be plagued by anxieties that an extended peace would lead to, as one author put it, "effeminate tendencies in young men," foremost among them the middle- and upper-class white men who enjoyed the many comforts of industrial society. Rather than easing their minds, the post–Spanish-American War valorization of the serviceman as the ideal citizen and political leader only underscored the question that had troubled them before the war: What would happen if the martial spirit dissipated in the United States? Theodore Roosevelt mentioned some of these concerns in 1901 in a letter to his English friend Cecil Arthur Spring Rice: "I do not wonder that you sometimes feel depressed over the future both of our race and of our civilization," he wrote. " . . . I should be a fool if I did not see grave cause for anxiety in some of the social tendencies of the day: the growth of luxury throughout the English-speaking world; and especially the gradual diminishing birth rate; and certain other signs of like import are not pleasant to contemplate." Fearful that the short Spanish-American War had not permanently rectified the softness wrought by industrialization, Roosevelt turned to empire as a more lasting remedy.

Imperialists like Roosevelt believed that holding colonies could prove to be a longer-term solution to modern civilization's seemingly dangerous tendency to make young, middle-class, and wealthy men soft, self-seeking, and materialistic. They thought that the experience of holding colonies would create the kind of martial character so valued in the nation's male citizens and political leaders (especially in the aftermath of the Spanish-American War), and that, in so doing, it would prevent national and racial degeneracy. James C. Fernald, who in less militant moments worked on abridging the *Standard Dictionary*, conveyed this idea in his expansionist tract *The Imperial Republic*, published in 1898. Imperial pursuits, he wrote, would "provide adventurous occupation for a host of sturdy men," thereby preventing the United States from retrograding "toward Chinese immobility and decay." Fervent imperialists joined with Fernald to contend that American men must embrace rigorous overseas challenges lest they lose their privileged position in a Darwinian world. "The law of evolution is pitiless and he who gets in its way will be run over," wrote one expansionist to his senator. "There is no standing still, forward or backward we must go." Sen. Jonathan Ross (R, Vt.) drew on similar logic in a speech advocating retention of the Philippines: "Stagnation is decay and ultimate death. Honest struggle, endeavor, and discussion bring light, growth, development, and strength." To such men, colonies held the key to character.

Imperialists wanted to build manly character not only because they were concerned about American men's standing relative to other races and nations but also because they were worried about American men's position vis-à-vis women. Fernald illustrates this point. Seven years before publishing *The Imperial Republic*, he published a tract titled *The New Womanhood* that deplored women who did not devote themselves to maternity and homemaking. In this tract, Fernald said that "for high manly health," boys needed "a certain roughness and severity of exercise," but that women would be destroyed by such strenuous endeavors. He was so committed to womanly delicacy that he deplored the style of dress that tried to give women the "high, square shoulders which are the beauty of the manly figure." He went on, "The tendency of man is toward authority, command, and penalty; of woman, toward tenderness, persuasion and reward" and concluded that women should be sheltered from the wider world for their moral well-being.

From Fernald's point of view, women who ceased to devote themselves to men and instead competed with them, who preferred "manly" self-assertion to "womanly" self-sacrifice, threatened the health of the race. But just as worrisome was women's threat to traditional male prerogatives. Warning that softness in men and assertiveness in women indicated degeneracy, Fernald offered imperial policies as a solution. He looked to overseas policies to solve domestic problems because he believed that the rigors of combat and challenges of establishing colonial control would test American men more thoroughly than domestic pursuits. Beyond that, they seemed certain to separate American men from effeminizing domestic influences. . . .

As the nation celebrated its victory, some observers concluded that American men had done more than prove their manhood in war—they had improved it. Manhood, they opined, was the greatest legacy of the war. The newspaper editor Henry Watterson conveyed this idea in his *History of the Spanish-American War.* "Above all, it [the war] elevated, broadened, and vitalized the manhood of the rising generation of Americans," he wrote. Similarly, an article in *Century Magazine* held that "exhibitions of the finer and rarer qualities of manhood, added to the record of bravery made by white and black, regular and volunteer, all these are national possessions that can never be taken away from us, that can never work us injury; they are of more real value than any territorial possessions that the war has brought or may bring to these United States. For it remains forever true that it is the manhood, the nobility, the character of its people, and not the extent of its territory, that makes a country great." Such statements implied that the war had been, above all, a wonderful and ultimately successful opportunity for American men to "vitalize" their manhood and then flaunt it before everyone who had doubted it. This included American men themselves. In the Republican convention of 1900, Sen. Chauncey M. Depew (R, N.Y.) applauded the war's effects on American men's psyches. Thinking of charges such as those made by Theodore Roosevelt on the eve of the war that "shilly-shallying and half-measures at this time merely render us contemptible in the eyes of the world; and what is infinitely more important in our own eyes too," Depew declared, "There is not a man here who does not feel four hundred percent bigger in 1900 than he did in 1896. Bigger intellectually, bigger hopefully, bigger patriotically, bigger in the grasp of the fact that he is a citizen of a country which has become a world power."

It was against this martial backdrop that the United States confronted the Philippine issue. The ascendant belief that martial endeavors were good for the nation because they vitalized American men made overseas colonies appear desirable not only for their economic and strategic benefits but also for their character-building potential. This assumption was particularly noticeable in the thought of the prominent imperialists Theodore Roosevelt, Albert

Beveridge, and Henry Cabot Lodge, all of whom regarded manly character as the bedrock of American democracy. . . .

Roosevelt, Beveridge, and Lodge had plenty of company in glorifying imperial policies for their effects on character. Similar strains of thought can be seen in the statements made by many of their fellow imperialists, including even President McKinley. After resisting the pressures for war with Spain in the early months of 1898, McKinley caught a mild dose of war fever. "What a wonderful experience," he said of the Spanish-American War. The success of the war and his own increased status made McKinley more receptive to taking and holding the Philippines. Though never an ardent imperialist, McKinley went along with the affirmations put forth by such imperialists as Roosevelt, Beveridge, and Lodge. Echoing their assertions, he explained his decision to take the Philippines by saying, "The progress of a nation can alone prevent degeneration. There must be new life or there will be weakness and decay." McKinley proffered the Philippines as a challenge with great potential, as "the mightiest test of American virtue and capacity." Like a number of other imperialists, he concluded that aggressive Philippine policies would build character in American men. "We have not only been adding territory to the United States," he declared in 1899, "but we have been adding character and prestige to the American name (continued applause)."

Driven by a desire to build character in American men, imperialists welcomed the Philippine War as a great challenge. Behind their noble-sounding talk of U.S. obligations to the Filipinos lay a self-serving motive: the belief that the Filipinos were opportunities as well as responsibilities. The imperialists' calls to duty, calculated to appeal to Americans' sense of mission, masked the less benevolent idea that conquering and governing the Philippines would benefit American men. The stereotypes of the Filipinos [mentioned] earlier can reveal much about these self-interested concerns if they are interpreted with their implications for American men foremost in mind. . . .

At the turn of the century, Lodge, Beveridge, and Roosevelt worried that American men were abdicating their domestic authority, thus causing women to become more active in public life. Like Fernald, the imperial publicist and exponent of domesticity for women, all three deplored women's growing political presence and insisted that electoral politics should remain a male preserve. . . .

Believing that the refinement and purity of such women as [his wife] Anna Lodge depended on their distance from ugly political and commercial struggles, Henry Cabot Lodge and his like-minded allies on the imperial issue preached men's responsibility to shelter and protect women. . . . For his part, Roosevelt maintained that a healthy state relied on women's domesticity as well as men's heroism. "The woman must be the housewife, the helpmeet of the homemaker, the wise and fearless mother of many healthy children," he wrote in "The Strenuous Life." "When men fear work or fear righteous war, when women fear motherhood, they tremble on the brink of doom." Fearing that "race suicide" would enfeeble the nation, Roosevelt told his turn-of-the-century audiences that women's primary political role was to bear and raise children.

Roosevelt, Beveridge, and Lodge wanted to build American men's governing capacity in part to counter women's increasing political activism. They believed that more authoritative men would dispel the pernicious "propaganda" of women's equality and cause women to return to domestic pursuits. These objectives contributed to their commitment to martial policies, for they assumed that by teaching American men to wield authority, such policies would teach them to govern their households with a firm, though benevolent, hand. Arduous struggles, they believed, would enable men to regain women's respect, devotion, and admiration. The same logic which held that an inability to govern household dependents served as evidence of Filipino men's political incapacity led Beveridge and other imperialists to think that shouldering responsibility for child-like or feminine colonial dependents would demonstrate American men's political fitness. . . .

By imperialist accounts, the [anti-annexationists] deserved little credibility in political debate because they were effeminate, homebound critics, not bold men of action. In "The Strenuous Life," Roosevelt blamed the "silly, mock humanitarianism of the prattlers who sit at home in peace" for costing the lives of American men in the Philippines. The timid antis, he maintained, spoke of liberty and the consent of the governed merely to "excuse themselves for their unwillingness to play the part of men." Roosevelt continued this theme in another address: "We need display but scant patience with those who, sitting at ease in their own homes, delight to exercise a querulous and censorious spirit of judgment upon their brethren who, whatever their shortcomings, are doing strong men's work as they bring the light of civilization into the world's dark places. . . ."

As they struggled to stigmatize antis as womanly, imperialists benefited from the widespread tendency to construe opposition to war as a sign of cowardice, weakness, or other supposedly unmanly attributes. Especially in the frenzy of militarism that followed the Spanish-American War, militance seemed to indicate manly character, and a lack thereof, effeminacy. Imperialists also benefited from the composition of the anti-imperialist forces. Women were, indeed, important to the anti-imperialist cause. Although the Anti-Imperialist League had no women in its elected leadership, women were highly visible among the ranks. In the first mass meeting to protest imperialism, held in June 1898, half of the people in attendance were women. The antis' campaign to recall volunteer troops from the Philippines in the spring of 1899 relied heavily on the energies of women, who lobbied to have the troops returned. Women also helped sustain the anti-imperialist movement financially. In the second meeting of the New

England Anti-Imperialist League, an officer reported that "noble-hearted ladies in Boston and New York" had contributed "ten or a dozen times each" to the league. . . .

By depicting the antis as women, imperialists suggested that the elderly, peaceable, seemingly female (if not literally female) antis did not represent the [founding] fathers as much as themselves, for, although older, the antis lacked the fathers' manly character. Despite their relative youthfulness, imperialists could say that they resembled the manly fathers more than the womanly antis did. Because of the martial ideal of citizenship that flourished in the aftermath of the Spanish-American War and the more fundamental assumption that manhood mattered in politics, these claims significantly benefited imperialists. The valorization of manly character in late-nineteenth-century U.S. politics meant that the "aunties," as the "old lady element" in public affairs, appeared less qualified to judge whether American policies were consistent with American principles than the imperialists, who might have seemed boyish but always seemed male.

PRIMARY SOURCES

The primary sources fall into several categories: cartoons from the popular press, writings of expansionists regarding the Philippines, selections from the congressional debates over Philippine annexation, and statistical tables related to U.S. overseas trade. As you evaluate these sources, remember that they may support different conclusions about the decision to annex the Philippines and thus may reinforce or contradict Kristin Hoganson's argument in Source 1. They will also help you come to your own conclusion about why the United States decided to keep the Philippines.

___

Cartoons on Philippine Annexation

This section contains cartoons related to the issue of the annexation of the Philippines. Political cartoons such as these were regular features in the late nineteenth-century popular press. Because they were a form of political commentary intended for a mass audience of paying readers, it is reasonable for historians to assume that they shaped *and* reflected popular views and prejudices. As you study these images, note the issues that they emphasize. Pay particular attention to images revealing attitudes toward masculinity or gender. Do these images reveal that proponents of annexation attempted to use gender as an effective weapon in the debate over the Philippines? Do any of these images suggest that the need to assert masculinity was connected in annexationists' minds to other issues?

This cartoon, originally published in the *Minneapolis Tribune,* comments on the opposition of Massachusetts senator George Hoar to Philippine annexation.

"Recommended by Hoar" (1899)

RECOMMENDED BY HOAR.

HOAR: "Give the child over to the nurse, uncle, and it will stop crying."—From the *Tribune* (Minneapolis).

Boston Athenaeum

3 This cartoon from *Judge* magazine also focuses on George Hoar's opposition to annexation. The figure on the lower left is John P. Altgeld,
   the former governor of Illinois who gained nationwide attention by
freeing three of the accused bombers in Chicago's Haymarket Square
bombing.

"The Anti-Expansion Ticket for 1900" (1899)

Boston Athenaeum

4   English poet Rudyard Kipling penned the poem "The White Man's Burden" in celebration of the U.S. Senate's ratification of the treaty with Spain. This cartoon, originally from the *Detroit Journal* and reprinted in the *Literary Digest*, illustrates the same theme.

"The White Man's Burden" (1899)

THE WHITE MAN'S BURDEN.—*The Journal, Detroit.*

Harvard College Library, Widener Library, P 267.3

Also from *Judge* magazine, this cartoon makes an obvious connection between cultural uplift and annexation. Note, too, the contrasting images of McKinley and Cuba, Puerto Rico, and the Philippines.

"The Filipino's First Bath" (1899)

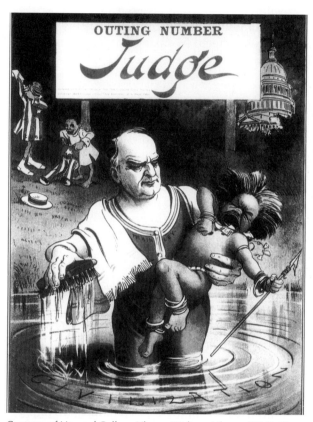

Courtesy of Harvard College Library, Widener Library, P 248.4F

Statements by Expansionists

Even before the start of the Spanish-American War, many American expansionists were vocal in their desire to see American influence expand overseas. After the U.S. Senate voted to ratify the treaty with Spain, which turned over the Philippines to the United States, they were equally vocal in support of a war against Filipino nationalists upset with the American decision to keep their country. This section contains excerpts from speeches, articles, and books written by some of the most prominent expansionists. As you read them, note the various justifications offered for taking—and then fighting to keep—the Philippines. Do any of these sources equate manliness with such a policy?

6   There was no more ardent or vocal expansionist than Theodore Roosevelt. As Assistant Secretary of the Navy, Roosevelt ordered Commodore Dewey, several months before the Spanish-American War started, to keep his fleet together and, in the event of war with Spain, engage the Spanish fleet in the Philippines. Roosevelt also wrote and spoke widely on the desirability of American overseas expansion. His essay "The Strenuous Life," originally delivered as a speech in April 1899, offers an especially forceful statement of Roosevelt's thinking about America's role in the world. It is also a vivid demonstration of his thinking about manliness and gender.

"The Strenuous Life" (1899)
THEODORE ROOSEVELT

A life of slothful ease, a life of that peace which springs merely from lack either of desire or of power to strive after great things, is as little worthy of a nation as of an individual. I ask only that what every self-respecting American demands from himself and from his sons shall be demanded of the American nation as a whole. Who among you would teach your boys that ease, that peace is to be the first consideration in their eyes—to be the ultimate goal after which they strive?. . . We do not admire the man of timid peace. We admire the man who embodies victorious effort; the man who never wrongs his neighbor, who is prompt to help a friend, but who has those virile qualities necessary to win in the stern strife of actual life. . . .

In the last analysis a healthy state can exist only when the men and women who make it up lead clean, vigorous, healthy lives; when the children are so trained that they shall endeavor, not to shirk difficulties, but to overcome them; not to seek ease, but to know how to wrest triumph from toil and risk. The man must be glad to do a man's work, to dare and endure and to labor; to keep himself, and to keep those dependent upon him. The woman must be the housewife, the helpmeet of the homemaker, the wise and fearless mother of many healthy children. . . .

When men fear work or fear righteous war, when women fear motherhood, they tremble on the brink of doom; and well it is that they should vanish from the earth, where they are fit subjects for the scorn of all men and women who are themselves strong and brave and high-minded. . . .

. . . In 1898 we could not help being brought face to face with the problem of war with Spain. *All* we could decide was whether we should shrink like cowards from the contest, or enter into it as beseemed a brave and high-spirited people; and, once in, whether failure or success should crown our banners. So it is now. We cannot avoid the responsibilities that confront us in Hawaii, Cuba, Porto [*sic*] Rico, and the Philippines. All we can decide is whether we shall meet them in a way that will redound to the national credit, or whether we shall make of our dealings with these new problems a dark and shameful page in our history. To refuse to deal with them at all merely amounts to dealing with them badly. We have a given problem to solve. If we undertake the solution, there is, of course, always danger that we may not solve it aright; but to refuse to undertake the solution simply renders it certain that we cannot possibly solve it aright. The timid man, the lazy man, the man who distrusts his country, the over-civilized man, who has lost the great fighting, masterful virtues, the ignorant man, and the man of dull mind, whose soul is incapable of feeling the mighty lift that thrills "stern men with empires in their brains"—all these, of course, shrink from seeing the nation undertake its new duties; shrink from seeing us build a navy and an army adequate to our needs; shrink from seeing us do our share of the world's work, by bringing order out of chaos in the great, fair tropic islands from which the valor of our soldiers and sailors has driven the Spanish flag. These are the men who fear the strenuous life, who fear the only national life which is really worth leading. They believe in that cloistered life which saps the hardy virtues in a nation, as it saps them in the individual; or else they are wedded to that base spirit of gain and greed which recognizes in commercialism the be-all and end-all of national life, instead of realizing that, though an indispensable element, it is, after all, but one of the many elements that go to make up true national greatness. . . .

. . . It is worse than idle to say that we have no duty to perform, and can leave to their fates the islands we have conquered. Such a course would be the course of infamy. It would be followed at once by utter chaos in the wretched islands themselves. Some stronger, manlier power would have to step in and do the work, and we would have shown ourselves weaklings, unable to carry to successful completion the labors that great and high-spirited nations are eager to undertake. . . .

Source: Theodore Roosevelt, *The Strenuous Life: Essays and Addresses* (New York: The Century Co., 1903), pp. 1–4, 6–8, 9–10, 17–18; original copyright © 1899 by The Century Company.

The problems are different for the different islands. Porto [*sic*] Rico is not large enough to stand alone. We must govern it wisely and well, primarily in the interest of its own people. Cuba is, in my judgment, entitled ultimately to settle for itself whether it shall be an independent state or an integral portion of the mightiest of republics. . . . The Philippines offer a yet graver problem. Their population includes half-caste and native Christians, warlike Moslems, and wild pagans. Many of their people are utterly unfit for self-government, and show no signs of becoming fit. Others may in time become fit but at present can only take part in self-government under a wise super-vision, at once firm and beneficent. We have driven Spanish tyranny from the islands. If we now let it be replaced by savage anarchy, our work has been for harm and not for good. I have scant patience with those who fear to undertake the task of governing the Philippines, and who openly avow that they do fear to undertake it, or that they shrink from it because of the ex-pense and trouble; but I have even scanter patience with those who make a pretense of humanitarianism to hide and cover their timidity, and who cant about "liberty" and the "consent of the governed," in order to excuse them-selves for their unwillingness to play the part of men. Their doctrines, if car-ried out, would make it incumbent upon us to leave the Apaches of Arizona to work out their own salvation, and to decline to interfere in a single Indian reservation. Their doctrines condemn your forefathers and mine for ever having settled in these United States.

In a meeting with a group from the Methodist Episcopal Church, Presi-dent William McKinley explained how he came to a decision about the desirability of annexing the Philippines.

William McKinley on Annexation (1899)

Hold a moment longer! Not quite yet, gentlemen! Before you go I would like to say just a word about the Philippine business. I have been criticized a good deal about the Philippines, but don't deserve it. The truth is I didn't want the Philippines, and when they came to us, as a gift from the gods, I did not know what to do with them. When the Spanish War broke out [Admiral George] Dewey was at Hongkong, and I ordered him to go to Manila and to capture or destroy the Spanish fleet, and he had to; because, if defeated, he had no place to refit on that side of the globe, and if the Dons were victorious they would likely cross the Pacific and ravage our Oregon and California coasts. And so he had to destroy the Spanish fleet, and did it! But that was as far as I thought then.

Source: Charles S. Olcott, *William McKinley* (Boston: Houghton Mifflin Company, 1916; reprinted in 1972 by AMS Press, New York), Vol. II, pp. 110–111.

When I next realized that the Philippines had dropped into our laps I confess I did not know what to do with them. I sought counsel from all sides—Democrats as well as Republicans—but got little help. I thought first we would take only Manila; then Luzon; then other islands perhaps also. I walked the floor of the White House night after night until midnight; and I am not ashamed to tell you, gentlemen, that I went down on my knees and prayed Almighty God for light and guidance more than one night. And one night late it came to me this way—I don't know how it was, but it came: (1) That we could not give them back to Spain—that would be cowardly and dishonorable; (2) that we could not turn them over to France and Germany-our commercial rivals in the Orient—that would be bad business and discreditable; (3) that we could not leave them to themselves—they were unfit for self-government—and they would soon have anarchy and misrule over there worse than Spain's was; and (4) that there was nothing left for us to do but to take them all, and to educate the Filipinos, and uplift and civilize and Christianize them, and by God's grace do the very best we could by them, as our fellow-men for whom Christ also died. And then I went to bed, and went to sleep, and slept soundly, and the next morning I sent for the chief engineer of the War Department (our map-maker), and I told him to put the Philippines on the map of the United States (pointing to a large map on the wall of his office), and there they are, and there they will stay while I am President!

8   Senator Albert J. Beveridge of Indiana was another vocal defender of American imperialism. In this speech before the Senate in January 1900, Beveridge defends the American effort to keep the Philippines in the face of both armed Filipino resistance and vocal critics at home of an increasingly costly Philippine-American War.

"In Support of an American Empire" (1900)
ALBERT J. BEVERIDGE

The Philippines are ours forever, "territory belonging to the United States," as the Constitution calls them. And just beyond the Philippines are China's illimitable markets. We will not retreat from either. We will not repudiate our duty in the archipelago. We will not abandon our opportunity in the Orient. We will not renounce our part in the mission of our race, trustee under God, of the civilization of the world. And we will move forward to our work, not howling out regrets like slaves whipped to their burdens, but with gratitude for a task worthy of our strength, and thanksgiving to Almighty God that He has marked us as His chosen people, henceforth to lead in the regeneration of the world.

This island empire is the last land left in all the oceans. If it should prove a mistake to abandon it, the blunder once made would be irretrievable. If it proves a mistake to hold it, the error can be corrected when we will. Every other progressive nation stands ready to relieve us.

But to hold it will be no mistake. Our largest trade henceforth must be with Asia. The Pacific is our ocean. More and more Europe will manufacture the most it needs, secure from its colonies the most it consumes. Where shall we turn for consumers of our surplus? Geography answers the question. China is our natural customer: She is nearer to us than to England, Germany, or Russia, the commercial powers of the present and the future. They have moved nearer to China by securing permanent bases on her borders. The Philippines gives us a base at the door of all the East.

Lines of navigation from our ports to the Orient and Australia; from the Isthmian Canal to Asia; from all Oriental ports to Australia, converge at and separate from the Philippines. They are a self-supporting, dividend-paying fleet, permanently anchored at a spot selected by the strategy of Providence, commanding the Pacific. And the Pacific is the ocean of the commerce of the future. Most future wars will be conflicts for commerce. The power that rules the Pacific, therefore, is the power that rules the world. And, with the Philippines, that power is and will forever be the American Republic.

China's trade is the mightiest commercial fact in our future. Her foreign commerce was $285,738,300 in 1897, of which we, her neighbor, had less than 9 per cent, of which only a little more than half was merchandise sold to China by us. We ought to have 50 per cent, and we will. And China's foreign commerce is only beginning. Her resources, her possibilities, her wants, all are undeveloped. She has only 340 miles of railway. I have seen trains loaded with natives and all the activities of modern life already appearing along the line. But she needs, and in fifty years will have, 20,000 miles of railway.

Who can estimate her commerce then? That statesman commits a crime against American trade—against the American grower of cotton and wheat and tobacco, the American manufacturer of machinery and clothing—who fails to put America where she may command that trade. . . .

It will be hard for Americans who have not studied them to understand the people. They are a barbarous race, modified by three centuries of contact with a decadent race. The Filipino is the South Sea Malay, put through a process of three hundred years of superstition in religion, dishonesty in dealing, disorder in habits of industry, and cruelty, caprice, and corruption in government. It is barely possible that 1,000 men in all the archipelago are capable of self-government in the Anglo-Saxon sense.

Source: U.S. Congress, Senate, "In Support of an American Empire," speech by Senator Albert J. Beveridge of Indiana, 56th Cong., 1st sess., Congressional Record 33 (January 9, 1900): pp. 704–712 passim.

My own belief is that there are not 100 men among them who comprehend what Anglo-Saxon self-government even means, and there are over 5,000,000 people to be governed. . . .

Mr. President, reluctantly and only from a sense of duty am I forced to say that American opposition to the war has been the chief factor prolonging it. Had Aguinaldo* not understood that in America, even in the American Congress, even here in the Senate, he and his cause were supported; had he not known that it was proclaimed on the stump and in the press of a faction in the United States that every shot his misguided followers fired into the breasts of American soldiers was like the volleys fired by Washington's men against the soldiers of King George his insurrection would have dissolved before it entirely crystallized. . . .

Mr. President, this question is deeper than any question of party politics; deeper than any question of the isolated policy of our country even; deeper even than any question of constitutional power. It is elemental. It is racial. God has not been preparing the English-speaking and Teutonic peoples for a thousand years for nothing but vain and idle self-contemplation and self-admiration. No! He has made us the master organizers of the world to establish system where chaos reigns. He has given us the spirit of progress to overwhelm the forces of reaction throughout the earth. He has made us adept in government that we may administer government among savage and senile peoples. Were it not for such a force as this the world would relapse into barbarism and night. And of all our race He has marked the American people as his chosen nation to finally lead in the regeneration of the world. This is the divine mission of America, and it holds for us all the profit, all the glory, all the happiness possible to man. We are trustees of the world's progress, guardians of its righteous peace. The judgment of the Master is upon us: "Ye have been faithful over a few things; I will make you rule over many things."

Senate Debate on the Treaty with Spain

In early 1899, the U.S. Senate debated the ratification of the Treaty of Paris, negotiated with Spain at the end of the Spanish-American War. The treaty called for the Philippines to be turned over to the United States, a key issue in the debates on the treaty in the Senate and the country at large. As you read the following excerpts from these debates, notice how annexationists counter objections to taking the Philippines. How did racial attitudes influence each side's arguments? What issues seem most important in the minds of the expansionist senators?

*Filipino nationalist Emilio Aguinaldo was the leader of the armed resistance to American occupation.

9   Selections from the Treaty Debate (1899)
SEN. [DONELSON] CAFFERY (*D, LOUISIANA*)

In the first place, any people that we take jurisdiction over, by taking the territory in which they live, ought not to be, and, in my opinion, cannot [*sic*] be, incorporated into our midst, to be bone of our bone and flesh of our flesh, without their free consent.

In the second place, if such a people are unfit and in all human probability never will be fit for the glorious privileges, franchises, and functions of an American citizen, we ought not in that case to even think of incorporating them into the United States, for we cannot [*sic*] establish the principle of despotic sway in America. . . .

Sir, when I look at the condition of the world to-day, when I review the history of the past, I am unalterably convinced that no permanent sway can ever be held by the white man over the colored races of the Tropics; and if sway is held, it is held under the power of unlimited, cruel despotism. That is the only way the white man can rule in the Tropics. It is the only way he has ever ruled. Whether it is providential or whether it is not, it is a fact. . . .

SEN. [ORVILLE H.] PLATT (*R, CONNECTICUT*)

Mr. President, what did we do with the Indians of this country? I said that that doctrine would have turned back the Mayflower from Plymouth Rock. We found here a continent in the hands of the Indians, aborigines, who did not want us to come here, who did not want to be governed by us without their consent, and with them incapable of consenting, we have, nevertheless, gone on and legislated for them and governed them, and now, at last, have brought many of them to a state where they have become citizens and incorporated with us. If you attempt to make a literal application of this doctrine, what answer have you to make when the Indian raises his voice and says: "I did not want to be legislated for, I did not consent to be governed by the United States; you violated your Declaration of Independence when you attempted to legislate for and to govern me without my consent"?. . .

. . . I am one who believes that we shall not have done a great wrong to humanity, that we shall not have imperiled our institutions, that we shall not have rung the doom knell of republican institutions if we extend over the people who reside in the territory which we may acquire those principles which protect them in their lives, which protect them in their property, which protect them in their efforts to secure happiness, and the American Senate and the American House of Representatives are not going to legislate in any other spirit, Mr. President. . . .

Source: Congressional Record, 55th Cong., 3rd sess., January 1899, pt. 1, pp. 436, 437, 502–503, 639, 640, 641, 959, 960.

I believe in Providence. I believe the hand of Providence brought about the conditions which we must either accept or be recreant to duty. I believe that those conditions were a part of the great development of the great force of Christian civilization on earth. I believe the same force was behind our army at Santiago and our ships in Manila Bay that was behind the landing of the Pilgrims on Plymouth Rock. I believe that we have been chosen to carry on and to carry forward this great work of uplifting humanity on earth. From the time of the landing on Plymouth Rock in the spirit of the Declaration of Independence, in the spirit of the Constitution, believing that all men are equal and endowed by their Creator with inalienable rights, believing that governments derive their just powers from the consent of the governed, we have spread that civilization across the continent until it stood at the Pacific Ocean looking ever westward. . . .

The English-speaking people, the agents of this civilization, the agency through which humanity is to be uplifted, through which despotism is to go down, through which the rights of man are to prevail, is charged with this great mission. Providence has put it upon us. We propose to execute it. We propose to proclaim liberty in the Philippines Islands, if they are ours. We propose to proclaim liberty and justice and the protection of life and human rights wherever the flag of the United States is planted. Who decries that? Who will haul down those principles?. . .

SEN. [JOHN LOWNDES] MCLAURIN (*D, SOUTH CAROLINA*)

I feel that a representative from South Carolina is peculiarly qualified to speak upon one phase of the question, and it is that pertaining to the incorporation of a mongrel and semibarbarous population into our body politic, a population that, so far as I can ascertain, is inferior to but akin to the negro in moral and intellectual qualities and incapacity for self-government. The experience of the South for the past thirty years with the negro race, is pregnant with lessons of wisdom for our guidance in the Philippines. It is passing strange that Senators who favored universal suffrage and the full enfranchisement of the negro should now advocate imperialism.

In other words, that territory can be acquired by conquest, held as a colony, and its inhabitants treated as vassals rather than citizens—governed by military rule or legislation not authorized by the Constitution. There is a glaring inconsistency in these positions. If they are sincere in their views as to the Philippines, they should propose an amendment to the Constitution which will put the inferior races in this country and the inhabitants of the Philippines upon an equality as to their civil and political rights, and thus forever settle the vexed race and suffrage questions in this country as well as the outlying territories.

How can they consistently, justly, and, I might add, constitutionally advocate a policy for outlying territories, embracing races so nearly akin to the negro, which differs so radically from the policy adopted as to that race in the South? There can be but one answer to that question, and that is that they substantially admit, in the light of a third of a century's experience, that universal suffrage is a monumental failure and that the time has come for the correction of this stupendous government error. . . .

Therefore, if the Philippine Islands were annexed and formed into States, this Chamber and the other House would contain about one-seventh Japanese, Malays, Chinese, or whatever mixture they have out there. We would have representatives with a voice in directing the affairs of this country from another continent, speaking another language, different in race, religion, and civilization—a people with whom we have nothing in common. For me, I cannot [sic] tolerate the thought. The great strength of our country is not merely its isolated position, washed on each side by the waters of a great ocean, but in a homogeneous population, speaking a common language, and with similar aspirations and ideas of liberty and civilization. . . .

In a commercial point of view, I believe the importance of the Philippines per se is greatly exaggerated. They are chiefly valuable as the key to the Orient, but we need not colonize to obtain that advantage. The exports of the Philippines, according to the Statistical Abstract, in 1896 amounted to $30,806,250. If this entire trade was monopolized by us it would be insignificant. We will have to teach them to wear shirts and breeches before we can trade with them much. But England and Germany have large trade interests in the Philippines, and under our agreement with Spain she must have equal trade privileges with the United States. As a matter of dollars and cents, I doubt its advantage. . . .

If we embark in a colonial system, it means the inauguration of a despotic power in Washington. It means a large standing army that will not only be used to rule outlying territories with an iron hand, but that sooner or later will be used at home to overawe and override the popular will. An imperialistic democracy, like an atheistic religion, is an impossible hybrid. . . .

SEN. [HENRY CABOT] LODGE (*R, MASSACHUSETTS*)

What our precise policy shall be I do not know, because I for one am not sufficiently informed as to the conditions there to be able to say what it will be best to do, nor, I may add, do I think anyone is. But I believe that we shall have the wisdom not to attempt to incorporate those islands with our body politic, or make their inhabitants part of our citizenship, or set their labor alongside of ours and within our tariff to compete in any industry with American workmen. I believe that we shall have the courage not to depart from those islands fearfully, timidly, and unworthily and leave them to anarchy among themselves, to the brief and bloody domination of some self-constituted dictator, and to the quick conquest of other powers, who will have no such hesitation as we should feel in crushing them into subjection by harsh and repressive methods. It is for us to decide the destiny of the Philippines, not for Europe, and we can do it alone and without assistance. I believe that we shall have the wisdom, the self-restraint, and the ability to restore peace and order in those islands and give to their people an opportunity for self-government and for freedom under the protecting shield of the United States until the time shall come when they are able to stand alone, if such a thing is possible, and if they do not themselves desire to remain under our protection. This is a great, a difficult, and a noble task. I believe that American civilization is entirely capable of fulfilling it, and I should not have that profound faith which I now cherish in American civilization and American manhood if I did not think so.

Take now the other alternative. Suppose we reject the treaty or strike out the clause relating to the Philippines. That will hand the islands back to Spain; and I can not conceive that any American should be willing to do that. Suppose we reject the treaty; what follows? Let us look at it practically. We continue the state of war, and every sensible man in the country, every business interest, desires the reestablishment of peace in law as well as in fact. At the same time we repudiate the President and his action before the whole world, and the repudiation of the President in such a matter as this is, to my mind, the humiliation of the United States in the eyes of civilized mankind and brands us as a people incapable of great affairs or of taking rank where we belong, as one of the greatest of the great world powers. . . .

There is much else involved here, vast commercial and trade interests, which I believe we have a right to guard and a duty to foster. But the opponents of the treaty have placed their opposition on such high and altruistic grounds that I have preferred to meet them there, and not to discuss the enormous material benefits to our trade, our industries, and our labor dependent upon a right settlement of this question, both directly and indirectly. For this reason I have not touched upon the commercial advantages to the country involved in the question of these islands, or the far greater question of the markets of China, of which we must have our share for the benefit of our workingmen. I have confined myself solely to the question which has been brought to the front here, and to the proposition that we could not be trusted to deal honestly with those islands of the East, for that is what the argument of the opposition, stripped of rhetoric and ornament, amounts to.

Tables on American Exports

As you examine these tables (which are better read from bottom to top), note the trend in manufactured exports and in the exports to particular nations or regions. Also compare the values of exports to Asia with those of exports to the Americas or Europe. Are these trends or values relevant in understanding the decision to annex the Philippines?

Value of Manufactured Exports, 1880–1900

[In millions of dollars]

Year	Manufactured foodstuffs[a]	Semi manufactures[b]	Finished manufactures
1900	320	153	332
1899	305	118	263
1898	285	102	223
1897	235	98	213
1896	219	76	182
1895	219	62	144
1894	250	67	136
1893	247	49	130
1892	250	50	133
1891	226	48	140
1890	225	46	133
1889	175	43	123
1888	170	40	114
1887	176	37	112
1886	163	34	112
1885	202	39	111
1884	195	38	118
1883	186	38	122
1882	178	37	125
1881	226	33	102
1880	193	29	93

[a]Processed food.
[b]Partially finished manufactured goods.

Source: Historical Statistics of the United States: Colonial Times to 1957 (Washington, D.C.: U.S. Bureau of the Census, 1960), pp. 544–545.

11 Value of U.S. Exports by Country of Destination, 1880–1900

[In millions of dollars]

Year	Total value	America						Europe					Asia				Australia and Oceania	Africa
		Total	Canada	Cuba	Mexico	Brazil	Other	Total	United Kingdom	France	Germany	Other	Total	China	Japan	Other		
1900	1,394	227	95	26	35	12	59	1,040	534	83	187	236	68	15	29	24	41	19
1899	1,227	194	88	19	25	12	50	937	512	61	156	208	49	14	17	18	29	19
1898	1,231	174	84	10	21	13	46	974	541	95	155	183	45	10	20	15	22	18
1897	1,051	159	65	8	23	12	51	813	483	58	125	147	39	12	13	14	23	17
1896	883	153	60	8	19	14	52	673	406	47	98	122	26	7	8	11	17	14
1895	808	143	53	13	15	15	47	628	387	45	92	104	18	4	5	9	13	6
1894	892	153	57	20	13	14	49	701	431	55	92	123	22	6	4	12	12	5
1893	848	152	47	24	20	12	49	662	421	47	84	110	17	4	3	10	11	5
1892	1,030	139	43	18	14	14	50	851	499	99	106	147	20	7	3	10	16	5
1891	884	131	38	12	15	14	52	705	445	61	93	106	26	9	5	12	18	5
1890	858	133	40	13	13	12	55	684	448	50	86	100	20	3	5	12	16	5
1889	742	125	41	12	11	9	52	579	383	46	68	82	19	8	5	6	16	4
1888	696	110	36	10	10	7	47	549	362	39	56	92	20	5	4	11	15	3
1887	716	104	35	11	8	8	42	575	366	57	59	93	20	6	3	11	14	3
1886	680	98	33	10	8	7	40	541	348	42	62	89	23	8	3	12	15	3
1885	742	104	38	9	8	7	42	599	398	47	62	92	21	6	3	12	14	4
1884	741	123	44	11	13	9	46	584	386	51	61	86	17	5	3	9	13	3
1883	824	129	44	15	17	9	44	660	425	59	66	110	17	4	3	10	14	4
1882	751	113	37	12	15	9	40	600	408	50	54	88	19	6	3	10	13	4
1881	902	108	38	11	11	9	39	766	481	94	70	121	13	5	1	7	10	6
1880	836	93	29	11	8	9	36	719	454	100	57	108	12	1	3	8	7	5

Source: Historical Statistics of the United States: Colonial Times to 1957 (Washington, D.C.: U.S. Bureau of the Census, 1960), pp. 550–551.

CONCLUSION

Whatever your conclusions about the reasons for the American decision to annex the Philippines, you probably have discovered that it may not necessarily be easy for historians to prove broad assertions. The U.S. Senate, of course, made the ultimate decision about the retention of the Philippines after the Spanish-American War, but that decision was not made in a vacuum. Senators may have been subject to numerous influences, including an assessment about markets for American goods, notions about the responsibilities of "civilized" nations toward "backward" ones, or even concerns about the character of the American people. The sources in this chapter suggest that these and other influences were present in 1899.

The sources also illustrate some important axioms of historical inquiry. First, historians seek the causes of things. They do not just want to know that the United States decided to keep the Philippines for itself in 1899, but why. The search for causes leads historians to consider the influence of ideas. In this case, that search has led historians to consider the influence of an American sense of mission and even ideas about gender and masculinity. It also requires them to ask whether history is better written "from the top down" or "from the bottom up," that is, from the point of view of leaders or followers. Thus, historians attempt to determine if the influence of elite individuals like William McKinley and Theodore Roosevelt or of a voting public aroused by press accounts, political cartoons, or speeches was more important in explaining the decision for annexation. Finally, the sources in this chapter make clear that the question of motivation is central to historical inquiry. Your conclusion about the role of fears regarding American masculinity or other factors in the decision for annexation involve a corresponding view about the motives of annexationists in and outside the Congress. The chapters that follow will consider these problems: historical causation, ideology and history, history written from the top and bottom of society, and, as we will see next, motivation in history.

FURTHER READING

H. W. Brands, *Bound to Empire: The United States and the Philippines* (New York: Oxford University Press, 1992).

Matthew Frey Jacobson, *Barbarian Virtues: The United States Encounters Foreign Peoples at Home and Abroad, 1876–1917* (New York: Hill and Wang, 2000).

Stanley Karnow, *In Our Image: America's Empire in the Philippines* (New York: Random House, 1989).

Paul A. Kramer, *The Blood of Government: Race, Empire, the United States and the Philippines* (Chapel Hill: University of North Carolina Press, 2006)

Walter LaFeber, *The New Empire* (Ithaca: Cornell University Press, 1963).

Stuart Creighton Miller, *"Benevolent Assimilation": The American Conquest of the Philippines, 1899–1903* (New Haven, Conn.: Yale University Press, 1982).

William Appleman Williams, *The Tragedy of American Diplomacy* (New York: Dell Publising Company, 1962).

NOTE

1. Ernest R. May, *Imperial Democracy: The Emergence of America as a Great Power* (New York: Harcourt, Brace and World, 1961), p. 159.

Chapter

5

The Problem of Historical Motivation: The Bungalow as the "Progressive" House

The documents in this chapter present various kinds of information on the craze for the bungalow style in the Progressive era.

Secondary Source

*I*n the first decades of the twentieth century, the bungalow transformed the appearance of neighborhoods throughout the United States. With its wide, low-pitched roof, overhanging eaves, prominent front porch, straight lines, "modern" kitchen, and economical use of space, it was the new ideal home for middle-class Americans. In drawings and photographs, it filled the pages of *Architectural Record, Ladies' Home Journal, Good Housekeeping,* and other magazines. One book on bungalows published in 1908 went through five editions in two years. To Progressive-era critics, the older Victorian house was now "aesthetically repulsive," an "architectural atrocity," "hideous," and a reflection of a "fatuous craze for the crudely ornate."[1] Suddenly nineteenth-century styles were out of date.

The bungalow was more than a fad. Many housing crusaders—architects, craftsmen, social reformers, home economists, feminists, and home builders—promoted this architectural style as a powerful means to transform American society. What exactly did the bungalow promoters hope to achieve with new designs and furnishings? What motivated them to assault older "Victorian" aesthetic standards? What values did they seek to promote? In this chapter, we examine the motives of the early twentieth-century housing reformers and the middle-class Americans whose tastes they influenced.

SETTING

The bungalow craze did not arise in a cultural vacuum, but was one expression of a broader artistic movement at the turn of the century known as Arts and Crafts. English Arts and Crafts enthusiasts in the late nineteenth century promoted simple architectural styles and handicraft production. In response to the spread of the factory, they drew inspiration from Oxford artist John Ruskin and his student William Morris, who argued that machines robbed work of its creativity and pleasure. By the early twentieth century the Arts and Crafts movement had come to America. It was taken up by a number of influential reformers, including Jane Addams, labor reformer Ellen Gates Starr, architect Frank Lloyd Wright, and naturalist Charles Keeler.

Middle-class magazines also popularized the bungalow. *Ladies' Home Journal* editor Edward Bok campaigned relentlessly to replace the "repellently ornate" Victorian home and its "machine-made ornamentation" with simplified home designs and decorations.[2] So did Gustav Stickley, founder of *The Craftsman* magazine, which published dozens of bungalow plans and promoted the Arts and Crafts style as the key to "right living." Other magazines, including *House Beautiful, House and Garden,* and *Country Life in America,* also publicized the Arts and Crafts style. As one observer put it, the nation seemed to have been swept by a "craftsman craziness."[3]

Although craftsmen promoters helped to popularize the bungalow, "craftsman craziness" was not foisted on an unsuspecting public by a cultural elite. Influenced by a variety of social and economic trends, an expanding middle class was very receptive to the new style. For instance, as the army of white-collar workers swelled between 1860 and 1900, so did the anxiety about loss of independence and masculinity. One popular magazine observed in 1903 that "the middle class is becoming a salaried class, and rapidly losing the economic and moral independence of former days."[4] Promoters of Arts and Crafts associated its rugged style with creative manual work, independence, and "the return of manhood to common work."[5] Theodore Roosevelt, who fretted about the decline of America's virility, was an enthusiastic supporter of the new style and called for "the overcivilized man" to cultivate "hardy virtues." Gustav Stickley was in turn an ardent supporter of Roosevelt and reprinted Roosevelt's "The Strenuous Life" in *The Craftsman*.

The bungalow's appeal was also related to dramatic changes overtaking women in the late nineteenth century. By the turn of the century, the weight of household chores had been lightened by such technological innovations as water heaters, running water, and washing machines. Moreover, urbanization had led to both lower middle-class birthrates and the ability to purchase more household goods outside the home. Gradually, the housewife's role had been transformed from producer to consumer. At the same time, smaller families and labor-saving products created greater opportunities for women to work outside the home. As work at typewriters and telephone switchboards drew the daughters of the middle class out of the house, the supply of domestic servants declined and fears about a household "crisis" rose.

These changes in women's roles stimulated varied responses, from alarm about the fate of the family to proposals for completely reorganizing the family. Some commentators called on housewives to become experts in spending. The new profession of home economics moved to transform housekeeping into a profession, a domestic science requiring special training in household and scientific management. Settlement house pioneer Jane Addams advocated public kitchens for working mothers. Feminist Charlotte Perkins Gilman, who believed that domestic architecture kept women enslaved, proposed new living arrangements involving cooperative housekeeping and homes without kitchens to free women to pursue careers outside the home.

To many Progressive-era Americans, however, the bungalow was the answer to the "woman question." Within its walls they could project their ideal middle-class woman and family. It was not an accident that bungalow "craziness" swept Americans in the midst of a discussion about work, families, and the role of women in society. Progressive-era Americans, from Edward Bok and Gustav Stickley to Theodore Roosevelt and Charlotte Perkins Gilman, had a deep desire to reshape institutions and values and an enormous faith in the power of the domestic environment to reform people. As one commentator put it: "Our works and our surroundings corrupt or refine our souls. The dwelling, the walls, the windows, the roof, the furniture, the pictures, the ornaments . . . all act constantly upon the imagination and determine its contents."[6] Like the tenement house movement, bungalow "craziness" reflected a Progressive impulse to view the home as an instrument of uplift. Examining this infatuation with the bungalow is thus a good way for historians to understand one generation's domestic hopes and fears.

INVESTIGATION

Americans embraced the bungalow for many reasons. Examining the ideas and designs of its promoters can reveal what they thought about family life and what they hoped to achieve by adopting this new style. One of their concerns was the changing status of women. The essay in this chapter examines the relationship between the popularity of the bungalow and changing gender roles. It is accompanied by a variety of primary sources, including house plans, illustrations of home decorations, and the writings of Progressive-era housing reformers. As you read the essay and study the primary sources, your main task is to determine what motivated Americans to adopt the bungalow style in the early twentieth century. To complete this assignment, use the secondary and primary sources to answer the following main questions:

1. **According to historian Gwendolyn Wright in Source 1, why were many Americans receptive to the bungalow style at the turn of the century?** What social and economic developments influenced their tastes in housing?

2. **Is Wright's argument supported by the primary sources?** What evidence do the primary sources provide about the motives of bungalow promoters? What family problems do they identify, and how do they think the bungalow would solve them?

3. **Was the bungalow craze prompted mostly by radical or conservative motives?** Did the bungalow hold out the promise of revamping domestic life completely, or of solving social problems without drastic change?

Before you begin, read the sections in your textbook on Progressive reform and cultural changes at the turn of the century. Although these sections may not mention the bungalow, they will provide additional background on the economic, social, and cultural trends in the Progressive era and about the goals of Progressive reformers.

SECONDARY SOURCE

In *Building the Dream: A Social History of Housing in America* (1981), from which the following selection was drawn, Gwendolyn Wright argues that Americans have long used domestic architecture to encourage certain kinds of family and home life, and that the bungalow was no exception. As you read this excerpt, note Wright's argument about the impact of changing gender roles on the popularity of the bungalow. What kind of home life did bungalow enthusiasts envision? Were they motivated by a desire to keep women in the home or to free them from it? How did their house plans reflect their desires?

The Progressive Housewife and the Bungalow (1981)
GWENDOLYN WRIGHT

In the early twentieth century, many different groups were campaigning for what they called a progressive approach to house design and upkeep. While their social goals often were based on conflicting values, public-health nurses, arts and crafts advocates, feminists, domestic scientists, and settlement-house workers favored the same simplified, standardized home to represent those values. . . .

In the arts and crafts movement of the early 1900s, architects and designers mixed with poets and writers, housewives and reformers, combining a sentimental reverence for hand-crafted goods with a more up-to-date endorsement of simplified, wholesome environments. Some designers acclaimed a self-consciously rustic aesthetic for the home, using massive tree trunks and uncut stone for structural elements, which they left exposed. While the fashionable family might display Indian handicrafts or folk art in the living room, most American arts and crafts enthusiasts simply called for "good taste" through quiet lines and minimal ornament. In contrast to their English counterparts who had initiated the arts and crafts movement as a reaction against the abuses of industrialization, most members of the numerous American organizations claimed that it was possible to produce pleasing forms in a factory as well as in a crafts workshop. They focused predominantly on the final product rather than on the actual conditions of making that product.

One of the most prominent popularizers of the arts and crafts movement in the United States was Gustav Stickley of Syracuse, New York. A furniture maker, Stickley had first redesigned the practices in his shop so that all work was done with hand tools. Simple, rectilinear lines and unvarnished oak became characteristic of his "Craftsman" furniture. In 1901 Stickley began publication

Source: From *Building the Dream* by Gwendolyn Wright, copyright © 1981 by Gwendolyn Wright. Used by permission of Pantheon Books, a division of Random House, Inc.

of a magazine, *The Craftsman*, hoping to lead a social and artistic revolution in America. The journal featured articles on tenements in New York City, . . . utopian anarchism, factory working conditions, flower arranging, and glass blowing. The following year, Stickley began to offer his readers model house designs, and continued to feature both interior and exterior plans until the magazine's demise in 1916. In 1903 he established the Craftsman Home Builder's Club, which gave free advice on "well-built, democratic, well-planned homes."

According to Stickley, "The Craftsman type of building is largely the result not of elaboration, but of elimination." The houses in his magazine had simple, rectilinear, built-in furniture, plain surfaces of native stone or wood, unpretentious plans and elevations. Stickley did not insist that every dwelling be a highly personalized design, even though he clearly enjoyed experimenting with the texture and variety of materials. To him, "democratic architecture" meant good homes available to all Americans through economy of construction and materials, together with necessary standardization. Though Craftsman designs suggested time-consuming construction techniques, the exposed beams were often simply tacked on under the eaves and the rough "clinker brick," produced in a factory to look like hand-molded brick.

Stickley claimed that his approach to design could remedy almost every problem facing the middle-class family, from lack of servants to the increased divorce rate. He also saw the well-crafted home as a key to solving larger social problems, such as crime and civil disorder. Small, inexpensive versions of the Craftsman house would make working-class families homeowners. Apprentice training programs in house construction and furniture making, run by the state and by private business, would provide uplifting employment for young men. The pages of *The Craftsman* carried the message that housing and social issues were related in their need for good design. Though Stickley's expectations of immediate, lasting social harmony through aesthetic reform were obviously unrealistic, he found a sizable audience that regarded residential architecture as the preferred American approach to reform.

Other magazines also offered detailed specifications for modern model houses, as well as more general advice on decoration and domesticity. By the time Edward Bok retired in 1919 as editor of *Ladies' Home Journal*, this magazine had a circulation of 2 million largely because of Bok's crusade for "model *Journal* houses." Bok wanted to encourage middle-class women to become more involved with the home, thereby relinquishing their recent tendencies to abandon domestic duties for jobs or women's club activities. He was emphatic about architectural standards for the modern home. The house should be free from "senseless ornamentation"; it should be equipped with the latest sanitary fixtures; it should be decorated with unpretentious furnishings and a few handmade niceties. These dicta did not, by any means, imply a spartan setting. The *Journal's* 1901 series of room designs by the St. Louis artist Will Bradley were opulent Art Nouveau décors. Yet Bok's taste was not all-embracing. He laid down exacting specifications for every detail, from pillows to room dimensions, often showing comparisons of "Good Taste vs. Bad Taste" in furnishings.

At first, no architects would deign to accept Bok's offer to design "model *Journal* houses," but with the depression of the 1890s, they became more willing. Beginning in 1895, suburban dwellings in Colonial Revival, Elizabethan, and Queen Anne styles, costing between $3,500 and $7,000, regularly appeared. In 1901, Bok launched the first of a series of modern model dwellings by Frank Lloyd Wright and his associates in Chicago. Thousands of readers sent in $5 for a complete set of plans and specifications, which would enable them to build duplicates of these model houses. As Theodore Roosevelt supposedly said of the *Journal*'s editor "Bok is the only man I ever heard of who changed, for the better, the architecture of an entire nation, and he did it so quickly and yet so effectively that we didn't know it was begun before it was finished."

While there were many words for the new house of the early twentieth century, "bungalow" was certainly the most widely used. It usually referred to a relatively unpretentious small house, although more exotic, expansive, hand-crafted dwellings created by architects like Charles and Henry Greene in southern California were also called bungalows. In general, though, the term implied a one-story or story-and-a-half dwelling of between six hundred and eight hundred square feet. Bedrooms were only bunk spaces. The kitchen, fitted like a ship's galley, accommodated a single person, and she (it was assumed) had a squeeze, . . .

. . . The kitchen replaced the parlor as the focus of attention in many builders' pattern books, and certainly in domestic science textbooks and women's magazines. Isabell McDougall, describing "An Ideal Kitchen" for readers of *The House Beautiful* in 1902, evoked the by-now familiar metaphors of impeccable laboratory order to be enforced by the housewife, or household administrator. "Everything in her temple is clean," she explained, "with the scientific cleanliness of a surgery, which we all know to be far ahead of any mere housewifely neatness."

The average kitchen in the turn-of-the-century bungalow or larger house was compact and carefully planned. It measured approximately 120 square feet, and everything had its place. The commodious Hoosier cabinet, with numerous wooden drawers and bins, stood against one wall. Wooden work-tables were positioned to cut down on unnecessary steps—a principle that domestic scientists borrowed from Taylorism. By 1910, the built-in breakfast nook had become popular; and in many houses, the kitchen had been reduced to a Pullman kitchen, or "kitchenette."

New appliances held center stage. The sink and drainboard were of shiny white porcelain or enameled iron. An automatic pump supplied hot and cold running water. If there was no brine-cooled or ammonia-cooled icebox on the back porch, where the iceman had easy access, a metal basin in one corner sufficed. A hood hung over the gas range to cut smells, and porcelain-enameled cookware hung on wall hooks. Unfortunately, the new appliances were not necessarily reliable. As one textbook on domestic architecture admitted, most laundry machines "are not economical on account of the severity of the process on the clothes being washed." Most households still used a washboard and hung the clothes in the yard to dry.

To many Americans, mechanical devices for the home were the essence of progressive improvements and a bright future. Writing in the *Congregationalist*, Henry Demarest Lloyd, the Chicago muckraking journalist, extolled the benefits he envisioned:

> Equal industrial power will be as invariable a function of citizenship as the equal franchise. Power will flow in every house and shop as freely as water. All men will become capitalists and all capitalists co-operators. . . . Women, released from the economic pressure which has forced them to deny their best nature and compete in unnatural industry with men, will be re-sexed. . . . Every house will be a center of sunshine and scenery.

According to Lloyd, technology promised individual freedom and social equality. Men and women of all classes would share the infinite power of electricity, the "modern servant." Lloyd envisioned women returning to their homes, leaving their jobs because of increased economic abundance brought about by electrical power. But other reformers, especially feminists, foresaw a future wherein more women would be able to take on jobs outside the home because electricity had freed them from household drudgery. . . .

In more and more cases, the housewife worked alone in her kitchen. Between 1900 and 1920, the number of domestic servants in the United States declined by half—from eighty per thousand families to thirty-nine. (Most of these were day workers, usually black married women rather than live-in servants.) Yet no builders considered opening up the kitchen and ending the housewife's isolation there. Rather, they praised the smaller, better-equipped kitchen, planned for the domestic scientist who had no need of a servant, since she had learned the most efficient techniques for housework. The kitchen was not to be a place for playing with children or visiting with neighbors but a modern "home laboratory."

One of the principal justifications for the smaller kitchen and the minimum-upkeep materials of the progressive house was the middle-class woman's demand for more time of her own outside the house. By 1900, women held jobs in almost every occupation listed in the census. Although most of these women were unmarried, and a quarter of them domestics or factory workers, college-educated women did enter the professions. Other young women donned the starched shirtwaist and ankle-length skirt of the Gibson girl* and entered offices as receptionists, clerical workers, and typewriters (the same word was used for the machine and the person working at it).

Middle-class women who did not hold regular jobs often worked as volunteers in charity or civic organizations, promoting the numerous improvement campaigns of the National Consumers' League or their local women's club, lobbying for reform legislation or neighborhood parks. These women still considered domestic issues their primary concern, but now the entire city was their home. In 1910, the president of the General Federation

* Idealized female image drawn by illustrator Charles Dann Gibson

of Women's Clubs declared that their platform was based on protecting "women and children, and the home, the latter meaning the four walls of the city as well as the four walls of brick and mortar."

Private homes were often the focus of debate, all the same. In order for women to have time for their non-domestic activities, they wanted both simpler houses that were easier to keep clean and more labor-saving appliances. The single-family dwelling was condemned in the pages of *Harper's Bazaar* as "a prison and a burden and a tyrant." The Philadelphia economist Robert E. Thompson and Charlotte Perkins Gilman and other radical feminists demanded kitchenless houses and public childcare facilities to ease the domestic demands on women.

There was some reservation about architectural changes that were tied to new sex roles. The restlessness that characterized "the modern woman" caused a stir among many conservatives. Journalists, physicians and politicians raised the issues of "race suicide" and "desexualization," which they connected to the declining birth rate among white women. In *The Foes of Our Own Household* (1917) and in articles for *Ladies' Home Journal*, Theodore Roosevelt spoke about the dangers of women abandoning the traditional roles of wife and mother for more exciting challenges outside the home. Higher education for women came under attack, since college-educated women often did not marry, and when they did, they had one or two children at most. The modern home and, even worse, the apartment, requiring as little time as they did, seemed to encourage these tendencies.

Despite their misgivings, architects, builders, and the editors of women's magazines recognized the growing market of working women. Even the married woman who worked was not necessarily considered a pariah. *Ladies' Home Journal* carried several articles on ways to earn one's living both inside and outside the home; and a full-page color spread in February 1911 considered the best house plan for a woman with a family and a career at home. Her bungalow had two separate entrances, a living room that doubled as a reception room for clients, and many built-in conveniences to accelerate housekeeping chores. Bungalows designed for single "business-girls" or "girl-bachelors" were featured in magazines and home-economics texts in the 1910s. Space allotted for cooking and laundering was minimal, for it was assumed that such tasks were done commercially, outside the private home. . . .

An elaboration of this model was the bungalow court—a group of ten or twenty almost identical dwellings, first designed as winter housing in southern California—which appeared in all parts of the country in the 1910s. Since the bungalows were quite small, there was usually a community "playhouse," where residents entertained guests and organized evening entertainments. Those who promoted the bungalow court as a modern living environment suggested that it could domesticate single working women, demonstrating to them the progressive side of home life. According to many advocates, this setting also represented "The Community Problem Solved." The harmonious uniform aesthetic and the shared outdoor spaces, playhouse, and garages were evidence that the residents had established strong social ties among themselves. . . .

While more than half the nation's farmers owned their homes in 1910, only one third of non-farm households did. . . . It was increasingly difficult for Americans to afford to become homeowners. In particular, the growing number of unmarried women and men usually rented rather than owned. The smaller, plainer dwelling, especially one set on a common court rather than on a large private yard, was an attempt to find a solution to the economic problem and to the seemingly related problem of a growing population of unmarried persons. Participants at the annual National Conference on City Planning, whose meetings began in 1909, and the National Conference on Housing, which commenced in 1911, hoped to find innovative ways to increase home-ownership without moving toward any sort of federal subsidies. They endorsed architectural solutions to economic and social dilemmas. The Model Street display at the St. Louis Exposition of 1904, the Model Bungalow installed at the Indiana State House for the 1913 National Conservation Congress, and the flurry of competitions for model suburban developments were all expressions of a nationwide enthusiasm for the "progressive house," which began to look much the same, wherever it appeared.

The uniform image appealed to a range of people who hoped that domestic architecture would encourage social cooperation. The Victorian suburb was branded as a "labyrinth of unreason," reflecting a time of "rabid democracy," of social and aesthetic license. Settlement workers Jane Addams and Graham R. Taylor, Jr., the domestic scientist Marion Talbot, the statistician Adna Weber, and the political journalist Herbert Croly concurred: houses conceived as individualistic display encouraged class differences and competition among neighbors. They argued for common architectural standards that would visually reinforce their ideal of a balanced, egalitarian social life for women and men. Both feminists and conservatives asserted that it was possible to solve "the woman question" through a more rational approach toward living environments. In 1912, Grosvenor Atterbury, who designed the model suburb of Forest Hills Gardens in Queens and championed planned industrial towns, wrote an appeal for progressive residential planning in *Scribner's*. He too argued that domestic architecture could reinforce the higher social values of residents, subordinating individual desires to the general good. "[T]he truth is that with any kind of control anarchy ceases," Atterbury claimed. "With the elimination of lawless eccentricity and disregard of architectural decency, the good elements begin to count."

PRIMARY SOURCES

There are several types of primary sources in this chapter: sketches and floor plans of a Victorian house and a Progressive-era bungalow, illustrations of old and new styles of household furnishings, and the writings of housing reformers and others. They may reflect a variety of motives for embracing a new architectural style.

Victorian and Craftsman Home Designs

The Craftsman magazine offered house plans and suggestions for home decorations to "simplify the work of home life." Compared to Victorian houses, such as those illustrated in Sources 2 and 4, what might Progressive-era Americans, especially women, have found especially appealing about the features of Craftsman houses and their interiors? Along with fears about "modern" women leaving the home and contributing to declining "Anglo-Saxon" birth rates, Progressives also voiced concerns about the impact of urban and industrial growth and declining manual labor on American male virility. *The Craftsman* magazine publisher Guvtav Stickley suggested that his own home reflected the personality of a man, in contrast to "the majority of modern houses . . . built to meet the ideas of women."[7] How may have the craftsman home, with its frequent use of rough-hewn, natural building materials, addressed fears about declining masculinity and made the Arts and Crafts bungalow even more appealing?

2   Elaborate and ornate, Victorian houses were often not based on any clear philosophy of design. By the turn of the century, they came under frequent attack for their excessive ornamentation.

A Victorian House (1875)

David P. Handlin, The American Home: Architecture and Society, 1815-1915 (Boston: Little, Brown and Company, 1979), p. 359; originally from Ec Gardner

3   *The Craftsman* magazine promoted this house as a "homelike cottage for a small family." A large lot with many trees, it declared, would provide "the ideal setting for a house like this."[8]

A Craftsman Cottage (1909)

Published in The Craftsman, February, 1905.

VIEW OF COTTAGE FROM THE FRONT

FIRST STORY FLOOR PLAN

Gustav Stickley, *Craftsman Homes: Architecture and Furnishings of the American Arts and Crafts Movement* (New York: Dover Publications, Inc., 1979; originally published by the Craftsman Publishing Company, New York, 1909), pp. 76, 77.

4   *The Craftsman* Contrasts Complexity and Confusion with Cohesion and Harmony (1907)

Courtesy of Frances Loeb Library, Harvard University Graduate School of Design, NA737.S65.A4

Craftsman bungalow promoters intended these homes to appeal to men as well as women.

Craftsman Home Interiors (1909)

Living room, showing fireplace of split boulders; nook with built-in bookcases and writing desk; division of wall spaces by wainscoting, stenciled panels and frieze, and effect of casements set high in the wall above the wainscot.

Kitchen and dining room combined, showing range set in a recess and hooded to carry off cooking odors; the decorative effect of an old-fashioned cupboard built into the wall and the placing of the dining table beneath a group of four windows.

Gustav Stickley, *Craftsman Homes: Architecture and Furnishings of the American Arts and Crafts Movement* (New York: Dover Publications, Inc., 1979; originally published by the Craftsman Publishing Company, New York, 1909), p. 77.

Gustav Stickley was one of the most influential promoters of the bungalow. Note the social ills that Stickley suggests will be solved by the adoption of this simple home style.

Gustav Stickley on the Craftsman Home (1909)

That the influence of the home is of the first importance in the shaping of character is a fact too well understood and too generally admitted to be offered here as a new idea. One need only turn to the pages of history to find abundant proof of the unerring action of Nature's law, for without exception the people whose lives are lived simply and wholesomely, in the open, and who have in a high degree the sense of the sacredness of the home, are the people who have made the greatest strides in the development of the race. When luxury enters in and a thousand artificial requirements come to be regarded as real needs, the nation is on the brink of degeneration. . . . Even in the rush and hurry of life in our busy cities we remember well the quality given to the growing nation by such men and women a generation or two ago and, in spite of the chaotic conditions brought about by our passion for money-getting, extravagance and show, we have still reason to believe that the dominant characteristics of the pioneer yet shape what are the salient qualities in American life.

To preserve these characteristics and to bring back to individual life and work the vigorous constructive spirit which during the last half-century has spent its activities in commercial and industrial expansion, is, in a nut-shell, the Craftsman idea. We need to straighten out our standards and to get rid of a lot of rubbish that we have accumulated along with our wealth and commercial supremacy. It is not that we are too energetic, but that in many ways we have wasted and misused our energy precisely as we have wasted and misused so many of our wonderful natural resources. All we really need is a change in our point of view toward life and a keener perception regarding the things that count and the things which merely burden us. This being the case, it would seem obvious that the place to begin a readjustment is in the home, for it is only natural that the relief from friction which would follow the ordering of our lives along more simple and reasonable lines would not only assure greater comfort, and therefore greater efficiency, to the workers of the nation, but would give the children a chance to grow up under conditions which would be conducive to a higher degree of mental, moral and physical efficiency.

Therefore we regard it as at least a step in the direction of bringing about better conditions when we try to plan and build houses which will simplify

Source: Excerpted from Gustav Stickley, *Craftsman Homes: Architecture and Furnishings of the American Arts and Crafts Movement* (Mineola, N.Y.: Dover Publications, 1979) by permission of Dover Publications.

the work of home life and add to its wholesome joy and comfort. We have already made it plain to our readers that we do not believe in large houses with many rooms elaborately decorated and furnished, for the reason that these seem so essentially an outcome of the artificial conditions that lay such harassing burdens upon modern life and form such a serious menace to our ethical standards. Breeding as it does the spirit of extravagance and of discontent which in the end destroys all the sweetness of home life, the desire for luxury and show not only burdens beyond his strength the man who is ambitious to provide for his wife and children surroundings which are as good as the best, but taxes to the utmost the woman who is trying to keep up the appearances which she believes should belong to her station in life. Worst of all, it starts the children with standards which, in nine cases out of ten, utterly preclude the possibility of their beginning life on their own account in a simple and sensible way. Boys who are brought up in such homes are taught, by the silent influence of their early surroundings, to take it for granted that they must not marry until they are able to keep up an establishment of equal pretensions, and girls also take it as a matter of course that marriage must mean something quite as luxurious as the home of their childhood or it is not a paying investment for their youth and beauty. Everyone who thinks at all deplores the kind of life that marks a man's face with the haggard lines of anxiety and makes him sharp and often unscrupulous in business, with no ambition beyond large profits and a rapid rise in the business world. Also we all realize regretfully the extravagance and uselessness of many of our women and admit that one of the gravest evils of our times is the light touch-and-go attitude toward marriage, which breaks up so many homes and makes the divorce courts in America a by-word to the world. But when we think into it a little more deeply, we have to acknowledge that such conditions are the logical outcome of our standards of living and that these standards are always shaped in the home.

That is why we have from the first planned houses that are based on the big fundamental principles of honesty, simplicity and usefulness—the kind of houses that children will rejoice all their lives to remember as "home," and that give a sense of peace and comfort to the tired men who go back to them when the day's work is done. Because we believe that the healthiest and happiest life is that which maintains the closest relationship with out-of-doors, we have planned our houses with outdoor living rooms, dining rooms and sleeping rooms, and many windows to let in plenty of air and sunlight.

---

7 As the editor of the *Ladies' Home Journal*, Edward Bok promoted a variety of Progressive causes. He also used the magazine to publicize the simple bungalow style. Note the ills Bok hoped to cure with the reform of home design, especially for women.

Edward Bok on Simplicity (1900)

There are no people on the face of the earth who litter up the rooms of their homes with so much useless, and consequently bad, furnishing as do the Americans. The curse of the American home to-day is useless bric-a-brac. A room in which we feel that we can freely breathe is so rare that we are instinctively surprised when we see one. It is the exception, rather than the rule, that we find a restful room.

As a matter of fact, to this common error of overfurnishing so many of our homes are directly due many of the nervous breakdowns of our women. The average American woman is a perfect slave to the useless rubbish which she has in her rooms. This rubbish, of a costly nature where plenty exists, and of a cheap and tawdry character in homes of moderate incomes, is making house-keeping a nerve-racking burden. A goodly number of these women are conscious of their mistakes. Others, if not absolutely conscious, feel that something is wrong in their homes, yet they know not exactly what it is. But all are loath, yes, I may say afraid, to simplify things. They fear the criticism of the outside world that their homes are sparsely furnished; they dread the possibility that their rooms may be called "bare." They fear to give way to common-sense. It is positively rare, but tremendously exhilarating, to find a woman, as one does now and then, who is courageous enough to furnish her home with an eye single to comfort and practical utility, and who refuses to have her home lowered to a plane of mediocrity by filling it with useless bric-a-brac and jimcracks, the only mission of which seems to be to offend the eye and accumulate dust. . . .

More simplicity in our homes would make our lives simpler. Many women would live fuller lives because they would have more time. As it is, hundreds of women of all positions in life are to-day the slaves of their homes and what they have crowded into them. Instead of being above in-animate objects of wood and clothes and silks, their lives are dominated by them. They are the slaves of their furniture and useless bric-a-brac. One hears men constantly complain of this. The condition is not a safe one for wives. No woman can afford to allow a lot of unnecessary furnishings to rule her life. . . . We need only to be natural: to get back to our real, inner selves. Then we are simple. It is only because we have got away from the simple and the natural that so many of our homes are cluttered up as they are, and our lives full of things that are not worth the while. We have bent the knee to show, to display, and we have lowered ourselves in doing it: surrounded ourselves with the trivial and the useless: and filling our lives with the poison of artificiality and the unnatural, we have pushed the Real: the Natural: the Simple: the Beautiful—the best and most lasting things—out of our lives. Now, I ask, in all fairness: Is it worth while?

Source: Reprinted from David E. Shi, *In Search of the Simple Life* (Layton, Utah: Gibbs M. Smith, 1986), by permission of the author.

The Bungalow Magazine provided readers with plans for inexpensive bungalows. What does this cover illustration suggest about the benefits of a simpler home style?

Cover from *The Bungalow Magazine* (1909)

The Bungalow Magazine, October 1909, Vol. 1 No. 8.

The Bungalow and the Efficient Homemaker

Christine Frederick, Annie Dewey, and other leaders of the home economics movement at the turn of the century frequently preached the need for simplicity, efficiency, and the application of scientific management in the home. Their work often revealed a progressive faith in social improvement through sanitation and rejuvenation through close contact with nature, just as their ideal homes often closely resembled the Arts and Crafts bungalow. As you read and examine these selections, note what Dewey and Frederick hoped to achieve by applying principles of efficiency and simplicity to the home. Do they advocate a change in gender roles?

"Standards of Living in the Home" (1912)
ANNIE DEWEY

The colonial houses of New England, with their large living-rooms and huge open fireplaces, illustrate an almost perfect type of family life. Each member had a share in the day's work, and to each it meant home in the truest sense. To-day the high cost of shelter is the greatest menace to the social welfare of the community. A house which cost $5,000 sixty years ago will to-day cost nearer $20,000. There is added pleasure in the home which we plan for ourselves, which expresses our individual ideas of comfort, happiness, and privacy, but with limited means we must shut out everything that is simply for show or for sham, making health, efficiency, and the general welfare of the family the first essentials, recognizing that true hospitality welcomes intimate friends to a share in the real home life rather than large numbers for occasional and costly entertainments. Four walls in a city block with paved streets, crowded sidewalks, the hurry and rush of city life, can never give the best environment for the symmetrical development of children. Let our ideal home be in the country or suburbs, with trees, shrubs, a garden or a few flowers, the companionship of animals, a safe playground for children where the nursemaid is not essential. Let there be a large general living-room, with open fireplace and broad hearth, comfortable chairs to fit all ages, low reading lights, ample table space for books and magazines adapted to all, hardwood floors with rugs, simple furnishings in harmonious colors, a few choice pictures and growing plants, no useless or meaningless ornaments as dust-catchers and time-absorbers. If means permit, a library or quiet room for reading, writing, and study is most desirable, that all ages and tastes may find expression. Have many and large windows, with morning sunshine in the dining-room where possible, and plants or ferns. The ideal country home will have ample piazza space, opening from both living

Source: Annie Dewey, "Standards of Living in the Home," *The Outlook* 101 (June 29, 1912), pp. 486, 488–489.

and dining room, permitting at least occasional meals out of doors. Life was so serious, so full of duties, to our colonial ancestors that time for outdoor life was hardly recognized. Much work can be done out in the fresh air, and piazzas may be inclosed in glass for winter use, also making a rainy-day playground for children. Sleeping balconies above are invaluable, for sun baths for invalids, brushing and airing bedding and clothing, and for the baby's nap out of doors. Closets with windows, rods, hangers, shelves, and hooks of most convenient height, all add greatly to the comfort of daily living. Where the bath-room is used by several persons, separate the fixtures. Have ample hooks and shelves and towel bars for each one.

In bedrooms there should be nothing which does not satisfy some need, spiritual or physical, of the one who occupies it. Let each person have a separate bed, if possible, with comfortable springs, good mattress, and ample light, warm bedding of sufficient length. . . . One-third of life is spent in bed, and yet this is usually the first place where economy in furnishing is practiced, instead of the last. There should be some place in each house for each one as his own. The demand for privacy increases with a rising scale of intelligence. Individuality may become selfish and self-centered to an extent that affects society perceptibly, but the line between comfort and luxury should be drawn for each where it best ministers to efficiency.

The modern kitchen should be a food laboratory, arranged in every detail for working convenience and sanitary conditions; with smooth surfaces, glass shelves and table tops, and modern saving devices. Some families spend on a few elaborate pieces of parlor furniture more than enough to equip a suitable kitchen or to give comfortable beds to all the family. . . . We need sane and wholesome living which shall leave time and energy free for intellectual pleasures, which are now so often sacrificed to the house itself as the symbol of social rank. It takes all the force of the man to supply money and of the woman to spend it.

The Efficient and Inefficient Homemaker (1920)
CHRISTINE FREDERICK

DIAGRAM 1—UNPLANNED CLEANING ORDER

Method: Worker gets tools from tool closet (1): and walks down hall and begins on living room (2); returns with trash to kitchen (3); and walks to dining room (4); after cleaning it, again returns to kitchen with trash, and proceeds to clean the study (5); she walks back to kitchen again, and last cleans hall (6); ending by bringing back tools and next refuse to kitchen again, before taking the final walk back to tool closet (1). That is not an exaggeration, but the method used by a so-called good worker.

DIAGRAM 2—PLANNED CLEANING ORDER

Method: Worker gets tools from tool closet (1): proceeds direct to study (2); from study through door to parlor (3); across parlor hallway to dining room (4); she then begins at upper end of hallway (5); and cleans its length back to the door opening on rear porch, carrying to waste and tools back directly ro service porch (6). Note that this method eliminates *all tracking to kitchen* and results in about two-thirds less unnecessary steps and walking.

Christine Frederick, *Household Engineering* (Chicago: American School of Home Economics, 1920), p. 74.

Charlotte Perkins Gilman and the Bungalow

Feminist Charlotte Perkins Gilman wrote extensively on the need to revamp domestic architecture. She advocated the replacement of traditional household arrangements so that women could enjoy work outside the home and the economic independence it would bring. Gilman called for the replacement of the traditional home with its isolated kitchen by kitchenless houses and apartments connected to central kitchens staffed by paid professionals. She also suggested the advantages of husbands and wives living in "separate establishments" such as those at Bowen Court, constructed in Pasadena, California, in 1910. Known as a bungalow court, Bowen Court contained twenty-two bungalows bordering a center garden. It also featured a sewing room and laundry for women tenants. Some of the units were double bungalows "planned for two or more persons who may wish to live under the same roof, but desire separate establishments."[9] Bowen Court was designed by architects who had been influenced by Gilman. As you read and examine these sources, note Gilman's response to the home economists' solution to the problem of "domestic economy." How do the motives behind the bungalow court compare to those of Stickley, Bok, and other bungalow promoters?

Domestic Economy (1904)
CHARLOTTE PERKINS GILMAN

One of the strongest intrenchments of our piously defended system of household industry is its supposed economy. "The careful housewife" is our ideal of a wise and judicious expender of money, some even going so far as to call her a "partner" in the business of housekeeping. . . .

Let us give a fair examination to this particular point, the economy of domestic industry. . . .

Merely as a matter of business, is it good business?

What is, exactly, the business we are to study?

It is that of catering to the personal physical needs of the human animal, caring for the health of the body, providing shelter, warmth, food and cleanliness. . . .

The home is intended to furnish shelter and protection to the family—sleeping accommodations, food, and those cleansing processes so essential to all civilized life. The business of the home is in the rent or purchase and replenishment of the place and plant; the provision of supplies for consumption; the preparation and service of food, and all kinds of cleaning. What is commonly called "housekeeping" really embraces this group of industries, arbitrarily connected by custom, but in their nature not only diverse, but grossly incompatible. . . .

Source: Charlotte Perkins Gilman, "Domestic Economy," *The Independent,* June 16, 1904, pp. 1359–1363.

Yet we carry on all these contradictory trades in one small building, and also live in it!

Not only do we undertake to have all these labors performed in one house, but by one person.

In full ninety per cent of our American homes there is but one acting functionary to perform these varied and totally dissimilar functions—to be cook, laundress, chambermaid, charwoman, seamstress, nurse and governess. . . .

The person who is expected to achieve this miracle is not some specially selected paragon of varied ability, but merely the average woman; neither is she prepared for her herculean tasks (Hercules was never required to perform his twelve labors all at once!) by a rigorous course of training, but is supposed to be fitted by nature for their successful achievement, aided perhaps by instruction from a similarly well prepared predecessor. Under these circumstances the wonder is that even half of us live to grow up, that our average of intelligence and ability is so good, and that our common standard of comfort and cleanliness, of health, vigor and peace of mind is as high as it is; that any degree of family happiness remains to us; and it is no wonder whatever, but an inevitable consequence, that the waste and incompetence manifested in this pitiful business constitute so huge a loss and injury. . . .

Double Bungalow Plan, Bowen Court

Schlesinger Library, Radcliffe Institute, Harvard University.

Changes in Middle-Class Life

By the turn of the century, industrial growth had had a profound impact on middle-class life. What changes do these tables reveal that may have made the bungalow more attractive to middle-class Americans?

Female Servants by Regions, per 1,000 Families, 1880–1920

United States	Per 1,000 families		
	1880	1900	1920
The North	92	80	39
New England	105	96	45
Middle Atlantic	121	99	49
Eastern North Central	74	68	32
Western North Central	61	61	32
The South	78	63	46
Northern South Atlantic	131	104	64
Southern South Atlantic	70	59	51
Eastern South Central	68	61	42
Western South Central	51	43	36
The West	43	49	28
Mountain, Basin, and Plateau	33	43	25
Pacific	49	53	29

Source: From *Seven Days a Week: Women and Domestic Service in Industrializing America,* edited by David M. Katzman. Copyright © 1978. Reprinted by permission of Oxford University Press.

14 Clerical Workers in the United States, by Sex, 1870–1920

Job Category	1870	1880	1890	1900	1910	1920
Bookkeepers, cashiers, and accountants						
Total	38,776	74,919	159,374	254,880	486,700	734,688
Male	37,892	70,667	131,602	180,727	299,545	375,564
Female	884	4,252	27,772	74,153	187,155	359,124
% Female	2.0	5.7	17.4	29.1	38.5	48.4
Office clerks						
Total	29,801	59,799	187,969	248,323	720,498	1,487,905
Male	28,878	59,484	163,686	229,991	597,833	1,015,742
Female	923	315	24,283	18,332	122,665	472,163
% Female	3.1	.5	12.9	7.4	17.0	31.7
Messenger, errand, and office boys/girls						
Total	8,046	12,818	47,183	66,009	108,035	113,022
Male	7,967	12,421	44,294	59,392	96,748	98,768
Female	79	397	2,889	6,617	11,287	14,254
% Female	.9	3.1	6.1	10.0	10.4	12.6
Stenographers and typists						
Total	154	5,000	33,418	112,364	316,693	615,154
Male	147	3,000	12,148	26,246	53,378	50,410
Female	7	2,000	21,270	86,118	263,315	564,744
% Female	4.5	40.0	63.6	76.6	83.1	91.8

Source: Alba M. Edwards, *Comparative Statistics for the United States, 1870–1940.* Part of the *Sixteenth Census of the United States: 1940* (Washington, D.C.: U.S. Government Printing Office, 1943), Tables 9 and 10.

CONCLUSION

As the bungalow craze illustrates, historians must often sort out a variety of motives. Housing reformers expressed fears about inflation, declining middle-class birthrates, rising divorce rates, women leaving the home, and the confinement of women in the home. They saw new housing styles as a way to reform domestic life. Because their views about domestic problems varied, so too did their motives for promoting the bungalow.

The sources in this chapter also illustrate that we cannot escape the influence of ideas. The bungalow reflected the influence of a Progressive ideology characterized by a belief in efficiency, faith in the power of the environment to transform people, and a distrust of concentrated wealth, class divisions, and urban life. It led Progressive reformers to take up such diverse causes as trust busting, housing reform, and conservation. It also led them to see common solutions for social problems. It was no coincidence, for instance, that Progressive conservationists promoted contact with nature at the same time that Progressive-era bungalow designers found rugged, natural houses aesthetically pleasing. As we shall see next, historians cannot fully understand motivations or any historical change without reference to ideologies.

FURTHER READING

Polly Wynn Allen, *Building Domestic Liberty: Charlotte Perkins Gilman's Architectural Feminism* (Amherst: University of Massachusetts Press, 1988).
Eileen Boris, "The Gendered Meaning of Arts and Crafts," in Janet Kardon, ed., *The Ideal Home, 1900–1920: The History of Twentieth-Century American Craft* (New York: Harry N. Abrams, 1993).
Clifford Edward Clark, Jr., *The American Family Home, 1800–1960* (Chapel Hill: The University of North Carolina Press, 1986).
Dolores Hayden, *The Grand Domestic Revolution: A History of Feminist Designs for American Homes, Neighborhoods, and Cities* (Cambridge: MIT Press, 1981).
David E. Shi, "Progressive Simplicity," in *The Simple Life: Plain Living and High Thinking in American Culture* (New York: Oxford University Press, 1985).
Gustav Stickley, *Craftsman Homes: Architecture and Furnishings of the American Arts and Crafts Movement* (New York: Dover Publications, 1979; reprint of 1909 edition).

NOTES

1. Quoted in Clifford Edward Clark, Jr., *The American Family Home* (Chapel Hill: University of North Carolina Press, 1986), pp. 132, 144.
2. Quoted in David E. Shi, *The Simple Life: Plain Living and High Thinking in American Culture* (New York: Oxford University Press, 1985), p. 186.

3. Quoted in Eileen Boris, *Art and Labor: Ruskin, Morris, and the Craftsman Idea in America* (Philadelphia: Temple University Press, 1986), p. 75.

4. Quoted in Eileen Boris, "Crossing Boundaries: The Gendered Meaning of Arts and Crafts," in Janet Kardon, ed., *The Ideal Home 1900–1920: The History of Twentieth-Century American Craft* (New York: Harry N. Abrams, 1993), p. 35.

5. Quoted in ibid., p. 36.

6. Quoted in Clark, *American Family Home*, p. 153.

7. Quoted in Eileen Boris, "The Gendered Meaning of Arts and Crafts," in Kardon, *The Ideal Home*, p. 44.

8. Gustav Stickley, *Craftsman Homes: Architecture and Furnishings of the American Arts and Crafts Movement* (New York: Dover Publications, Inc., 1979; originally published by the Craftsman Publishing Company, New York, 1909), p. 77.

9. Quoted in Dolores Hayden, *The Grand Domestic Revolution: A History of Feminist Designs for American Homes, Neighborhoods, and Cities* (Cambridge, Mass.: MIT Press, 1981), p. 239.

Chapter

6

Ideology and History: Advertising in the 1920s

The sources in this chapter offer evidence about advertising's messages in the 1920s.

Secondary Source

1. *Advertising the American Dream* (1985), ROLAND MARCHAND

Primary Sources

2. "The Poor Little Bride of 1860" (1920)
3. Listerine Advertisement (1923)
4. Ford Motors Advertisement (1924)
5. Kotex Advertisement (1927)
6. Calvin Coolidge on the Economic Aspects of Advertising (1926)
7. Earnest Elmo Calkins, *Business the Civilizer* (1926)
8. Walter Dill Scott on Effective Advertisements (1928)
9. *Advertising to Women* (1928), CARL A. NAETHER

*I*n 1931, historian Frederick Lewis Allen wrote a popular account of the 1920s that is still read today. Though "only yesterday," the booming postwar years already seemed far from the Great Depression's hard times. Allen used that sense of distance to spot some defining features of the 1920s. One of them was the new power of advertising. In the 1920s, automobiles, radios, refrigerators, vacuum cleaners, and other consumer products poured from American factories. As a new consumer-driven economy emerged in these years, the advertising industry assumed a more important position in American life than ever before. Evidence of that was everywhere, from a surge in advertising revenue to the transformation of advertising practitioners into what Allen called prosperity's "evangels."[1] In fact, Allen concluded with only slight exaggeration, a wise person in the 1920s would have cared more about who wrote the advertising than who wrote the laws.

Nothing offers better evidence of advertising's coming of age in the 1920s than advertisements themselves. National advertisers responded to a growing need to sell products directly to consumers with new techniques and new messages. Until the 1920s, advertisements generally touted the quality of a product. Now, many began to focus on the desires of consumers. More and more, they did that by presenting small dramas in which consumers could easily place themselves. These dramas, Allen concluded, were designed to teach consumers a "lesson": how someone's life was altered by using a product, or which cigarette people smoked "in the most fashionable circles."[2] Allen was not the only early observer to notice this new sales approach. As one study declared in 1929, advertising seemed aimed to make consumers "emotionally uneasy."[3]

Many historians since Allen's time have also turned their attention to advertisements. They realize that advertising's messages may not be easy to detect and that advertisements do not necessarily offer accurate depictions of Americans' material conditions or diversity. Yet this pervasive form of communication is in many ways a cultural mirror. Advertisements reflect people's aspirations and possibly even some basic assumptions about the society. They may even reveal an ideology—a complex of beliefs, values, fears, and prejudices that serves to justify or support a political or economic system. In this chapter, therefore, we analyze advertising in the 1920s. Its messages and those of the advertising industry's practitioners promise to tell us something about Americans' values in these years—and about the ideology behind a new and powerful postwar marketing system.

SETTING

If the advertising industry reached maturity in the 1920s, it was partly due to significant developments in the field since the late nineteenth century. These changes moved advertising well beyond its nineteenth-century patent medicine roots and made it easier for advertising practitioners to think of their work as a profession. Coupled with some important trends in American society, they also made it possible for the industry to have unprecedented impact in the postwar decade. By the turn of the twentieth century, for instance, advertising by big manufacturers and department stores had changed the role of advertising agencies from mere buyers of space in magazines and newspapers to creators of advertising campaigns. At the same time, the rise of mass-circulation magazines had created a powerful new advertising vehicle. By 1905, twenty such magazines already had a combined circulation of 5.5 million. Meanwhile, improvements in printing gave magazine advertising a new, "modern" character. By the 1890s, for example, photoengraving allowed photographs to be reproduced in magazines, eliminating the need for hand-drawn illustrations.

By the turn of the century, advertising practitioners also began to justify their work in terms of its ability to stimulate consumer demand. As one advertising agent vividly put it, "The fear of germs has to be *put* into the minds of most people."[4] The industry's growing confidence was bolstered further by its discovery of psychology. Led by Walter Dill Scott, a professor at Northwestern University, advertising agents in the early twentieth century began to see the insights from this field as powerful weapons to manipulate consumers. In *The Theory and Practice of Advertising* (1903), Scott advanced concepts such as mental imagery, suggestion, and association, and probed the effects of color, emotion, and repetition on an advertisement's appeal. A good advertisement, he concluded, should appeal to the senses rather than reason. Numerous textbooks on sales and advertising advanced and refined these ideas. As one early advertising manual declared, "The advertiser who approaches his problem with a well-defined idea that all human beings are essentially prone to act as children act is much closer to a solution than he who assumes that his prospective customers are endowed with superior reasoning abilities."[5]

It was a short jump from academic theory to advertising practice. Armed with the lessons of psychology, advertisers turned to market research and laboratory testing of advertisements' "pulling power." Already before World War I, old-fashioned, cluttered advertisements touting in great detail the merits of a product gave way to the simplified appeals that even today look "modern" by comparison. These changes proved useful to the industry during World War I, when the Wilson administration's Committee on Public Information turned to advertisers to help it sell the war to the American people. They also came in handy after the war as the nation entered an unprecedented economic boom centered around the mass production of consumer goods.

Meanwhile, broad economic and social trends further enhanced advertising's influence by the 1920s. Since the nineteenth century, industrial expansion had spurred rapid urban growth. By the 1920s, the city's bright lights and beckoning opportunities had lured millions of Americans away from farms and small towns. In cities, the enticements of mass-produced goods were not only more evident, but also large numbers of residents had more disposable income to spend on them. Here, too, newcomers found themselves uprooted from settled communities, familiar relationships, and traditional sources of authority. Often at work in corporations, they now lived in a far less personal world, where good impressions and success frequently rested on the right image. The impact of these changes is difficult to chart. They may have left many Americans uncertain about new standards of taste and judgment. They certainly created an audience far more receptive than ever to advertising's messages at the very time that advertising practitioners were better equipped than ever to provide consumers an authoritative voice and proper guidance.

INVESTIGATION

If advertising is a cultural or social mirror, it reflects much about the society that created it. Given the pervasiveness of advertising by the 1920s, though, sorting out the reflections and making sense of them is not easy. Just as advertisements distort most consumers' material conditions, they do not accurately reflect social realities. In the 1920s, for instance, they frequently pictured upscale consumers and almost never members of the working class or non-whites. Easier to see is advertising's vision of the American dream—the material ideals and aspirations that advertisements reflect.

This chapter explores Madison Avenue's version of that dream in the 1920s. It does so by using advertisements and the pronouncements of advertising practitioners as historical sources. Advertisers, of course, create messages to which consumers can relate. Your challenge, then, is to determine what their work tells us about popular attitudes and values. More specifically, this chapter examines one historian's thesis that advertisements from the 1920s "carried an ideological bias toward 'system reinforcement.'"[6] In other words, you will consider whether advertising's messages worked to reinforce the American social and economic system by helping consumers adjust themselves to it. As you read the secondary source and consider the primary sources, including a small set of advertisements from the 1920s, the following questions will help you focus your investigation:

1. **What does historian Roland Marchand, the author of the secondary source, see as the defining characteristics of advertisements of the 1920s?** What new techniques did advertisers deploy in the decade to influence consumers?

2. **In what ways, according to Marchand, did advertising in the 1920s help adjust Americans to the changes in "modern" American society?** How did advertising's "ideology" in this period, according to Marchand, work to reinforce certain values?

3. **Do the primary sources support the conclusions in the secondary source about some of the defining characteristics of advertisements from the 1920s?** Do the primary sources reflect embedded attitudes toward the social or economic system of the sort discussed in the secondary source?

4. **What attitudes toward the public do the primary sources reveal?** What do the advertisements or pronouncements of those in the advertising industry reveal about their attitudes toward consumers in general and toward women or other groups?

Before you begin, make sure you have read the sections in your textbook on the economic and social changes in the 1920s, including its discussion of the emergence of a postwar consumer economy and advertising's role in it.

SECONDARY SOURCE

Roland Marchand was a leading late twentieth-century student of advertising during the 1920s and 1930s. In the following essay, he discusses some of the new messages of advertisements in the 1920s and the biases they reveal. As you read this selection, keep in mind what he identifies as the most important changes in advertisers' appeals during the decade. Also, pay particular attention to the evidence he uses. According to Marchand, how did advertising in the 1920s help adjust consumers to a "modern" society?

Advertising the American Dream (1985)
ROLAND MARCHAND

Most advertisements, even into the first years of the 1920s, still retained the quality of announcements. While they did occasionally show people enjoying the product—dancing to the phonograph or riding in the car—they rarely invited the reader's engagement and empathy with detailed vignettes of group conversations, family activities, or moments of social triumph or humiliation. In contrast to the dominant mode of ads after the mid-1920s, they provided more objective information about the product than subjective information about the hopes and anxieties of the consumer.

In an attempt to define what was new about advertising content and technique in the 1920s, *Printers' Ink* retrospectively pointed to such criteria as the

Source: From Roland Marchand, *Advertising the American Dream: Making Way for Modernity, 1920–1940*, pp. 11–12, 13–16, 18, 20, 22–24, 66, 69, 207–210, 212, 214, 227, 234. Copyright © 1985 Regents of the University of California. Reprinted by permission of the publisher, the University of California Press, and the Family of Roland Marchand: Betsy, Suzanne and Jeanette.

shift from the "factory viewpoint" to concern with "the mental processes of the consumer," from "the objective to the subjective," from "descriptive product data" to "talk in terms of ultimate buying motives."... People rather than products dominated illustrations as advertisers sought to induce the potential customer to play a vicarious, scripted role as protagonist in the ad. A 1928 headline, "Be the Leading Lady in this Little Modern Drama," only made explicit the invitation to consumer participation that many advertisers now sought to imbed in their illustrations and copy....

World War I brought an end to widespread distrust of big business, and postwar legislation curtailed the influx of immigrants. But perceptions of a quickened tempo of change in the 1920s intensified people's fears of failing to keep pace with new complexities and of becoming "lost in the crowd." ... NOW, increasingly, many Americans pursued their search for a secure identity, for "self-realization," by seeking clues and advice in those sources most conveniently and ubiquitously available—the mass media. Advertisers gradually recognized, consciously or subconsciously, that the complexities of an increasingly urbanized, specialized, interdependent mode of life were creating a residue of unmet needs. Perceiving new vacuums of guidance and personal relationships, they stepped forward to offer their products as answers to modern discontents....

Advertisements in the new copy styles set forward a model of life's struggles that was well-tailored to strike a responsive chord among people conscious of the increasing dependence of their life ambitions on large organizations and impersonal judgments. This model portrayed the typical life-situation as that of an individual facing an external task or goal. An objective test or impersonal decision determined whether the protagonist of the story—the consumer's stand–in—successfully met the challenge. Disinterested, judgmental people would determine whether one succeeded in contests for business success, popularity, social standing, beauty, even love. "They" would determine by rigid standards—without the possibility of personal favoritism or the sympathetic excusing of faults—whether one's teeth, breath, "intestinal vigor," bathroom fixtures, silverware, or automobile polish "met the test." Having scripted a confrontation between the consumer and an impersonal test, the advertiser quickly befriended the consumer. Assuming the role of coach and confidante, he offered the consumer advice and encouragement as together they faced the external challenge.

As copywriters evolved from salesmen to confidantes, they began to perceive other advantages in this new "side-by-side" [with the consumer] approach. Argument, no matter how amiable and persuasive, had a polarizing tendency that pitted advertising persuasiveness against buyer resistance. Too much argumentative reliance on reasons induced the reader to generate counter-reasons. Advice or "coaching," on the other hand, aligned advertiser and potential consumer on the *same side* in opposition to a task or problem confronting the consumer. As society's increasing pressures and complexities made the consumer uneasy, the advertiser intervened with sympathetic advice on how to triumph over the impersonal judgments of the modern world.

"Scare copy," which became increasingly prominent as the 1920s progressed, was simply one variant of this side-by-side positioning. Known in trade jargon as the "negative appeal," scare copy sought to jolt the potential consumer into a new consciousness by enacting dramatic episodes of social failures and accusing judgments. Jobs were lost, romances cut short, and marriages threatened. Germs attacked, cars skidded out of control, and neighbors cast disapproving glances. In each instance, the product stepped forward—not to argue with the reader, but to offer friendly help. Scare copy posited a universe in which the fate of each consumer lay in the hands of external disinterested forces and unsympathetic, judgmental observers, a world of normative expectations applied with unmerciful severity. By contrast, the advertiser was solicitous and caring, a friend in need.

Increasingly during the 1920s, this friend was recognizable by name. It might be Betty Crocker or Mary Hale Martin or Nurse Ellen Buckland or any of a score of (usually fictitious) advisers and confidantes who "personally signed" their company's ads. Or it might be someone you "knew well"—a prominent society figure or movie star whose familiar presence could give you a sense of receiving advice from a real person. . . .

Readers hungered for a personal touch. Mobility, greater generational separation, and modern complexities of living had created a vacuum of personal advice. In responding to that need, advertisers explored new ways to personalize their relationship with the consumer. . . .

Listerine was not a new product in 1920. For years it had been merchandised perfunctorily as a general antiseptic. Initially, the three men who transformed Listerine into the marvel of the advertising world—the copywriters Milton Feasley and Gordon Seagrove and the company president Gerard B. Lambert—did not so much convert the product to a new use as induce the public to discover a new need. After a year of comparatively awkward and old-fashioned human-interest ads for Listerine as a mouthwash, the copywriters hit upon a winning formula. The picture of a lovely girl introduced a story cryptically entitled "He Never Knew Why." The hero of the story, a rising young businessman, was spurned by the "luminous" but "charmingly demure" girl of his dreams after a single romantic encounter. He seemed to have every advantage in life, but labored under one insurmountable handicap. He had "halitosis."

The term "halitosis" (exhumed from an old medical dictionary) had a scientific sound, and thus took some of the coarseness out of a discussion of bad breath. Mimicking the tabloids' personal-interest stories and advice to the lovelorn columns, the ads took the form of quick-tempo sociodramas in which readers were invited to identify with temporary victims in tragedies of social shame. Now the protagonist was not the product but the potential consumer, suffering vicariously a loss of love, happiness, and success. As *Printers' Ink* reflected in a tribute to the copywriter Milton Feasley: "He dealt more with humanity than with merchandise. He wrote advertising dramas rather than business announcements—dramas so common to everyday experience that every reader could easily fit himself into the plot as the hero or culprit of its action." ...

The promoters of Listerine were not the first to discover the sociodrama as an advertising technique—just as they had not pioneered the appeal to social shame or personal fear. In advertisements headlined "Within the Curve of a Woman's Arm," the deodorant Odo-ro-no had earlier confronted the threats to romance posed by underarm perspiration. But Listerine purchased larger space in a wider variety of publications. Its expanding appropriations and spectacular profits impressed the business community. The J. Walter Thompson Company summarized the new perception of proper advertising techniques in 1926: "To sell *goods* we must also sell *words*. In fact we have to go further: we must sell *life.*" Listerine had vividly demonstrated how to "befriend" consumers by inducing them to experience vicariously the barriers and the avenues to "a romantic way of living" through the ads....

In the mid-1920s the more subjective, intimate style of advertising campaign still represented only the leading edge of change in a diverse body of advertising. Some advertisers, concerned about the prestige of their products and the status of their profession, found such copy too reminiscent of the patent medicine era. The sales figures were impressive, but could "participatory" copy work for most products?

By the end of the 1920s, the answer to that question by the advertising business was unquestionably Yes. Negative or scare appeals might often be inappropriate, but empathetic depiction of consumer experiences, instead of the product itself, gained steadily in favor. "Show consumer satisfactions" increasingly became the rallying cry for advertisers. The organizer of a J. Walter Thompson door-to-door survey returned early in the decade from the land "behind the doorbell" to report breathlessly that "members of the Consumer Family do not want for its own sake the product which they buy." Soap ads should sell "afternoons of leisure," advised one copywriter. Copy should wrap the product "in the tissue of a dream." The *Chicago Tribune* provided a lesson in the new orthodoxy for anyone who had missed the message. It demonstrated the potential of its ... section for radio advertising with a sample illustration captioned, "Here is a picture, not of a radio, but of keen enjoyment."

Obviously the illustrations for such ads should emphasize people more than products. They should picture situations of fulfillment or cautionary scenes of humiliations easily avoided by use of the product. Advertising agencies prided themselves on having begun to modernize industry by introducing the consumer's point of view to correct the producer's self-centered myopia. "The happiness of the reader should be the real topic of every advertisement," concluded Earnest Calkins in 1926. "The happiness of the advertiser should be carefully camouflaged." Writers in the advertising journals recounted a standard scenario of modernization in advertising: it began with ads depicting the bewhiskered founder and his factory, then moved to illustrations of the housewife pushing a vacuum cleaner or otherwise using the product, and finally arrived at scenes of fulfillment—the housewife's friends blinded by her gleaming floor or her children enjoying her company on an outing to pick wildflowers....

Demographically, of course, women comprised no more than a razor-thin majority of the nation's population—or of any of its ... segments. But statistics indicated that women did the bulk of the nation's retail buying. A constant agency cliché referred to women as the "purchasing agents" of their families, an analogy that suggested near-total responsibility for expenditures. The advertising trade journals commonly attributed 85 percent of all consumer spending to women. Scarcely anyone estimated women as comprising less than 80 percent of the consumer audience.

Once the audience was understood to be overwhelmingly female, certain implications for copy content and selling appeal seemed evident. Advertisers could draw upon a long tradition, British and French as well as American, for viewing women as fickle and debased consumers. In a tone of scientific assurance, advertising leaders of the 1920s and 1930s added that women possessed a "well-authenticated greater emotionality" and a "natural inferiority complex." Since women were "certainly emotional," advertisements must be emotional. Since women were characterized by "inarticulate longings," advertisements should portray idealized visions rather than prosaic realities. Copy should be intimate and succinct, since "women will read anything which is broken into short paragraphs and personalized."...

Academic psychologists had been stressing the efficacy of the emotional appeal in advertising ever since Walter Dill Scott's *The Theory of Advertising* in 1903. Throughout the 1920s advertising agencies intensified their rival claims to superiority in creating emotional copy. One agency claimed that it based its effort to dramatize each advertising story on the scientific fact that "for every act based upon *reasoning* we perform *twenty* acts as a result of our emotions." William Esty of J. Walter Thompson reminded his colleagues that the unanimous conclusion of all the experts they had recently consulted on public opinion was "that it is futile to try to appeal to masses of people on an intellectual or logical basis." Emotion, or what one of those experts had referred to as the public's "childish love of ... raw sensation," was the only sure avenue of influence.

This growing consensus about audience emotionality helped fuse the other observed audience traits into a composite conception. Popular convention defined emotion as a particular characteristic of women—and the advertising audience was overwhelmingly female. In fact, nearly every characteristic commonly attributed to the masses was also conventionally a "feminine" trait—capriciousness, irrationality, passivity, and conformism.

A blatant appeal to the emotions, moreover, epitomized the vulgarity in taste that was common to the masses. Emotional appeals succeeded because only by seeking this lowest common human denominator could the advertiser shake the masses from their lethargy without taxing their limited intelligence. Despite occasional protests against this audience image, advertisers of the 1920s became increasingly committed to a view of "consumer citizens" as an emotional, feminized mass, characterized by mental lethargy, bad taste, and ignorance....

Several advertising parables were so frequently repeated and so effectively reduced to formulas that their entire story could eventually be suggested by a phrase or two. These I have designated the "great parables" of the age. They did not directly invite interpretation on more than one level or challenge the audience to accept a new moral logic. Yet they did, in spite of their narrow, practical intent, incorporate some wider dimension of meaning. They reinforced (and even encouraged conversions to) a modern, secular "logic of living," as we shall see once we have examined... one.

A flush of anticipation colored the cheeks of the beautiful young lady as her escort seated her at the elegant table. It was her first important dinner among the fashionables of the city's smart set. But as the butler served the first course, her thrilled excitement turned to terror. "From that row of gleaming silver on either side of her plate, which piece shall she pick up?" Suddenly she sensed, as a knowledgeable mother would have been able to advise, that her chance of being invited to such an affair again—in fact, her whole future popularity—would be determined by this crucial first impression of her "presence." As her social destiny hung in the balance, "She could feel every eye on her hesitating Hand."

Even if she passed the test of "the Hesitating Hand," a young lady was certain to encounter many other fateful first-impression judgments. In "the Open Door" she and her husband faced the greatest social crisis of their five-year marriage: they had taken the bold step of inviting the vice-president in charge of sales and his wife to dinner. For days, the eager young wife planned the dinner menu. Her husband researched and rehearsed several topics for appropriate conversation. But both completely forgot about their tasteless front doorway, with its lack of beautifully designed woodwork. And neither realized how dreary and out-of-date was the furniture they had purchased soon after their marriage. Thus, all of their efforts at preparation came to naught, for their guests formed an indelible impression during "those few seconds" from "the touch of the bell" to their entrance into the living room. No feats of cooking or conversation could counteract that first impression of dowdy tastelessness and lack of modernity. It fatefully bespoke a deficiency in character and ambition. Twenty years later, with the husband still third-assistant for sales at the small branch office, they anxiously passed on to their children a hard-won bit of wisdom: "Your Future may rest on what the Open Door reveals."

These re-enacted conflations of late 1920s "tragedy of manners" advertisements suggest the drama and pathos with which copywriters could recount the popular parable of the First Impression. According to such tableaux, first impressions brought immediate success or failure. Clearly, the scenarios were fantastical. Yet the parable of the First Impression, for all its exaggerated dramatics, drew much of its persuasive power from its grounding in readers' perceptions of contemporary realities. In a relatively mobile society, where business organizations loomed ever larger and people dealt far more often with strangers, many personal interactions were fleeting and unlikely to be repeated. In large organizations, hiring and promotion decisions now often seemed arbitrary and impersonal. No longer were they generally predictable on the basis of accumulated personal connections and past interactions. The reasons why one man gained a promotion or one woman suffered a social snub had become less explicable on grounds of long-standing favoritism or old family feuds. In the increasingly anonymous business and social relationships of the age, one might suspect that anything—including a first impression—had made the crucial difference.

Warren Susman and Daniel Rodgers suggest the context of popular ideas within which the parable of the First Impression found ample sustenance when they describe the new advice manuals of the early twentieth century. These manuals revealed a fundamental shift: from a nineteenth-century "culture of character," which stressed morality and work discipline as prerequisites for success, to a new "culture of personality," which emphasized the cultivation of one's ability to please others. Paula Fass's study of the peer society of college students in the 1920s indicates a high potential susceptibility to the parable of the First Impression among these business-oriented youths. She notes their emphasis on "externals of appearance and the accessories of sociability," their "scrupulous attention to grooming," and their heavy reliance on instantly recognizable displays of status calculated to create a desired impression. Like many others, they perceived that the rapid tempo of the age, and the larger scale and relative impersonality of business and social life, invited decisions based on anonymous judgments and quick impressions. One was never sure what minor and superficial considerations one's casual acquaintances might take into account.

Sensing its power in these circumstances, a variety of advertisers made use of the parable of the First Impression. Often they modified the basic formula of the tableau slightly to fit their particular product. Clothing manufacturers stressed overall appearance; gum, toothpaste, and toothbrush makers promised a "magic road to popularity in that first winning smile." Williams Shaving Cream recommended that powerful initial impact of "the face that's fit" for the "double-quick march of business." All agreed that "it's the 'look' of you by which you are judged most often." One of the most important effects of preparing carefully for that crucial first impression, many of the ads suggested, was the sense of self-confidence it created. "The man who looks like business, meets *better* business more than half-way," assured Williams Shaving Cream. A lovely frock, washed in Lux, would enable any woman to overcome an inferiority complex and feel a "deep, sure, inner conviction of being charming," Dorothy Dix counseled readers of the Ladies' Home journal. The House of Kuppenheimer confided to the up-and-coming young man that "someday your father may tell you how a certain famous letter 'k' in his inner coat pocket ... put confidence in his heart ... the confidence born of good appearance. And so helped him land his first job."

The disastrous results of a similar case, in which the leading man had failed to prepare himself for a positive first impression, were graphically displayed by the Cleanliness Institute of the Association of American Soap and Glycerine Producers. In the tableau, a salesman sitting in front of the desk of a business executive glanced back nervously over his shoulder at a huge specter of himself posed with one hand to his face in an embarrassed, self-conscious gesture. As the executive's impression formed, the salesman realized why he was failing to "put it over."

Capitalizing on an increasing public uncertainty that true ability and character would always win out in the scramble for success, advertising parables of the First Impression stressed the narrowness of the line that separated those who succeeded from those who failed. Many men possessed relatively equal abilities. The intensity and evenness of the competition gave great import to every detail of one's appearance. Far from deploring the apparent trend toward judging people on superficial externals, advertising tableaux often suggested that external appearance was the best index of underlying character. People were always—necessarily and appropriately—looking for quick clues to your taste and character. If they found these in the cut of your clothes, the brightness of your teeth, the age and taste of your furniture, your inept choice of silverware, or the closeness of your shave, they judged appropriately in a world of quick decisions. If your outer appearance, and that of your home, failed to reflect your true qualities of taste and character, you had no one to blame but yourself.

The power of the parable of the First Impression stemmed from the presumption that these impressions, any one of which might constitute a crucial victory or defeat, occurred constantly and almost instantaneously. Only because she was constantly prepared could the heroine of a Dr. West's toothbrush tableau pass "The Smile Test" during that moment when a handsome man picked her up from a fall off a speeding toboggan. "How often trivial incidents change the whole course of our existence," philosophized Dr. West. Such "great moments" allowed no opportunity for last-second preparations and no second chances. Like death or the "Second Coming," the impression that might determine one's opportunity for social acceptance, marriage, or a promotion might come at any time, in its terrible swiftness and finality, catching one unprepared for social salvation. "In the flicker of an eyelid," warned Camay soap, "a man—another woman—will appraise your looks." A "charming hostess" who failed to obtain stylish new furnishings would henceforth be condemned to "lonely afternoons, dreary evenings" for being unprepared for acquaintances who "called once out of courtesy" but never came again. One ardent suitor completely destroyed the good impression he had built up over months "when she noticed a hint of B.O." as he knelt to pop the question. There was no appeal from such judgments, no way to escape the constant surveillance. Throughout life, the Cleanliness Institute counseled, "Everywhere we go the people we meet are sizing us up. Very quickly they decide whether we are, or are not, from nice homes." ...

Externals *were* more significant in a mobile, urban, impersonal society. As a leading citizen of "Middletown" commented to a member of Robert and Helen Lynd's research staff in the mid-1920s, "You see, they [people] know money; they don't know you." By applying that money, through products, to your wardrobe, your face, your automobile, or your bathroom, you might manipulate their judgments in your favor. It might have been pure fantasy to suggest, as Tumbler Car Polish did, that a woman would break a social appointment because her husband had bought the wrong car polish and thus invited a bad first impression through "motor car dullness," or to imply, as Paris garters did, that a woman would reject the marriage proposal of an otherwise desirable mate simply because his socks sagged. But the parable of the First Impression would never have appeared in such extreme variations if advertisers had not sensed that it reflected a common public perception of how society really worked in an age of shifting relationships....

The ideology of advertising is an ideology of efficacious answers. No problem lacks an adequate solution. Unsolvable problems may exist in the society, but they are nonexistent in the world glimpsed through advertisements.... [T]he parable offered catharsis by promising that these particular ills of civilization—and by implication, all perils arising from modernity—could be cured by advertised products.

Thus, although the great parables were employed on each occasion for a specific merchandising purpose, their cumulative effect was to educate consumers to the modernity epitomized by the advertising agent. In a manner far less radical than the biblical parables, they invited readers to a new "logic of living" in which the older values of discipline, character-building, self-restraint, and production-oriented achievement were subordinated to the newer values of pleasure, external appearance, and achievement through consumption. These were not the parables of a radical gospel, but of an optimistic and mildly therapeutic ministry. Rather than challenging entrenched values and ideas, they brought a modern cast to the American dream by subtly redefining the terms of its fulfillment.

PRIMARY SOURCES

This chapter contains two types of primary sources: advertisements from the 1920s and sources written by those associated with the advertising industry during the decade. As you consider them, keep in mind Roland Marchand's argument in Source 1. What values do these sources reveal? Do the advertisements provide evidence for the existence of an ideology that guided or shaped a postwar American marketing system?

Sources 2–5

As you examine these advertisements, keep in mind what historian Roland Marchand calls advertising's "therapeutic ministry" to consumers. In other words, do these ads offer solutions to various anxieties without challenging "entrenched" ideas about society? Why do you think advertisers believed advertisements such as these would be so effective in the 1920s? Is the same approach evident in present-day advertising?

This pancake mix advertisement appeared in the *Ladies' Home Journal*. Note its use of drama and the various associations it makes.

"The Poor Little Bride of 1860" (1920)

Image courtesy of The Advertising Archives.

3   This advertisement was part of a broader ad campaign in the 1920s for Listerine mouthwash. As a result of that campaign, the manufacturer Lambert Pharmaceutical Company saw its profits skyrocket from $100,000 in 1921 to more than $4 million by 1927, leading other firms to take note of the company's advertising strategy.

Listerine Advertisement (1923)

Image courtesy of The Advertising Archives.

The Model T, Henry Ford's "car for the great multitude," was known for its simple design and reliability. Note the ways that this ad appeals to female consumers and how it associates the car with "modern" life.

Ford Motors Advertisement (1924)

Her habit of measuring time in terms of dollars gives the woman in business keen insight into the true value of a Ford closed car for her personal use.

This car enables her to conserve minutes, to expedite her affairs, to widen the scope of her activities. Its low first cost, long life and inexpensive operation and upkeep convince her that it is a sound investment value.

And it is such a pleasant car to drive that it transforms the business call which might be an interruption into an enjoyable episode of her busy day.

TUDOR SEDAN, $590   FORDOR SEDAN, $685   COUPE, $525   (All prices f. o. b. Detroit)

Ford
CLOSED CARS

May 1924 Good Housekeeping

MPI/ Archive Photos/Getty Images

Note the ways in which this advertisement associates the product with both "modern" life and consumer aspirations.

Kotex Advertisement (1927)

Image courtesy of The Advertising Archives.

6   This speech, delivered by President Calvin Coolidge to the American Association of Advertising Agencies, was ghostwritten by Bruce Barton, perhaps the most prominent advertising man in the 1920s. How does it defend advertising? How does it associate advertising with modern society?

Calvin Coolidge on the Economic Aspects of Advertising (1926)

When we stop to consider the part which advertising plays in the modern life of production and trade we see that basically it is that of education. It informs its readers of the existence and nature of commodities by explaining the advantages to be derived from their use and creates for them a wider demand. It makes new thoughts, new desires, and new actions. By changing the attitude of mind it changes the material condition of the people....

In former days goods were expected to sell themselves. Oftentimes they were carried about from door to door. Otherwise they were displayed on the shelves and counters of the merchant. The public were supposed to know of these sources of supply and depend on themselves for their knowledge of what was to be sold. Modern business could neither have been created nor can it be maintained on any such system. It constantly requires publicity. It is not enough that goods are made; a demand for them must also be made. It is on this foundation of enlarging production through the demands created by advertising that very much of the American industrial system rests....

The uncivilized make little progress because they have few desires. The inhabitants of our country are stimulated to new wants in all directions. In order to satisfy their constantly increasing desires they necessarily expand their productive power. They create more wealth because it is only by that method that they can satisfy their wants. It is this constantly enlarging circle that represents the increasing progress of civilization.

A great power has been placed in the hands of those who direct the advertising policies of our country, and power is always coupled with responsibilities. No occupation is charged with greater obligations than which partakes of the nature of education. Those engaged in that effort are changing the trend of human thought. They are molding the human mind. Those who write upon that tablet write for all eternity....

Advertising ministers to the spiritual side of trade. It is a great power that has been entrusted to your keeping which charges you with the high responsibility of inspiring and ennobling the commercial world. It is all part of the greater work of the regeneration and redemption of mankind.

Source: Calvin Coolidge on the Economic Aspects of Advertising.

Earnest Elmo Calkins was an advertising agency president who also promoted the advertising industry in the 1920s. How does Calkins associate advertising with modern conditions?

Earnest Elmo Calkins, *Business the Civilizer* (1926)

The question before the house is simply this: Is advertising a benefit to the public as a whole, is it necessary to retain the desirable phases of our present system of living, does it impose an unnecessary burden of cost on the ultimate consumers of goods, becoming thereby an economic waste, or does it, in short, add to the sum of human happiness?

When I was a boy, about fifty years ago more or less, mother used to buy a bar of Castile soap half a yard long and four inches square and saw it up into cakes an inch thick. The cake was hard as Stonehenge, the corners sharper than a serpent's tooth. It took weeks of use to wear it down so that it comfortably fitted the hand.

To-day we have a cake of toilet soap—a great many of them, in fact—just the right shape to fit the hand, just as pure as Castile, scented if we like, tinted to match the bathroom decorations if we prefer, reasonable in price; and when we want another cake we go to the nearest grocery or drug store, and there it is.

And not only toilet soap. We have seen the evolution of shaving creams, safety razors, and tooth pastes, as well as soap powders, laundry chips, washing machines, vegetable shortenings, self-rising flours, electric sad-irons, vacuum cleaners, hot-water taps, aluminum cooking utensils, refrigerators, kitchen cabinets—everything, in short, that constitutes the difference between our mothers' kitchens and our wives'.

The amount of sheer drudgery that has been taken out of housekeeping in fifty years can be realized only by comparison, by drawing the illuminating parallel. An iron, soft-coal cookstove; a reservoir at the back the only source of hot-water supply; the green-painted iron pump in the wooden corner sink for cold; drinking water from the pump outside; saleratus instead of baking powder; hog lard instead of vegetable shortening; butter and milk hung down the well by a string to keep them cold; heavy iron pots and skillets to be lifted, to say nothing of the coalhod; dishes washed by hand; no device to alleviate the frightful labor—no rubber scrapers, scouring mops, metal-ring dishrags, no wire brushes, or drying racks, or cleansing powders; baked beans an eighteen-hour job; oatmeal an overnight operation; sugar, salt, dried fruit, pickles, crackers, rice, coffee,

Source: "Business the Civilizer" from Earnest Elmo Calkins *Business the Civilizer*, 1926, pp. 11–15, 18.

pepper, spices, lard, bought in bulk, scooped out of open boxes or barrels ... exposed until sold, dumped on a sheet of paper laid on the scales. Molasses and vinegar drawn from the wood, and between whiles the gallon measures standing around, proving the adage that molasses attracts more flies than vinegar. Food was unclean, there was no sponsor for its quality, and it came to the kitchen almost in a state of nature. The housemother became a miniature manufacturing plant before the food was ready for the family to eat. And the preparation of meals was but a small portion of the housewife's burden. There was cleaning with no other implements but a rag, a broom, and a turkey wing. Clothes were washed with a rub-rub-rub that wore the zinc from the washboard. ...

The amelioration that has come about in fifty years is due directly and indirectly to advertising. These things did not come into existence because women demanded them. Women did not know that they were possible. They exist because there was a method of distributing them, of teaching possible buyers what a help they would be, of educating the housewife while offering her the means of applying what she learned, and of doing it on a large scale. And the strongest urge to invent desirable labor-saving devices has been this same possibility of distributing them—that is, selling enough of them to make it worth while.

Sometimes advertising supplies a demand, but in most cases it creates demand for things that were beyond even the imagination of those who would be most benefited by them. A woman knew the use of a broom, but she could not imagine a vacuum cleaner. Therefore she could not demand one, save with that vague unspoken desire which has existed from the beginning for some lightening of the terrible drudgery of keeping a house livable. The vacuum cleaner was introduced by educational advertising. The advertising was done partly by manufacturers anxious to sell vacuum cleaners, and partly by electric-light companies anxious to sell current. The spread of electrical housekeeping devices has followed the increase in the number of houses wired for electricity, and that too has been brought about by advertising, by the selfish desire to do more business, to sell more goods. But the result has been a public benefit, an increasing willingness to spend money to lighten the human burden, to cut down the waste of human energy spent in the operation of living. ...

The point is that we cannot eat our cake of accessible and convenient apparatus of living and still have our cake of freedom from advertising, freight trains, industrial villages, steel and cement construction, riveting hammers, congested highways, and the many other annoyances of a prosperous, material, and mercantile age. It's a fair question whether or not our modern life is worth while, but it has nothing to do with this question, which is, If our modern life is worth while and we want to continue it, is advertising necessary to that end?

8   Walter Dill Scott was the pioneer in applying new insights from psychology to advertisements in the early twentieth century. In this excerpt from one of his books on the psychology in advertising, Scott discusses the role of emotional appeals in ads. How does he suggest that advertisers should appeal to consumers? Do you detect any of the appeals to what Scott calls "fundamental instincts" in Sources 2–5?

Walter Dill Scott on Effective Advertisements (1928)

The wise salesman induces his customer to try on the clothing, to drive the automobile, to play the musical instrument, etc. The wise advertiser presents the goods, so far as possible, in such a way that the customer will not be compelled to use any original thought in conceiving of all the steps involved in the securing of the goods.

Much advertising fails to get at the feelings and emotions, the instincts and sentiments. It must not only convince the public that they OUGHT to act, but it must present its proposition so that it will make them WANT to act.

We are late in reaching the pew but early at the bleachers. We put off writing to cousins and aunts, but the fiancée is answered by "return mail." The dictates of reason may be resisted but not the promptings of sentiment and emotions.

We put off the things we know we OUGHT to do but not the things we WANT to do.

Almost every one who reads the advertisements of automobiles hankers after a machine, but unless his income is adequate his better judgment convinces him that it would be foolish extravagance to make the purchase. In this case we seem to have hesitation produced by the judgment even when the purchase is prompted by intense feelings. But the judgment is easily convinced of the wisdom of any act which excites intense desire. In the case of the automobile the judgment easily recognizes a fanciful need and yields to the promptings of desire.

A current advertisement takes advantage of this psychological situation and makes a most clever appeal to possible purchasers of automobiles. The following extract from the text of the advertisement is very adroit: "You may think you don't WANT a motor car. But there isn't any question about your NEEDING one. There is a difference between wanting a thing and needing it.... There is nothing that you could invest the money in that will pay you such a big dividend in the saving of your time in business and the saving of your health for years, as the purchase of a motor car. A good thing is a better thing the sooner you get it."

Source: From Walter Dill Scott, *Influencing Men in Business: The Psychology of Argument and Suggestion,* 1911, 1938, pp. 130–133.

If this advertisement is able to convince a man that he OUGHT to get the car he will do so at once because he already WANTS to purchase it. When desire is surging we are easily convinced that we ought to act, and hence the act follows immediately. When the judgment is convinced but no desire is enkindled, procrastination keeps the intended act from taking place. Many articles of merchandise may be so presented that the public will DESIRE to purchase them. Or they may be so presented that the public will merely be convinced that the goods OUGHT to be secured. The practical problem then arises as to methods of making the public WANT to act and WANT to follow out specific directions.

Advertisers have been successful in accomplishing this purpose in various ways. Some of these successful methods are worthy of consideration. Goods offered as means of gaining social prestige make their appeals to one of the most profound of the human instincts. In monarchies this instinct is regarded as a mere tendency to imitate royalty. In America, with no such excuse, the eagerness with which we attempt to secure merchandise used by the "swell and swagger" is absurd, but it makes it possible for the advertiser to secure more responses than might otherwise be possible. As an illustration of this fact we need but to look at the successful advertisements of clothing, automobiles, etc. The quality of the goods themselves does not seem to be so important as the apparent prestige given by the possession of the goods.

Goods which are presented as supplying a need long felt by the public are purchased without delay. In the case also of objects which supply any of the fundamental instinctive needs, the chances are that we shall act unhesitatingly. The instinctive desire to win social approval is but a typical illustration of an appeal to the fundamental instincts.

Our feelings may be awakened by the ideas themselves, by the manner in which the ideas are presented, or by a combination of the two. The idea of savory viands is pleasing in itself and the manner of presenting the idea may add much to its pleasing value when presented as is done, for example, by the National Biscuit Company in placing Nabisco before the public. In the advertisements of Nabisco an attempt was made for many months to please by means of fairy maids serving the product, by means of alluring verbal descriptions of the goods and by perfect harmony between the illustration and the type matter.

The man with the proper imagination is able to conceive of any commodity in such a way that it becomes an object of emotion to him and to those to whom he imparts his picture, and hence creates desire rather than a mere feeling of ought. It would be hard to conceive of any more prosaic things than correspondence schools, dental cream, billiard tables, tobacco, soap, flour, fountain pens, foods, musical instruments, automobiles, heating plants, radiators, financial securities, and insurance. In the mind of the artist these homely commodities are transformed into objects that awaken our sentiments and aesthetic feelings.

9   Written by a University of Southern California professor, *Advertising to Women* was intended for the "business man who wants thoroughly practical information on how to appeal to women." What advice does the author offer here regarding the stimulation of what he calls the female "sex ego"? What is his view of women?

Advertising to Women (1928)
CARL A. NAETHER

I find evidence of the sex appeal in advertisements, letters, and booklets which merchandisers of complexion powders, toilet soaps, perfumes, so-called tissue builders and tissue destroyers, hair tonics, and the multitude of other similar artificial expedients employ to further sales. Through these media woman is freely told that the acquisition in sufficient quantity and the use in prescribed manner of certain beauty builders will enable her to keep or in due course of time will endow her with a certain amount of that bodily charm she longs to retain or to attain. And since, seemingly, there is hardly a woman in youth or in middle age who is not at once willing and eager to be made physically more attractive, the market for the aids to beauty has assumed large and apparently profitable proportions.

The sex appeal varies only in so far as its final expression is either blunt or subtle. That is to say, either directly or indirectly the advertiser gives woman to understand that, through the use of his product or services, she can procure or retain certain physical characteristics—commonly spoken of as physical "charms"—effective in subjugating and dominating the affections of men. In magazine advertisements the appeal is often veiled; in booklets and sales letters—these are meant only for actual prospects—it is more personal, more detailed, less subtle, and more direct.

In toiletry advertising the far-reaching sex appeal is based on two assumptions. The one is that every woman is physically unattractive in one or more respects and that, therefore, she requires the supposedly beneficial use of the seller's wares; the other, that advancing years, necessarily shadowing and to some extent even marring every woman's beauty, necessitate a more or less continual application of preservatives of physical youth and physical charm. The method of procedure followed is simply to make woman *conscious* in word and picture of a definite need for the goods on either or both grounds. Thus is feminine consciousness of sex, already well developed in most American women to-day, heightened and made more constant. The extent to which a woman may at times become aware of her lack of physical charm

Source: Carl A. Naether, *Advertising to Women,* 1928, pp. 244–246.

is shown by the following letter, written by a country woman in answer to an advertising offer of a bottle of hair tonic. The advertisement appeared in a farm paper. The letter reads:

> Kind Friend:
>
> My hair is awful thin and falling out daily. I have beautiful coal-black curly hair which stays in waves all the time. Everyone is crazy about it. If I could only find something that would bring it back again as it was when I was 20 years old. I am now 34.
>
> I am heartbroken when I think and see how thin my beautiful curly hair is. I have to stay at home all the time. I could cry my eyes out. Kind friend, if you think your hair treatment will do my hair any good and bring it back thick and beautiful again, please send me a bottle free of charge by return mail.
>
> May God bless you. Please let me hear from you at once.

Even though this very frank letter is written in poor English, its lines lay bare a wealth of human pathos, a profound yearning for the restoration of a woman's proverbial "crown of glory." Nor was this human document an exception—a spirit of personal frankness and sincere humanness pervaded nearly all the letters received in response to the farm paper advertisement.

To strengthen woman's awareness of sex in relation to *herself*, to *other women*, and to *man*, the advertiser of toiletries relies on both the picture and the printed word. Especially in advertisements do we find the picture allusive to sex attraction. Here it serves as an attention-getter and, strategically and almost without exception, is made to occupy the upper part of the advertisement so as to be sure to catch the fleeting glances of the magazine reader as trippingly they fall on this page or that. Undeniably, the Woodbury advertisement, originally a full-page spread in warm but subdued colors ... ranks high as an attention lure, because its pictorial appeal fascinates. Inserted as it was in a periodical found almost exclusively on the reading tables of women, its illustrative message is intended to suggest a partial solution at least of one of woman's lifelong problems—that of retaining man's affections. The frankness with which the artist has ... depicted the soap seller's theme—the man kissing the hand of a woman he is holding in his arms, that portion of her body which is shown in the picture almost nude—cannot fail to strike vividly and sympathetically the imagination of every woman who chances to see this advertisement. The whole is nothing more than an ostensibly refined version of sex appeal pure and simple. It is a lure to make woman believe that, by using the soap in question, she will be able to cultivate a skin sufficiently beautiful to constitute an infallible safeguard against the waning of male affection. This advertisement is to impress upon the reader mainly the affection-retaining powers which a certain soap has when it is used for toilet purposes! Because of the overwhelming pictorial appeal to woman's strongest emotion, consisting here of an ingenious, sensuous portrayal of the workings of sight and touch, the illustration may succeed in laming the reader's reasoning faculties for the moment so completely as to nullify their influence. In other words, so deadly in its effect is the picture's suggestive power as to make woman believe the unreasonable assertion that she will be able to keep warm and active her man's feelings toward her by bringing the advertised soap in contact with her skin at stated intervals! Such is the "logical" conclusion which the feminine reader of this message is to reach. As if the love of man for woman depended solely on the charm of the latter's skin! As if the material factor—the presence to senses of sight and touch of a lovely skin— were the only one sufficiently potent to attract the one sex to the other.

CONCLUSION

A wise person once noted that fish did not discover water. Like fish in the sea, we are immersed in advertising. Thus, we take it for granted. Rarely do we step back to examine it, except as consumers. And more rarely still do we actually analyze it. In other words, we do not ask the sorts of questions that this chapter's sources pose. Yet this chapter demonstrates a point about primary historical sources reflected in earlier chapters: The range of historical sources is practically limitless. We only need to look at them with critical eyes.

This chapter is also an example of the way historians turn to the past for evidence regarding ideas or values. Sometimes these things are easy to spot. That is especially true when sources—the Declaration of Independence, for instance—were created for the purpose of stating ideas or affirming values. Sometimes, though, they are more elusive. That is usually the case when sources were created for some other purpose, such as selling mouthwash. In that case, finding evidence for ideas or values usually requires careful analysis and many examples.

Finally, if advertising is a mirror, as historian Roland Marchand suggests, this chapter reminds us that history is as well. Just as it is difficult to see water while swimming, sometimes it is easier to see pervasive influences while looking from afar. That is true even when we encounter ideas and practices in the past that seem familiar to us. In many ways, advertising in the 1920s is indistinguishable from that of today. Turning to history helps us to understand what separates us from people in the past and also what unites us with them. In other words, we begin to comprehend recent influences and those inherited from long ago. As we move closer to the present in the second half of this volume, we will encounter evidence of recent changes and old inheritances. Whether we examine one person at the top of the society or many at the bottom, the lessons of war or ideas about gender, we will see the impact of both old and new influences. A recognition of them helps us see how the past has shaped us and how we have moved beyond it.

FURTHER READING

Stuart Ewen, *Captains of Consciousness: Advertising and the Social Roots of the Consumer Culture* (New York: McGraw-Hill, 1976).

Stephen Fox, *The Mirror Makers: A History of American Advertising and Its Creators* (New York: Vintage Books, 1984).

Daniel Delis Hill, *Advertising to the American Woman: 1900–1999* (Columbus: Ohio State University Press, 2002).

Daniel Pope, *The Making of Modern Advertising* (New York: Basic Books, Inc., 1983).

Juliann Sivulka, *Soap, Sex, and Cigarettes: A Cultural History of American Advertising* (Belmont, Calif.: Wadsworth Publishing Company, 1998).

NOTES

1. Frederick Lewis Allen, *Only Yesterday: An Informal History of the 1920s* (New York: Harper & Row Publishers, 1959), p. 140.
2. Ibid., p. 142.
3. Robert S. and Helen Merrell Lynd, *Middletown: A Study in American Culture* (New York: Harcourt, Brace and Company, 1929), p. 82.
4. *Printer's Ink* 72 (August 18, 1891), p. 17.
5. William Shryer, *Analytical Advertising* (Detroit: Business Service Corporation, 1912), p. 47.
6. Roland Marchand, *Advertising the American Dream: Making Way for Modernity, 1920–1940* (Berkeley: University of California Press, 1985), p. xviii.

Chapter

7

History "From the Top Down":
Eleanor Roosevelt, First Lady

The sources in this chapter enable the reader to evaluate the activities of Eleanor Roosevelt and to assess their relevance to the times.

Secondary Source

1. Eleanor Roosevelt as First Lady (1996), ALLIDA M. BLACK

Primary Sources

2. Transcripts of Eleanor Roosevelt's Press Conferences (1933–1938)
3. "The Negro and Social Change" (1936)
4. Letter to Her Daughter (1937)
5. This I Remember (1949), ELEANOR ROOSEVELT
6. My Parents: A Differing View (1976), JAMES ROOSEVELT
7. Letter from Barry Bingham to Marvin McIntyre (1934)
8. Excerpts from Letters to Franklin Roosevelt (1935)
9. It's Up to the Women (1933)
10. Eleanor Roosevelt on the Equal Rights Amendment (1933)

*D*uring the Great Depression in 1932, unemployed World War I veterans marched on Washington, D.C. to demand early payment of their service bonuses. In response Herbert Hoover called out the army, which routed the desperate marchers out of their shantytown and then burned it down. Shortly after Franklin Roosevelt took office in 1933, a second "bonus army" descended on Washington. This time the First Lady drove out to talk to them. When she arrived, they asked her who she was and what she wanted. She told them her name and that she wanted to see how they were doing. "I did not spend as much as an hour there; then I got into my car and drove away," she said. "Everyone waved and I called, 'Good luck,' and they answered, 'good-by and good luck to you.'"[1]

Before the Depression was over, Eleanor Roosevelt had visited coal miners, Civilian Conservation Corps boys, women in Works Progress Administration sewing rooms, tenant farmers, and many others. As she traveled around the country, the First Lady gave a human face to numerous New Deal relief programs. At the same time she was her paralyzed husband's eyes and ears, reporting to him Americans' struggles to survive the Depression. She was also his conscience, fighting amid much criticism to extend the boundaries of the New Deal to blacks and women.

By sharing the public spotlight with her husband, Eleanor Roosevelt was the first "modern" First Lady. As a political activist, she redefined the role of the president's wife. At the same time, there was also something old-fashioned about her. A Victorian upbringing gave her what one historian called "an uncynical sense of duty and moral purpose."[2] It also left her with a traditional view of women as mothers and wives. Eleanor believed that women were agents of moral good and needed protection more than equality. She never went to college or pursued a career. Self-reliance grew only slowly, nurtured by the pain of rejection.

Eleanor Roosevelt's struggle for independence is a compelling story for biographers, but there is another reason to examine her life. Like her, there is something "old-fashioned" about biography itself. Although not always the case today, traditionally it was written about people at the "top" of their society, wealthy and influential people like Eleanor. Moreover, as one writer put it, biography "moves to the pace and powers of individual human beings and not to the impersonal dictates of markets and masses."[3] During the Depression, of course, few Americans had escaped the dictates of either. FDR was president because markets had collapsed and the "masses" had chosen him to lead the nation. At first glance, biography's personal approach to history might seem ill-suited to a time dominated by such impersonal forces. Yet the Depression era is actually a good time to see how one person's life illuminates the past, because biographers deal with the important historical developments as well as with individual lives. Biographies show us the forces that shaped their subjects' lives and how, in turn, their lives influenced history. This chapter, therefore, examines how one exceptional woman both reflected and affected her times.

SETTING

Anna Eleanor Roosevelt was born in 1884 into a world of privilege. The daughter of two families who could trace their wealth to colonial times, she grew up sheltered from both the masses and the marketplace. Yet her childhood was hardly blissful. Eleanor's mother was cold, distant, and disappointed by her only daughter's plain appearance. As Eleanor later realized, she grew up shy and lonely, "entirely lacking in the spontaneous joy and mirth of youth."[4] Her affectionate but alcoholic father was the one bright spot in her childhood. Unfortunately, he died when she was ten, two years after diphtheria had claimed her mother. Eleanor and her younger brother lived with their grandmother, who reared them "on the principle that 'no' was easier to say than 'yes.'"[5]

Escape came in the form of an English finishing school. There Eleanor learned more than the social graces that upper-class Americans considered "education" for their daughters. Headmistress Marie Souvestre encouraged her students to think critically and to challenge conventional ideas. Souvestre took special interest in Eleanor, who seemed burdened with a sense of inferiority. She taught her to champion the underdog. Together they traveled through Europe. "Whatever I have become since," Eleanor later confided, "had its seeds in those three years of contact with a liberal mind and strong personality."[6]

Still, exposure to Madame Souvestre's "liberal" ideas did not prevent Eleanor from becoming a New York society debutante when she returned home, or from being depressed about her appearance. "I was the first girl in my mother's family who was not a belle," she confessed, "and . . . I was deeply ashamed."[7] Eleanor had not forgotten Souvestre's lessons, however. After her debut, she joined the National Consumers' League, which fought for better conditions for female workers in sweatshops and clothing factories. She also joined the Junior League, recently founded by charity-minded socialites. She taught classes at a community center on the Lower East Side, where she was at first terrified at the sight of "foreign-looking people, crowded and dirty."[8] In time, however, Eleanor discovered she preferred social work to the social whirl.

Marriage to distant cousin Franklin in 1905 ended Eleanor's trips to the tenements. For the next fifteen years she was occupied with her five children and her husband's budding political career. Gradually, though, she was again drawn out of her private sphere. After World War I, Eleanor joined the League of Women Voters and the Women's Trade Union League, which fought for legislation regulating women's wages and hours of labor. Personal shocks furthered a growing sense of independence and self-confidence. In 1918 she discovered Franklin's affair with her personal secretary. "The bottom dropped out of my . . . world and I faced myself, my surroundings, my world honestly for the first time," she later wrote.[9] Their marriage continued, but marital relations did not. Eleanor began to spend more time in reform causes and discovered her own political skills. Franklin's paralyzing bout with polio four years later further encouraged her independence.

Eleanor began to represent her husband in public and became active in New York Democratic party politics. She organized women voters, fought for numerous social reforms, and developed associations with many female reformers. In 1928, while teaching part-time at a private girls' school in New York City, Eleanor worked for Al Smith's unsuccessful campaign for the presidency, running the New York headquarters of the Democratic Party's National Women's Committee. When Franklin was elected governor of New York the same year, Eleanor decided to keep her teaching job and be First Lady in Albany only part-time.

Eleanor nevertheless played an influential role as the governor's wife, advising him on policies and appointments, and when FDR ran for the presidency four years later, she put her experience to work campaigning around the country. It was on the campaign that she also began an intimate friendship with reporter Lorena Hickok. During Eleanor's years in the White House, the two women sustained a furtive relationship that some historians claim was both passionate and romantic. Although historians are unsure of the level of intimacy between the two women, it is clear that Eleanor freely confided in Hickok, including her fears about becoming First Lady. Eleanor was fearful for her husband and children, but mostly she was worried about her own fate. She knew that, far more than in the governor's mansion, she would have to sacrifice her autonomy and tend to social obligations as the nation's First Lady. Right after FDR's sweeping victory in 1932, Eleanor confided to Hickok that she was "sincerely" glad for her husband. "Now," she added, "I shall have to work out my own salvation."[10]

INVESTIGATION

This chapter examines Eleanor Roosevelt's efforts to "work out" her "salvation" as First Lady. Thus your main task is to evaluate Eleanor Roosevelt as an activist First Lady during the Depression. Your evaluation should address the following main questions:

1. **What do Eleanor Roosevelt's activities reveal about the limitations on women in the early twentieth century?** Do the sources reveal that she had power, or only influence with other people?

2. **Do the sources reveal that Eleanor challenged or reinforced traditional conceptions of women's proper role?** Did she challenge her role as helpmate to her husband or channel her energies in only socially acceptable directions?

3. **In what ways was Eleanor Roosevelt's struggle unique and how did it reflect the situation of women generally?** What do the sources reveal about the influence of Eleanor's social background on her attitudes?

4. **Do you agree with historian Allida Black's conclusions in Source 1 about Eleanor's achievements?** What were her greatest achievement and biggest failure as First Lady? Was she able to change the lives of women and blacks, or only her own?

Before you begin, review the sections in your textbook on the status and role of women in American society in the first decades of the twentieth century, as well as the chapter on the New Deal. Although Eleanor Roosevelt may not be mentioned, these sections will provide useful background for evaluating her activities and achievements.

SECONDARY SOURCE

1   In this selection, historian Allida M. Black examines Eleanor Roosevelt's role as First Lady during the 1930s. Note how Black uses ER's life to examine important social issues during the Depression. What impact did she have on these issues? Do you think a biography of an exceptional, upper-class woman like Eleanor Roosevelt reveals a lot or a little about historical developments and the lives of ordinary Americans in the early twentieth century?

Eleanor Roosevelt as First Lady (1996)

ALLIDA M. BLACK

Questions "seethed" in ER's mind about what she should do after March 4, 1933. Realizing that FDR would not allow her the same mobility she had when he was governor, ER worried that she would be confined to a schedule of teas and receptions and tried to create a less restrictive place for herself within the White House. She volunteered to "do a real job" for FDR. . . . The president rebuffed the first lady's offer. Trapped by convention, she begrudgingly recognized that "the work [was FDR's] work and the pattern his pattern." Frustrated and disappointed, she acknowledged that she "was one of those who served his purposes."

Nevertheless, ER refused to accept a superficial and sedentary role. She wanted "to do things on my own, to use my own mind and abilities for my own aims" and struggled to carve out an active contributory place for herself in the New Deal. This was not to be a challenge easily met. Dejected, she found it "hard to remember that I was not just 'Eleanor Roosevelt,' but the 'wife of the President.'" Yet within her first two years in the White House, she had turned her "joblessness" into the freedom to investigate a variety of issues and the power to advance specific programs which she hoped would ease the problems she detected. . . .

She was lonely. . . . "First Friend" Hickok, who continued to travel as an investigative reporter for the Federal Emergency Relief Administration after she resigned her position with the Associated Press, tried to fill the gap. By May, ER's frustration had given way to immense depression. "My zest in life is rather gone for the time being," ER confessed to Hickok. "If anyone looks at me, I want to weep . . . my mind goes round and round like a squirrel in a cage. I want to run and I can't, and I despise myself. . . .

. . . On March 6, two days after her husband became president, Eleanor Roosevelt held her own press conference to announce that she would "get together" with women reporters once a week. She asked for the reporters' cooperation. ER hoped that together they not only could discuss her duties as first lady but also explain "what goes on politically in the legislative national life" and encourage women to become active in the New Deal programs in their community. "The idea," she said, "largely is to make an understanding between the White House and the general public."

Initially ER tried to weight the discussion more in favor of her traditional social duties and away from her views of the problems the nation confronted. However, as she expanded her role, the topics covered during the press conferences also expanded. Her statements to the press notwithstanding, political issues soon became a central part of the weekly briefings.

FDR, at [his adviser Louis] Howe's urging, had asked his wife to travel the nation as his "ambassador." Within three months, ER had logged 40,000 miles. Her observations during these tours only reinforced the impressions she had formed during the final days of the campaign. She returned to Washington convinced that relief programs alone could not counteract the Depression and that basic economic reforms were essential. She began to share these views with the women assigned to cover her.

By May she discussed the White House protocol for serving 3.2 percent beer, her opposition to sweat shops and child labor, the problem confronting those living in the Bonus Army encampment and poverty-stricken Appalachia, and her support for the Veterans National Liaison Committee and higher salaries for teachers. By early June she proclaimed that "very few women know how to read the newspapers," argued that they should pay close attention to international economic news, and delivered a tutorial on how "a busy woman" could keep track of the news "at a time when every one of us ought to be on [our] toes."

These pronouncements, when coupled with the image she made when she visited those the Depression affected most, encouraged political reporters to cover her. This fostered an in-house rivalry between reporters assigned to cover hard news and those assigned to the women's pages. Society reporters complained that her meetings with the press did not cover enough social news and many eventually stopped attending her weekly briefings.

Some political journalists, worried that such unorthodox comments would encourage criticism, urged ER to go off the record when she discussed political issues. Grateful for their concern, she nevertheless rejected their advice and argued that she knew that some of her statements would "cause unfavorable comment in some quarters," but, she told Emma Bugbee, "I am making these statements on purpose to arouse controversy and thereby get the topics talked about."

By 1934 ER's press conferences had become one of the major ways she defended her own activity and the programs she championed. Although she never issued a formal statement to the reporters and met with the press only to answer their questions, she soon learned to use these conferences as a way to appeal directly to the people. As [reporter] Bess Furman later recalled, "at the President's press conference, all the world's a stage, at Mrs. Roosevelt's, all the world's a school. . . . Give Mrs. Roosevelt a roomful of newspaper women, and she conducts classes on scores of subjects, always seeing beyond her immediate hearers to the 'women of the country.'"

ER, not satisfied with just disseminating information, also wanted to know how the public responded to the positions she advocated and those positions promoted by FDR's major critics, Huey Long and Father Charles Coughlin. Consequently, when *Women's Home Companion* asked her to write a monthly column, she gladly accepted. Announcing that she would donate her monthly thousand dollar fee to charity, ER then proceeded to ask her readers to help her establish "a clearinghouse, a discussion room" for "the particular problems which puzzle you or sadden you" and to share "how you are adjusting yourself to new conditions in this amazing changing world." Entitling the article "I Want You to Write to Me," ER reinforced the request throughout the piece. "Do not hesitate," she wrote in August 1933, "to write to me even if your views clash with what you believe to be my views." Only a free exchange of ideas and discussion of problems would help her "learn of experiences which may be helpful to others." By January 1934, 300,000 Americans had responded to this solicitation, more than the total number of letters received by Abraham Lincoln and Woodrow Wilson in their first year in office and equal to the weekly circulation of Long's *American Progress*.

This was not a token offer. ER had personal and political reasons for appealing for public input. Worried that Long and Coughlin supporters felt neglected by the New Deal, she wanted to make herself available to them.

Also concerned that the Federal Emergency Relief Administration programs did meet enough of people's needs, she pressured FERA administrator Harry Hopkins to hire Hickok to tour different parts of the nation, observe FERA programs, and report to him on their effectiveness. Hickok sent copies of these honest, harsh field reports to ER, daily confirming the many obstacles those seeking relief encountered. Plus, she was bored. "Your job is much more interesting than mine," she complained to Hickok that winter. She desperately wanted an assignment that was hers alone, an arena in which she could judge for herself the effectiveness of her husband's programs.

Yet her appeal to the public was not motivated solely by her dissatisfaction. Her commitment to free and unrestricted public discussion was heartfelt and intense. She considered the free exchange of information and ideas central to democracy's success. The more informed the public about the issues it confronted, the more educated the society would become, and the more opportunities democracy would have to be realized. . . .

The cornerstone of ER's emerging political philosophy was as simple as it was powerful: if the nation was to flourish, Americans must accept the responsibility of living in a democracy. They must study the issues and develop informed opinions about the best ways to solve the nation's problems because "knowledge will forever govern ignorance." Americans "must arm themselves with the power that knowledge gives" because government could only be as good as its people. Democracy was a two-way street. It not only "must have leaders who have the power to see farther, to imagine a better life but it must also have a vast army of men and women capable of understanding these leaders.". . .

Although most historians focus on ER's enthusiastic support for the model subsistence homestead community in Arthurdale, West Virginia, as the clearest example of ER's pressuring FDR toward a more encompassing relief effort, other New Deal programs, when examined as a group, offer a more thorough illustration of ER's democratic principles. While she doggedly advocated programs which would ensure "that a family shall have sufficient means of livelihood and the assurance of an ability to pay their expenses covering a stand which we hope to establish as something to shoot at," in her vision, the responsibilities of a democratic state were not to be confined to improving the lot of only one socioeconomic group. . . .

The huge numbers of unemployed youth of the 1930s underscored several fears adults had about society. Conservatives saw disgruntled young people as a fertile ground for revolutionary politics while progressives mourned the disillusionment and apathy spreading among American youth. Indeed, concern over the political susceptibility of youth concerned some within the administration so much that they wondered "whether the New Deal ought to establish a democratic alternative to the Hitler Youth." Educators feared that without some type of financial aid, colleges would suffer irreversible damage. Eleanor Roosevelt agreed with the progressives, telling the *New York*

Times that "I live in real terror when I think we may be losing this generation. We have got to bring these young people into the active life of the community and make them feel that they are necessary."

ER insisted that government had the responsibility to keep these young people from becoming even more "stranded." Although many in the White House agreed with her, New Deal officials differed over the means to reduce joblessness among high school and college-age youth and debated whether or not student aid should be provided as part of the relief package. Public opinion, fearful that students would take jobs that might otherwise help adult workers, was ambivalent over which course the government should pursue. Moreover, understanding the sensitivity of this issue, FDR proved reluctant to institute a program which might backfire. Although he wanted to put young people to work and believed that action must be taken to shore up youth's commitment to democracy, the president "never approved of ideological training for American youth." Furthermore, he did not want to be accused of favoritism or despotism. While everyone agreed there was a major problem, there was no consensus on how to address it.

FDR signed the executive order creating the National Youth Administration (NYA) in the summer of 1935, two years after telling the press that he objected to "channeling direct federal aid to high school graduates or their teachers." He insisted that he had "pretty serious" disagreements with a program that would "do anything in the way of sending boys and girls to college." And lastly, he categorically rejected any proposal which would provide widespread vocational training. Instead he championed a more traditional approach that emphasized physical labor, strict supervision, and limited job training. In short, FDR promoted the Civilian Conservation Corps (CCC) as the model agency for youth relief.

ER, who could not have disagreed more strongly with her husband, emphatically rejected the CCC model. Although it certainly helped adults, she argued that it failed youth. Its camps were too militaristic to encourage independence and its instruction was limited to forestry. This was no way to bring disgruntled and disillusioned youth back into society. The specific problem facing youth needed to be recognized, but in a way that not only fostered self-worth but also encouraged faith in democratic capitalism. The government must show American youth that they had more options than the military and the dole.

By 1934, ER decided that the government had to develop a program tailored to the special economic, educational, and vocational needs of youth, and she dedicated herself to seeing a comprehensive program implemented. She lobbied the press and administration officials, appealed to the public to recognize the social and political benefits the program could offer, and coaxed student leaders into setting realistic goals. Having met regularly with student leaders and relief officials, she understood both sides of the argument. And she strove to form a consensus that could satisfy most needs of both groups. . . .

Although not the legislative architect of the NYA, ER nevertheless helped establish its priorities, and in so doing left an indelible imprint upon the agency's development. When FDR issued the executive order June 26, 1935, he authorized the NYA to administer programs in five areas: work projects, vocational guidance, apprenticeship training, educational and nutritional guidance camps for unemployed women, and student aid. Clearly ER's preference for vocational guidance and education triumphed over his earlier support of the CCC relief model. Even historian James Kearney, who believed that the first lady's sole contribution to political thought was her "goodness," acknowledged that over time, "the NYA moved toward [her] preferences." As the agency progressed from its initial emphasis on relief to placing more emphasis on recreation and clerical training to providing educational loans, this shift in emphasis was "more than coincidental." . . .

Indeed, ER took such satisfaction in the NYA that when she briefly acknowledged her role in forming the agency, she did so with an uncharacteristic candor. "One of the ideas I agreed to present to Franklin," she wrote in *This I Remember*, "was that of setting up a national youth administration. . . . It was one of the occasions on which I was very proud that the right thing was done regardless of political consequences." . . .

Despite the fervor with which ER campaigned for a more democratic administration of relief through the NYA. . . , these efforts paled in comparison to the unceasing pressure she placed upon the president and the nation to confront the economic and political discrimination facing Black America. In seeking to educate the public on the evils of racial discrimination, she underscored the moral imperative of the civil rights agenda. Although the first lady did not become an ardent proponent of integration until the 1950s, throughout the thirties and forties she nevertheless persistently labeled racial prejudice as undemocratic and immoral. Black Americans recognized the depth of her commitment and consequently kept faith with FDR because his wife kept faith with them. . . .

ER's racial policies attracted notice almost immediately. Less than a week after becoming first lady, she shocked conservative Washington society by announcing she would have an entirely black White House domestic staff. And even though the staff would be supervised by the "bigoted" Henrietta Nesbit, White House maid Lillian Rogers Parks recalled that "it was the first time it was great to be black. It meant you could hang on to your job at the White House."

By late summer 1933, photographs appeared showing ER discussing living conditions with black miners in West Virginia and the press treated her involvement in the anti-lynching campaign as front page news. Rumors of ER's "race-baiting" actions sped across the South with hurricane force. In August 1934, Barry Bingham, son of the publisher of the *Louisville Courier-Journal*, wrote FDR aide Marvin McIntyre that ER "has made herself offensive to Southerners by a too great affection for Negroes." Although Bingham claimed not to believe the rumor, he needed reassurance. The first lady refused to comply completely, responding that while she was "very much interested in the Negroes and their betterment," the story that she "drove through the streets of a town with a negro woman beside me happens to be untrue." Yet she warned Bingham that while she "probably would not do it in North Carolina," she "would, however, not have a single objection to doing so if I found myself in a position where it had to be done."

ER refused to be intimidated by rumor. In 1935, she visited Howard University's Freedman Hospital, attended the University's fundraising banquet, lobbied Congress for increased appropriations, and praised the institution in her press conferences. After intensive briefing by [NAACP secretary] Walter White ER toured the Virgin Islands with Lorena Hickok investigating conditions for herself only to return agreeing with White's initial assessments. When White asked her to address the 1934 and 1935 national NAACP conventions, FDR vetoed her appearance, fearing political backlash from southern Democrats. ER acceded to his wishes; however, FDR's cautiousness did not affect her support of the organization. "I deeply regret that I was obliged to refuse to attend the conference," she telegraphed the delegates. Her commitment had not waned. She continued, "I am deeply interested . . . [and] I hope that ways can be found to accomplish some of the things that you and I both desire." She then joined the local chapter of the NAACP and the National Urban League, becoming the first white District of Columbia resident to respond to the membership drives.

She mobilized cabinet and congressional wives for a walking tour of the slum alleys of Southeast Washington to increase support for housing legislation then before Congress. Lady Bird Johnson* accompanied ER on this tour and recalled that as accustomed as she was to rural poverty, she "hadn't seen anything like this." The first lady strode "along streets . . . [which] you usually kept off" and shamed her companions into following her example, hoping that if they saw such deprivation, they would be spurred to action. And, in a truly unique outreach, enlisted her mother-in-law's assistance in pressuring FDR to speak out in favor of the Costigan-Wagner anti-lynching bill. FDR's refusal to make anti-lynching legislation a priority did not dissuade her from actively seeking its passage. Indeed, when the bill finally came to the floor for a vote in 1937, ER's presence in the Senate gallery throughout the entire seven-day filibuster stood in stark contrast to FDR's cautious endorsement of the bill.

Unlike his wife, the president saw civil rights as more a political than a moral issue. Therefore, as the 1936 election approached and Eleanor Roosevelt continued her very public inspections, she finally convinced FDR to let her address the NAACP and National Urban League annual conventions by arguing that he needed the black vote. When *The New Yorker* published the famous cartoon of miners awaiting her visit, ER aggressively defended her outreach to minorities and the poor in a lengthy article for

---

*Wife of the congressman and future president, Lyndon Baines Johnson.

The Saturday Evening Post. Directly she attacked those who mocked her interest. "In strange and subtle ways," she began, "it was indicated to me that I should feel ashamed of that cartoon and that there was certainly something the matter with a woman who wanted to see so much and know so much." She refused to be so limited, she responded to those "blind" critics who refused to be interested in anything outside their own four walls. In a more subdued tone, she argued the same point when questioned by high school students about her "excitement" over discrimination. "People say I become 'too excited' about conditions," she replied. "Not at all. It is simply that I prefer to have my excitement in advance when it may do some good.". . .

By 1939, ER's support of civil rights was so well known that she could have dodged the controversy surrounding [singer] Marian Anderson's [proposed] performance [at Constitution Hall] and have few question her commitment to racial justice. But she did not sidestep the affair. Indeed, her bold actions on the diva's behalf not only "gave her opponents something [more] to talk about" but also provided her with unquestionable proof of her own political power.

Marian Anderson, the world's greatest contralto, was black. She had entertained all the crowned heads and elected officials of Europe, had won the highest awards her profession could bestow, and entertained the Roosevelts in the White House. Her previous performances in the District of Columbia before sold-out racially mixed audiences had received rave reviews. In January, Howard University had asked Anderson to perform a benefit concert for its School of Music on Easter weekend 1939. Anderson gladly accepted.

The problem surfaced when the Daughters of the American Revolution (DAR) refused to rent its auditorium, Constitution Hall, to Anderson because she was black. While at first the DAR denied that race was the reason preventing her leasing the hall, the truth soon emerged; and the University and the NAACP launched an immense lobbying campaign to force the DAR to change its policy. The DAR refused. Prominent black and white Washingtonians then formed the Marian Anderson Citizens Committee and petitioned the District of Columbia School Board for permission to use the Armstrong High School Auditorium for the concert. Following the DAR's lead, the school board denied the request.

ER debated what action to take on Anderson's behalf. By early January, she already had agreed to present the Spingarn Medal to the artist at the National NAACP convention, met with NAACP Secretary Walter White and conference chair Dr. Elizabeth Yates Webb to discuss the broadcast of the awards ceremony, invited Anderson to perform for the British King and Queen at the White House in June, and telegraphed her support to Howard University. Although initially she thought she should not attack the DAR's decision, she changed her mind and resigned from the organization in late February. Still angry and embarrassed at the treatment Anderson received, ER worked behind the scenes to arrange for the concert to be held at the Lincoln Memorial.

As important as ER's interventions on Anderson's behalf were they pale in comparison to the pivotal role she played in highlighting the discriminatory conduct of such a prestigious organization as the DAR. The power of under-statement displayed in her "My Day" column of February 28, 1939, revealed ER's hand on the pulse of the nation. Carefully portraying the situation in impersonal, nonthreatening terms with which the majority of her readers would identify, she refrained from naming the issue or the organization that had caused her distress.

She introduced the dilemma simply: "I have been debating in my mind for some time a question which I have had to debate with myself once or twice before in my life. Usually I have decided differently from the way in which I am deciding now." She then outlined the problem and her response to it. "The question is, if you belong to an organization and disapprove of an action which is typical of a policy, shall you resign or is it better to work for a changed point of view within the organization?" Telling her readers that she preferred to work for change, she "usually stayed in until I had at least made a fight and been defeated." When she lost, she "accepted my de-feat and decided either that I was wrong or that I was perhaps a little too far ahead of the thinking of the majority of that time." Indeed, she "often found that thing in which I was interested was done some years later." But this case did not fit that pattern because this organization is one "in which I do no active work." Moreover, "they have taken an action which has been widely talked of in the press. To remain as a member implies approval of that action, and therefore, I am resigning."

The next day, the column splashed across the front pages of American newspapers from San Francisco to New York City. Although others had re-signed from the DAR over this issue, although other major public figures had publicly lamented the DAR's policy, Eleanor Roosevelt put Marian Anderson, the DAR, and racial discrimination on a national stage. By placing her politi-cal clout and personal popularity squarely behind Anderson and in front of the DAR, she moved the conflict into another arena. . . .

Although the history of Eleanor Roosevelt's actions as first lady is far from complete, all studies of both her life and the Roosevelt Administration agree that she redefined the role of president's wife and set the standard by which all future presidential spouses would be judged. So strong an imprint on contemporary American culture did this woman's struggle for self-reliance and independent action leave that when Katharine Hepburn was struggling to find the appropriate demeanor with which to approach her most famous character, the prim, but feisty missionary Rose Sayer who rode the rapids on *The African Queen*, her director John Huston simply instructed, "Play her like Eleanor Roosevelt."

PRIMARY SOURCES

Many of the sources in this section are the kinds of evidence that biographers often use to learn about people's lives: personal letters, autobiographies, memoirs, and speeches or transcriptions. They will help you evaluate Eleanor Roosevelt's effectiveness as First Lady, the challenges she faced in that role, and whether she challenged or reinforced traditional conceptions of women's proper role.

2   In 1933, Eleanor Roosevelt began to hold regular press conferences limited to female reporters. What do Eleanor's answers to reporters' questions reveal about her efforts to change the role of women during the Depression?

Transcripts of Eleanor Roosevelt's Press Conferences (1933–1938)

June 15, 1933

TOPIC: Need for women to understand news.

Mrs. Roosevelt: "It is an awfully good thing to stress that this is a time when women have a special stake in watching national and international news. Every woman should have a knowledge of what is going on in economic conferences. It does affect the future amicable relations between the nations of the world. It has been stated the debt question is not to be discussed. But whatever does come out will be vitally important to every woman in her own home. Very few women know how to read newspapers and they miss what could give a new point of view. If more women would get in the habit of reading first the headlines, then the first paragraph,—often the whole gist of the article is in the first paragraph—that way a busy woman can count on keeping track at a time when every one of us ought to be on our toes to get what is happening every minute of time.

"The average woman today ought to read one paper that gives her point of view and two opposing points of view to draw her own conclusions. One's own prejudices and own ideas go into interpretation of public events. Women should train themselves to see both sides, then decide what they really think.

"Many people will never read editorials at all. It is grand to read editorials and opinion but not to accept without thought. All writing and all opinion is only good when you make it your own."

Source: Excerpted with permission from *The White House Press Conferences of Eleanor Roosevelt,* edited by Maurine Beasley. Copyright © 1983 by Garland Publishing, Inc.

May 15, 1936

TOPIC: Garden party at the White House for inmates of the National Training School for Girls, a District of Columbia reformatory for Negroes. [Note by Strayer*] Mrs. Roosevelt went alone [on a visit to the reformatory] and told her press conference about it after her visit.

Mrs. Roosevelt: "I know of no place else where conditions exist like I found there. They have no psychiatrist. I think Dr. [Carrie] Smith [superintendent] said two girls were locked in cells when she came to the institution. I think she said 26 of the girls had syphilis and almost every girl had gonorrhea.

"There are no facilities to separate them from each other in cottages, each with one type of disease, but Dr. Smith separates them as far as possible. Every possible precaution is taken, but in those circumstances, what can you do? That is why Judge [Fay] Bentley [of the District of Columbia Juvenile Court] hasn't been willing to send any girls out there. She hasn't sent any girls there for a year.

"There was no teacher when Dr. Smith came. They now have one teacher that they are going to get a government appropriation for. Most of these girls are still school age. The youngest is 14. They go up to 21. Some of them have been there five years. The school has discarded library books that are falling to pieces.

"The girls have to be taken to Juvenile Court three times before they are committed out there. This is because of the physical conditions. The place has had no program to fit the girls to earn a living except doing the work of the institution, which, of course, is some preparation.

"They were making dresses to wear to the [White House] party when I was there the other day. They have always done the mending and sewing and made their own clothes because they always have to. They also were making gym suits of different colors for the different cottages. That, I thought, was beginning to give them a little more interest in life."

June 16, 1938

TOPIC: Married women in the labor force.
. . . **Mrs. Weed:** "Do you think there is a greater moral obligation on women to give up their work, when they have other means of support, than there is on men in the same circumstances, married or single?"

Mrs. Roosevelt: "I think if the single woman has to support herself, the question does not arise if she is under more moral obligation than a man.

"So I think it boils down to a married woman, and then comes the question whether the man or woman should be the main support in a family. My own instinct is a feeling that most women, if it comes to a decision, have

*Martha Strayer was one of the reporters.

more ability to find employment for themselves than most men have. But that doesn't always hold true.

"I happen to know of a couple where the woman earns money and the man runs a farm. It's the kind of work which doesn't bring in a large amount of income but which makes living a very pleasant, happy thing, and he is happy and does the kind of thing he enjoys. It's a happy family. My instinct is to say that, as a rule, a woman is more adjustable."

May [Craig?]: "What is a woman's duty? Her first duty is to stay home and take care of her family, and the other is to take a job in the economic situation when jobs are scarce."

Mrs. Roosevelt: "Who is going to be the person to decide whether it is a woman's duty to stay at home and take care of her family?

"Second, who should say that where the skills of the woman were such that she could do that particular job better than anybody else, better than she could do any other, probably it would be economically sound as well as spiritually a good thing? On the other hand, there may be a great many people for whom it would neither be spiritually or economically the best thing for their children or for that individual."

December 27, 1938

TOPIC: National League of Women Voters [report that number of women legislators dropped from 149 in 38 states to 130 in 28 states over the last ten years and from nine to five in Congress].

Mrs. Roosevelt: "I think what that benefits, really, is the fact that was emphasized for me very much yesterday by talking to a man who is here form France. He said he was quite appalled by the apathy in youth and amongst women, their lack of interest in social questions.

"I think, in spite of that, we have been very good. We haven't suffered sufficiently to get to the point that something has to be done, and we have to be part of it.

"I think the reason why there are so many men in our state legislatures and Congress is not so much that women would be unwilling to run but the fact that women as a whole do not back women's running and do not back them for positions and are not really trying to get them to represent the woman's point of view.

"I think just as soon as you have found a genuine demand among women for the representation of their point of view, you would find plenty of women capable and willing to run; and untill there is a genuine demand, you don't find women who are willing to go out and do that.

"I think we will probably have something jolting us into waking up some day. We waste our energy so many times. I think there are plenty of capable women."

3 As the transcripts of her White House press conferences reveal, ER was interested in the condition of African Americans. What does this speech to the National Urban League reveal about her racial views? Were they conservative or progressive?

"The Negro and Social Change" (1936)

Much that I am going to say tonight would apply with equal force to any of us living in this country. But our particular concern tonight is with one of the largest race groups in the country—the Negro race.

We have a great responsibility here in the United States because we offer the best example that exists perhaps today throughout the world, of the fact that if different races know each other they may live peacefully together. On the whole, we in this country live peacefully together though we have many different races making up the citizenry of the United States. The fact that we have achieved as much as we have in understanding of each other is no reason for feeling that our situation and our relationship are so perfect that we need not concern ourselves about making them better. In fact we know that many grave injustices are done throughout our land to people who are citizens and who have an equal right under the laws of our country, but who are handicapped because of their race. I feel strongly that in order to wipe out these inequalities and injustices, we must all of us work together; but naturally those who suffer the injustices are most sensitive of them, and are therefore bearing the brunt of carrying through whatever plans are made to wipe out undesirable conditions.

Therefore in talking to you tonight, I would like to urge first of all that you concentrate your effort on obtaining better opportunities for education for the Negro people throughout the country. You *must* be able to understand the economic condition and the changes which are coming, not only in our own country, but throughout the world, and this, without better education than the great majority of Negro people have an *opportunity* to obtain today, is not possible. And without an improvement which will allow better work and better understanding, it will be difficult to remove the handicaps under which some of you suffer.

I marvel frequently at the patience with which those who work for the removal of bad conditions face their many disappointments. And I would like to pay tribute tonight to the many leaders amongst the colored people, whom I know and admire and respect. If they are apt at times to be discouraged and downhearted, I can only offer them as consolation, the knowledge that all of us who have worked in the past, and are still working for

Source: Eleanor Roosevelt, "The Negro and Social Change," *Opportunity*, January 1936. Reprinted by permission of the Eleanor Roosevelt Literary Estate.

economic and social betterment, have been through and will continue to go through many periods of disappointment. But as we look back over the years, I have come to realize that what seemed to be slow and halting advances in the aggregate make quite a rapid march forward.

I believe, of course, that for our own good in this country, the Negro race as a whole must improve its standards of living, and become both economically and intellectually of higher calibre. The fact that the colored people, not only in the South, but in the North as well, have been economically at a low level has meant that they have also been physically and intellectually at a low level. Economic conditions are responsible for poor health in children. And the fact that tuberculosis and pneumonia and many other diseases have taken a heavier toll amongst our colored groups, can be attributed primarily to economic conditions. It is undoubtedly true that with an improvement in economic condition it will still be necessary not only to improve our educational conditions for children, but to pay special attention to adult education along the line of better living. For you cannot expect people to change overnight, when they have had poor conditions, and adjust themselves to all that we expect of people living as they *should* live today throughout our country. . . .

So that I think I am right when I say that it is not just enough to give people who have suffered a better house and better wages. You must give them education and understanding and training before you can expect them to take up their full responsibility.

I think that we realize the desirability today of many social changes; but we also must realize that in making these changes and bridging the gap between the old life and the new, we have to accept the responsibility and assume the necessary burden of giving assistance to the people who have not had their fair opportunity in the past.

One thing I want to speak about tonight because I have had a number of people tell me that they felt the Government in its new efforts and programs was not always fair to the Negro race. And I want to say quite often, it is not the intention of those at the top, and as far as possible I hope that we may work together to eliminate any real injustice.

No right-thinking person in this country today who picks up a paper and reads that in some part of the country the people have not been willing to wait for the due processes of law, but have gone back to the rule of force, blind and unjust as force and fear usually are, can help but be ashamed that we have shown such a lack of faith in our own institutions. It is a horrible thing which grows out of weakness and fear, and not out of strength and courage; and the sooner we as a nation unite to stamp out any such action, the sooner and the better will we be able to face the other nations of the world and to uphold our real ideals here and abroad.

We have long held in this country that ability should be the criterion on which all people are judged. It seems to me that we must come to recognize this criterion in dealing with all human beings, and not place any limitations upon their achievements except such as may be imposed by their own character and intelligence.

This is what we work for as an ideal for the relationship that must exist between all the citizens of our country. There is no reason why all of the races in this country should not live together each of them giving from their particular gift something to the other, and contributing an example to the world of "peace on earth, good will toward men."

 Eleanor Roosevelt and Anna, her first child and only daughter, corresponded regularly. What does the letter on the following page reveal about the difficulties Eleanor had as First Lady?

Letter to Her Daughter (1937)

20 East 11th Street
New York City
March 3d [1937]

Darling,

. . . Pa is both nervous & tired. The court hue & cry [the Supreme Court packing controversy] has got under his skin. I thought stupidly his little outburst of boredom on meals was amusing & human & used it in my column & it was taken up by papers & radio & over the ticker & Steve [Early, press secretary] & Jimmy got hate letters & were much upset & Pa was furious with me. James came & reproved me & said I must distinguish between things which were personal & should not be said or none of them would dare to talk to me & he thought I should apologize to Father. I did before McDuffie [FDR's valet] Monday night before leaving as I couldn't see him alone & Pa answered irritably that it had been very hard on him & he would certainly say nothing more to me on any subject! So it has become a very serious subject & I am grieved at my poor judgment & only hope it won't be remembered long. Will I be glad when we leave the W.H. & I can be on my own!

A world of love to you all & much to you darling.

Mother

Source: Bernard Asbell, ed., *Mother and Daughter: The Letters of Eleanor and Anna Roosevelt* (New York: Coward, McCann, and Geoghegan, 1982), p. 79.

5   *This I Remember,* the second volume of Eleanor Roosevelt's autobiography, deals with her life from the early 1920s until her husband's death in 1945. In the following selections, she discusses the nature of her influence on FDR and her interest in several reforms. How much influence did Eleanor appear to have with FDR?

This I Remember (1949)

ELEANOR ROOSEVELT

Always, when my husband and I met after a trip that either of us had taken, we tried to arrange for an uninterrupted meal so that we could hear the whole story while it was fresh and not dulled by repetition. That I became, as the years went by, a better reporter and a better observer was largely owing to the fact that Franklin's questions covered such a wide range. I found myself obliged to notice everything. For instance, when I returned from a trip around the Gaspé, he wanted to know not only what kind of fishing and hunting was possible in that area but what the life of the fisherman was, what he had to eat, how he lived, what the farms were like, how the houses were built, what type of education was available, and whether it was completely church-controlled like the rest of the life in the village.

When I spoke of Maine, he wanted to know about everything I had seen on the farms I visited, the kinds of homes and the types of people, how the Indians seemed to be getting on and where they came from.

Franklin never told me I was a good reporter nor, in the early days, were any of my trips made at his request. I realized, however, that he would not question me so closely if he were not interested, and I decided this was the only way I could help him, outside of running the house, which was soon organized and running itself under Mrs. Nesbitt.

In the autumn I was invited by the Quakers to investigate the conditions that they were making an effort to remedy in the coal-mining areas of West Virginia. My husband agreed that it would be a good thing to do, so the visit was arranged. I had not been photographed often enough then to be recognized, so I was able to spend a whole day going about the area near Morgantown, West Virginia, without anyone's discovering who I was.

The conditions I saw convinced me that with a little leadership there could develop in the mining areas, if not a people's revolution, at least a people's party patterned after some of the previous parties born of bad economic conditions. There were men in that area who had been on relief for from three to five years and who had almost forgotten what it was like to have a job at which

Source: Pages 177–179, 191–193 from *The Autobiography of Eleanor Roosevelt.* Copyright 1937, 1949, © 1958, 1961 by Anna Eleanor Roosevelt. Copyright © 1958 by Curtis Publishing Company. Reprinted by permission of HarperCollins Publishers.

they could work for more than one or two days a week. There were children who did not know what it was to sit down at a table and eat a proper meal.

One story which I brought home from that trip I recounted at the dinner table one night. In a company house I visited, where the people had evidently seen better days, the man showed me his weekly pay slips. A small amount had been deducted toward his bill at the company store and for his rent and for oil for his mine lamp. These deductions left him less than a dollar in cash each week. There were six children in the family, and they acted as though they were afraid of strangers. I noticed a bowl on the table filled with scraps, the kind that you or I might give to a dog, and I saw children, evidently looking for their noonday meal, take a handful out of that bowl and go out munching. That was all they had to eat.

As I went out, two of the children had gathered enough courage to stand by the door, the little boy holding a white rabbit in his arms. It was evident that it was a most cherished pet. The little girl was thin and scrawny, and had a gleam in her eyes as she looked at her brother. She said, "He thinks we are not going to eat it, but we are," and at that the small boy fled down the road clutching the rabbit closer than ever.

It happened that [Assistant Secretary of State] William C. Bullitt was at dinner that night and I have always been grateful to him for the check he sent me the next day, saying he hoped it might help to keep the rabbit alive.

This trip to the mining areas was my first contact with the work being done by the Quakers. I liked the theory of trying to put people to work to help themselves. The men were started on projects and taught to use their abilities to develop new skills. The women were encouraged to revive any household arts they might once have known but which they had neglected in the drab life of the mining village.

This was only the first of many trips into the mining districts but it was the one that started the homestead idea. . . . It was all experimental work, but it was designed to get people off relief, to put them to work building their own homes and to give them enough land to start growing food.

It was hoped that business would help by starting on each of these projects an industry in which some of the people could find regular work. A few small industries were started but they were not often successful. Only a few of the resettlement projects had any measure of success; nevertheless, I have always felt that the good they did was incalculable. Conditions were so nearly the kind that breed revolution that the men and women needed to be made to feel their government's interest and concern. . . .

Franklin did not talk a great deal about the work he was doing, either at meals or in private family conversations. Most of us felt that when he was with his family he should have a respite from the concerns of his office.

When an administration bill was up before Congress, we often found that the number of Congressmen coming to his study in the evenings increased. I learned that I must make an evaluation of the bills on which he had to get support. He calculated votes closely on what was known as the administration policy, and considered "must" legislation.

Only bills that were "must" legislation got full administration support. In the first years these were largely economic measures; later on, they were measures for defense. While I often felt strongly on various subjects, Franklin frequently refrained from supporting causes in which he believed, because of political realities. There were times when this annoyed me very much.

I also remember wanting to get all-out support for the anti-lynching bill and the removal of the poll tax, but though Franklin was in favor of both measures, they never became "must" legislation. When I would protest, he would simply say: "First things first. I can't alienate certain votes I need for measures that are more important at the moment by pushing any measure that would entail a fight." And as the situation in Europe grew worse, preparations for war had to take precedence over everything else. That was always "must" legislation, and Franklin knew it would not pass if there was a party split.

Often people came to me to enlist his support for an idea. Although I might present the situation to him, I never urged on him a specific course of action, no matter how strongly I felt, because I realized that he knew of factors in the picture as a whole of which I might be ignorant.

One of the ideas I agreed to present to Franklin was that of setting up a national youth administration. Harry Hopkins, then head of the WPA, and Aubrey Williams, his deputy administrator and later head of the National Youth Administration, knew how deeply troubled I had been from the beginning about the plight of the country's young people. One day they said: "We have come to you about this because we do not feel we should talk to the President about it as yet. There may be many people against the establishment of such an agency in the government and there may be bad political repercussions. We do not know that the country will accept it. We do not even like to ask the President, because we do not think he should be put in a position where he has to say officially 'yes' or 'no' now."

I agreed to try to find out what Franklin's feelings were and to put before him their opinions and fears. I waited until my usual time for discussing questions with him and went into his room just before he went to sleep. I described the whole idea, which he already knew something of, and then told him of the fears that Harry Hopkins and Aubrey Williams had about such an agency. He looked at me and asked: "Do they think it is right to do this?" I said they thought it might be a great help to the young people, but they did not want him to forget that it might be unwise politically. They felt that a great many people who were worried by the fact that Germany had regimented its youth might feel we were trying to do the same thing in this country. Then Franklin said: "If it is the right thing to do for the young people, then it should be done. I guess we can stand the criticism, and I doubt if our youth can be regimented in this way or in any other way."

I went back to Harry Hopkins and Aubrey Williams the next day with Franklin's message. Shortly after, the NYA came into being and undoubtedly benefited many young people. It offered projects to help high school and college youngsters to finish school, and provided training in both resident and nonresident projects, supplementing the work of the Civilian Conservation Corps in such a way as to aid all youth.

It was one of the occasions on which I was proud that the right thing was done regardless of political considerations. As a matter of fact, however, it turned out to be politically popular and strengthened the administration greatly.

James Roosevelt was Franklin and Eleanor's oldest son. What does this passage from his memoir reveal about his mother's struggle for independence?

My Parents: A Differing View (1976)
JAMES ROOSEVELT

After [FDR's 1932] election, mother also confided to her friend Lorena Hickok that she never wanted to be a president's wife. And yet she may have been the best. She was the first First Lady to hold press conferences. In fact she held her first press conference two days before father held his first as president. She did so to ease the demand on her for individual interviews, but she avoided discussion of directly political topics. However, from the time beer was made legal again—the first of the thrusts that would lead to the repeal of Prohibition—and she announced at her regular press conference that she would serve it in the White House, hard news with a political angle began to emerge from these sessions.

Later she began to do magazine articles, magazine and newspaper columns ("My Day") and even books. While these were not purely political, they had a political impact. Father was aware of this. He edited her book *This Is My Story* rather ruthlessly and would have edited, or had written for her, the columns and articles in his favor if she had given him the opportunity. But she was becoming independent. When there were complaints about her receiving $1000 an article, she ignored them because she did not consider the complaints justified. I doubt that today a president's wife would be permitted to receive pay for articles unless she donated the cash to charity, but mother treasured her private income. She did give much of it away, but only as she wished.

Source: James Roosevelt, *My Parents: A Differing View* (Chicago: Playboy Press, 1976), p. 179.

Attacks on Eleanor Roosevelt

As Eleanor Roosevelt began to champion a variety of reforms, she was assaulted by critics. What do their attacks reveal about the constraints on her?

 Barry Bingham was the son of Robert W. Bingham, the publisher of the Louisville *Courier-Journal* and FDR's ambassador to Great Britain; McIntyre was FDR's appointments secretary.

Letter from Barry Bingham to Marvin McIntyre (1934)

The old propaganda story is being passed around in Louisville to the effect that Mrs. Roosevelt has made herself offensive to Southerners by a too great affection for Negroes. The tale is that she was visiting in South Carolina recently, and was scheduled to make a speech in one of the larger towns. She is said to have ridden to the auditorium, through the streets of the town, in an open car in which she sat next to a Negro woman, with whom she conversed sociably all the way.

Source: Joseph P. Lash, *Eleanor and Franklin.*

 ## Excerpts from Letters to Franklin Roosevelt (1935)

From Fort Wayne, Indiana

[The First Lady] "would be rendering her country a far greater service if she would but uphold the dignity of the White House,". . .

From a New York woman

". . . is it not humanely [*sic*] possible to muzzle that female creature, known to the world as your wife?"

From a Philadelphia man

Mrs. Roosevelt should cease "gadding about the country and butting into matters that are no concern of hers. . . . My God, what a woman!"

Source: James R. Kearney, *Anna Eleanor Roosevelt: The Evolution of a Reformer* (Boston: Houghton Mifflin Company, 1968), pp. 228–229; originally from "President's Personal File #2," Box 1, Franklin D. Roosevelt Library.

Eleanor Roosevelt on Feminism

Eleanor Roosevelt was frequently asked about her stands on equality for women and the proposed equal rights amendment, which the National Woman's Party lobbied Congress to pass every year starting in 1923. What are her positions on these issues? Do these sources reveal contradictions in her views about female equality? Do they reveal attitudes shaped by class as well as gender?

 Eleanor Roosevelt addressed this advice book to women coping with the Depression.

It's Up to the Women (1933)

If a woman does her own work, the vital thing for her to do is to organize it so well that when her husband returns home she is not an exhausted human being, but can still meet him with a smile and enter into whatever interests he may wish to discuss with her.

If she has a domestic helper in her household, she must remember that she is dealing with a human being, and it is well for her to try everything herself before she lays down her rules for any one else. I have a theory that, under our modern system in which it is rare for any one to have more than one maid in the house, if a young woman will systematize her own work, she can greatly assist whoever is working for her. For instance, if when she gets up she immediately puts her bedclothes to air, it will save either her or her maid the necessity of coming up to do it later on, or of making up the bed without airing. Habits of neatness can be formed by the mistress so that she keeps her own part of the house tidy, and when she enters the kitchen to give an order, or to do some piece of work, she does not leave behind her a trail of work for somebody else to do. Then the household will run smoothly, the maid will come to her for advice and she will soon find if she does her own part of the work, that there is no shirking on the part of those who work with her. . . .

. . . I have often thought that it sounded so well to talk about women being on an equal footing with men and sometimes when I have listened to the arguments of the National Woman's Party and they have complained that they could not compete in the labor market because restrictions were laid upon women's work which were not laid upon men's, I have been almost inclined to agree with them that such restrictions were unjust, until I came to realize that when all is said and done, women are different from men.

Source: Eleanor Roosevelt, *It's Up to the Women,* Frederick A. Stokes Company, 1933, pp. 25–26, 201–202.

They are equals in many ways, but they cannot refuse to acknowledge their differences. Not to acknowledge them weakens the case. Their physical functions in life are different and perhaps in the same way the contributions which they are to bring to the spiritual side of life are different. It may be that certain questions are waiting to be solved until women can bring their views to bear upon those questions. . . .

In this excerpt from one of her press conferences, Eleanor Roosevelt expressed her views about the proposed Equal Rights Amendment.

Eleanor Roosevelt on the Equal Rights Amendment (1933)

TOPIC: [National Woman's Party and the Equal Rights Amendment.]

[Note by Furman:] Here, probably due to a question, she spoke out against the National Woman's Party [feminist group pushing for the Equal Rights Amendment].

Mrs. Roosevelt: "I think the National Woman's Party ignores the fact that there is a fundamental difference between men and women. I don't mean by that women can't make as great a contribution, nor if they do the same work they not be paid the same wages. The mere fact that women basically are responsible for the future physical condition of the race means for many restrictions. It is a physical difference, not a mental.

"In my mail the most violent protestation against employment of married women comes from women themselves.

"There is from my point of view a value in work. It is un-American to say anybody should not work. It is class legislation of the very worst kind to say that any particular class of people can't work.

"Women do need a certain amount of protection. I'm not sure I'd think so if women were well enough developed to run their own unions. But they are run by men and the women can't defend themselves and are exploited. They work for a very limited high type group of women who are able to defend themselves. The rest work at anything until they marry. They don't see far enough ahead either to be unionized or to prepare themselves for better jobs.

"I'm in perfect sympathy with many things the National Woman's Party stands for."

Source: Maurine Beasley, ed., *The White House Press Conference of Eleanor Roosevelt* (New York: Garland Publishing, Inc., 1983), pp. 13-14.

CONCLUSION

Few students would disagree with one historian's claim that "the behavior of . . . individuals is more interesting . . . than their behavior as groups or classes."[11] Maybe that is why the biographical approach to history remains popular, even though historians today reject the idea that history is merely the biography of great people. Yet Eleanor Roosevelt's life demonstrates that biography does more than create an enjoyable path to the past. Rather, it shows the power of individuals to move at great odds against impersonal forces. As First Lady, Eleanor struggled against the social and economic forces that shaped the lives of people who had no biographers. As she sought her own "salvation," she also struggled with the cultural forces influencing her own life. Her successes and failures as a reformer thus reveal as much about her times as they do about her life.

Still, neither Eleanor Roosevelt's background nor her public activities made her typical. Few girls had the opportunity to grow up in late nineteenth-century high society. Far fewer had the opportunity to become First Lady. In the past, that did not matter to most historians, who were more interested in people at the top of society than at the bottom. Today, however, many historians are interested in the lives of ordinary people. By writing history "from the bottom up," they reveal the historical significance of people who traditionally have lacked distinct voices. So in Chapter 8, we turn to people whose lives were a world removed from Eleanor Roosevelt's.

FURTHER READING

Blanche Wiesen Cook, *Eleanor Roosevelt, 1884–1933* (New York: Viking, 1992).
———, *Eleanor Roosevelt, 1933–1938* (New York: Viking, 1999).
Tamara K. Hareven, *Eleanor Roosevelt: An American Conscience* (Chicago: Quadrangle Books, 1968).
Stella K. Hershan, *The Candles She Lit: The Legacy of Eleanor Roosevelt* (Westport, Conn.: Praeger Publishers, 1993).
Joseph P. Lash, *Eleanor and Franklin: The Story of Their Relationship, Based on Eleanor's Private Papers* (New York: W. W. Norton and Company, 1971).
Eleanor Roosevelt, *The Autobiography of Eleanor Roosevelt* (New York: Harper and Brothers, 1961).

NOTES

1. Eleanor Roosevelt, *This I Remember* (New York: Harper and Brothers, 1949), p. 113.
2. Doris Kearns Goodwin, "The Home Front," *The New Yorker*, August 15, 1994, p. 51.

3. Nelson W. Aldrich, *Old Money: The Mythology of America's Upper Class* (New York: Vintage Books, 1989), p. 212.

4. Quoted in William H. Chafe, "Biographical Sketch," in Joan Hoff-Wilson and Marjorie Lightman, eds., *Without Precedent: The Life and Career of Eleanor Roosevelt* (Bloomington: Indiana University Press, 1984), p. 4.

5. Eleanor Roosevelt, *This Is My Story* (New York: Harper and Brothers, 1937), p. 24.

6. Quoted in William H. Chafe, "Biographical Sketch," in Hoff-Wilson and Lightman, *Without Precedent*, p. 5.

7. Quoted in Lois Scharf, *Eleanor Roosevelt: First Lady of American Liberalism* (Boston: Twayne, 1987), p. 28.

8. Eleanor Roosevelt, *This Is My Story*, p. 40.

9. Quoted in Joseph P. Lash, *Eleanor and Franklin: The Story of Their Relationship, Based on Eleanor Roosevelt's Private Papers* (New York: W. W. Norton, 1971), p. 220.

10. Quoted in ibid., p. 355.

11. Quoted in Edward H. Carr, *What Is History?* (New York: Alfred A. Knopf, 1962), p. 56.

Chapter

8

History "From the Bottom Up": The Detroit Race Riot and Los Angeles Zoot Suit Riots of 1943

The documents in this chapter offer facts and theories about the participants of the Detroit Race Riot and Los Angeles Zoot Suit Riots of 1943.

Secondary Source

1. The Detroit Rioters of 1943 (1991), DOMINIC J. CAPECI, JR., and MARTHA WILKERSON

Primary Sources

2. A Handbill for White Resistance (1942)
3. Black Employment in Selected Detroit Companies, 1941
4. Black Workers Protest Against Chrysler (1943)
5. A Complaint About the Police (1939)
6. Changes in White and Black Death Rates, 1910–1940
7. An Explanation for Mexican Crime (1942)
8. "Zoot Suiters Learn Lesson in Fights with Servicemen" (1943)
9. Testimony of Zoot Suiters (1943, 2000)
10. Views of the News, by Manchester Boddy (June 11, 1943)
11. A Governor's Citizen's Committee Report on Los Angeles Riots (1943)

A t 6:30 P.M. Monday, June 21, 1943, Moses Kiska, a 58-year-old African American, waited for a streetcar at Mack Avenue and Chene Street in Detroit. Kiska may have noticed a car drive by him and then turn around. Inside the car were four white youths, aged 16 to 20. Earlier, they had been looking for something to do and decided to drive around to see the fighting between blacks and whites that was turning Detroit into a bloody racial battleground. Late the night before, black and white youths had clashed on Belle Isle, a public park in the Detroit River. Less than a day later, rampaging African American and white mobs were assaulting one another, beating innocent motorists, pedestrians, and streetcar passengers, burning cars, destroying storefronts, and looting businesses.

As the four white youths drove around, one of them said, "Let's go out and kill us a nigger."[1] They continued to drive, but they couldn't find a target. They saw a lot of blacks, but they were in groups. They wanted someone by himself. Then on Mack Avenue they saw what they were looking for. The driver of the car grabbed his companion's gun, turned the car around, pulled up to the lone man, and pulled the trigger. As Moses Kiska fell to the ground, the car carrying the four boys sped off. "We didn't know him," one of the youths later testified. "He wasn't bothering us. But other people were fighting and killing and we felt like it, too."[2]

Thirty-four people lay dead after three days of rioting in Detroit. Moses Kiska was one of them.

The same month, violence struck Los Angeles when off-duty servicemen and young Latinos engaged in a series of violent and bloody confrontations known as the Zoot Suit Riots. Characterized by long coats and high-waisted baggy pants that tied in at the ankle, zoot suits drew attention to the young Latinos, or as they called themselves, *pachucos,* perhaps after the Pachuco district of Mexico. Ignoring the restriction on the manufacture of zoot suits due to wartime rationing, *pachucos* became a target of scorn among servicemen, many of whom had little exposure to Hispanic culture. After a group of sailors engaged in a street brawl with *pachucos* on June 3, the next night several hundred servicemen rode into the East Lost Angeles barrio where they descended on young Mexican Americans and beat and stripped them. After a half-hearted police response to these assaults, sailors and other service personnel as well as some civilians invaded the barrio three more nights, assaulting young Latinos whether clad in zoot suits or not.

The wartime riots in Detroit and Los Angeles served as brutal reminders to Americans in 1943 of the deep racial and ethnic divisions in their society. Today these riots remind historians that they must know something about the lives of ordinary people in places like Detroit and Los Angeles if they are to fully understand the impact of World War II on American society. Before the mid-twentieth century, that was usually not the case. Most historians did not write such "grassroots" history. They relied mostly on written sources produced by an educated elite, and their histories were written without reference to the lives of people at society's bottom. When historians did examine ordinary people, it was usually within the context of movements or organizations. If they studied labor history, for instance, they focused on unions, not the lives of workers. Of course, there is much more to the lives of common people than their involvement in political or labor organizations. By the 1950s, such scholars as George Rudé, Eric Hobsbawm, and Christopher Hill began to explore "an unknown dimension of the past," that is, the lives of ordinary people.[3] These historians had been influenced by the Great Depression and World War II, powerful examples of the masses' involvement in history. They were often guided as well by the Marxist conviction that history was made in the peasant's hut as well as in the castle.

Unfortunately, these historians did not have a ready-made body of sources at hand. Since people at the bottom of society rarely leave written records to explain their lives, much of their history was initially restricted to riots and revolutions. Such events as European peasant revolts or the French and American revolutions brought to public notice many people who rarely attracted attention. These uprisings left historians with documentation of otherwise obscure lives.

Today, historians with tape recorders and computers can preserve the memories of ordinary people and analyze massive amounts of data from a census or legal documents. Such technology helps them explore "bottom up" history far removed from riots or revolutions. As a result, many scholars are now interested in the lives of everyone from seventeenth-century slaves to late twentieth-century migrant farm workers. At the same time, historians have not abandoned the study of civil disturbances such as the Detroit and Zoot Suit Riots. Like other social upheavals, these riots thrust people at the bottom of the society into the public arena. For that reason, they remain good places to explore the lives of people mostly absent from the pages of history.

SETTING

In the months after Pearl Harbor, many observers saw trouble ahead on the home front. As black, white, and Hispanic workers converged on booming defense plants, racial and ethnic tensions began to rise. In 1943, more than 200 riots and racial conflicts had erupted across the country. In Los Angeles, a large war production center, the Zoot Suit Riots lasted four days and ended only when military authorities intervened. In May, black and white workers clashed in a Mobile, Alabama, shipyard. Several weeks later, a white mob attacked the black section of Beaumont, Texas, leaving two dead. Then in August, a race riot in New York City resulted in five deaths and millions of dollars in property damage.

On one level, the racial and ethnic violence on the home front reflected the destabilizing effects of wartime mobility. During the war, four million workers and five million family members relocated to war-production centers. In Los Angeles, many of them were African Americans who streamed into the city at the rate of 300–400 a day. Meanwhile, the city's Mexican-American population had been rising steadily as well. From World War I until the late 1920s, thousands of Mexicans had crossed the border into southern California to work on farms or elsewhere. By the early 1940s, many of them had settled in Los Angeles. During the war, thousands of Mexican Americans, mostly women, landed jobs in aircraft factories. Growing up in squalid barrios and caught between two cultures, many young Latinos were attracted to the *pachuco* culture, which conspicuously flouted the social norms with flamboyant dress and defiant attitudes and sometimes involved crime and drug use.

On another level, of course, the wartime riots also reflected deep-seated racial prejudice. In Los Angeles, tensions and paranoia had already flared after the Japanese attack on Pearl Harbor, leading to the internment of thousands of Japanese and Japanese Americans. Living apart and ostracized, Mexican Americans became easy target of fear and suspicion as well. In a racially charged climate, it was easy for white authorities to associate "zoots" with delinquency and lack of patriotism. Dressed in their emblems of *pachuco* culture, they quickly drew the attention of police and military personnel. In fact, despite a Mexican-American juvenile delinquency rate that was no higher than that of other groups, ethnic hostility and fears of a Latino crime wave had already been stoked by the press. That was especially true after the well-publicized death of a young Latino in 1942, the result of alleged gang activity. After a media campaign demanding action against zoot suiters, police rounded up six hundred suspects in the death. Seventeen of them were eventually put on trial, during which a sheriff's office bureau chief declared that Mexicans had a "biological predisposition" to crime. Twelve of the defendants were convicted, despite evidence suggesting that the young man's death had been the result of an automobile accident. By the spring of 1943, while local papers continued to raise fears of a "Mexican" crime wave, police launched repeated attacks on Mexican Americans.

Born in this hostile environment, the Zoot Suit Riots represented the largest outbreak of violence between Anglos and Latinos during the war. Although named after the garb worn by some young Latinos, blacks, and even occasionally whites, the violence in these "riots" was actually perpetrated primarily by whites: military personnel, police, and civilians. By the time it was over, many young Latinos, Latinas, and blacks had become targets of violence or harassment whether or not they were a "zoot" or even associated with them. As the mayor of Los Angeles declared, "They all look alike to us."[4] Initially confined to Los Angeles, the riots quickly spread to Long Beach, Ventura, and elsewhere in southern California. Similar outbreaks of violence against "zoots" also appeared in major cities outside California. After a week of violence in Los Angeles, one hundred and fifty people were injured and at least five hundred Latinos arrested. As in Detroit, order was restored only after military intervention.

After the riots, the city's leaders and other Americans offered explanations and pointed fingers. Frequently, they placed blame on the zoot suiters. While lauding the rioters in military uniforms, the local press condemned young Latinos as gangsters. Convinced that "zoots" were the heart of the problem, the Los Angeles City Council passed a resolution banning the clothing style.

Meanwhile, Latinas did not escape suspicion either. The local press reinforced a widespread belief that they were violence prone, reprinting rumors, for instance, that they sometimes hid knives in their hair. At the same time, suggestions that they were in their own way to blame for the riots also surfaced in the press. The repeated rumor that Latinas appealed to servicemen frequently accompanied the observation that servicemen felt white women were threatened by young Latinos. If nothing else, such talk hinted at the sexual tensions in wartime Los Angeles, where thousands of servicemen were stationed before shipping out to the Pacific. As one African American journalist put it, "Some of the boys in uniform were very much taken with some of the Mexican girls, because of their pretty ways and faces." The result, he concluded, was conflicts with "some of the Mexican-American boys."[5]

Amid the chorus of voices blaming Mexican Americans, a few dissenters stood out. Governor Earl Warren accused the local press of exaggerating the threat from zoot suiters while a governor's citizen's committee concluded that wearers of zoot suits should not automatically be linked with crime. Meanwhile, Eleanor Roosevelt called the riots a racial protest and said that she had long been worried about the "Mexican racial situation." Such analyses did not sit well with many white observers, though. Responding to ER, a *Los Angeles Times* headline declared that "Mrs. Roosevelt Blindly Stirs Racial Discord," while an editorial in the paper accused her of Communist sympathies.

Compared to wartime racial tensions in Los Angeles, those in Detroit, if anything, seemed far worse. In fact, before 1943 many observers had predicted that the greatest racial strife would be there. As automobile and other factories converted to defense production, thousands of Depression-ravaged people descended on the Motor City. Many were from the South, and most were poor. Eighteen months after Pearl Harbor, Detroit's population had surged by 350,000 people, 50,000 of them black. They joined the 160,000 African Americans already living in the city's slums. "Detroit," declared *Life* magazine, "is dynamite." The city, it predicted, "can either blow up Hitler or it can blow up the U.S."[6]

In June, America's greatest "Arsenal of Democracy" exploded. After three days of rioting, state and federal troops finally restored order. By then, property damage had run into the millions of dollars and war production had been halted for days. But the greatest toll was that suffered by African Americans. Twenty-five blacks had lost their lives, 17 of them killed by police. Blacks made up more than 75 percent of the approximately 600 injured people and 85 percent of the roughly 1,800 people arrested.

When the riot was over, Detroiters joined other Americans in the search for explanations. There were plenty of convenient targets: "thugs," Axis agents, the Ku Klux Klan, the police, Polish Americans, Italian Americans, Syrian Americans, and "hillbillies." One Mississippi newspaper even blamed Eleanor Roosevelt. The most popular scapegoat, however, was the African American. The lure of wartime jobs had drawn large numbers of Southern blacks to northern cities like

Detroit, where they were often scorned by longtime residents. Many observers thought that they were unable to adjust to northern life. Franklin Roosevelt's attorney general, for instance, recommended that the president limit the migration of blacks into cities that could not "absorb" them for "cultural" reasons. "It would seem pretty clear," he declared, "that no more Negroes should move to Detroit."[7]

After the riot, Detroit's white city leaders were also quick to point fingers. The mayor declared that the riots were started by young African American hoodlums. The Wayne County prosecutor charged that the leaders of the National Association for the Advancement of Colored People "were the biggest instigators of the race riot" and "would be the first indicted" if a grand jury were called.[8] A committee of city, county, and state law enforcement officials agreed with that assessment. It concluded that the "exhortation by many Negro leaders to be 'militant' in the struggle for racial equality played an important part in exciting the Negro people to violence."[9] Just as quickly, black leaders pointed to other causes: job discrimination in Detroit's booming defense plants, housing discrimination that forced blacks into expensive but run-down housing, police brutality, and the daily animosity of Detroit's white residents. Explanations of the riot revealed battle lines that were as clearly drawn as those in the riot itself.

INVESTIGATION

If residents of Detroit and Los Angeles had ready answers to the causes of the riots in their cities, the sources in this chapter offer some as well. Those sources include a discussion of the Detroit riot in Source 1. That source also provides a brief discussion about the theories of collective violence that may be applied to the riots in Detroit and Los Angeles. Your main assignment is to determine who the rioters were in each case, why they rioted, and whether the two riots differed in any significant ways. A good analysis of the riots should address the following questions:

1. **How would you compare the riots in Detroit and Los Angeles?** Were the conditions in each city and the expectations of those involved in these riots the same or different?

2. **What is the explanation of historians Dominic Capeci and Martha Wilkerson for the Detroit riot?** Was the riot for personal gain, an irrational act, or a form of protest?

3. **Can Capeci and Wilkerson's explanation for the Detroit riot be applied to the Zoot Suit Riots?** Do the chapter's sources offer evidence that World War II changed the expectations of African Americans and Mexican Americans?

4. **What does the primary source evidence reveal about the characteristics and motives of the rioters?** Do their voices contradict or support contemporary observers' explanations for the riots?

SECONDARY SOURCE

In this essay, Dominic Capeci and Martha Wilkerson examine who rioted in Detroit and offer an explanation for their behavior. They rely on evidence from Detroit's criminal court records to study the background and assess the actions of some of the rioters. Their work reflects the challenge that historians often face when trying to establish the motives of people who leave few written records to explain their behavior. Your analysis of the Detroit riot should begin with a careful reading of the authors' argument. Pay particular attention to their explanation for the behavior of the rioters, and look for evidence for the motives of the rioters. Also note whether the authors offer evidence that World War II changed the attitudes of Detroit's black and white residents. Do you agree with the authors' characterization of rioters or with the assessment of Gustave Le Bon and other European scholars of collective violence?

The Detroit Rioters of 1943 (1991)

DOMINIC J. CAPECI, JR., AND MARTHA WILKERSON

To Charles "Little Willie" L.—and, no doubt, to many others who rose on Sunday morning to clear, sunny skies, summerlike temperatures, and a day free from monotonous work, the tension that made Detroit "dynamite" seemed ever-present. Twenty years old and single, L. lived with his brothers and sisters at 5815 Brush Street.... His apartment sat in the east side, black Detroit's oldest, most congested, run-down community, one extending from downtown Adams Street north to Leicester Court, bounded by Woodward Avenue on the east and St. Aubin Street on the west. [See Detroit map.] His world, like that of most of the city's 185,000 black residents, consisted of dilapidated accommodations rendered "almost intolerable" by time and in-migration. Since his arrival from Brookhaven, Mississippi, five years earlier, Charles L. had witnessed an enormous influx of black newcomers, which had swelled to 2,100 per month since the previous year and increased the black population by 24 percent.

Detroit Riot Map in "Race Relations in Wartime Detroit" by Dominic J. Capeci. Cartography by Eric C. Fuller/Reprinted by permission of The Detroit Rioters of 1943.

Packed into a ghetto three-and-one-half miles square, which contained several viable institutions, diverse classes, and close-knit families, Charles L. and his neighbors found employment in the war-boom economy. He had worked as a laborer in grocery stores and factories for the past two years, no doubt denied access to well-paying defense jobs because of low skills, limited education, and "marked racial feelings." "Little Willie," who stood 5 feet 4 inches, weighed 140 pounds, and appeared dark-skinned, was considered "aggressive" and "antisocial"—perhaps the result of his diminutive size and ghetto experience. He seemed "criminalistic" to the Recorder's Court psychiatrist, although he boasted no arrest record. He knew discrimination first-hand, however, and had clashed recently with white youths and lawmen.

Seeking escape from the east side's confines, where the temperature broke 90 degrees on Sunday afternoon, Charles L. headed for Belle Isle. Perhaps he brooded along the way, angered by Detroit's inadequate recreation area and agitated by memories of Eastwood Park six days earlier. On Tuesday evening, he was one of fifty black teenagers and zoot suiters accosted by nearly 200 white high school students and servicemen at the privately owned amusement park in East Detroit. He lost the fight, as policemen arrested several whites and ejected all blacks. Charles L. had traveled over seven miles from his home to this amusement park, deep into lily-white territory. Consciously or otherwise, he also did so to protest the restrictive and humiliating conditions placed upon him—upon all black Detroiters. He embodied the "zoot effect," adopting expressive dress—broad shouldered, long-waisted coats, and bloused, pegged pants—behavior, and language that stroked his ego, parried racism, and affronted many of both races, who labeled such antics as abnormal, even gangsterlike, and mocked them in caricatures.

Small wonder that today Charles L. ventured more than three miles to Belle Isle—an island park in the Detroit River connected to the mainland by the Jefferson Avenue bridge—where 100,000 Detroiters converged to escape sultry weather and, ironically, wartime tensions. He arrived in midafternoon, one of many blacks who made up fully 80 percent of the crowd that jammed the isle's 985 acres of ball fields, beaches, and boardwalks, hiking trails and canoe livery, playgrounds and picnic areas. The large proportion of blacks present may have emboldened him, or the growing resentment of many whites, who objected to close racial associations, may have raised his own bitterness. In any event, around 3:30 P.M. he led a milling crowd of blacks in a series of altercations with whites, which officials said "fanned the flame of hatred" and led ultimately to the death of thirty-four persons.

Charles L. shot craps with several youths, both black and white, before a fight broke out over the question of crooked dice. The white cheaters fled the scene, and Charles L. and his friends were unable to catch them. Frustrated, he exhorted seven teenagers to avenge their humiliation in Eastwood Park and "take care of the Hunkies." Quickly he led them in a series of forays, assaulting whites, breaking up their picnics, and consuming their food. In thus evening the score, L. and his marauders reflected the racial tone of other confrontations that began to break out with increasing regularity (blacks and whites scuffling for pony rides or picnic grills). By 9:30 P.M. the exchange of blows and epithets escalated, recording the first hospital casualty—a white teenager assaulted three times within twenty minutes—and Charles L. surfaced again. At the playground, he and his pack attacked fourteen-year-old Gus Niarhos and stole his carfare. Failing to hail a homeward bus or chase down another white target, they headed across the crowded bridge to Detroit. It was now 10:45 P.M. Soon L. brushed against thirty-eight-year-old Joseph B. Joseph, called him a "white mother-fucking son of a bitch," and slammed him to the pavement, where other black youths kicked him and suggested hurling him into the river. As the victim struggled to his feet and raced into the path of two white sailors and their dates at the island end of the bridge, L. and his cohorts moved toward Jefferson Avenue.

Pushing and name calling—"black bitch," "white bastard"—turned to mayhem as one of the sailors blew his whistle and rallied some fifty blue-jackets stationed at the armory on Jefferson Avenue. Fighting broke out all along the bridge and spilled onto the thoroughfare, where one of Charles L.'s gang unsuccessfully urged blacks to enter the fray, claiming, "a colored woman and her baby had been drowned." By 11:30, however, white numbers had soared and comprised most of the 5,000 persons in the area. Sailors, still smarting from a racial brawl the previous morning, bridge crossers, and nearby residents fought to reclaim the park and reestablish social distance: "We don't want any niggers on Belle Isle." They beat and chased blacks, spreading their vengeance one block either side of Jefferson Avenue and four blocks north on Grand Boulevard. During the next two and a half hours, the crowd dispersed as police officers flooded the intersection and took control without serious loss of life. They handled the disorder, said blacks, by "beating and arresting Negroes while using mere persuasion on whites."

Charles L. was neither among the twenty-eight blacks arrested nor the five injured. He made his way back to the east side and, along with several witnesses frightened by the crazed-looking white toughs, alerted others in the black community. He, or someone else, arrived at the east-side Forest Club at 12:30 A.M. and informed Leo T. of the fighting across-town on Jefferson Avenue.

Thirty-five-year-old T. lived with his wife at 976 Wilkins Street. A resident of Detroit since the age of three, he was familiar with past racial conflicts—the Ossian Sweet incident (1925), the Black Legion terrorism (1930s), and the Sojourner Truth housing disorder (1942). He had brushed with the law as a way of life: thirteen arrests for unarmed robbery, breaking and entering, disturbing the peace, frequenting a gambling place, destruction of property, and, as recently as May 1941, carrying concealed weapons; four convictions, two prison terms, and one probation violation. He had worked as a handy man at the Forest Club, a popular recreation center, since his last police encounter, operating a sound truck, selling dance tickets, and manning the coat room. Literate but crime-prone, he doubtlessly experienced alienation toward white society and especially its gendarmes. His victims, however, had hitherto been fellow blacks.

At the Forest Club that night, Leo T. made his way through the crowd of 700 dancers, climbed atop the bandstand, and stopped the music. Dressed in a dark suit and carrying a briefcase, he identified himself as Sergeant Fuller and announced that a riot was in progress on the island, where whites had thrown "a colored lady and her baby" off the bridge. Everyone "get your guns" and "go out there," he instructed; free transportation awaited outside. Then, having directed his anger against whites, he disappeared, and pandemonium broke out.

Leo T.'s shocking news stampeded Forest Club patrons into the street, but no vehicles idled at the curb for their convenience. Their numbers were unusually large because the night spot, which contained a bowling alley, dance floor, and skating rink, provided one of the few recreational outlets for blacks, and, on June 20, was holding a "big dance" that drew several hundred youths. Galvanized by the rumor of whites killing a black woman and child, which linked a specific violation of sacred mores with general hostile beliefs in white violence, dancers and pedestrians became vengeance-seeking mobs. They filled the intersection of Forest Avenue and Hastings Street, stoning white motorists and trolley passengers while taunting policemen who came to rescue them. One thousand persons of both sexes and various classes struck human targets and overwhelmed lawmen, whose depleted wartime ranks and Belle Isle emergency assignments made answering 500 east-side calls impossible. Unchecked, blacks beat, hit, and stabbed whites who crossed their path, sending one injured person every minute to Receiving Hospital.

Soon rioters roamed throughout "the colored district," flush with victory and, like counterparts of a later generation, "commonality of purpose." South of Canfield on Brush, they knocked unconscious a twenty-seven-year-old white man, who became the first fatality when crushed accidentally by a cab. North of Grand Boulevard on Holbrook, they fought fifty Chevrolet Gear and Axle shift workers, and created disturbances along Oakland Avenue at Owen and Westminster. In this section, a mile above the boulevard, black residents like John T. clashed with police and forced them to detour streetcars. Most in their early twenties, married, and employed as laborers— and well aware of the "hate strikes" that had rocked Detroit for the previous six months, denying promotion of blacks to more skilled, better paying jobs—they might have been pursuing white workers out of revenge.

As police sealed the ghetto and whites avoided it, rioters turned their attention to stores, and, sometime before dawn of June 21, began to loot them. In fact, within one hour of Leo T.'s announcement, they were smashing windows on Hastings Street. Their fury now spread out of control along all the major commercial streets: St. Antoine, Beaubien, Brush, and John R, east to Hastings; Rivard, Russell, Riopelle, and Dequindre, west to St. Aubin. From Adams Street north to Grand Boulevard and ultimately beyond, residents shifted from an interracial or communal upheaval to a riot against property. Hemmed in by physical boundaries, they concentrated on symbols of white domination—lawmen, property, and goods—as white citizens, absentee landlords, and shop owners slept beyond their reach. They confronted officers, injured several, and killed one, but drew deadly, often indiscriminate gunfire, which would ultimately claim seventeen black lives. More often, rioters demolished store fronts and showcases, strewed mannequins and merchandise around the streets in the midst of broken glass, and left large segments of the business district looking as if it "had been bombed from the air with block busters." Looters, in turn, swept through drug and grocery stores, haberdasheries, pawnshops and taverns, confiscating everything from aspirin to liquor. Some stole alone, others in groups; some acted crazy, others deliberate; some targeted any store, but a great majority spared known "colored" establishments or those later identified by hastily painted signs.

At 4:00 a.m., whites began to retaliate along Woodward Avenue, probably having heard of the upheaval from escaping passersby and laborers. Adolescents and young men gathered about the Roxy and Colonial theaters, stoning the cars of blacks that passed along the thoroughfare, which separated black ghetto and white west side, itself characterized by substandard dwellings and transient populations. They also assaulted black patrons exiting from the all-night cinemas and tried to push their way into the black community at Alfred, but were driven back by police officers. In close residential proximity to east siders and competing with them for jobs and status, white assailants, like their predecessors in earlier interracial riots, sought to kick blacks back into their place. And, despite a lull in their activities around 6:30 a.m., they—again like earlier rioters—seemed proud of themselves and threatened further bloodshed....

... White gangs controlled Woodward Avenue, halting traffic to drag blacks from trolleys and automobiles, beat them viciously, sometimes senseless, overturn and incinerate their cars—all pay-back for east-side attacks. They roamed about, with little interference from bluecoats, whose numbers never exceeded 1,000, were divided between two war zones, and generally harbored racial prejudice. Inside the ghetto, where most officers found themselves assigned, blacks continued to break into stores, forage for possessions, and run afoul of patrolmen. Looters represented older, more mature residents, albeit no less resentful than the ruffians led by Charles L.

Rudolph M. certainly would have fought at Belle Isle. A twenty-three-year-old native of Louisiana, who had come to Detroit only thirteen months before the disturbance, he lived with his wife on Edmund Place, two blocks

east of Woodward Avenue and midway between Forest Avenue and downtown. He worked in a store stocking shelves for wages far below those
paid in the defense industry. Perhaps angered by his environment—slums
largely built before 1915, often lacking indoor plumbing, and cruelly
dubbed "Paradise Valley"—he turned his anger against absentee owners
responsible for his plight. Rather than destroy his own dwelling, however,
he selected a more practical target over a half mile from home: Paul's Drug
Store at Hastings and Leland. He hurled first a brick and then, moments later,
a bottle through the plate-glass window. He was only one of many in the
missile-throwing crowd, but he alone drew the attention of police officers,
who apprehended him after a short chase. He was found to be carrying a
7-inch butcher knife, a concealed weapon. Though he made no effort to slash
his captors, his possession of the blade indicated fear and possibly Southern
tradition. Significantly, his presence on the street and repeated attacks on the
pharmacy revealed deep alienation and purposeful protest—the combination of ghetto isolation, oppression, numbers, and solidarity with wartime
opportunities and anxieties.

Looters carried this racial complaint further. Their early morning plunder
seemed symbolically defiant, and soon became wholesale theft by usually
law-abiding citizens. Roy S., for instance, watched as several people tossed
armfuls of merchandise out of a grocery store at 4717 St. Antoine, half a mile
from his home on East Ferry. He and a companion were loading several
pounds of pork loins, smoked ham, canned salmon, and cheese—then rare
and rationed items—into their car, when police arrested them for larceny.
Born in Gregory, Arkansas, but a Detroit resident for the past five years,
S. lived with his wife and child and earned good money at Ford Motor Company. Approaching thirty years of age, seeming less disaffected and more
established than window smashers like Rudolph M., he nonetheless helped
himself to food thrown into the street. Possibly he considered such actions
righteous redistribution and redefinition of property—as would some ghetto
rioters a generation later. Yet S. never hinted at motivation; he told officers
only that he had picked up the goods and indicated which store they came
from. That a man like this should engage in behavior normally unlawful—
but momentarily acceptable by many in the community—disclosed the
drawing power and the grievance of mob activity; that he should collect
mostly perishables that would have spoiled if left in the gutters and could
have been purchased in the expensive but equitable rationing system, exhibited the ambivalence of moral standards and the anomie among oppressed
people. Experiencing mixed emotions and motives in a wholly unregulated
and opportunistic setting, Roy S. stole, but he did so for much more than
"fun and profit."

Neither Rudolph M. nor Roy S. knew the proprietors of the stores they
sacked, despite later contentions by observers that such actions manifested
anti-Semitism. Living half a mile away and possessing little if any knowledge

of which stores were Jewish-owned, they delivered symbolic attacks on "the white caste." They probably knew that German and, more recently, Russian Jews had occupied the east side before them and still controlled many of its apartments and businesses, yet the antagonisms that fueled the violence were customer-merchant rather than ethnic. They believed themselves exploited by all shopkeepers, not simply the white druggist and the Russian Jewish grocer. Certainly black anti-Semitism—growing out of socioeconomic competition and cultural conflict, which enjoyed a long tradition in the ghetto, and intensified in the face of Nazi propaganda—heightened tensions, but M. and S. reacted as opportunists seizing the moment rather than as ideologues punishing Semites. They struck at accessible, safe targets, emblems of white exploitation and black humility, and they struck as everyday residents, who had neither police records nor apparently political doctrines....

... Concentrated in an enormous rectangle, stretching from downtown Detroit north to the city of Highland Park, running through the heart of the 1st, 13th, and 9th precincts and spilling over east and west into adjacent zones, upheaval also occurred in the black west side and above the Polish city of Hamtramck. Approximately three miles west of Woodward Avenue at Ironwood and Tireman, deep in the black middle-class community to which those who escaped the ghetto had moved, Thomas H. disturbed the peace. Like many living in this stable, upwardly mobile area of homeowners, he was married and employed in a skilled job; unlike most of those milling in the street, he had brushed with the police once before. He might have been displaying anger over reports of DPD brutality in the east side and indifference to white assaults downtown. At thirty-nine years of age, H. and his cohorts were older than most rioters elsewhere, possibly venting frustration over white society's disregard for their socioeconomic achievements and disdainful rejection of them as mere "niggers."...

The numbers and characteristics of those apprehended between June 21 and June 30 affected how the riot was interpreted by many people. Of nearly 2,000 arrestees, young, black males comprised the overwhelming majority, followed by far fewer white males and black and white females. These participants recorded a median age of twenty-five years; surprisingly few of the scores of juveniles seen at the riot were arrested. Regardless of age or gender, blacks filled the ranks of arrestees in greater proportions than their population in metropolitan Detroit. Their spokespersons attributed this gross imbalance to police bias, while bluecoat officials explained it in terms of black aggression....

Those who witnessed or read about the rampage also blamed Southern newcomers. When [Mayor Edward] Jeffries stated that an influx of migrant workers contributed to the riot, he sparked the ire of editors like Ralph McGill of the *Atlanta Constitution*, who protested "the cheap and easy habit of blaming any and all racial troubles on the South." Such conflict grew out of civil injustices and economic inequities found in both Detroit and Dixie, lectured McGill, noting also that teenagers, not Southern laborers, had ignited the outburst. Despite McGill's logic, most Detroiters thought like their mayor. Popular *News* columnist W. K. Kelsey ascribed the disorder to scores of Southerners who encountered liberal conditions in the city, where blacks experiencing newfound freedom clashed with whites clinging to "Jim Crow notions."...

... Of course, more than black hooligans and Southern newcomers participated in the Detroit riot of 1943. Despite contemporary studies and public opinion, hoodlums and migrants shared the streets with lawful, longtime Detroiters. Rioters, in fact, included multitudes of ordinary men and women of both races. Their experiences, as well as those of teenagers, identify more completely those arrested for having been in the crowd....

... The largest percentage of black men, slightly more than a quarter, fell between the ages of twenty-eight and thirty-seven, and the median age for all black male participants stood at twenty-seven years. Nearly 63 percent were married, and nearly 75 percent lived in Paradise Valley. Most were literate and employed, and over 85 percent had benefited from the war boom and worked as laborers; 9 percent of the black rioters worked as skilled and semiskilled operatives, suggesting even higher and more stable social standing. Significant also for understanding the spontaneous actions of normally upright residents, most black transgressors were arrested alone and for the first time in their lives. They rioted in their home precincts and within a half mile of their east side addresses.

Information from probation records indicated further social stability for black males. Overwhelmingly born and bred in Alabama, Georgia, and Mississippi, fully half of them had resided in Detroit for nine years or more—the median stay, just short of a decade. Most were married, nearly 40 percent were raising children, and over 50 percent had secured meaningful jobs within the past year; they represented working-class people hopeful of bright futures. Indeed, having endured the Great Depression and blatant racism, they must have sensed the potential for personal and racial advancement: Weekly wages of fifty dollars, median educations of eight years, and several successful protests over housing and employment had surely raised their expectations....

In sum, usually law-abiding and hard-working men stood side-by-side with lawbreakers. No doubt many of both kinds were politically astute and racially proud. Black laborers and skilled workers, particularly those married, with children and education levels approaching that of whites, knew of—might even have participated in—recent DSR* incidents, housing controversies, or hate strikes that sharpened racial animus. Very likely their riot activity arose from the accumulation of blocked socioeconomic opportunities, which they attributed to white racists. They deemed the Belle Isle

*Detroit Street Railway.

rampage and accompanying rumors as final provocation in a series of real and occasionally perceived wrongs. Fearful for their newfound prosperity and status, they struck as much to protect their stake in society as to destroy their enemy, as much out of pride as anger. Black repeat offenders probably clashed with lawmen on familiar ground over perennial grudges. Slightly over 25 percent of all black male participants, however, exhibited calculated or mindless theft as they looted east-side stores, expressly those on Hastings Street. And a minute number of arrestees attacked white citizens or patrolmen, perhaps displaying a bloodlust that predated wartime frustrations. In essence, no single profile or motivation moved black males to action. Protestors and lawbreakers alike took part in several different kinds of riot for equally diverse reasons....

Unsurprisingly, white male rioters were as diverse as their black counterparts. Nearly 65 percent of all white men were younger than twenty-three years old. Their ages extended from seventeen to fifty-four, the median age at twenty years—less extreme than the black range of fourteen to sixty-four and significantly younger than the black midpoint of twenty-seven. Consequently, over 70 percent of the white arrestees were single and over 55 percent worked as laborers, with 4 percent as clericals, 5 percent as semi-skilled, 23 percent as skilled operatives, and the rest service employees or domestics. And, regardless of marital status or occupation, slightly more than 50 percent of all white participants lived relatively close to Belle Isle or on the fringes of Paradise Valley, and 40 percent more traveled over two miles to riot along its boundaries. Fully three quarters of all white offenders left their home precincts, determined to secure the perimeters of Detroit's color line against integrated housing and black upward mobility. Young adults, ordinarily law-abiding, mobilized to avenge past affronts aboard public conveyances, in municipal parks, and at downtown theaters, stores, and eateries.

Probation data reveals that almost all white arrestees were individuals with roots, on the make, and yet insecure. Most—53 percent—identified their home state as Michigan, and only one named the South as his origin; obviously far fewer white Southerners participated in the upheaval than was believed by officials, black leaders, and residents. Surprisingly, white in-migrants, Southern born or otherwise, stayed pretty clear of the disturbance. Neither Bedford B. nor Leonard O., placed on probation for carrying concealed weapons, qualified as "hillbillies"—those allegedly clannish, dirty, ignorant newcomers from Dixie. One came from a border state, the other from Michigan. Neither possessed police records, and both worked as machinists. They lived with their families, respectively, east of Cass in a neighborhood of white transients and north of Grand Boulevard in a mixed area rapidly becoming an extension of the black ghetto. Separated by nearly twenty years of life (forty-two versus twenty-three) and eight years of education (third grade versus eleventh), they shared little save their whiteness, offenses, and convictions. Both carried weapons, one a butcher knife, the other a nickel-plated revolver, and received sentences of short probation. Occasional drinking problems aside, both met the terms of probation. Having reported regularly, worked steadily, and provided a "suitable home," they were discharged with improvement. Their experiences belied the dominance of Southern or other groups of newcomers among white participants.

Despite ... Southern cultural deprivation theories, over 80 percent of the white felons had resided in the city more than six years. In fact, 50 percent had lived as Detroiters for over seventeen years. Except for being significantly more single than black felons, they registered similar education levels, time of employment, and wages. They competed with blacks for jobs and status, which personalized and sharpened the racial rivalry. Most probably, they recalled the hardships of depression and, facing black competition on every front, feared slipping backward....

Personal characteristics and riot activity also distinguished black female rioters from males of both races. (No data exist for white women, whose participation in the disturbances was completely ignored for the first two days out of the prejudice or chivalry of out-numbered, overtaxed lawmen.) Ranging from seventeen to forty-five years of age, black women tallied a median age of twenty-four and one-half years. Over 65 percent were single, yet almost half of those had been separated, divorced, or widowed. Regardless of marital status, 69 percent of all black females worked outside the home: 43 percent as domestics, cooks, or similar service workers, and 19 percent as common laborers. Their ages, marital statuses, employment rates, occupational categories, and police records identified most of them as predominantly older, mature, working class, and law-abiding....

Prior to the 1960s, European scholars of collective violence in England and France followed the lead of Gustave Le Bon. They characterized early rioters as criminal, maladjusted, and riffraff, unstable persons fulfilling emotional needs and selfish, apolitical aims. Lacking quantifiable evidence and drawing on psychological interpretations, they posited breakdown and contagion theories: Urbanization and industrialization promoted antisocial behavior in some individuals, and these misfits exploded, drawing others into a "mental unity" of excitement, destruction, and anonymity.

Le Bon's theory is still quite popular with some officials and private citizens, but it began losing its credibility among scholars in the early 1960s. Some, like E. J. Hobsbawm and E. P. Thompson, resurrected and revised Karl Marx's solidarity theory, and interpreted collective violence as the struggle of working-class people for political power. Non-Marxist historians also explained riot as protest and participants as ordinary people seeking redress. Perhaps most influential is George Rudé's synthesis of preindustrial crowds, which posits violence as collective behavior evolving through a precise set of determinants. Rudé presented history from the bottom up and suggested similarities between food rioters and political rebels. He also encouraged further investigation of the mob in other eras and locales as a "living and many-sided historical phenomenon." Slightly more than a decade later, a comparative history of upheavals in England, France, and Germany between 1830 and 1930 by Charles Tilly, Louise Tilly, and Richard Tilly extended the revised history of collective violence into modern times and suggested parallels for the recent civil disorders in the United States....

In fact, the Detroit rioters of 1943 provided the necessary example for understanding successive generations of white and black participants in riots dating back to the turn of the century and, particularly for blacks, forward to the 1960s. Taken together and allowing for distinctions of time, place, and riot patterns, ... Detroit profiles have dashed officials' self-serving descriptions of earlier white rioters as riffraff and raised anew the possibility that rioters in other cities ... represented several classes and ethnic groups. While additional research is needed of all those who erupted before World War II, Detroiters ... came from the general populace and shared certain traits with them.

Indeed, participants in the 1943 Detroit outburst desired greater participation in society. White rioters felt threatened and their black counterparts resentful, for members of both races had made enough gains to want much more. Unlike more successful residents, they were too impatient to mark time amid democratic rhetoric and wartime change. Younger, more energized, and less influential than those who avoided violence, they sought redress in the streets; they rioted to improve rather than destroy the system. They came forth as neither mainstream nor misfit, but as desperate people seeking respectability through protest that shed blood and ironically reinforced their disrepute in the eyes of the public.

PRIMARY SOURCES

The Detroit Riot

The sources in this section reflect the social and economic conditions of Detroit's African American population and their view about those conditions. What, if anything, does this evidence reveal about the causes of the Detroit riot and the motives of the rioters?

2   In 1942, African Americans were accepted as tenants in the Sojourner Truth Homes, a public housing project located in a black–Polish neighborhood. When they arrived to move in, they were greeted by white mobs who beat them and stoned their cars.

A Handbill for White Resistance (1942)

Walter P. Reuther Library, Wayne State University.

Black Employment in Selected Detroit Companies, 1941

Aeronautical Products, Inc.	0.02 percent
Briggs Manufacturing Company	7.0 percent
Chrysler	2.5 percent*
Hudson Motor Company	1.8 percent
Murray Corporation of America	5.0 percent
Packard Corporation	11.0 percent*
Vicker, Inc.	3.0 percent*

*Most were foundry workers or janitors.

Source: Data from Richard W. Thomas, *Life for Us Is What We Make It* (Bloomington: Indiana University Press, 1992), p. 157.

In March 1943, 600 black male workers at the Chrysler Highland Park plant walked out to protest the working conditions of black women at the factory. Here two female workers offer their explanations for the protest.

Black Workers Protest Against Chrysler (1943)

We are not given the same opportunities for promotions that white women are given. In the first place, … the superintendent has stated that we have got to do the hard work, such as pulling steel, running jitneys and heavy mopping. Many of us were hired as elevator operators but have never run an elevator at the plant because the men on the elevators refuse to transfer to work we are doing. They say the work is too hard for them. We have taken our complaints to the union—to the proper sources—but there has been no action.…

Many of us have trained for skilled jobs, hired as matrons but our jobs soon developed into common labor in the shop—labor for which the company is unable to hire men. White girls turn these jobs down and are given other work, but Negro women are told … they must do these jobs or ring their cards and go home. I was fired from my job because I wanted to change my clothes before going out to sweep around the building at 6 a.m. on a cold morning. I had been working in a hot place all night and would have been exposed to catching a severe cold.…

We are constantly being intimidated because we insist on eating in the regular places. When we first went to the plant they gave us separate toilets—far from our work—and we were told that we would have to eat

Source: Michigan Chronicle, May 8, 1943. Reprinted by permission.

our lunch in these restrooms. There is nothing but two benches and a low table in them. We don't know what they were used for before we were hired. Once when a colored girl changed her clothes in a white girl's restroom, she went back and found out that the buttons had been cut off her coat and her galoshes cut into shreds. We complained to the plant committeeman about this but have not heard anything from him.

This editorial ran in the *Detroit Tribune*, a black newspaper, in 1939. Note black Detroiters' complaints about the police department.

A Complaint About the Police (1939)

The Detroit Police Department is apparently trying to establish a national record for brutality to Negro citizens. In spite of the many protests made to those in authority, the brutality continues.... Since January 1, this year, the number of Negroes slain in cold blood and savagely beaten and clubbed by local police officers has steadily mounted.... In addition to these and other murders by Detroit policemen in recent months, many other members of our race have been brutally clubbed and beaten by officers of the law, without just cause.... Policemen are paid by the taxpayers to preserve law and order and to protect human lives and public and private property, but they have no right to take the law into their own hands, as so many of them do. It is not their duty to act as judges, juries and executioners, in their dealings with Negroes. Policemen have no legal or moral right to let their racial or religious prejudices lead them to persecute members of our race or any other racial group, and when policemen ... forget their duty as to indulge in such lawless acts of violence, they should be curbed, reprimanded, and in flagrant cases they should be dismissed from the Police Department and punished by the courts of justice.

   Colored citizens of Detroit have been protesting for some time to those in local authority, and appealing to them to put a stop to this police brutality, but our protests thus far seem to have fallen on deaf ears.

Source: Detroit Tribune, July 15, 1939.

Declining death rates are usually an indication of improving living conditions. Do these tables provide evidence about the expectations of blacks in Northern cities like Detroit? Do they reveal a difference between Detroit and the rest of the nation in that regard?

Source: Richard W. Thomas, *Life for Us Is What We Make It* (Bloomington: Indiana University Press, 1992), pp. 104–105.

Changes in White and Black Death Rates, 1910–1940

Changes in White and Black Death Rates in Detroit,
1915–1940 (per 1,000)

Year	White Death Rate	Black Death Rate
1915	12.8	14.7
1920	12.8	24.0
1925	10.4	19.4
1930	8.7	15.6
1940	8.0	12.2

Changes in National Black and White Death Rates,
1910–1940 (per 1,000)

Year	White Death Rate	Black Death Rate
1910	14.5	21.7
1920	12.6	17.7
1930	10.8	15.6
1940	10.4	13.9

Richard W. Thomas, Life for Us Is What We Make It (Bloomington: Indiana University Press, 1992), pp. 104–105. Reprinted with permission of Indiana University Press.

The Zoot Suit Riots

The sources in this section reflect the social and economic condition of the Mexican-American population of Los Angeles, evidence regarding racial or ethnic prejudice, and views of the zoot suiters, themselves. What does this evidence reveal about possible causes of the violence in Los Angeles?

7   Lieutenant Edward Ayres of the Los Angeles County Sheriff's Department testified before the grand jury investigating the death of a young Latino in the so-called Sleepy Hollow Murder Case in 1942. That death ultimately led to the trial of seventeen Mexican-American youths. His testimony, which came to be known as the Ayres Report, was supported by the Los Angeles police chief, who called it an "intelligent" assessment of the "psychology of the Mexican people."[10] To what does Ayres attribute crime and violence in the community?

Source: Luis Alvarez, The Power of the Zoot: Youth Culture and Resistance during World War II (Berkeley: University of California Press, 2008), p. 48; originally from Carey McWilliams Papers, Department of Special Collections, University of California, Los Angeles.

An Explanation for Mexican Crime (1942)

Representatives of the Mexican colony will [be] loathe to admit that it is in any way biological,… but the fact remains that the same factors, discrimination, lack of recreation facilities, economics, etc, have also always applied to the Chinese and Japanese in California, yet they have always been law abiding and have never given our authorities trouble except in that of opium among the Chinese, and that of gambling among both the Chinese and Japanese, but such acts of violence as now are in evidence among the young Mexicans has been entirely unknown among these two Oriental peoples. On the other hand, among the Filipinos crime and violence in proportion to their population is quite prevalent, and practically all of it over women. This is due to the fact that there are so few Filipino women here, and also the biological aspect enters into it, as the Filipino is a Malay, and ethnologists trace the Malayan people to the American Indian, ranging from the south-western part of the United States down through Mexico, Central America and into South America. The Malay is even more vicious than the Mongolian, to which race the Japanese and Chinese, of course belong. In fact, the Malay seems to have all the bad qualities to the Mongolian and none of the good qualities. As for the Negro, we also have a biological aspect, to which the contributing factors are the same as in respect to the Mexican—which only aggravates the condition, as to the two races.

This *Los Angeles Times* article on one encounter between servicemen and zoot suiters was typical of much of the press coverage of the riots. As you read, note how the zoot suiters are characterized.

"Zoot Suiters Learn Lesson in Fights with Servicemen" (1943)

Those gamin dandies, the zoot suiters, having learned a great moral lesson from servicemen, mostly sailors, who took over their instruction three days ago, are staying home nights.

With the exception of 61 youths booked in County Jail on misdemeanor charges, wearers of the garish costume that has become a hallmark of juvenile delinquency are apparently "unfrocked."

These were the conclusions reached last night by Capt. David Croushorn, commanding Sheriff's men at the Hall of Justice during night patrols, and Capt. Harry Seager, night Chief of Police.

Source: Los Angeles Times (June 7, 1943).

Street Fights Rage

The officers have directed some 200 extra police and 100 deputies who for the last 72 hours maintained vigils at widely scattered points in the eastern sections of the city during a long series of more or less bloody encounters between gangs of zooters and servicemen.

Strife between the two factions arose as a result of beatings of individual sailors by juvenile street bands and in two cases, assaults on women relatives of servicemen.

These attacks by zooters occurred over a period of several days. The counterattack did not last as long.

None in Sight

Main St. from First to Sixth, California and Temple Sts., Carmelita and Brooklyn and other focuses of habitual zoot-suit congregation all were empty of male zooters last evening, the authorities reported.

On Saturday night, however, an entire truckload of youths - 16 of them all armed with some sort of bludgeon - were arrested at Carmelita and Brooklyn Aves. after they assertedly tried to keep Deputy Sheriffs Foster Kellogg and E. N. Smith from arresting one of their number.

Booked at County Jail

The entire lot was booked in County Jail on riot charges after flying squadrons of officers arrived on the scene.

The suspects said they acquired the truck and were on their way to "have it out" with a bunch of sailors who had sent word they would be at California and Temple Sts., to accommodate any of the zooters who thought Uncle Sam's fighting men aren't just that.

Other zoot suspects, including a group of six in the 300-block on Ford Blvd., were rounded up during the night of warfare and joined the others in Sheriff Biscailuz's bastile.

9 | This source contains the accounts of two zoot suiters. In the first, Rudy Sanchez related events leading up to the riots in a letter shortly after they ended. In the second, Bob Rodriguez recalled fights between zoot suiters and military personnel in an oral history conducted in 2000. How do these accounts, especially the first written shortly after the riots ended, differ from those generally presented in the media?

Source: Luis Alvarez, *The Power of the Zoot: Youth Culture and Resistance during World War II* (Berkeley: University of California Press, 2008) Alvarez, pp. 169–170, 170–171.

Testimony of Zoot Suiters (1943, 2000)

I am writing this letter, in behalf of the so called "zoot suiters." We all got, together (the so-called zoot suiters) a few weeks ago. Boys from each neighborhood were present, Lee Chapman a detective, and a few business men around the neighborhood are all helping us to keep out of trouble, by trying to make a club for us (zoot suiters) to keep us out of the street, and we were all for it. We went to four straight meeting's [sic], trying to make some progress, to keep us out of trouble. Everything was going along very nicely in fact there hasn't been a fight between a gang of "zoot suiters" for quite some time. In spite the fact rumors have it that the so-called "zoot suiters" always start everything, meaning all these gang fights that have taken place lately, but its not true, they only fight back to defend there selfs, and that's only natural. Last Thursday we had a meeting at the Central jail on first street between Broadway and Hill, to see what could be done about getting us that club. After the meeting a former "zoot suiter" (now a sailor) came to the meeting to warn us, that about fifty sailors were walking and riding around our neighborhood with sticks, boards, clubs, rocks, and even guns looking for any "zoot suiters" they could find to use their weapons on. When we got back to our neighborhood, (Alpine and Figueroa) we saw a crowd of people in front of our neighborhood theatre (Carmen) we stopped to see what had happened. The girls, boys, ladys, men and manager of the theatre informed us that forty or fifty sailors broke in the show and beat up "zoot suiters," grown up men and even boys as young as twelve and thirteen years old. Men and "zoot suiters" getting beat up is pretty bad, in fact its bad enough like it was before "zoot suiters" fighting each other, but when the sailors of the United States of America beat up twelve and thirteen year old kids of the same country just because their Mexicans, you can imagine how brave they must be. Some of the sailors victims twelve and thirteen year old kids were taken to hospitals for injuries they suffered at the hands of the pitiless sailors.

. . . .

One night they [sailors and soldiers] came down [to the neighborhood around Alpine] and we wondered what the hell was going on. We never seen [that many] sailors or soldiers down there. So there was three or four of us that were hanging together, you know, at one of those restaurants down by the corner with the nightclubs. The bar, that's where all the prostitution happened. . . . It was bad enough that we seen a bunch of white cats, and we said what the hell's going on? So they go to this restaurant and somebody comes out and says, "Hey, you guys are Mexicans, you guys better go." "Why?" "They come looking for Mexicans." I says, "Oh, yeah? Well let 'em come. Come on." So as [the sailors and soldiers] are coming out, boom bang boom, you know. There was only about seven or eight of them. There was four of us, but we kicked some good ass, you know. And they left. All that started. That was on a Monday or Tuesday evening. Come Friday, man, five hundred guys coming through there.

10   Manchester Boddy, publisher of the *Los Angeles Daily News*, acknowledged the influence of Mexican culture in California and cast blame for the riots. In his front-page column, he also printed a Mexican-American mother's letter, which pointed to other causes of the riots. How would you compare the two analyses?

Views of the News, by Manchester Boddy (June 11, 1943)

All general rules, including this one, are false. Nevertheless there is one that has held true in so many situations that it deserves consideration. It is this: "Out of every evil comes some good." Certainly it applies to the current zoot suit trouble.

Police and court records prove that only a ridiculously small percentage of the local Mexican population is involved in the so-called "gang" demonstrations.

The vast majority of local Mexicans are just as distressed over the unfortunate brawls as is any other section of our citizenship. More so, in fact, because the admitted activities of a few irresponsible Mexican youths cast reflections on the many who are not in the least involved.

Every true Californian has an affection for his fellow citizens of Mexican ancestry that is as deep-rooted as the Mexican culture that influences our way of living—our architecture, our music—our language and even our food.

There are those who fear that the current trouble will cause a permanent strain on this friendship. In our opinion just the opposite will be the case. That is the good that will come from the admitted evil.

Today we received the following letter:

"Dear Mr. Boddy:

"Being a subscriber of the *Daily News*, I have been reading about the socalled 'zoot suiter.' Being the mother of four children, I want to express my feelings.

"My children and myself are of Mexican descent, born and raised in this country. We are 100 percent Americans. My oldest son is serving our country and the youngest is about to join the United States navy.

"In this morning's paper the socalled 'pachucos' are called Hitler's agents. To that I am expressing my belief. This racial discrimination they

Source: From Los Angeles Daily News (June 11, 1943), P 1. Reprinted with permission.

have in schools is where the youngsters' pride is hurt and hatred is started — always being called Mexicans. In schools there are all nationalities, but only Mexicans are called by their ancestors' blood. There are Irish, Jews, English, French, Swedes, etc., but as long as they are born in this country they are Americans. Why not those of Mexican descent? They are treated as rare specimens. My two girls and my young son are going to high school. Yesterday, the principal had an auditorium call just for Mexicans. These youngsters resent the way they were taken out of their classes. 'All Mexicans report to the auditorium,' with emphasis on the 'all Mexicans.'

"My children were in tears when they told me. 'Mother, how do you think we felt, being the only Mexicans in a class and having to walk out. Everybody stared at us.' These youngsters naturally are hurt, and hatred gets the best of them.

"If the principal of this school had called everybody to the auditorium, those of Mexican blood would have understood, and would not have felt like they were all hoodlums.

"If you care to publish this you are welcome to do so. Many Mexican mothers feel just like I do but are afraid to express their opinions. Thank you."

 After the Los Angeles riots, Governor Earl Warren formed a citizens' committee to investigate the causes of the Zoot Suit Riots. To what does the report issued by the committee in 1943 attribute them?

A Governor's Citizen's Committee Report on Los Angeles Riots (1943)

There are approximately 250,000 persons of Mexican descent in Los Angeles County. Living conditions among the majority of these people are far below the general level of the community. Housing is inadequate; sanitation is bad and is made worse by congestion. Recreational facilities for children are very poor; and there is insufficient supervision of the playgrounds, swimming pools and other youth centers. Such conditions are breeding places for juvenile delinquency. . . .

Mass arrests, dragnet raids, and other wholesale classifications of groups of people are based on false premises and tend merely to aggravate the situation. Any American citizen suspected of crime is entitled to be treated as an individual, to be indicted as such, and to be tried, both at law and in the

Source: Steven Mintz, ed., *Mexican-American Voices: A Documentary Reader* (Malden, Mass.: Wiley-Blackwell, 2009), pp. 160–162; originally in *Governor's Citizen's Committee Report on Los Angeles Riots* (1943).

forum of public opinion, on his merits or errors, regardless of race, color, creed, or the kind of clothes he wears.

Group accusations foster race prejudice, the entire group accused want revenge and vindication. The public is led to believe that every person in the accused group is guilty of crime.

It is significant that most of the persons mistreated during the recent incidents in Los Angeles were either persons of Mexican descent or Negroes. In undertaking to deal with the cause of these outbreaks, the existence of race prejudice cannot be ignored. . . .

On Monday evening, June seventh, thousands of Angelenos, in response to twelve hours' advance notice in the press, turned out for a mass lynching. Marching through the streets of downtown Los Angeles, a mob of several thousand soldiers, sailors, and civilians, proceeded to beat up every zoot-suiter they could find. Pushing its way into the important motion picture theaters, the mob ordered the management to turn on the house lights and then ranged up and down the aisles dragging Mexicans out of their seats. Street cars were halted while Mexicans, and some Filipinos and Negroes, were jerked out of their seats, pushed into the streets, and beaten with sadistic frenzy. If the victims wore zoot-suits, they were stripped of their clothing and left naked or half-naked on the streets, bleeding and bruised. Proceeding down Main Street from First to Twelfth, the mob stopped on the edge of the Negro district. Learning that the Negroes planned a warm reception for them, the mobsters turned back and marched through the Mexican east side spreading panic and terror.

Throughout the night the Mexican communities were in the wildest possible turmoil. Scores of Mexican mothers were trying to locate their youngsters and several hundred Mexicans milled around each of the police substations and the Central Jail trying to get word of missing members of their families. Boys came into the police stations saying: "Charge me with vagrancy or anything, but don't send me out there!" pointing to the streets where other boys, as young as twelve and thirteen years of age, were being beaten and stripped of their clothes . . . not more than half of the victims were actually wearing zoot-suits. A Negro defense worker, wearing a defense-plant identification badge on his workclothes, was taken from a street car and one of his eyes was gouged out with a knife. Huge half-page photographs, showing Mexican boys stripped of their clothes, cowering on the pavement, often bleeding profusely, surrounded by jeering mobs of men and women, appeared in all the Los Angeles newspapers. . . .

At midnight on June seventh, the military authorities decided that the local police were completely unable or unwilling to handle the situation, despite the fact that a thousand reserve officers had been called up. The entire downtown area of Los Angeles was then declared "out of bounds" for military personnel. This order immediately slowed down the pace of the rioting. The moment the Military Police and Shore Patrol went into action, the rioting quieted down.

CONCLUSION

"There's a monotony about the injustices suffered by the poor ..." the critic Dwight Macdonald once wrote. "Everything seems to go wrong with them. They never win. It's just boring."[11] Although there was nothing boring about the Detroit and Los Angeles riots, Macdonald had a point. Unless eruptions had occurred in those cities in 1943, Detroit's wartime slums and conditions confronting Mexican Americans in Los Angeles would draw relatively little notice today. Macdonald's observation points to a problem facing historians looking at history "from the bottom up." The poor are not at the center of power. They normally do not make decisions affecting the lives of millions, and often their lives appear to change little until violence breaks the monotony. Historians would seem to find little worthy of study in them.

Yet wartime Detroit and Los Angeles show that historians must see beyond the "monotony" of everyday life. Those cities slums and barrios reflected important changes in the lives of many Americans. Historians who wish to understand how World War II changed American society need to understand the lives of those in many groups on the home front, including those considered at the time as outsiders or those at society's bottom. Because historians make generalizations about historical influences, they cannot lose sight of these people. Otherwise, they may explain less than they claim to. That is a good point to remember as we turn next to one historian's explanation regarding the influence of a single factor—anticommunism—on America's postwar culture.

FURTHER READING

Luis Alvarez, *The Power of the Zoot: Youth Culture and Resistance during World War II* (Berkeley: University of California Press, 2008).

Earl Brown, "The Detroit Race Riot of 1943," in Herbert Aptheker, ed., *A Documentary History of the Negro People in the United States, 1933–1945* (Secaucus, N.J.: Citadel Press, 1974).

Kevin Allen Leonard, *The Battle for Los Angeles: Racial Ideology and World War II* (Albuquerque: University of New Mexico Press, 2006).

Alfred McClung Lee and Norman D. Humphrey, *Race Riot, Detroit 1943* (New York: Octagon Books, 1968).

Elaine Latzman Moon, *Untold Tales, Unsung Heroes: An Oral History of Detroit's African-American Community, 1918–1967* (Detroit: Wayne State University Press, 1994).

Catherine S. Ramirez, *The Woman in the Zoot Suit: Gender, Nationalism, and the Politics of Memory* (Durham: Duke University Press, 2009).

George Rudé, *The Crowd in History: A Study of Popular Disturbances in France and England, 1730–1848* (New York: John Wiley & Sons, 1964).

Richard W. Thomas, *Life for Us Is What We Make It* [A history of black Detroit] (Bloomington: Indiana University Press, 1992).

NOTES

1. Quoted in Alfred McClung Lee and Norman D. Humphrey, *Race Riot, Detroit, 1943* (New York: Octagon Books, 1968), p. 38.
2. Ibid.
3. Eric J. Hobsbawm, "History from Below—Some Reflections," in Frederick Krantz, ed., *History from Below: Studies in Popular Protest and Popular Ideology in Honour of George Rudé* (Montreal: Concordia University, 1985), p. 65.
4. Luis Alvarez, *The Power of the Zoot: Youth Culture and Resistance during World War II* (Berkeley: University of California Press, 2008), p. 185.
5. Ibid., p. 179.
6. Quoted in Robert Conot, *American Odyssey: A Unique History of America Told Through the Life of a Great City* (New York: William Morrow, 1974), p. 379.
7. Quoted in Earl Brown, "The Detroit Race Riot of 1943," in Herbert Aptheker, ed., *A Documentary History of the Negro in the United States, 1933–1945* (New York: Citadel Press, 1969), p. 453.
8. Quoted in Conot, *American Odyssey*, p. 386.
9. Quoted in ibid.
10. Alvarez, op. cit., p. 49.
11. Quoted in Michael Sragow, "The Individualist," *The New Yorker*, September 12, 1994, p. 90.

Chapter

9

Popular Culture as History:
The Cold War Comes Home

The documents in this chapter deal with the anticommunist climate of the Cold War era.

Secondary Source

1. The Culture of the Cold War (1991), STEPHEN J. WHITFIELD

Primary Sources

2. Advertisement for *I Married a Communist* (1949)
3. Promotional Material for *Walk East on Beacon* (1952)
4. A Game Show Producer Remembers the Red Scare (1995)
5. A Playwright Recalls the Red Scare (1995)
6. "This Land Is Your Land" (1956), WOODY GUTHRIE
7. A Folk Singer Remembers the Early Fifties (1995)
8. Pogo (1952), WALT KELLY
9. *On the Road* (1957), JACK KEROUAC

*I*n March 1947, the House Un-American Activities Committee (HUAC) came to Hollywood to expose communist influence in the film industry. Ronald Reagan, Gary Cooper, Robert Taylor, Adolph Menjou, and other stars testified as "friendly" witnesses at HUAC's hearings. Menjou declared, "I am a witch hunter if the witches are Communists. . . . I would like to see them all back in Russia."[1] Other witnesses also shared evidence of subversion in Hollywood's studios. Animator Walt Disney told the committee of a communist plot to turn Mickey Mouse into a Marxist. Fervid anticommunist author Ayn Rand pointed to evidence of subversive influence in *Song of Russia* (1943), one of several pro-Soviet wartime films produced when the United States and the Soviet Union were allies in World War II. Rand declared that the movie made her "sick." It showed Russian schoolchildren smiling, and, in Russia, Rand pointed out, children never smiled.

The committee, chaired by Representative Parnell Thomas, also heard from ten "unfriendly" witnesses. All of them refused to cooperate with HUAC, and Thomas had armed guards drag them from the hearing room. Later that year, all were cited for contempt by the Congress and indicted by a grand jury. By 1950, the "Hollywood ten" were in prison. Two of the ten, screenwriters Ring Lardner, Jr., and Lester Cole, served time in the federal prison at Danbury, Connecticut. By the time they arrived, former HUAC chairman Thomas was already there, convicted in 1949 of padding his office payroll. One day Cole passed Thomas, who was in charge of the prison farm's chicken yard. "I see," Cole observed, "that you're still shoveling chicken shit."[2]

Cole and the other "Hollywood ten" did not get the last laugh with the communist hunters, however. In 1949, communists led by Mao Zedong had come to power in mainland China, creating the world's most populous communist state. The same year, the Soviets detonated an atomic bomb—years before American experts had expected. News of the Soviet bomb blast hit during the trial of Alger Hiss, a former State Department official accused of passing (nonatomic)—secrets to Soviet agents. Then, in 1950, little-known Wisconsin Senator Joseph McCarthy emerged, claiming to possess names of known communists working in the State Department. Those charges quickly led to a series of investigations into alleged communist espionage in the government, with McCarthy frequently leading the charge.

By the time the "Hollywood ten" were released from prison in 1951, anticommunist hysteria had only grown. That year, HUAC returned to Hollywood to ferret out more communists and communist sympathizers. The committee obtained more than 300 names. By then, the major studios had begun blacklisting actors, screenwriters, and technicians, making it virtually impossible for them to find work. And the hunt for subversives had also spread well beyond Hollywood. The unexpected Soviet test of an atomic bomb, the conviction of the accused spy Alger Hiss in 1950, and the outbreak of the Korean War the same year had fed a growing fear of communism. So had Senator Joseph McCarthy's shocking accusations of a communist underground in the government. By 1950, the effort to root out alleged communist subversion had spread from Hollywood and the government to television, radio, and schools. When McCarthy was censured by the U.S. Senate four years later, McCarthyism had become a household word and thousands of lives and careers had been ruined.

The postwar anticommunist witch hunt tarnished reputations, sent people to prison for their political convictions, and even led some to commit suicide. Because many of the accused were writers and performing artists, it also dramatically affected the postwar era's films, television programs, novels, and other expressions of popular culture. Producers of entertainment—and messages—for mass consumption were visible targets of the communist hunters' investigations. Many were liberal, some were communists, and most had been enthusiastic supporters of America's alliance with the Soviet Union during World War II. It was not an accident that Hollywood was one of the first places to be searched for subversives, or that the search would quickly turn to television and radio networks and to other producers of popular entertainment.

Because of the vulnerability of writers, artists, and entertainers to anticommunist hysteria, popular culture is one of the best places to see the impact of the Cold War on American society. To understand the Cold War's impact on the popular messages in that era, historians must synthesize or combine evidence from such diverse sources as films, plays, songs, television programs, novels, and even comics. In this chapter, we piece together some of this evidence to create a picture of American popular culture in a period of anticommunist hysteria.

SETTING

As is true today, popular culture in the 1950s meant primarily movies, television programs, and recorded music as well as fiction, drama, and even fashion and comics. In the postwar years, however, spreading affluence, new technology, and growing numbers of children and teenagers made this culture more pervasive than ever. Its growing influence was evident in the new medium of television and in new forms of popular entertainment, from TV's situation comedies to rock 'n' roll. And many postwar commentators were appalled by what they saw and heard. Surveying postwar radio, television, movies, and novels, one critic declared popular culture to be "non-art."[3] Other observers lamented the homogenization of culture pitched to a mass audience.

Since the 1950s, scholars have continued to debate the limits and limitations of popular culture. Yet most of them would probably agree about its important characteristics. If "high" culture conforms to rigorous artistic standards, demands some effort to enjoy, and appeals to a limited audience, popular culture adheres to no fixed rules, requires no effort to enjoy, and little training to understand, and thus appeals to a broad audience. At the same time, popular culture differs from folk culture: stories, songs, dances, and other forms of artistic expression usually created by a society's illiterate, lower classes. Folk culture is preserved in memory and is passed down orally, often over centuries. By contrast, popular culture is created and marketed by an entertainment industry and transmitted through channels of mass communication, both of which are dominated by large corporations. In other words, it is a commodity to be bought and sold for profit in the marketplace. Like other marketable commodities, it has a short "shelf life." Popular culture, then, travels instantly and disappears quickly, but often not before it has touched all levels of society.

Today, historians who study postwar popular culture are less interested in judging people's tastes than in understanding what its messages reveal about the period. They also see much more variety in the popular culture of the 1950s than did contemporary critics, who often focused on the burgeoning white, middle-class suburbs. Historians also recognize numerous influences on postwar popular culture: growing middle-class affluence, the spread of suburbia, the increasing importance of the automobile, the "baby boom," and the Cold War. Thus their task is to understand popular culture's messages and determine the role of varied influences in shaping them.

The glorification of mothers and homemakers, a dominant theme of postwar popular culture, illustrates the challenge. Undoubtedly, the baby boom and the growth of suburbs played a large role in fashioning this domestic ideal, which was broadcast widely in the movies, television, and magazines of the 1950s. Yet so may have other factors, including the Cold War. The domestic ideal was a comforting image and a useful tool in the battle against communism. The image of the suburban home with its contented homemaker seemed to be compelling evidence of American superiority in the Cold War. Thus when Richard Nixon engaged Soviet leader Nikita Khrushchev in their famous "kitchen debate" at an exhibition of American goods in Moscow in 1959, the vice president praised the American way of life because it had eased the domestic burden of women. Standing in front of a washing machine, Nixon told Khrushchev, "What we want is to make easier the life of our housewives."[4]

The postwar domestic ideal illustrates that popular culture's influence can run in many, often unexpected, directions. It also demonstrates that popular culture can be shaped by numerous influences. To understand its many messages, historians must draw from myriad, often unrelated, sources. And, as with any historical analysis, they must be careful not to attribute too much influence to a single cause.

INVESTIGATION

In the movie *Blackboard Jungle* (1955), an idealistic teacher played by Glenn Ford tells a high school class filled with rebellious students, "All your lives you're gonna hear stories—what some guy tells you, what you see in books and magazines—but you gotta examine these stories, look for the real meaning, and most of all . . . you gotta think for yourselves."[5] It was easy for postwar Americans to enjoy their favorite television programs, movies, music, or popular fiction without thinking much about them. Few perceived in them a common frame of reference. Now, with the advantage of hindsight, historians can synthesize a variety of sources into a coherent picture. In this chapter, we examine a wide array of cultural artifacts to determine the messages, assumptions, and values they reveal. The main problem is to determine what impact the fear of communism had on postwar American popular culture. Your analysis of the culture of the Cold War should address the following questions:

1. **Did the Cold War narrow postwar popular culture?** How did it "distort and enfeeble" cultural expression, according to historian Stephen Whitfield? How did it undermine challenges to the status quo?

2. **Did Cold War politics affect all forms of popular culture the same way, or were some forms more resistant to political influences?** Why?

3. **Is Whitfield's argument in Source 1 about the impact of anticommunism on postwar popular culture supported or contradicted by the primary sources?** Do the sources reflect a cultural consensus, or do they demonstrate a clash of discordant messages and resistance to dominant standards? Is popular culture an influential force in American society, or is it merely a commodity that is influenced by other developments?

Before you begin, read the section in your textbook about the Cold War, especially its impact on American society in the 1950s. It will provide background that will help you analyze this chapter's sources. What is its view about the Cold War's impact on cultural expression?

SECONDARY SOURCE

In this selection, Stephen Whitfield explores the impact of anticommunism on various forms of popular culture. Pay particular attention to his argument about the main messages conveyed by postwar popular culture. What is the most important evidence that anticommunist hysteria influenced popular culture? Are Whitfield's examples representative?

The Culture of the Cold War (1991)
STEPHEN J. WHITFIELD

In 1951, one of the prisoners in a New York jail awaiting sentencing under the Smith Act for conspiring to advocate the violent overthrow of the American

Source: Whitfield, Stephen J., *The Culture of the Cold War*. 1996. pp. 1, 2, 10–12, 34, 35, 37, 53, 71, 127, 131–133, 144, 200–203. © 1996 The Johns Hopkins University Press. Reprinted with permission of The Johns Hopkins University Press.

government was George Charney. The chairman of the state's Communist party and a member of the national committee, he became acquainted with an Italian-American hoodlum named Bob Raymondi, who since his teens in Brooklyn had associated with Murder, Inc., and was a veteran of seventeen years as an inmate of Dannemora. While dominating the prison population, Raymondi also sought to compensate for his poor formal education by chatting with the Marxist-Leninists who had been inserted among the other prisoners. One Saturday, Raymondi's sister visited him and was startled to learn how close he had gotten with Charney and others convicted under the Smith Act. "My God, Bob," she warned. "You'll get into trouble."

In this era, a specter was haunting America—the specter of Communism. Trying to exorcise it were legislators and judges, union officials and movie studio bosses, policemen and generals, university presidents and corporation executives, clergymen and journalists, Republicans and Democrats, conservatives and liberals. The specter that, a century earlier, Marx and Engels had described as stalking the continent of Europe was extending itself to the United States. . . . By introducing ideological politics, Communism became more loathed than organized crime, exacerbating fears that were to distort and enfeeble American culture throughout the late 1940s and the 1950s. . . .

. . . Censors endorsed the boycott of films that they had not seen; vigilantes favored the removal from library shelves of books that they had not read.

The confusion of the public and private realms was also characteristic of the era. Thus, the Federal Bureau of Investigation compiled dossiers on novelists who seemed unduly critical of their native land, and the bureau got into the movie business by secretly filming the patrons of a left-wing bookstore, Four Continents, in New York. At the same time, some representatives of Hollywood presented themselves to Congress as authorities on the theory and tactics of Marxism-Leninism. An awed member of the House Committee on Un-American Activities (HUAC) hailed even the mother of musical star Ginger Rogers as "one of the outstanding experts on communism in the United States," for example. While legislators were interrogating musicians and actors about their beliefs, university administrators were using political instead of academic criteria to evaluate the fitness of teachers. Even as some clergymen were advocating ferocious military measures to defeat an enemy that was constantly described as "atheistic," government officials were themselves asserting that the fundamental problem presented by Communism was not political but spiritual. . . .

. . . [T]he effect was . . . the suffocation of liberty and the debasement of culture itself. Even by the narrowest chauvinistic criteria of the Cold War, the United States thus diminished its ability in the global struggle to be seen as an attractive and just society. The politicization of culture might win the allegiance of those who cherished authority, but not of those who valued autonomy. The politicization of culture might appeal to reactionaries abroad, but not to foreigners who appreciated creativity or critical thought.

And though the state was intimately involved in restricting liberty, it acted with popular approval and acquiescence; the will of the majority was not thwarted. In effect, Americans imposed a starchy repression upon themselves. . . .

. . . One response can be explored at the murkier edges of popular sensibility, the locale of novelist Mickey Spillane. . . .

On the top ten fictional bestsellers of the decade of the 1950s, Spillane wrote an astounding six of them: number three, *The Big Kill* (1951); number five, *My Gun Is Quick* (1950); number six, *One Lonely Night* (1951); number seven, *The Long Wait* (1951); number eight, *Vengeance Is Mine* (1950); and number nine, *Kiss Me, Deadly* (1952). This catalogue does not count his most popular novel, *I, the Jury*, which had been published prior to the decade. By 1953, the New American Library had sold seventeen million paperbacks of his first six novels, which meant that having Spillane on the firm's list of authors was like a license to print money.

I, the Jury (1947) introduced a private investigator named Mike Hammer, a World War II veteran of such magnanimity that he harbors no hostility toward Nazis. Though he chose not to become a cop because a "pansy" bureaucracy was emasculating policemen with its rules and regulations, his real contempt is reserved for the professional and intellectual classes, for homosexuals, and above all for swarthy criminals like "the Mafia. The stinking slimy Mafia. An oversized mob of ignorant, lunk-headed jerks who ruled with fear and got away with it because they had the money to back themselves up."

The detective's hairy-chested heroics would have made such novels enormously popular even if they had been devoid of any explicit politics, but the overt anti-Communism of Spillane's fiction engraved it with the signature of the period. Two decades earlier, Hammer might have combated only organized criminals spawned in the lower depths; two decades later, the adversaries would have been a cabal of Third World terrorists. In the early 1950s, however, the Red Scare required his special skills. For the comrades and conspirators in *One Lonely Night*, Hammer has reserved kicks that can shatter bone on impact, bursts of lead from his .45, and the sadistic pleasures of strangulation.

In that novel, which sold more than 3 million copies, the detective seduces a millionaire's estranged granddaughter, whom boredom has driven to Communism. At first Hammer cannot fathom why Ethel Brighton, despite her early exposure to the attractions of capitalism, can embrace the twisted creed of Bolshevism. He suspects that she needs only the substitute of *his* embrace. Confident that his virility can transform her politics, he has her spend one night in his apartment, and concludes, "Now that she had a taste of life[,] maybe she'd go out and seek some different company for a change." He is wrong—or at least seems to be, and realizes that Ethel Brighton has continued to associate with the scum and perverts who comprise the Communist movement. So he strips and whips her. Eventually Hammer poses as a member of the Soviet intelligence apparatus; since no one in this supposedly very clandestine organization thinks of challenging his credentials, he considers these conspirators as "dumb as horse manure." These malignant dreamers of world conquest "had a jackal look of discontent and cowardice." When they are not merely credulous cretins, they are either vicious hypocrites or else clinically insane. The supreme villain in *One Lonely Night* is Oscar Deamer, who is both a Communist and a psychopath. Hammer tells this master criminal, just before choking him to death: "You were a Commie, Oscar, because you were batty. It was the only philosophy that would appeal to your crazy mind. It justified everything you did and you saw a chance of getting back at the world." The explanation for the appeal of Communism is, apparently, insanity.

In destroying such motiveless, psychopathic malevolence, Hammer personifies the rejection of liberalism. The cure for the plague of Communism cannot be the diffusion of New Deal programs to relieve economic misery, or the extension of the Four Freedoms to amplify the meaning of an open society, or more resonant calls to lighten the burden of social injustice. The solution, the creator of Hammer seems to fantasize, is violent prophylaxis. After the detective has saved his naked fiancée from hysterical Bolshevik flagellants, he murders them all, . . . "I killed more people tonight than I have fingers on my hands," he later boasts. "I shot them in cold blood and enjoyed every minute of it. . . . They were Commies. . . . They were red sons-of-bitches who should have died long ago. . . . They never thought that there were people like us in this country. They figured us all to be soft as horse manure and just as stupid.". . .

To appraise the literary significance of such fiction would be utterly irrelevant, to sermonize against such appalling crudeness equally pointless. What needs underscoring is that, at least in the night battles of the Cold War for which Spillane recruited more Americans than any other author, the procedural rules and legal guarantees that helped make a civil society worth defending were treated with savage contempt. Justice was imagined as coming from the barrel of a pistol, and cruelty was not confined to Party headquarters but was exalted in the exploits of Mike Hammer. Because of the official limitations under which formal authority chafed, vigilante ruthlessness was the only effective antidote to unmitigated evil. . . .

The search to define and affirm a way of life, the need to express and celebrate the meaning of "Americanism," was the flip side of stigmatizing Communism; to decipher the culture of the 1950s requires tracing the formulation of this national ideology. It was not invented but inherited, and some of its components were intensified under the political pressures of the era. The belief system that most middle-class Americans considered their birthright—the traditional commitment to competitive individualism in social life, to the liberal stress on rights in political life, and to private enterprise in economic life—was adapted to the crisis of the Cold War. . . .

. . . [By the 1950s] the bounties pouring forth from American factories and laboratories, made available in such profusion in stores and markets, had become perhaps the chief ideological prop—the most palpable vindication—of "the American way of life." Success and virtue were so easily equated that, after *Life* magazine published *The Old Man and the Sea* (1952), the industrialist who became Eisenhower's secretary of the treasury was puzzled by the popular fascination with Hemingway's story. "Why would anybody be interested in some old man who was a failure," George M. Humphrey wondered, "and never amounted to anything anyway?"

Such assumptions help account for Barbie (b. 1958), the most popular doll in history. With her own national fan club, she received five hundred letters a week. Eleven and one-half inches tall, this late adolescent was endowed with a three-and-one-quarter-inch bust that smashed an anatomical taboo in the toy market. But what made her something of an icon of the Cold War were the fantasies of consumption that she evoked. Barbie came cheap: three dollars. But her full wardrobe cost more than one hundred dollars, and her appetite for more was insatiable: party dresses and casual attire, prom gowns and eventually a wedding ensemble (her boyfriend's name was Ken), outdoor outfits, professional uniforms. Barbie lived in a split-level house, patronized a beauty parlor, drove a Corvette. She "seemed to be only a product," one scholar concluded, "but she turned out to be a way of life," an affirmation of national supremacy. The capitalist "fetishism of commodities" that Marx found so repellent had advanced to the first line of defense. . . .

. . . The movie industry was conscripted into the Cold War in 1947 when HUAC was invited to Los Angeles. The committee's host was the Motion Picture Alliance for the Preservation of American Ideals, an organization that struck a typical postwar stance in asserting that "co-existence is a myth and neutrality is impossible . . . anyone who is not FIGHTING Communism is HELPING Communism." About fifteen hundred members of the film community had founded the alliance three years earlier; they included John Wayne, Gary Cooper, Walt Disney, Adolphe Menjou, and Cecil B. De Mille. Its first president was director Sam Wood, who felt so strongly about the subject that his will imposed as a condition of inheritance that his relatives (other than his wife) file affidavits in court that they "are not now, nor have they ever been, Communists.". . .

. . . [By the 1950s] it was safer to produce films without any political or economic themes or implications at all. Although *Broken Arrow* (1950) had presented Cochise sympathetically as a peace-loving Apache, Monogram Studios abandoned its plans for a movie on Hiawatha, whose efforts to achieve peace among the Iroquois nations might be interpreted as a boost to Communist peace propaganda. Because novelist Theodore Dreiser had formally converted to Communism shortly before his death in 1945, Paramount got the jitters in adapting his classic of a generation earlier, *An American Tragedy*. So director George Stevens toned down the social analysis and highlighted the romance in *A Place in the Sun* (1951). Stevens's protagonist (Montgomery Clift) is no longer a victim of certain class relationships that Dreiser had shown motivating Clyde Griffiths toward homicide. Then even the inflated love story posed a problem when supporting actress Anne Revere took the Fifth Amendment, so Paramount cut out most of her major scenes. . . .

. . . [I]t was prudent to avoid overtly political films. Consider, for instance, the fate of Universal's *The Senator Was Indiscreet* (1947), a satire about a bumbling Senator (William Powell) who does not realize that a new income tax bill applies to him as well. He runs for the presidency on a platform that includes adding his relatives to the payroll and giving every citizen the right to attend Harvard. The movie also dares to suggest that White House aspirants can be packaged with images that can maximize their appeal to the electorate. *The Senator Was Indiscreet* was written by Charles MacArthur, was rewritten and produced by Nunnally Johnson, and was the only movie that George S. Kaufman ever directed. None of the three was a political activist. All were renowned for their wit, which was lost on Congresswoman Clare Boothe Luce (R-Conn.) when it was screened for her. "Was this picture made by an American?" she demanded to know. *Life,* which her husband published, retracted its own favorable review of the film in a column called "On Second Thought." Editorials in other forums, plus the American Legion, also attacked the un-American propaganda of *The Senator Was Indiscreet.* Having approved the script, the Motion Picture Association of America had somehow missed its incendiary implications, leaving the trade organization with only the option of prohibiting the showing of *The Senator Was Indiscreet* overseas, which it did.

Partly as a result, the few dozen political films that were released in the postwar era bristled with titles like *The Iron Curtain* (1948), *The Red Menace* (1949), *The Red Danube* (1949), *Red Snow* (1952), and *The Steel Fist* (1952). The election year of 1952 was the peak, when twelve explicitly anti-Communist films were produced. Though Elizabeth Taylor and Robert Taylor were featured in *Conspirator* (1950) and John Wayne glamorized HUAC in *Big Jim McLain,* very few of these movies had large budgets or major stars. They were shot on the cheap and usually ended up as the second features on double bills. Because strongly ideological films were considered unlikely to attract the masses anyway, the studios apparently reasoned that anti-Communist pictures might mollify the American Legion and right-wingers in Congress without losing too much money. And although Menjou had predicted to HUAC that such movies "would be an incredible success," the studios' apprehensions proved correct: most of them bombed at the box office.

How was domestic Communism depicted in the films of the Cold War? Its adherents show no respect for national sanctums and symbols, which Party members traduce. They treat the Stars and Stripes with contempt. They conspire to meet one another by carrying an edition of *Reader's Digest* or a TWA flight bag and by picking such agreeable settings as the Boston Public Garden amid the swan boats. Communists are rude, humorless, and "cruel to animals," Nora Sayre noticed. "But we don't know how they treat children, since they never have any." Women in the Party are either disturbingly unfeminine, downright unattractive, or nearly nymphomaniacs. Bereft of the experience of "normal" love, they use sex for political seduction. A Party target in Republic Pictures' *The Red Menace* tells a blonde *femme fatale:* "I always thought the Commies peddled bunk. I didn't know they came as cute as you." After the comely comrade lets the dupe kiss her, she teasingly withdraws, then gives him a copy of *Das Kapital.* . . .

X
   . . . When one independent, left-wing film was produced in 1954, it was unclear what was more impressive—the fact that in so politically parched an atmosphere *Salt of the Earth* could be made at all, or the fact that it faced so many barriers imposed by those who believed that liberty was an ornament of American life.

The movie was based on a 1951–52 strike by Mexican-American zinc miners, who demanded better safety regulations as well as equal treatment with Anglo employees. The strike was conducted by the International Union of Mine, Mill, and Smelter Workers, which the CIO had expelled in 1950 because it was Communist-controlled. Since no Hollywood studio would have touched such a subject in the 1950s, *Salt of the Earth* was a venture of the blacklisted. Director Herbert Biberman was a member of the Hollywood Ten, scenarist Michael Wilson took the Fifth Amendment before HUAC in 1951, and producer Paul Jarrico had co-written *Song of Russia.* . . .

   . . . The fragility of the left-wing popular culture that faced extinction during the Cold War was symbolized by an encounter in 1956 in a New Jersey hospital. Harold Leventhal, a Communist who once plugged songs for Irving Berlin, went to Greystone Park to visit one of the inmates. A psychiatrist rummaged through the files on his desk, then exclaimed: "Guthrie, Guthrie, ah, Guthrie! A very sick man. Very sick. Delusional! He says he has written more than a thousand songs! And a novel too. And he says he has made records for the Library of Congress." Leventhal's reply was terse: "He has.". . .

   . . . Born in 1912, Woody Guthrie had proudly cultivated an ardent pro-Communism by the late 1930s and did not waver thereafter. . . . A drifter and a loner, Guthrie was even jailed and given a six-month sentence in 1948 for writing obscene letters to a Los Angeles woman. His drinking and self-destructive rages were awful preludes to the congenital disease called Huntington's chorea that would eventually deprive him of control of mind and body. The atrophy would gradually worsen until he would quiver into horrifying disintegration, his brain utterly depleted.

Guthrie was functioning well enough to attend a major concert held in New York in 1956 to honor his work. Over a thousand people filled Pythian Hall, and at the end of the program the entire cast sang "This Land Is Your Land. "Guthrie sat in the balcony, and the audience cheered him when it too joined in "This Land Is Your Land." Within a few months of that consolidation of the political culture to which Guthrie had contributed for two decades, he was committed to Greystone Park, and five years later to

Brooklyn State Hospital. One pilgrim who came east to visit the hospitalized Guthrie early in 1961 would quickly become his most dazzling successor, taking audiences far beyond the "progressive" confines within which Guthrie had operated. Bob Dylan idolized Guthrie, sang and dressed like him, concocted a similar past, and recorded a "Song to Woody" on his first album in 1962. Born in 1941, the University of Minnesota dropout was immune to Guthrie's pro-Soviet politics. But Dylan transmitted an outrage against social injustice and war in such early songs as "Blowin' in the Wind" and "A Hard Rain's Gonna Fall" that outstripped the appeal of Guthrie's music a generation earlier, though the successor himself soon abandoned the leftist orientation to which Guthrie himself had been so faithful. . . .

In the 1950s, when dissent was too easily equated with disloyalty, the influence of such figures sharply diminished. As a result, talents were thwarted, creative possibilities were stifled, and the development of a more vital and various national culture was unrealized.

PRIMARY SOURCES

This section contains a variety of sources, from movie advertisements to popular songs, reflecting postwar popular culture. Together, the primary sources offer important clues about the impact of anticommunism on the popular culture of the period. All of them may not support the same conclusion.

Movie Advertising and the Anticommunist Hysteria

After Germany invaded the Soviet Union in 1941, Hollywood movie studios produced numerous pro-Soviet films. Warner Brothers' *Mission to Moscow* (1943), based on former U.S. Ambassador Joseph Davies's memoir, was a good example. In the movie, Davies (Walter Huston) tells Stalin, "I believe, sir, that history will record you as a great benefactor of mankind."[6] By 1947, the Soviet Union was no longer an ally in the battle against Nazism and the HUAC was investigating alleged communist subversion in Hollywood. Studios were under intense pressure to demonstrate their anticommunist credentials. One result was the blacklisting of actors and other studio personnel. Another was a stream of B-grade movies exposing the dangerous menace of communist subversion. Although never big hits at the box office, these films showed that Hollywood took seriously the growing fear of domestic subversion. As you examine material produced to market several of these movies, determine what messages they give. Think about their impact on the public. Are these movies evidence of Hollywood's influence, or of its vulnerability to outside influences?

2   *I Married a Communist* was a drama about a newly wed shipping executive who is targeted by communists operating on the San Francisco waterfront because of his past association with the Communist Party. When audiences resisted the title, RKO Radio Pictures released the film under the titles *The Woman on Pier 39* and *Beautiful but Dangerous.*

Advertisement for *I Married a Communist* (1949)

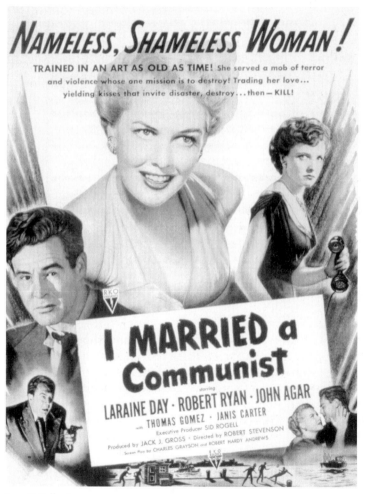

Everett Collection.

3   In this movie from Columbia Pictures, the FBI battles a vast communist spy network in Boston, where spies hope to steal the results of "an extraordinary scientific experiment" involving a new computer. The movie opens with the narrator praising the FBI for "protecting" Americans and then shows FBI agents opening other people's mail.

Promotional Material for *Walk East on Beacon* (1952)

"Walk East on Beacon" 1952, renewed 1980 Columbia Pictures Industries, Inc. All Rights Reserved. Courtesy of Columbia Pictures.

4   Mark Goodson was a producer of television game shows, including *What's My Line*, *I've Got a Secret*, *Password*, and *Family Feud*. Before he died in 1992, Goodson was the subject of an oral history, a tape-recorded interview designed to preserve an individual's experiences and to share them with a broader audience. What does this portion of Goodson's oral history reveal about the forces that made television particularly vulnerable to the communist hysteria?

A Game Show Producer Remembers the Red Scare (1995)

I'm not sure when it began, but I believe it was early 1950. At that point, I had no connection with the blacklisting that was going on, although I

Source: From *Red Scare: Memories of the American Inquisition, an Oral History* by Griffin Fariello. Copyright © 1995 by Griffin Fariello. Used by permission of W. W. Norton & Company, Inc., the author and the Sandra Dijkstra Literary Agency.

had heard about it in the motion picture business and heard rumors about things that had happened on other shows, like *The Aldrich Family*. My first experience really was when we settled into a fairly regular panel on *What's My Line?* in mid-1950. The panel consisted of the poet Louis Untermeyer, Dorothy Kilgallen, Arlene Francis, and Hal Block, a comedy writer. Our sponsor was Stopette, a deodorant.

A few months into the show, I began getting mail on [left-wing poet] Louis Untermeyer. He had been listed in *Red Channels*.* He was one of those folks who had supported the left-wing forces against Franco in Spain. I know that he also had allowed his name to be affiliated with the Joint Anti-Fascist Refugee Committee and had been a sponsor of the 1948 May Day parade. Back in the early 1920s, he had written articles for *The Masses*. But he was certainly not an active political person, at least as far as I knew.

CBS and Stopette also began receiving letters of protest. First, it was just a few postcards. Then it grew. Members of the Catholic War Veterans put stickers on drugstore windows, red, white, and blue stickers, warning "Stop Stopette Until Stopette stops Untermeyer."

We didn't pay too much attention until we got the call from CBS. Untermeyer and I were summoned to Ralph Colin's office, who was the general counsel for CBS at the time. Louis and Colin knew each other. Ralph asked him why he lent his name to the group. "I thought it was a good cause," Untermeyer said. "Louis, you're being very naive. These are very difficult times and you've put us in a bad spot. We're going to have to drop you." Untermeyer was very apologetic, but the decision had been made. He was let go.

I remember leaving that office feeling embarrassed. Untermeyer was in his sixties, a man of considerable dignity. He was a good American poet and I liked him; he was funny and articulate on the show. What's more, I had no political ax to grind.

That was the last of that kind of meeting. Soon afterwards, CBS installed a clearance division. There wasn't any discussion. We would just get the word—"Drop that person"—and that was supposed to be it. Whenever we booked a guest or a panelist on *What's My Line?* or *I've Got a Secret*, one of our assistants would phone up and say, "We're going to use so-and-so." We'd either get the okay, or they'd call back and say, "Not clear," or "Sorry, can't use them." Even advertising agencies—big ones, like Young & Ribicam and BBD&O—had their own clearance departments. They would never come out and say it. They would just write off somebody by saying, "He's a bad actor." You were never supposed to tell the person what it was about; you'd just unbook them. They never admitted there was a blacklist. It just wasn't done.

Red Channels: The Report of Communist Influence in Radio and Television was a private publication that listed names of people affiliated with communist "causes." After it appeared in June 1950, it quickly became known as "the Bible of Madison Avenue." Advertising agencies, the television networks, and sponsors used it to remove "subversives" from the airwaves.

Some fairly substantial names were off-limits—big stars like Leonard Bernstein, Harry Belafonte, Abe Burrows, Gypsy Rose Lee, Judy Holliday, Jack Gilford, Uta Hagen, and Hazel Scott. Everyone, from the stars to the bit-part actors, was checked. We once did a show in California called *The Rebel*, and we used wranglers to take care of the horses—we had to clear all of their names. CBS, in particular, asked for loyalty oaths to be signed by everybody, making sure that you were not un-American. So far as I know, no one ever refused.

In 1952, *I've Got a Secret* got a new sponsor, R. J. Reynolds Tobacco Company, with its advertising agency, William Este. When they came aboard, someone from the agency called me and said, "Please get rid of Henry Morgan," one of the regular panelists on the show. Morgan had been named in *Red Channels*. I had known Henry for a long time; he was one of those young curmudgeons who was acidic at times, but he was by no means a Communist. His wife was involved with radical politics, but they were getting a divorce, and to some extent his name was just smeared.

I went to the agency and told them that they were crazy to try and get rid of Henry Morgan. They agreed that the charge in *Red Channels* was absurd, but they said they couldn't take the risk. That was the main thing—mail accusing them of being pro-Communist was not going to sell cigarettes. They gave me an ultimatum: dump Morgan or face the show's cancellation.

So I went to Garry Moore, the MC of the show and an established comedian. He was a conservative, a Republican from Maryland. I know that he liked Morgan. I said that if he'd be willing to back me up, I'd tell the agency I'd do the show without a sponsor. He agreed without hesitation. I phoned up William Este and said, "We're not going to do the show without Henry." The people at the agency were flabbergasted. It was virtually unheard-of to have this kind of confrontation. They told me they'd think about it, and in the end, they actually backed down. The show was not canceled, and some weeks later Morgan's name simply vanished from *Red Channels*.

Morgan never even knew. When I wrote the article about my experience, Henry called me. "I did not know that I was about to be dropped," he said. "I knew I was in *Red Channels* and I was outraged about that, but I didn't know I was about to be dropped." It was a revelation for him.

The Morgan episode was my first act of resistance. It was not something my lawyers ever encouraged. The watchword in the business is "Don't make waves."

The studios and the advertising agencies didn't have to subscribe to *Red Channels*. It was one of about a dozen publications. There were several private lists, and the major agencies and networks exchanged lists, most of which had several names each. I'd help you out by giving you my list and you'd help me out by giving me your list. There was a big interchange of listings. A fellow called Danny O'Shea was in charge of the listings at CBS, an ex-FBI man. *Red Channels* would maybe have a couple of hundred names, but there might be on the other list at CBS several hundred more. Anybody could show up on a list, stars, technicians, cowboys.

5   Arthur Miller, author of *Death of a Salesman* (1949), *The Crucible* (1953), and other plays, discusses anticommunist pressures on Broadway in this oral history. In 1956, Miller appeared before HUAC. Refusing to testify, he was convicted for contempt of Congress, a decision later overturned by a higher court. Note Miller's explanation for Broadway's relative immunity from the anticommunist hysteria. Do the previous sources reflect his point about the difference between Broadway, on the one hand, and Hollywood and the broadcasting industry, on the other?

A Playwright Recalls the Red Scare (1995)

I drew some attention when I became involved with the Conference for Peace at the Waldorf in 1949. That was a kind of crossroads, I guess, at the time: when the Russians were—in fact, up to that moment almost—our allies and then suddenly they were turned into our enemy, and that conference was very important from that point of view.

At the time I was not working in films or for any broadcasting companies, or advertisers, so the effect on me was more obscure. It was simply that I would be attacked in the press from time to time. But I had no job to lose, so it was quite a bit different than it was for a lot of other writers who had either actual jobs that they would be thrown out of, or contracts with publishers that would have been affected. I didn't have anything like that, and obviously the Broadway situation was quite different, because we didn't have any big corporations investing in Broadway, there were just a lot of small investors who threw in their money to put a play on. So they were not so easily tampered with as the big companies were in Hollywood or the broadcasting industry. They could maintain more independence.

They had blacklists of writers, and as it later turned out, practically every American writer was on it. But not all of them were out front the way I found myself, because they weren't putting plays on, especially not in the Middle West. So the impact was greater on me than it would have been on, let's say, Steinbeck or somebody else.

We had a road company of *Death of a Salesman* in the Middle West that we finally had to close down. The American Legion especially, and I think the Catholic War Veterans, picketed it so heavily everywhere that people were intimidated and they didn't come. So there wasn't much business. They were attacking the play and me as being an anti-American.

Source: From *Red Scare: Memories of the American Inquisition, an Oral History* by Griffin Fariello. Copyright © 1995 by Griffin Fariello. Used by permission of W. W. Norton & Company, Inc., the author and the Sandra Dijkstra Literary Agency.

Death of a Salesman questioned the ethos of the business civilization, which the play intimates has no real respect for individual human beings, whereas the going mythology was quite the opposite: in that nobody of any competence ever fails and that everything was pretty sound and terrific for everybody. So to put a play on where somebody who believes in the system, as Willy Loman does to his dying minute, ends up a suicide, it was rather a shock.

In fact, when they made the film they made Willy appear crazy. That was the whole drift of the film; that's why it was such a bad film in my opinion. They made him into a lunatic, and consequently you could observe him with the same distance you observe any crazy person, you don't really identify with him. In my opinion that was to make the play politically more palatable, but there were other artistic problems with that production which I disagreed with, but certainly this was the major one.

Columbia Studios actually made a short, cost them a couple of hundred thousand dollars, which they wanted to run before each showing of the film in the movie theaters. The short was shot at City College in New York City and was basically a very boring set of lectures by business administration professors who made it clear that Willy Loman represented nobody and that the play was really quite absurd and that the system was altogether different than as it was portrayed in the play and that the salesman's job was one of the best imaginable careers that a person could have and indeed that the system was based on salesmanship. When they got finished with this kind of analysis you wondered why they had produced the play at all as a film. I managed to make an empty threat that I would sue them if they did this, but in fact I think they themselves saw that the absurdity of the whole thing was even too much for them. They may have shown it, somebody told me that he had seen it once in some theater, but I don't think it was very widespread.

---

6   Folk singer Woody Guthrie wrote the lyrics to this song in 1940 after he had encountered poverty and injustices while traveling through California and Texas during the Great Depression. He originally titled it "God Blessed America" in response to a popular recording of Irving Berlin's "God Bless America." Recorded in 1944 as "This Land Is My Land," Guthrie continued to change the lyrics, some of which expressed sympathy to Communism, and eventually made two other recordings of the song. The song was professionally published in 1956. Guthrie continued to perform the song in the 1950s, as would other folk singers. Does the endurance of this song in the 1950s suggest anything about the resilience of some popular cultural expression in the face of the anticommunism of the period?

"This Land Is Your Land" (1956)

WOODY GUTHRIE

This land is your land This land is my land
From California to the New York island;
From the red wood forest to the Gulf Stream waters
This land was made for you and Me.

As I was walking that ribbon of highway,
I saw above me that endless skyway:
I saw below me that golden valley:
This land was made for you and me.

I've roamed and rambled and I followed my footsteps
To the sparkling sands of her diamond deserts;
And all around me a voice was sounding:
This land was made for you and me.

When the sun came shining, and I was strolling,
And the wheat fields waving and the dust clouds rolling,
As the fog was lifting a voice was chanting:
This land was made for you and me.

As I went walking I saw a sign there
And on the sign it said "No Trespassing."
But on the other side it didn't say nothing,
That side was made for you and me.

In the shadow of the steeple I saw my people,
By the relief office I seen my people;
As they stood there hungry, I stood there asking
Is this land made for you and me?

Nobody living can ever stop me,
As I go walking that freedom highway;
Nobody living can ever make me turn back
This land was made for you and me.

7   Ronnie Gilbert was the only female member of The Weavers, a popular folk music quartet whose hit *Goodnight Irene* sold two million records in the early 1950s. As you read this excerpt from Gilbert's oral history, note what effect the anticommunist crusade had on the group. Was popular music more or less susceptible to blacklisting than Hollywood, television, or Broadway?

A Folk Singer Remembers the Early Fifties (1995)

My interest in the Weavers was political as well as musical. We sang for unions. We sang for the Henry Wallace campaign.* I was all of eighteen or nineteen at the time. My background was political. My mother was a rank-and-file unionist, belonged to the International Ladies Garment Workers Union, and she was a singer. She taught me all the songs. So I come from a very proud, political union background. That was part of my nature and my life, you know. I still sing political songs. There's a different style and shape, I'm not so much a "folksinger" as I was then. I sing a wide variety of musical styles. But the lyrics that attract me are lyrics about something.

We incubated most of our material at the Village Vanguard. We were there for six months. It was a small club in New York that did all kinds of stuff, radical stuff, nonradical stuff, jazz. . . .

We sang everything that we sang later on. But we were very aware that we were entertainers. We would never even think of singing a song that wasn't good fun to do. Sure, we sang Spanish Civil War songs, one or two of them, 'cause they were musically exciting. And we would refer to them and say that this was a song that was written during the Spanish Civil War, and that perhaps if Hitler had been turned back during that war, we would never have had World War Two. We said really "subversive" things like that. And every now and then we'd sing something that related to a union. Very subversive, you know. You bet, that's the kind of thing we did. But when we appeared on television, we knew that we were singing for a very broad audience that wouldn't sit still for the explanation of a song. The song had to be directly of interest to them, and we sang what we thought was best in American folk music, and that was what we represented.

*FDR's vice president and Progressive Party candidate for president in 1948.

Source: From *Red Scare: Memories of the American Inquisition, an Oral History* by Griffin Fariello. Copyright © 1995 by Griffin Fariello. Used by permission of W. W. Norton & Company, Inc., the author and the Sandra Dijkstra Literary Agency.

The Weavers were headline-makers. We were the hottest thing to come along in a long time in the music industry. . . . Had we not made "Goodnight Irene," had we not become hot performing artists, it's very possible that we would never have been caught up in the blacklist, because we wouldn't have been worth anything to anybody.

I mean, why are entertainers picked up in a blacklist like that? 'Cause they made headlines for the committee. The headlines you see in these old movies from the thirties—the Criminal or the Hunted Person comes into a hotel lobby, and everybody's reading the papers: "So-and-So Wanted," you know? Well, that actually happened to us. We were playing a nightclub engagement in Springfield, Illinois. And we came into the hotel lobby, and there were people reading the newspaper, and it said "Weavers Named Reds!" [Laughs.] And there we were! . . .

We were being followed all the time. I remember walking down the street in some place in Ohio, it might have been Akron, with these two guys following us behind. I was terrified. By that time it was very scary, because it involved groups like the American Legion, the Catholic War Veterans, and a very patriotic kind of macho. I was present at Peekskill, at the Paul Robeson concert, where people were badly injured by rock-throwing goons, with the police standing by doing absolutely nothing. So I knew that kind of thing could happen very easily. These guys followed us a long ways. I stopped and turned around and confronted them. One of them seemed very surprised, and he said, "Well, do you want your subpoena here, or in the club, while you're performing?" I said, "I'll take it now!" [Laughs.] . . .

I never did get subpoenaed again. Very quickly our work came down to nothing, there was no work to be had. We stuck together as long as we possibly could, and then it was pointless. Decca was not going to do any more recording. Decca was in the red when we recorded for them and we pulled them right out. It didn't help. It didn't make them loyal to us. [Laughs.] The music industry is the music industry. The Weavers were merchandise. Our songs were merchandise, just the way people are now.

8 In his popular animal comic strip, Walt Kelly often targeted political figures. In the strip on the following page, Kelly introduces a lynx named Simple J. Malarkey, who bears a striking resemblance to Joseph McCarthy. Malarkey takes over the Okefenokee Swamp's Bird Watching Club. Note Kelly's message about Malarkey's methods. Why was Kelly able to get away with such criticism while other popular artists and entertainers were not?

Pogo (1952)

WALT KELLY

9   Jack Kerouac was a college dropout and leading figure in the Beats, a movement of poets and writers that rejected both literary and middle-class conventions. *On the Road,* which sold a half million copies, was Kerouac's semi-autobiographical novel about the travels of Sal Paradise and Dean Moriarty, characters based on Kerouac and fellow Beat Neil Cassady. Accompanied by plenty of sex and drug and alcohol use, their spontaneous trips around the country reflected a distinct lack of purpose. Is there a political message in Kerouac's work or does its message reside in its very lack of political content? Does this excerpt from *On the Road* provide evidence of the constriction of popular culture in the 1950s?

On the Road (1957)

JACK KEROUAC

It was drizzling and mysterious at the beginning of our journey. I could see that it was all going to be one big saga of the mist. "Whooee!" yelled Dean. "Here we go!" And he hunched over the wheel and gunned her; he was back in his element, everybody could see that. We were all delighted, we all realized we were leaving confusion and nonsense behind and performing our one and noble function of the time, *move*. And we moved! We flashed past the mysterious white signs in the night somewhere in New Jersey that say SOUTH (with an arrow) and WEST (with an arrow) and took the south one. New Orleans! It burned in our brains. From the dirty snows of "frosty fagtown New York," as Dean called it, all the way to the greeneries and river smells of old New Orleans at the washed-out bottom of America; then west. Ed was in the back seat; Marylou and Dean and I sat in front and had the warmest talk about the goodness and joy of life. Dean suddenly became tender. "Now dammit, look here, all of you, we all must admit that everything is fine and there's no need in the world to worry, and in fact we should realize what it would mean to us to UNDERSTAND that we're NOT REALLY worried about ANYTHING. Am I right?" We all agreed. "Here we go, we're all together. . . . What did we do in New York? Let's forgive." We all had our spats back there. "That's behind us, merely by miles and inclinations. Now we're heading down to New Orleans to dig Old Bull Lee and ain't that going to be kicks and listen will you to this old tenorman blow his top"—he shot up the radio volume till the car shuddered—"and listen to him tell the story and put down true relaxation and knowledge.". . .

* * *

We arrived in Washington at dawn. It was the day of Harry Truman's inauguration for his second term. Great displays of war might were lined along Pennsylvania Avenue as we rolled by in our battered boat. There were

B-29s, PT boats, artillery, all kinds of war material that looked murderous in the snowy grass; the last thing was a regular small ordinary lifeboat that looked pitiful and foolish. Dean slowed down to look at it. He kept shaking his head in awe. "What are these people up to? Harry's sleeping somewhere in this town. . . . Good old Harry. . . . Man from Missouri, as I am. . . . That must be his own boat."

Dean went to sleep in the back seat and Dunkel drove. We gave him specific instructions to take it easy. No sooner were we snoring than he gunned the car up to eighty, bad bearings and all, and not only that but he made a triple pass at a spot where a cop was arguing with a motorist—he was in the fourth lane of a four-lane highway, going the wrong way. Naturally the cop took after us with his siren whining. We were stopped. He told us to follow him to the station house. There was a mean cop in there who took an immediate dislike to Dean; he could smell jail all over him. He sent his cohort outdoors to question Marylou and me privately. They wanted to know how old Marylou was, they were trying to whip up a Mann Act* idea. But she had her marriage certificate. Then they took me aside alone and wanted to know who was sleeping with Marylou. "Her husband," I said quite simply. They were curious. Something was fishy. They tried some amateur Sherlocking by asking the same questions twice, expecting us to make a slip. I said, "Those two fellows are going back to work on the railroad in California, this is the short one's wife, and I'm a friend on a two-week vacation from college."

The cop smiled and said, "Yeah? Is this really your own wallet?"

Finally the mean one inside fined Dean twenty-five dollars. We told them we only had forty to go all the way to the Coast; they said that made no difference to them. When Dean protested, the mean cop threatened to take him back to Pennsylvania and slap a special charge on him.

"What charge?"

"Never mind what charge. Don't worry about *that*, wise guy."

We had to give them the twenty-five. But first Ed Dunkel, that culprit, offered to go to jail. Dean considered it. The cop was infuriated; he said, "If you let your partner go to jail I'm taking you back to Pennsylvania right now. You hear that?" All we wanted to do was go. "Another speeding ticket in Virginia and you lose your car," said the mean cop as a parting volley. Dean was red in the face. We drove off silently. It was just like an invitation to steal to take our trip-money away from us. They knew we were broke and had no relatives on the road or to wire to for money. The American

*The Mann Act, passed in 1910, prohibited the transportation of women across state lines for immoral purposes.

Source: From *On the Road* by Jack Kerouac, copyright © 1955, 1957 by Jack Kerouac; renewed © 1983 by Stella Kerouac, renewed © 1985 by Stella Kerouac and Jan Kerouac. Used by permission of Viking Penguin, a division of Penguin Group (USA) Inc.

police are involved in psychological warfare against those Americans who don't frighten them with imposing papers and threats. It's a Victorian police force; it peers out of musty windows and wants to inquire about everything, and can make crimes if the crimes don't exist to its satisfaction.

CONCLUSION

Before historians can judge the importance of historical developments, they need to determine their influence. As this chapter makes clear, to do that they must often examine a wide variety of historical artifacts and evidence. Thus, to understand the impact of anticommunist hysteria on American popular culture after World War II, historians must consider everything from images in comic books to trends in popular music. Indeed, one of the biggest challenges confronting historians is to make sense of such seemingly unrelated evidence. To do this, they must synthesize, or combine various parts into a whole. Historical synthesis, in turn, depends on skills emphasized in earlier chapters: the ability to evaluate evidence carefully, to detect causal influences, to understand the role of ideology in history, and to examine the past from many perspectives. In the case of the postwar period, this ability to synthesize allows us to reconstruct what one historian called the "mentality of the fifties" and to understand its impact on American society. This skill, however, can be applied to any historical problem. As we shall see in Chapter 10 on the civil rights movement, for instance, historians must often reconstruct events primarily from the memories of individuals who took part in them. As we shall also see, synthesizing such evidence into a coherent and meaningful story often leads to new insights into the past.

FURTHER READING

Thomas Doherty, *Cold War, Cool Medium: Television, McCarthyism, and American Culture* (New York: Columbia University Press, 2003).

Griffin Fariello, *Red Scare: Memories of the American Inquisition: An Oral History* (New York: W. W. Norton and Company, 1995).

Cyndy Hendershot, *Anti-Communism and Popular Culture in Mid-Century America* (Jefferson, N.C.: McFarland and Company, Inc., 2003).

Edward Pessen, *Losing Our Souls: The American Experience in the Cold War* (Chicago: Ivan R. Dee, 1993).

Nora Sayre, *Running Time: Films of the Cold War* (New York: Dial Press, 1982).

Judith Smith, *Visions of Belonging: Family Stories, Popular Culture, and Postwar Democracy, 1945–1960* (New York: Columbia University Press, 2004).

Wendy L. Wall, *Inventing the "American Way": The Politics of Consensus from the New Deal to the Civil Rights Movement* (New York: Oxford University Press, 2008).

NOTES

1. Quoted in David Caute, *The Great Fear: The Anti-Communist Purge Under Truman and Eisenhower* (New York: Simon and Schuster, 1978), p. 493.
2. Quoted in Griffin Fariello, *Red Scare: Memories of the American Inquisition: An Oral History* (New York: W. W. Norton and Company, 1995), p. 263.
3. Dwight Macdonald, *Against the American Grain: Essays on the Effects of Mass Culture* (New York: Vintage Books, 1952), p. 4.
4. Quoted in Elaine Tyler May, *Homeward Bound: American Families in the Cold War Era* (New York: Basic Books, 1988), p. 16.
5. Quoted in Peter Biskind, *Seeing Is Believing: How Hollywood Taught Us to Stop Worrying and Love the Fifties* (New York: Pantheon Books, 1983), p. 6.
6. Quoted in Nora Sayre, *Running Time: Films of the Cold War* (New York: Dial Press, 1982), p. 61.

Chapter 10

History and Popular Memory: The Civil Rights Movement

The documents in this chapter relate to civil rights activity in Mississippi in the early 1960s and provide perspective on contemporary popular images of the civil rights movement.

Secondary Source

1. *I've Got the Light of Freedom* (1995), CHARLES M. PAYNE

Primary Sources

2. A SNCC Founder Discusses Its Goals (1966)
3. Amzie Moore: Farewell to the N-Double-A (ca. 1975), HOWELL RAINES
4. Chronology of Violence, 1961 (1963)
5. A Sharecropper's Daughter Responds to the Voter Registration Campaign (ca. 1975), FANNIE LOU HAMER
6. A Black Activist Endorses White Participation (ca. 1975), DAVE DENNIS
7. A SNCC Organizer Recalls Federal Intervention (ca. 1975), LAWRENCE GUYOT
8. "A Letter from a Freedom Summer Volunteer" (1964)
9. Freedom School Student Work (1964)
10. An "Insider" Recalls the Divisions in SNCC (1966)
11. Fannie Lou Hamer on the Lessons of 1964 (1967)
12. "What We Want" (1966), STOKELY CARMICHAEL

*O*n August 28, 1963, Martin Luther King, Jr., approached the podium on the steps of the Lincoln Memorial. Before him lay a vast human sea. Perhaps a quarter of a million people, mostly black, sprawled around the Capitol Mall's reflecting pool. The massive assembly had gathered to pressure Congress into passing a civil rights bill that President John Kennedy had proposed earlier that summer. By now, their march on Washington had become, in the words of its organizer A. Philip Randolph, "the largest demonstration in the history of the nation."[1] As he stepped to the microphone, even King was amazed at the size of the crowd.

The civil rights leader was determined not to give Congress any excuse for not passing Kennedy's bill. Thus, his speech was designed to move the throng without sparking civil unrest. He also wanted it to be short, a "sort of Gettysburg Address." Both summoning and echoing Lincoln, King began: "Five score years ago, a great American, in whose symbolic shadows we stand today, signed the Emancipation Proclamation."[2] Like Lincoln's famous battle-field address a hundred years before, King's speech was carefully crafted, but hardly moved his audience. Then the voice of gospel singer Mahalia Jackson called out from behind him: "Tell them about your dream, Martin! Tell them about your dream!"[3] King began again, this time extemporaneously. When he was finished, he had shared his dream for America with his listeners and had given the nation another Gettysburg Address.

King's delivery of his "I Have a Dream" speech remains nearly four decades later one of the most vivid images to emerge from the 1960s. It has become emblematic not only of the march on Washington in 1963, but of the civil rights movement itself. Just as this protest in the summer of 1963 is today associated in the public mind with one man, so increasingly is the entire movement of which King and the Washington march were a part. Yet, as King's popular image has sharpened, other images surrounding the fight for black equality in the 1950s and 1960s have dulled. In other words, the popular memory of the struggle for civil rights has become highly selective. In this chapter, therefore, we examine the struggle for civil rights, how it is remembered today, and the accuracy of our collective memories about it.

SETTING

As the civil rights movement recedes into the past, public interest in it grows. Today, Martin Luther King Day provides Americans an annual reminder about the black fight for equality. Responding to rising popular interest, Hollywood has produced several hit movies in the last several decades about the black struggle in the 1960s. Meanwhile, students of the civil rights movement have written numerous academic and popular accounts since the late 1960s. Historians' views regarding the movement have not remained static, though, and many of them now question the contemporary popular views of it.

In the last three decades or so, most popular and many scholarly examinations of the civil rights movement have focused mainly on its leaders, especially Martin Luther King, Jr. In these accounts, the movement's main goal was to secure federal action in the area of civil rights and the primary initiative for black rights came from a few men—civil rights leaders and, sometimes, even white politicians. It was directed, furthermore, by the leaders of such national organizations as the National Association for the Advancement of Colored People (NAACP), the Congress of Racial Equality (CORE), and the Southern Christian Leadership Conference (SCLC), a view supported by the prominent role that these groups played in some important events in the struggle for black rights. Since its founding by W. E. B. Du Bois and others in 1909, the NAACP had engaged in a long series of legal battles against racial discrimination, including the one that led to the landmark public school desegregation ruling in *Brown v. Board of Education* in 1954. Founded in 1942, CORE began a battle for integration during World War II using nonviolent protests to desegregate public facilities. By 1962, the Chicago-based organization had launched the Freedom Rides, during which black and white riders attempting to desegregate the South's interstate bus systems were met with mob violence. The SCLC, founded by King and other black activists in the wake of the Montgomery bus boycott of 1956, had deep roots in Southern black churches. By the early 1960s, the Atlanta-based and King-led organization was engaged with other groups in nonviolent direct action to promote desegregation, most noticeably in Albany, Georgia, in 1961 and 1962 and in Birmingham, Alabama, in 1963.

Prominent though these groups were in a number of civil rights battles, some historians in the 1980s began to challenge the view that the movement could be understood primarily as the work of a few national organizations or their leaders. Without denying the important—even heroic—role played by King, they criticized accounts of the civil rights movement that presented him as its creator and leader. They also charged that these accounts too often concentrated on such big events as the Montgomery bus boycott, the Birmingham marches, and the march on Washington, and thus overlooked the deep roots of the movement in the community-organizing efforts of determined activists as early as the 1930s. In fact, historians' complaints often echoed those voiced by many former civil rights activists, who charged that a complex and multifaceted struggle was frequently oversimplified and distorted in history books and in the news media. As a result, they said, the concerns and contributions of thousands of men and women who participated in the black struggle were ignored. Some critics were especially disturbed by popular accounts that portrayed the federal government—even the Federal Bureau of Investigation—as collaborators of the movement, as did *Mississippi Burning*, the 1989 movie about the murder of three civil rights workers in 1964. As one civil rights activist (and wife of another) expressed it in 1988, "I have three children, and I have read interpretations that make me cry, to think that my boys would be left with such ridiculous explanations of what their mother and father were doing in those days. . . ."[4]

Sharing these concerns, some scholars began to take a closer look at the civil rights movement at the local level. The leaders of national civil rights organizations, they concluded, did not initiate some of the well-publicized demonstrations—or countless other protests in communities throughout the South. Nor did King and other leaders control the men and women who did. Rather, there was frequent tension between local and national leaders over tactics, goals, and ideology. Local leaders were not that interested in launching protests to gain national attention and spur the passage of civil rights legislation in Congress. Instead, they were often more concerned with empowering blacks in their own communities, building local institutions, and—in the words of historian Clayborne Carson—creating "new social identities for participants and for all Afro-Americans."[5] In fact, as they studied these local struggles, some scholars began to question the appropriateness of the very term "civil rights movement" to describe these broader goals. More accurate, suggested Carson, is the term "black freedom struggle."[6]

Increased interest in the local roots of the civil rights struggle naturally led historians to look more closely at such organizations as the Student Nonviolent Coordinating Committee (SNCC—pronounced "Snick"), which launched numerous grassroots organizing efforts across the South in the early 1960s. Founded by students who sat in the "whites only" sections of North Carolina lunch counters and waited to be assaulted and arrested, SNCC quickly moved from sit-ins to a broad challenge to the racial status quo. It is perhaps best known for its efforts to register black voters in Mississippi. There, SNCC activists worked with CORE and the NAACP to set up the Council of Federated Organizations (COFO) in 1962 to engage in a Voter Education Project. The COFO had registered more than a half million black voters in the South by 1964, but it had made little headway in Mississippi, where fewer than 4,000 voters had been registered and SNCC organizers had become the victims of vigilante and police attacks. Attempting to turn the tide in 1964, SNCC launched the Mississippi Freedom Summer Project, which brought nine hundred college students into the state. The students assisted with voter registration and enlisted support for the Mississippi Freedom Democratic Party, established to challenge the state's white Democratic Party. By one tally, Freedom Summer was marked by a thousand arrests, thirty bombings, eighty beatings, and at least six murders of civil rights workers, including those of COFO local organizers Michael Schwerner and James Chaney and summer volunteer James Goodman. By that fall, about 17,000 blacks had filled out registration forms, but only 1,600 had been allowed to register. Nonetheless, the involvement of affluent white college students in Freedom Summer had focused national attention on conditions in Mississippi. By then, SNCC's efforts in Mississippi had brought other changes as well. Listening to the people involved in them, many historians argue, provides a different view of the civil rights struggle than traditionally presented in history books—or on Martin Luther King Day.

INVESTIGATION

Because the postwar black struggle for civil rights spanned many years, encompassed a variety of concerns, and involved numerous organizations and literally hundreds of thousands of participants, it is not surprising that scholars' assessments of it differ. Nor is it surprising that they have often looked primarily at Martin Luther King, Jr., and other leaders who operated on a broad stage and eventually captured national attention. This chapter, however, focuses on lesser-known participants operating in a narrower place and time—Mississippi in the early 1960s. More specifically, it considers the activities of the Student Nonviolent Coordinating Committee and its efforts to register voters and mobilize blacks in other ways. Much of the history presented here is based on the recollections of individuals who helped to make it. As you evaluate these sources, keep in mind that historians must treat such firsthand accounts with the same care that they exercise with any historical evidence. As we saw in earlier chapters, primary sources often reflect the biases or point of view of those who created them. Furthermore, many of these sources are recollections of events years after they occurred, and, as we all know, time often changes our perspective on events. Nonetheless, the participants in the civil rights movement have valuable experiences and memories that can help us evaluate *popular* memories of it. Your main job, then, is twofold. You must first determine what a grassroots view reveals about the origins of the civil rights struggle, its goals, and impact. Then you can assess the concerns raised by one historian about Americans' collective memories about it. Addressing the following questions will assist your investigation:

1. **According to historian Charles Payne in Source 1, how have many popular and scholarly accounts distorted our understanding of the civil rights movement?** According to Payne, how does an understanding of grassroots civil rights organizing efforts in Mississippi offer a more accurate view of the movement than focusing on such leaders as Martin Luther King, Jr.?

2. **What do Payne's essay and the primary sources reveal about the goals of the civil rights movement?** To what extent were the goals of those involved in the civil rights organizing efforts in Mississippi in the early 1960s achieved?

3. **What do these sources reveal about the most important obstacles confronting the civil rights movement?** What do they reveal about the divisions within it?

4. **How does a "bottom-up" approach offer a different view of the black struggle from one that focuses on the movement's leaders?** How did the sources in this chapter alter *your* views about the civil rights movement?

Before you begin, read your textbook's discussion of the civil rights movement. Pay particular attention to its treatment of Martin Luther King, Jr., and other leaders of the movement. Note what it says about the Student Nonviolent Coordinating Committee and about grassroots organizing of blacks in the South. In your textbook's account, does the impetus for the civil rights struggle come from above or below, that is, from leaders of civil rights organizations or from the efforts of many less prominent African Americans to change the racial status quo?

SECONDARY SOURCE

In this selection, historian Charles Payne examines the organizing efforts of SNCC activists who participated in the Council of Federated Organizations' Voter Education Project in Mississippi, which began in 1962. This excerpt from his study of SNCC's grassroots organizing in Mississippi focuses on the work that led up to Freedom Summer in 1964 and some of the accomplishments of the organizers there. In it, Payne discusses the activities of such COFO organizers as SNCC's Robert Moses, a Harvard University graduate student and director of the Voter Education Project; Dave Dennis of CORE, who served as Moses's assistant; and COFO president Aaron Henry of the Mississippi NAACP. Payne's account also includes many other people: SNCC staff member Fannie Lou Hamer, a sharecropper's daughter who had been shot at and beaten for her attempts to register to vote; Ella Jo Baker, a founder of SNCC and organizer of the North Carolina student sit-ins in 1960; and other less prominent SNCC workers. As you read this discussion, determine what Payne sees as the most important effects—and lessons—of the SNCC/COFO Mississippi organizing activity. What roles do Martin Luther King, Jr., and other civil rights leaders play in these efforts? What are the main goals of the Mississippi organizers? What accounts for the distortions in the popular and media accounts of the civil rights movement, according to Payne?

I've Got the Light of Freedom (1995)
CHARLES M. PAYNE

As late as 1960, fewer than two percent of Mississippi's Black adults were registered to vote. During the early summer of 1962, a handful of youthful organizers fanned out across the state to stimulate voter-registration drives. Seldom more than two or three to a county at first, they went into towns that

Source: From Charles Payne, *I've Got the Light of Freedom: The Community Organizing Tradition in the Mississippi Freedom Struggle,* 1995. Copyright © 1995 Regents of the University of California. Reprinted by permission of the publisher, the University of California Press.

few Americans had ever heard of—Greenwood, Hattiesburg, Holly Springs, Ruleville, Greenville. The organizers represented a coalition of civil rights groups, but most owed their primary allegiance to the Student Nonviolent Coordinating Committee, . . . the organization that had, under the watchful eye of Ella Baker, grown out of the sit-ins of 1960.

Wherever they were sent, the civil rights activists found that their initial reception by local Blacks was less than enthusiastic. The movement was generally dismissed as "dat mess." Reprisals were virtually certain. Those who were even thought to be interested in the movement might lose their jobs. Those who did join could expect to be shot at and to have their churches bombed and their homes targeted by arsonists. People who were able to survive the winter months only because of surplus commodities from the federal government could expect to lose them. Farmers who needed loans to get their crops started in the spring could expect their credit to be withdrawn. People who needed medical care could expect it to be refused. As one white landowner said, with completely unintended irony, to a Black family as he kicked them off his land, "Your food, your work and your very lives depend on good-hearted white people."

Nonetheless, a significant number of the Black residents in towns across the state eventually chose to cast their lot with the movement. The first organizers to come to Greenwood, near the heart of the Mississippi Delta, had to sleep catch-as catch can. Within a year, the level of movement activity was sufficient to bring the normal functioning of the city to a virtual standstill. Within two years, Black Greenwood was so much behind the movement that it could have slept a small army of civil rights workers (and did). It was one of the decade's earliest successful campaigns in the rural South. . . .

. . . The forty-one workers [of the Mississippi field staff] comprised about one-third of the total SNCC staff in the Deep South. Thirty-five of them were Black. Two of the six whites and twenty-five of the Blacks came from the Deep South. The white youngsters and most of the northern Blacks came from middle-class homes; their fathers were ministers or teachers or civil-service workers. All of the southern workers came from homes where the mothers had been maids or domestic workers, and most of the fathers had been farmers, factory workers, truck drivers, and construction workers. The ages ran from fifteen to over fifty, but most were in their late teens or early twenties. The staff, then, was mostly Black, mostly southern, mostly from working-class backgrounds. . . .

. . . By July [1963], thirteen hundred county residents had attempted to register, unsuccessfully, of course, in all but a few cases. COFO found an alternative way of encouraging political participation. Some volunteer law students found a Reconstruction era law that allowed unregistered citizens to vote provided they submitted an affidavit asserting they were qualified to vote. On that basis, COFO decided to participate in the gubernatorial primary scheduled for August 6.

The idea was to encourage as many people as possible to vote by affidavit. COFO people would serve as poll watchers. People reluctant to go to the polls could cast a freedom ballot that would be collected and disposed of by COFO. For six weeks, they explained the idea through canvassing and mass meetings, teaching people to prepare sample affidavits, how to find polling places, and the like. Response was good. During the week before the primary mass meetings were held nightly with an average attendance of two hundred. . . .

The night of the election, SCLC's Andy Young and SNCC chairman John Lewis spoke at [a] mass meeting that reflected the celebratory air of the day. "Difficult to capture," SNCC's Mike Miller wrote, "is the mood of the day—the air of jubilation at going to vote, and the infusion of this spirit in the Greenwood staff.". . .

. . . Encouraged by the participation in the primary, COFO decided to take part in the election that fall by holding its own registration and running its own candidates. The Freedom Vote was intended, first, to show that the masses of Negroes did in fact want to vote. (Polls at the time showed that forty percent of white southerners did not think Negroes really wanted to vote.) Second, it was intended to mock the legitimacy of the regular election by making the point that the candidates elected did not represent hundreds of thousands of Negroes. Aaron Henry ran for governor, with Ed King, a white native Mississippian and chaplain at Tougaloo, as his running mate. If Henry had suffered less than other leaders from repression in the 1950s, he made up for it in the sixties. He was arrested for leading a boycott of Clarksdale stores, his wife lost her job, he was arrested on allegations of child molestation, his home had been either firebombed or hit by lightning, and in July 1963 he spent a week on the chain gang, for parading without a permit.

Those who were registered—fewer than twenty-five thousand Negroes statewide—were encouraged to vote in the regular election and write in the names of the Freedom candidates. Everyone else was encouraged to vote in COFO's mock election, allowing them to register their opinions without exposing themselves to much danger.

There was nothing mock about the way COFO approached the election. They set up an elaborate statewide campaign organization, took out newspaper and television ads, and held rallies across the state. By October, Aaron Henry was making a speech a night. In mid-month, the campaign received some extra manpower. Eighty to ninety college students recruited by Allard Lowenstein from Stanford and Yale took two weeks off to help with the campaign. . . .

The vote was a great success across the state. Perhaps eighty thousand Freedom ballots were cast in COFO's first statewide organizing campaign, less than half of what COFO had hoped for but enough to make the point. National media coverage was considerable, due in no small part to the media's considerable interest in the white students from Yale and Stanford. Given that, why not bring an even larger number of students into the state for the following summer? The idea was first fully broached at a meeting in Greenville in November 1963. More media attention could lead to a greater degree of protection for civil rights workers. Most COFO staff . . . opposed the idea. Even before the idea was raised, there had been some discomfort among veteran staff about the slowly growing role of whites in the movement. It contradicted the principle of developing organizers where they found them. Given their education, whites coming into the movement were going to gravitate to leadership positions, supplanting local people, who were beginning to take on more leadership responsibility. If lives were at risk, it was largely the lives of COFO organizers, and most COFO staff preferred continuing running that risk to risking the long-term viability of their community-building efforts. Tactical issues aside, there were some who just plain didn't want to be bothered with a bunch of white folks on a daily basis. For that matter, the idea of bringing in outsiders, had that been Black staff from the Atlanta office, didn't sit well with some veteran staff members, mostly southern Blacks, who had done the most and risked the most to build a viable movement.

Bob Moses, Lawrence Guyot, Mrs. [Fannie Lou] Hamer, and CORE's Dave Dennis were among the proponents. Mrs. Hamer told opponents, "If we're trying to break down segregation, we can't segregate ourselves." Other proponents saw real risks in the idea but thought that the potential benefits outweighed them and that some way had to be found to offer some protection to the local people with whom they were working. Older local leaders were generally very much in favor of bringing the students in. The debate, in SNCC style, went on over the course of that winter.

SNCC's initial community-organizing venture in the state had been brought to a halt by the murder of Herbert Lee.* Another series of killings in the same part of the state, the Southwest, ultimately ended the arguments over Freedom Summer. . . .

. . . They had watched Herbert Lee get gunned down and couldn't do anything about it. Now at least they were in a position to force some national attention onto Mississippi, thereby putting pressure on the federal government to protect Black life in the state. It was self-consciously an attempt to use the nation's racism, its tendency to react only when white life was endangered, as a point of leverage. Moses and Dave Dennis put all of their authority behind the Summer Project. . . .

Since the summer involved large numbers of white people, we have a great deal of literature on it, far more than on the three years of organizing that preceded it. [One aspect] of that period [is] especially interesting here: Freedom Schools. . . . When Ella Baker first went to New York in 1927 she organized a Negro history club for youngsters at the Harlem Y. This may have been her first "political" act in the city. No doubt, she saw it as a way to raise

---

*Herbert Lee, who assisted Robert Moses in voter registration, was killed in September 1961 by a Mississippi state legislator, who was acquitted by a coroner's jury.

consciousness, to help people develop themselves. The Freedom Schools in Mississippi were an experiment in the same tradition. By late 1963, strategic thinking in SNCC was increasingly concerned with "parallel institutions."

If existing institutions did not meet the needs of Black Mississippians, what kinds of institutions would? Freedom Schools were one reflection of that thinking, but they also exemplified a much older tendency within the community-organizing tradition. During one of the early planning sessions for the summer, Charlie Cobb, the Howard University student who had first come to the Delta in the fall of 1962, proposed a summer Freedom School program "to fill an intellectual and creative vacuum in the lives of young Negro Mississippians, and to get them to articulate their own desires, demands and questions . . . to stand up in classrooms around the state and ask their teachers a real question." The schools were expected to be "an educational experience for students which will make it possible for them to challenge the myths of our society, to perceive more clearly its realities and to find alternatives and ultimately, new directions for action." Cobb envisioned the schools handling perhaps a thousand students of high school age. In fact, somewhere between twenty-five hundred and three thousand students actually showed up, and their ages ranged from seven to seventy. Cobb's original idea of having one teacher for every four or five kids had to be dropped, and the number of schools was increased from twenty-five to forty-one.

Part of the classwork consisted of traditional academic subjects. In Mississippi, though, traditional subjects were often not available in Black schools. Publicly supported Black schools tended not to offer typing, foreign languages, art, drama, or college-preparatory mathematics. Apart from whatever intrinsic interest they held, these subjects were popular with students partly because they symbolized equality. It was the Citizenship Curriculum that made the schools distinctive. It was built around a set of core questions, including:

1. What does the majority culture have that we want?
2. What does the majority culture have that we don't want?
3. What do we have that we want to keep?

One unit of the curriculum asked students to compare their social reality with that of others in terms of education, housing, and employment; one section called for them to compare the adjustment of Negroes to Mississippi with the adjustment of Jews to Nazi Germany. Another unit was intended to convince students that "running away" to the North wasn't going to solve anything. The "Introducing the Power Structure" unit tried "to create an awareness that some people profit by the pain of others or by misleading them." The unit on poor whites tried to help students understand how the power structure manipulated the fears of poor whites. "Material Things and Soul Things" was a critique of materialism. The last area of the curriculum was a study of the movement itself. The section on nonviolence made sure to present it as something beyond a mere refraining from doing anyone physical harm; students were admonished to practice nonviolence of speech and thought as well. The curriculum reflects how far discussion within SNCC had progressed beyond a narrow concern with civil rights. . . .

. . . The questions SNCC was raising about the nature of leadership and how leadership potential might be developed, the sheer persistence of organizers, the continuity of 1960s organizing with that done in earlier years, the questioning of the basic premises of American society—none of these were likely to become a key part of the story as framed by the press, and partly for that reason they never became a part of collective consciousness about the movement in the way that the "Big Events" did. . . .

. . . Much of SNCC's organizing was a response to their assumption that national institutions, including the press, were more interested in what happened to whites than to Blacks. The press had shown little interest in the mock elections that SNCC was running in Mississippi in the fall of 1963, but when white volunteers—the students from Yale and Stanford—came, the elections became a "story." Freedom Summer, of course, was predicated on the idea that privileged white volunteers would bring the concern of the nation with them. The unprecedented media coverage of the summer concentrated not on local Blacks or experienced organizers but on the volunteers. That surprised no one in SNCC, but it was nonetheless embittering. . . .

The undervaluation of the leadership role played by ordinary people corresponded to an overconcentration on the role of national leaders, Dr. King in particular. In 1963, when SCLC was about to announce the accords that had been reached with the power structure in Birmingham, it was decided that Fred Shuttlesworth, by far the most important local leader, should speak first at the press conference. The national press corps had hardly assembled to hear Fred Shuttlesworth. "Although Shuttlesworth announced the terms of the settlement, the reporters would not be satisfied until they heard it from King himself, as most of their readers knew nothing of Shuttlesworth.". . . In deciding that Shuttlesworth was not a part of the story, the press missed an opportunity to learn something about the historical depth of the struggle and the variety of leadership styles that sustained it. . . .

Scholarly and popular histories of the movement have traditionally reflected the same underlying analytical frames as did contemporaneous media. That has begun to change within the last decade, encouraged by a chorus of complaints from movement participants that they could not recognize their own movement in most histories. Even taking recent improvements into account, we are far short of what we might hope for. The issues that are invisible to the media and to the current generation of Black activists are still almost as invisible to scholars. . . .

As academic histories come to reflect a greater variety of social perspectives, it is not clear how popular culture will be affected. It may be that the top-down . . . conception of the movement is so deeply ingrained in popular culture, so constantly reinforced and so consistent with our national vanities, that new scholarship will be unable to dent it. We are likely to soon see a wave of scholarship that paints a more careful conception of Martin Luther King's role, but nonetheless, every January, the airwaves will be filled with "I Have a Dream."

Most of us who study the movement want to believe that our work can have some impact. Addressing an audience of scholars and movement activists, CORE's James Farmer said:

> I think that knowledge of the past is vital but historical knowledge is not an end in itself. The more we learn about the past, the more we must recognize that we learn about it in order to bring a more humane society into being in this country. Otherwise, historical knowledge is meaningless.

None of us understands fully how to use what we know of the past to shape a more just present, but we can be sure that social analysis which does not somehow make it clear that ordinary, flawed, everyday sorts of human beings frequently manage to make extraordinary contributions to social change, social analysis which does not make it easier for people to see in themselves and in those around them the potential for controlling their own lives takes us in the wrong direction. . . . Alice Walker has written that if the movement has done nothing else it has given Blacks a history of men (and women) better than presidents. Perhaps not. Even at this late date, at the level of popular culture the history has been largely homogenized, the men and women better than presidents largely forgotten, which may make it more difficult to produce any more like them.

PRIMARY SOURCES

Most of the sources in this section deal with the grassroots organizing efforts in Mississippi before and during Freedom Summer in 1964. Many of the sources are from the memoirs or oral histories of the participants in this activity. In other words, they reflect the *personal* memories of those involved in the civil rights struggle. As you read them, ask yourself whether they support Charles Payne's argument in Source 1 that journalists and historians have distorted our *collective* memory of the black struggle for equality by focusing too narrowly on civil rights leaders.

SNCC and the Early Efforts to Organize Mississippi

The sources in this section deal with SNCC's roots in the student sit-ins and with the attempts of civil rights activists to organize Mississippi in the years before the Freedom Summer in 1964. As you read these sources consider what they reveal about the differences between SNCC and other civil rights organizations. What do they demonstrate about the obstacles confronting those who challenged the racial status quo? What impact did this early organizing have? Why was SNCC more effective at grassroots organizing than other civil rights organizations, according to these participants in early civil rights activity?

> **2** Ella Jo Baker called the conference that led to the founding of SNCC and exercised a strong influence on it in its early years. In an oral history conducted by a Harvard University graduate student in 1966, Baker discussed the organization's move from the sit-ins to other activities, its goals, and its differences from other civil rights organizations.

A SNCC Founder Discusses Its Goals (1966)

Q. What is the basic goal of SNCC?

A. To change society so that the have-nots can share in it. . . .

Q. Could you discuss in detail SNCC's move from the sit-ins to other things?

A. In the early days, there was little communication, except on a highly personal basis, as between friends and relatives, in the sit-in movement. I had originally thought of pulling together 120–125 sit-in leaders for a leadership training conference—but the rate of spread of the sit-ins was so rapid and the response so electrifying, both North and South, that the meeting ended up with 300 people. Many colleges sent representatives; there was a great thrust of human desire and effort. The first sit-in took place February 1, 1960; the meeting in Raleigh was around April 17, 1960, for three days. Nineteen colleges above the Mason-Dixon Line sent representatives, most of them white. There were so many Northerners that at the meeting it was decided that Northerners could not participate in decision-making. This decision was made sort of by mutual agreement after discussion, because the Northerners recognized that the thrust of the action came from the South. They had been drawn magnetically to the movement because of their great admiration for the wonderful, brave Southerners. The Southerners wanted it that way, at that meeting, because of the divergent levels of political thinking both

Source: Reprinted with the permission of the publisher from Emily Stoper, *The Student Nonviolent Coordinating Committee: The Growth of Radicalism in a Civil Rights Organization* (Brooklyn, N.Y.: Carlson Publishing Inc., 1989).

within the Northern group and between the North and the politically unsophisticated Deep South. (There were many representatives from Georgia, Louisiana, Alabama, although only token representation from Mississippi.) There was an outstanding leadership group from Nashville. It was a basic insecurity that caused the South to keep the North out of decision-making. The North and South used different terminology, had trouble communicating. This has cropped up again in SNCC. It became more subdued in the summer of '64 when there was a real program to be carried out. . . .

Moreover, some of those who took part (I realize in retrospect) saw a basic difference in the role of leadership in [SCLC and SNCC]. In SCLC, the organization revolved around King; in SNCC, the leadership was group-centered (although I may have had some influence). Southern members of the movement were somewhat in awe of each other. There was a feeling that it was the "dawn of a new era," that something new and great was happening and that only they could chart the course of history. A strong equalitarian philosophy prevailed. There was a belief you could just go into an area and organize if you had had no leadership experience. SNCC rejected the idea of a God-sent leader. A basic goal was to make it unnecessary for the people to depend on a leader, for them to be strong themselves. SNCC hoped to spread into a big movement, to develop leadership from among the people. At first it had a rotating chairmanship, for periods of about two months. Marion Barry was the first chairman. He was selected at the Raleigh meeting as temporary chairman with no opposition. This was in deference to the role of the Nashville movement, of which he was a leader. (Nashville had already had mass arrests after which the demonstrators had decided to stay in jail.) Marion had already demonstrated his capacity both to suffer and to confront the white man. He was seen as a real martyr. The Nashville group brought with it the influence of the Reverend James Lawson, who believed in nonviolence as a religious principle. . . .

Q. What is SNCC's basic goal, that makes it unique?

A. The NAACP, Urban League, etc., do not *change* society, they want to get in. It's a combination of concern with the black goal for itself and, beyond that, with the whole society, because this is the acid test of whether the outs can get in and share in equality and worth. By worth, I mean creativity, a contribution to society. SNCC defines itself in terms of the blacks but is concerned with all excluded people.

Q. Has there been a change in SNCC's goal over time?

A. During the sit-in movement, we were concerned with segregation of public accommodations. But even then we recognized that that was only a surface goal. These obvious "irritants" had to be removed first; this was natural. Some people probably thought this in itself would change race relations; others saw deeper. . . .

Q. Would you tell in detail how SNCC's policy changed after the sit-ins?

A. From the start, there were those who knew sitting-in would not bring basic changes. Youngsters who had not thought it through had not bargained with the intractable resistance of the power structure. The notion of "appeals to the conscience" assumed that there is a conscience, and after a while the question began to be raised, *is* there a conscience? Students, because they were most out front in the movement, began to see this and its political connotations. People began asking who *really* controlled things.

<table>
<tr><td>3</td><td>Amzie Moore was a World War II veteran and an early leader in the black struggle in Mississippi. In this oral history conducted by a white Southern journalist in the mid-1970s, Moore recalled his early involvement with the NAACP and later with SNCC. (Those parts of the interview that are indented and set off with a line in the left margin are out of sequence. They were transposed by the original author for greater clarity.)</td></tr>
</table>

Amzie Moore: Farewell to the N-Double-A (ca. 1975)
HOWELL RAINES

When did you get involved in the NAACP?

Well, I came out of the Army in nineteen hundred and forty-six, and in nineteen hundred and fifty-one, somebody held a meeting in a church and elected me president of the NAACP, and I'd never been [to a meeting]. Well, I think at that time they were just passing the buck, getting rid of it as a hot potato. And I decided maybe I wasn't going to serve, and then finally it was kinda forced upon me, and I just went on.

Forced upon you in what way?

Well, by people I suppose. I clearly understood that the individuals who met and had me elected were people who just really didn't wanna fool with it, 'cause they weren't gonna fall out with their white friends on account of it. So they just said, "Well, here's what we'll do. We'll just move it off to

Source: "Amzie Moore", from *My Soul Is Rested* by Howell Raines, copyright © 1977 by Howell Raines. Used by permission of G. P. Putnam's Sons, a division of Penguin Group (USA) Inc.

him. He's young and able to take it." I think that's how I became involved. Finally enrolled about six hundred members, became vice president-at-large of the state conference of the NAACP branches, and up until SNCC came in, it was a matter of legal maneuvering. Nobody dared move a peg without some lawyer advisin' him.

Were you able to really accomplish much in the Delta through that sort of . . .

I don't think so really, because, you see, the base of operations was too far away. We met in Jackson. That's a hundred and thirty sumpin' miles from here. We had a nice crowd, but we didn't know about methods and procedures for demanding things. . . .

Anyway, in nineteen hundred and fifty-five, Emmett Till was found dead in the Tallahatchie River, and they had newspapers from all over the continent North America, some from India, and it was the best advertised lynching that I had ever heard. Personally, I think this was the beginning of the Civil Rights Movement in Mississippi in the twentieth century. . . . From that point on, Mississippi began to move.

Following the Freedom Bus Ride in nineteen hundred and sixty-one, I was invited to Atlanta by Bob Moses.

How did you meet him?

He came down and spent a while and invited me to the meeting in Atlanta. It must have been the spring before I went over the following fall.

Why did he come to you?

Now, that's the sixty-four-thousand-dollar question, and I don't know until yet why Bob came to me, but he found me and spent most of the time that summer at my house. In the fall of that year, I went to Atlanta to the meeting of the Student Nonviolent Coordinating Committee and invited them to come to Mississippi. So they came, set up their first office in Jackson, Mississippi, and then kind of spread it out all over the state. Activities were going on in McComb, Jackson, Indianola, Cleveland, Ruleville. . . . They had more courage than any group of people I've ever met. . . .

In that initial meeting that you had with Moses, did y'all discuss voter-registration tactics?

Well. . . Moses and I talked about it when he was here visiting me in the summer. The first thing we had to try to figure out: How can we expose the conditions in Mississippi with reference to people voting? How can we uncover what is covered? So then we got together, we went into homes, we persuaded people to go up and register. We had cameras from everywhere, television, the newspapers, and the whole thing was brought out. . . .

You knew they would be turned away?

Oh, we were well aware of that. . . .

Was it generally known that you were working with SNCC?

I think so. Of course, there was a little jealousy at that time between the N-Double-A-C-P and SNCC. The N-Double-A-C-P at that time seemed to have been a legal organization that required going to court and this type thing.

SNCC was an organization of strong, intelligent, young people who had no fear of death and certainly did not hesitate to get about the business for which they came here. It wasn't a matter of meeting in the Masonic Order or office or at a church to do this. They met anywhere, at any time. One great thing I think was introduced in the South with reference to SNCC's tactics was the business of organizing leadership. If 'leven people went to jail this evening who the power structure considered leaders, tomorrow morning you had 'leven more out there. [Laughs] And the next morning 'leven more.

I found that SNCC was for business, live or die, sink or swim, survive or perish. They were moving, and nobody seemed to worry about whether he was gonna live or die. [Laughs]

. . . Are you gonna sit here and tell me that didn't cross your mind?

Sho' I was scared to death. Now don't misunderstand me. [Laughs] Yeah. . . . It came across my mind because I was constantly threatened. I was called at night and told, "In five minutes, your house gon' blow up." If I'd run out, I coulda been shot, and if I had stayed in, I coulda been blown to pieces. So then, here I am between two opinions. I've got to decide to stay in the house or run out. I mean, What's "safe" . . .?

Did you get any adverse reaction from your N-Double-A-C-P associates when you . . .

[Laughs] When I went over to SNCC? Well, naturally.

What form did it take?

Well . . . it was like, "Maybe these kids don't know what they're doing. . . . It could get a lotta people hurt." I think what I really did was stayed away from N-Double-A-C-P meetings for years. Now, I didn't join an organization with SNCC. I just worked with 'em. That's more or less how it was. Now, the NAACP certainly has done a lot of great things. Don't misunderstand me. . . . Mr. Wilkins, he's a fine man. He'd fly down and hold our conferences and hold our annual "days" and raise our freedom money and be advised by different people outa New York office. And that was it. . . .

> But when an individual stood at a courthouse like the courthouse in Green-wood and in Greenville and watched tiny figures [of the SNCC workers] standing against a huge column . . . [against white] triggermen and drivers and lookout men riding in automobiles with automatic guns . . . how *they* *stood* . . . how gladly they got in the front of that line, those leaders, and went to jail! It didn't seem to bother 'em. It was an awakening for me. . . .

Why did SCLC never create the kind of impact on Mississippi that it did in other Southern states?

Well, SCLC had a group of preachers following it. Now don't misunderstand me, I think the world and all of ministers. I don't have anything against ministers, but their outlook was entirely different from SNCC's young people. Kids wore blue jeans, and I used to have sleeping in my house six and eight and ten, twelve, who had come. I bought a lots [*sic*] of cheese, and always we'd eat cheese and peaches, and sometimes we would get spaghetti and ground chuck or ground beef and make a huge tub of meatballs and spaghetti to fill everybody up. And this is how we were, and everybody knew they were there, wasn't any secret. They'd eat that without complaining. . . . You *know* they're being really persecuted and pushed to the wall, and they always had a smile and was always ready to try to do something. . . . To me, it was just a new leader. . . .

SNCC's civil rights organizing drew a quick response from many white Mississippians, as this record indicates.

Chronology of Violence, 1961 (1963)

AUGUST 15, AMITE COUNTY: Robert Moses, Student Nonviolent Coordinating Committee (SNCC) registration worker, and three Negroes who had tried unsuccessfully to register in Liberty, were driving toward McComb when

Source: From Papers of the Highlander Education and Research Center, State Historical Society of Wisconsin. Reprinted by permission.

a county officer stopped them. He asked if Moses was the man ". . . who's been trying to register our niggers." All were taken to court and Moses was arrested for "impeding an officer in the discharge of his duties," fined $50 and spent two days in jail.

AUGUST 22, AMITE COUNTY: Robert Moses went to Liberty with three Negroes, who made an unsuccessful attempt to register. A block from the courthouse, Moses was attacked and beaten by Billy Jack Caston, the sheriff's first cousin. Eight stitches were required to close a wound in Moses' head. Caston was acquitted of assault charges by an all-white jury before a justice of the peace.

AUGUST 26, MC COMB, PIKE COUNTY: Hollis Watkins, 20, and Elmer Hayes, 20, SNCC workers, were arrested while staging a sit-in at the F. W. Woolworth store and charged with breach of the peace. They spent 36 days in jail.

AUGUST 27 AND 29, MC COMB, PIKE COUNTY: Five Negro students from a local high school were convicted of breach of the peace following a sit-in at a variety store and bus terminal. They were sentenced to a $400 fine each and eight months in jail. One of these students, a girl of 15, was turned over to juvenile authorities, released, subsequently rearrested, and sentenced to 12 months in a state school for delinquents.

AUGUST 29, MC COMB, PIKE COUNTY: Two Negro leaders were arrested in McComb as an aftermath of the sit-in protest march on city hall, charged with contributing to the delinquency of minors. They were Curtis C. Bryant of McComb, an official of the NAACP, and Cordelle Reagan, of SNCC. Each arrest was made on an affidavit signed by Police Chief George Guy, who said he had information that the two ". . . were behind some of this racial trouble."

AUGUST 30, MC COMB, PIKE COUNTY: SNCC workers Brenda Travis, 16, Robert Talbert, 19, and Isaac Lewis, 20, staged a sit-in in the McComb terminal of the Greyhound bus lines. They were arrested on charges of breach of the peace and failure to obey a policeman's order to move on. They spent 30 days in jail.

SEPTEMBER 5, LIBERTY, AMITE COUNTY: Travis Britt, SNCC registration worker, was attacked and beaten by whites on the courthouse lawn. Britt was accompanied at the time by Robert Moses. Britt said one man hit him more than 20 times. The attackers drove away in a truck.

SEPTEMBER 7, TYLERTOWN, WALTHALL COUNTY: John Hardy, SNCC registration worker, took two Negroes to the county courthouse to register. The registrar told them he ". . . wasn't registering voters" that day. When the three turned to leave, Registrar John Q. Wood took a pistol from his desk and struck Hardy over the head from behind. Hardy was arrested and charged with disturbing the peace.

SEPTEMBER 13, JACKSON, HINDS COUNTY: Fifteen Episcopal ministers (among them three Negroes) were arrested for asking to be served at the lunch counter of the Greyhound bus terminal. They were charged with inviting a breach of the peace. They were found not guilty of the charge on May 21, 1962, by County judge Russell Moore.

SEPTEMBER 25, LIBERTY, AMITE COUNTY: Herbert Lee, a Negro who had been active in voter registration, was shot and killed by white state representative E. H. Hurst in downtown Liberty. No prosecution was undertaken, the authorities explaining that the representative had shot in self-defense.

OCTOBER 4, MC COMB, PIKE COUNTY: The five students who were arrested as a result of the August 29 sit-in in McComb returned to school, but were refused admittance. At that, 116 students walked out and paraded downtown to the city hall in protest. Police arrested the entire crowd, but later released all but 19, all of whom were 18 years old or older. They were charged with breach of the peace and contributing to the delinquency of minors and allowed to go free on bail totalling $3,700. At the trial on October 31, Judge Brumfield, finding the students guilty, and sentencing each to a $500 fine and six months in jail, said: "Some of you are local residents, some of you are outsiders. Those of you who are local residents are like sheep being led to the slaughter. If you continue to follow the advise [*sic*] of outside agitators, you will be like sheep and be slaughtered."

---

5 Fannie Lou Hamer, one of twenty children of a sharecropper, was typical of the poor, black Mississippians targeted by SNCC. She also came to epitomize the political commitment that organizers hoped to see develop in them. (The part of the interview that is indented and set off with a line in the left margin is out of sequence. It was transposed by the original author for greater clarity.)

A Sharecropper's Daughter Responds to the Voter Registration Campaign (ca. 1975)
FANNIE LOU HAMER

Well, we were living on a plantation about four and a half miles east of here. . . . Pap had been out there thirty years, and I had been out there eighteen years, 'cause we had been married at that time eighteen years. And you know, things were just rough. . . . I don't think that I ever remember working for as much as four dollars a day. Yes, one year I remember working for four dollars a day, and I was gettin' as much as the men, 'cause I kept up with the time. . . .But anyway, I just knowed things wasn't right.

So then that was in 1962 when the civil rights workers came into this county. Now, I didn't know anything about voter registration or nothin' like

Source: Howell Raines, *My Soul Is Rested.* Copyright © 1977 by Howell Raines. Used by permission of G. P. Putnam's Sons, a division of Penguin Group (USA) Inc., pp. 249–252.

that, 'cause people had never been told that they could register to vote. And livin' out in the country, if you had a little radio, by the time you got in at night, you'd be too tired to listen at what was goin' on. . . . So they had a rally. I had gone to church that Sunday, and the minister announced that they were gon' have a mass meeting that Monday night. Well, I didn't know what a mass meeting was, and I was just curious to go to a mass meeting. So I did. . . and they was talkin' about how blacks had a right to register and how they had a right to *vote.* . . . Just listenin' at 'em, I could just see myself votin' people outa office that I know was wrong and didn't do nothin' to help the poor. I said, you know, that's sumpin' I really wanna be involved in, and finally at the end of that rally, I had made up my mind that I was gonna come out there when they said you could go down that Friday to try to register.

> *She remembers the date precisely: August 31, 1962. She and seventeen others climbed aboard an old bus owned by a black man from neighboring Bolivar County. SNCC had chartered it for the thirty-mile ride to the county seat in Indianola. Once there, she was the first into the registrar's office.*
>
> . . . He brought a big old book out there, and he gave me the sixteenth section of the Constitution of Mississippi, and that was dealing with de facto laws, and I didn't know nothin' about no de facto laws, didn't know nothin' about any of 'em. I could copy it like it was in the book. . . but after I got through copying it, he told me to give a reasonable interpretation and tell the meaning of that section that I had copied. Well, I flunked out. . . .

So then we started back to Ruleville and on our way back to Ruleville, this same highway patrolman that I had seen steady cruisin' around this bus stopped us. We had crossed that bridge, coming over from Indianola. They got out the cars, flagged the bus down. When they flagged the bus down, they told all of us to get off of the bus. So at this time, we just started singing "Have a Little Talk with Jesus," and we got off the bus, and all they wanted then was for us to get back on the bus. They arrested Bob [Moses] and told the bus driver he was under arrest. So we went back then to Indianola. The bus driver was fined one hundred dollars for driving a bus with too much yellow in it. Now ain't that ridiculous?

For what?

Too much yellow. Said the bus looked too much like a school bus. That's funny, but it's the truth. But you see, it was to frighten us to death. This same bus had been used year after year hauling cotton choppers and cotton pickers to Florida to try to make a livin' that winter, and he had never been arrested before. But the day he tried . . . to carry us to Indianola, they fined him a hundred dollars, and I guess it was so ridiculous that they finally cut the fine down to thirty dollars, and all of us *together—not* one, but all us together—had enough to pay the fine. So we paid the fine, and then we got back on the bus and come on to Ruleville.

So Rev. Jeff Summers, who live on Charles Street, just the next street over, he carried me out there on the Marlowe Plantation where I had worked for eighteen years. And when I got out there, my little girl—she's dead now, Dorothy—she met me and one of Pap's cousins, and said that man [who owned the plantation] had been raising a lot of Cain ever since we left, that he had been in the field more times than he usually come a day, because I had gone to the courthouse. See, the people at the courthouse would call and tell it. So they was kinda scared, and quite natural I began to feel nervous, but I knowed I hadn't done nothin' wrong. So after my little girl told me, wasn't too long 'fore Pap got off, and he was tellin' me the same thing that the other kids had told me.

I went on in the house, and I sat down on a little old bed that belonged to the little girl, and when I sat down on the bed, this man [who owned the plantation] he come up and he asked Pap, "Did you tell Fannie Lou what I said?" And Pap said, "Yessir, I sho' did." And I got up and walked to the door, and then he asked me, "Did Pap tell you what I said?" I said, "He told me." And he said, "I mean that. You'll have to go back to Indianola and withdraw, or you have to leave this place." So I said, "Mr. Dee, I didn't go down there to register for you. I went down there to register for myself." And that made him madder, you know.

So he told me, "I want your answer now, yea or nay." And he said, "'They gon'"—now, I don't know who the *they* were, whether it was the white Citizens Council or the Ku Klux Klan, 'cause I don't think one is no worse than the other—"they gon' worry me tonight. They gon' worry the hell outa me, and I'm gon' worry hell outa you. You got 'til in the mornin' to tell me. But if you don't go back there and withdraw, you got to leave the plantation."

So I knowed I wasn't goin' back to withdraw, so wasn't nothin' for me to do but leave the plantation. So Pap brought me out that same night and I come to Mrs. Tucker's, a lady live over on Byron Street. I went to her house, and I stayed, and Pap began to feel nervous when he went to the [plantation maintenance] shop and saw some buckshot shells. And they don't have buckshot shells to *play* with in August and September, because you ain't huntin' or nothin' like that.

On September tenth—again she recalls the date precisely—came the nightrider attack. . . . The riders shot into the McDonald home, where the SNCC workers were staying, and into the Tucker home, where Mrs. Hamer had been given shelter. "They shot in that house sixteen times, tryin' to kill me," she remembers. She fled to the home of a niece in Tallahatchie County when the nighttime terrorism continued on into the fall.

I stayed away, 'cause things then—you could see 'em at night. They would have fires in the middle of the road. . . . You wouldn't see no Klan signs, but just make a fire in the middle of road. And it was *so dangerous*, I stayed in Tallahatchie County all of September and then October, and then November I come back to Ruleville. I was comin', I didn't know why I was comin', but I was just sick of runnin' and hadn't done nothin'. . . . I started tryin' to find a place to stay, 'cause we didn't have nothin'.

The woman who had been her sixth-grade school teacher put her in touch with a black woman who had a three-room house for rent "for eighteen dollars a month and that was a lotta money." She and her family moved in on December 3.

That was on a Sunday, and that Monday, the fourth of December, I went back to Indianola to the circuit clerk's office and I told him who I was and I was there to take that literacy test again.

I said, "Now, you cain't have me fired 'cause I'm already fired, and I won't have to move now, because I'm not livin' in no white man's house." I said, "I'll be here every thirty days until I become a registered voter." 'Cause that's what you would have to do: go every thirty days and see had you passed the literacy test. . . . I went back then the tenth of January in 1963, and I had become registered. . . . I passed the second one, because at the second time I went back, I had been studying sections of the Mississippi Constitution, so I would know if I got one that was simple enough that I might could pass it.

I passed that second test, but it made us become like criminals. We would have to have our lights out before dark. It was cars passing that house all times of the night, driving real slow with guns, and pickups with white mens in it, and they'd pass that house just as slow as they could pass it. . . three guns lined up in the back. All of that. This was the kind of stuff. Pap couldn't get nothin' to do. . . .

So I started teachin' citizenship class, and I became the supervisor of the citizenship class in this county.* So I moved around the county to do citizenship education, and later on I become a field secretary for SNCC—I guess being about one of the oldest people at that time that was a field secretary, 'cause they was real young.

*Hamer taught in an SCLC voter-education program.

Freedom Summer

In 1964, COFO organizers decided to bring hundreds of mostly white, affluent, Northern college students to Mississippi to participate in the Mississippi Freedom Summer Project, whose main goal was black voter registration. What do these sources reveal about the reasons for the Freedom Summer, the broader goals of its organizers, and the dangers and obstacles confronting the participants?

6   In the spring of 1964, CORE's Dave Dennis and SNCC's Robert Moses discussed the wisdom of bringing white college students to Mississippi to register black voters. Their decision, as recalled here by Dennis in a later oral history, led to Freedom Summer.

A Black Activist Endorses White Participation (ca. 1975)
DAVE DENNIS

We knew that if we had brought in a thousand blacks, the country would have watched them slaughtered without doing anything about it. Bring a thousand whites and the country is going to react to that in two ways. First of all is to protect. We made sure that we had the children, sons and daughters, of some very powerful people in this country over there, including Jerry Brown, who's now governor of California, for instance . . . we made sure of that . . . . The idea was not only to begin to organize for the Democratic Convention, but also to get the country to begin to respond to what was going on there. They were not gonna respond to a thousand blacks working in that area. They would respond to a thousand young white college students, and white college females who were down there. All right? And that's the reason why, and if there were gonna take some deaths to do it, the death of a white college student would bring on more attention to what was going on than for a black college student getting it. That's cold, but that was also in another sense speaking the language of this country. What we were trying to do was get a message over to the country, so we spoke their language. And that had more to do with that decision to bring 'em in by the two of us at the top than anything else.

You [and Bob Moses] discussed it that clearly?

Uh-mm, the two of us did. The two of us discussed it. That was not opened up to the staff and everything else in the meetings, because the fact is that we didn't know who was working for the press or whatever, and most things that happened in staff meetings always got out. And that's something we didn't want to. Now I guess it can be told. . . . We didn't plan anything that happened, for it to happen. That's what the Klan and the rest of 'em did, you know. We didn't plan any of the violence. [Pauses] But we just wanted the country to respond to what was going on.

What sorts of problems, if any, did that decision cause you and Moses?

Source: Howell Raines, *My Soul Is Rested.* Copyright © 1977 by Howell Raines. Used by permission of G. P. Putnam's Sons, a division of Penguin Group (USA) Inc., p. 274.

Well, I can't speak for Bob. It caused problems—I mean, psychologically—for me in terms of the fact that you felt responsible for what happened to people, you know, and I still do. I mean, it's the price that I had to pay and the price that I still pay for the decision. [Pauses] But it was something that had to be done. You see, one of the things is that we were in a war, and it wasn't very romantic for those people involved in it.

7   SNCC's Lawrence Guyot, a member of the COFO staff, recalled in an oral history the violence dealt civil rights workers during Freedom Summer and the federal government's response to it. Note what Guyot saw as the only protection from white violence. (The part of the interview that is indented and set off with a line in the left margin is out of sequence. It was transposed by the original author for greater clarity.)

A SNCC Organizer Recalls Federal Intervention (ca. 1975)
LAWRENCE GUYOT

Oh, man, look . . . [claps his hands for emphasis] . . . we were an open book. The phones were tapped, people knew where we were going, people knew where we bought our gas, where we lived . . . you name it. Fortunately, we didn't operate internally as though we had something to hide. I mean, our protection was the black community. We never doubted that and we knew it and we acted like it. I have no doubt that the twenty-five [black] people who really made decisions in that state politically at that time could have been wiped out in a day—*and would have been*. I mean, what's to prevent it?

I don't know, you may think I'm overstating my case, because I was individually involved, but I have no doubt about it. Logically that's the way the state deals with that kinda situation; that's the way it woulda been dealt with. But the national attention, the involvement of the President, the concern of the CIA. Allen Dulles came to Mississippi.* The FBI then began its infiltrating of the Klan and the Civil Rights Movement. I'm sure this was when the surveillance and tapping of King was stepped up.

> The only time that I really have opposition to the role of the federal government in Mississippi was when Allen Dulles came to Mississippi and met with myself, Aaron Henry, Bob Moses, Dave Dennis, a couple

*Allen Dulles, former director of the Central Intelligence Agency, came to Mississippi as a special representative of President Lyndon Johnson.

Source: Howell Raines, *My Soul Is Rested.* Copyright © 1977 by Howell Raines. Used by permission of G. P. Putnam's Sons, a division of Penguin Group (USA) Inc., pp. 288–289.

of other people, and said, "Look, I'm going to meet with the governor in an hour"—this was when they were looking for the bodies of Schwerner, Chaney, and Goodman—"and we want this mess cleaned up."

And Aaron Henry stood up and said, "What do you mean?"

Dulles said, "Well, these civil rights demonstrations are causin' this kind of friction, and we're just not gonna have it, even if we have to bring troops in here."

Fortunately, Aaron Henry took the right position, 'cause he said, "You talkin' to the wrong people. . . . Everything we're trying to do is constitutionally protected and we oughta be having more help from the federal government rather than you, as an agent of the federal government, come and tell us to be quiet." *Now that happened.*

8   In letters to friends and family members back home, the college students involved in Freedom Summer often discussed their experiences in Mississippi. As you read this letter, consider what it demonstrates about the civil rights workers' goals—and obstacles they confronted.

"A Letter from a Freedom Summer Volunteer" (1964)

Dear folks,   Mileston, August 18

One can't move onto a plantation cold; or canvas a plantation in the same manner as the Negro ghetto in town. It's far too dangerous. Many plantations—homes included—are posted, meaning that no trespassing is permitted, and the owner feels that he has the prerogative to shoot us on sight when we are in the house of one of *his* Negroes.

Before we canvas a plantation, our preparation includes finding out whether the houses are posted, driving through or around the plantation without stopping, meanwhile making a detailed map of the plantation.

We're especially concerned with the number of roads in and out of the plantation. For instance, some houses could be too dangerous to canvas because of their location near the boss man's house and on a dead end road. In addition to mapping, we attempt to talk to some of the tenants when they are off the plantation, and ask them about conditions. The kids often have contacts, and can get on the plantation unnoticed by the boss man, with the pretense of just visiting friends.

Our canvassing includes not only voter registration, but also extensive reports on conditions—wages, treatment by the boss man, condition of

Source: From Leon Friedman, ed., *The Civil Rights Reader: Basic Documents of the Civil Rights Movement,* 1967.

the houses, number of acres of cotton, etc. Much more such work needs to be done. The plantation system is crucial in Delta politics and economics, and the plantation system must be brought to an end if democracy is to be brought to the Delta. . . .

Love, Joel

---

9   Besides voter registration, one of the major activities of Freedom Summer participants was organizing and teaching in the Mississippi Freedom Schools. Directed by Staughton Lynd, a white history professor at Spelman College, the Freedom Schools were established to teach black students in such basic skills as reading, writing, and arithmetic. The schools had a broader impact on many of the students, though, as these examples of their work reveal.

Examples of Freedom School Student Work (1964)

What the Summer Project Has Meant by [ZH]

The Summer Project Ment So Much to Me. I Met New people. They taught us New things about our people, things that we hadnt realized about. The life of famous colored people. We also learned about writing different letter, that was a big help. What I liked very much was learning the meaning of lots of words. Words that I had been over but not nowing the real meaning. The project ment much to me discussing health, food that prevent different diseases. And if you dont get enough of food containing these vitamins, you may come in conact with these diseases. The Library means a great deal of help. We learn steps on how to use the library, which was very important. All of the SNCC student was just what we needed. I pray that they come back again.

In Freedom Schools

I like to go to Freedom School. You would like it too. If you want to come and don't have a way, let us know.

I think we should all have our equal rights. We Negroes have been beaten, but we will never turn back until we get what belongs to us.

We just want what belongs to us. We don't want anything else. I think we as Negroes ought to have the right to vote for justice, equal rights, freedom, jobs, we need better books to read. In the stores uptown and down here we have to pay tax. That is a crying shame.

Source: Freedom School Curriculum Website, http://www.educationanddemocracy.org/FSCfiles/B_18_ExcerptsOfStudentWork.htm

God is looking down on people now. We try to hid things form people, but we can't hide things from God. We pay tax. I think we should have a right to vote. All of our colored men are getting beaten and put in jail. This unfair I think, don't you?

[RMC] age 11.

DECLARATION OF INDEPENDENCE
By the
Freedom School Students of
St. John's Methodist Church,
Palmer's Crossing, Hattiesburg, Miss.

In this course of human events, it has become necessary for the Negro people to break away from the customs which have made it very difficult for the Negro to get his God-given rights. We, as citizens of Mississippi, do hereby state that all people should have the right to petition, to assemble, and to use public places. We also have the right to life, liberty, and to seek happiness.

The government has no right to make or to change laws without the consent of the people. No government has the right to take the law into its own hands. All people as citizens have the right to impeach the government when their rights are being taken away.

All voters elect persons to the government. Everyone must vote to elect the person of his choice; so we hereby state that all persons of twenty-one years of age, whether back, white or yellow, have the right to elect the persons of their choice; and if theses persons do not carry out the will of the people, they have the right to alter or abolish the government.

The Negro does not have the right to petition the government for a redress of these grievances:

For equal opportunity.
For better schools and equipment.
For better recreation facilities.
For more public libraries.
For schools for the mentally ill.
For more and better senior colleges.
For better roads in Negro communities.
For training schools in the State of Mississippi.
For more Negro policemen.
For more guarantee of a fair circuit clerk.
For integration in colleges and schools.

The government has made it possible for the white man to have a mock trial in the case of a Negro's death.

The government has refused to make laws for the public good.
The government has used police brutality.

The government has imposed taxes upon us without representation.

The government has refused to give Negroes the right to go into public places.

The government has marked our registration forms unfairly.

We, therefore, the Negroes of Mississippi assembled, appeal to the government of the state, that no man is free until all men are free. We do hereby declare independence from the unjust laws of Mississippi which conflict with the United States Constitution.

SNCC and Political Change

As a result of SNCC's and the COFO's organizing efforts in Mississippi, the Mississippi Freedom Democratic Party sent 68 delegates to the Democratic National Convention in Atlantic City in August 1964. At the convention, the delegates challenged the legitimacy of Mississippi's regular Democratic delegates, whose party had excluded blacks from the polls and office holding. Although Fannie Lou Hamer and other delegates were able to advance their case at nationally televised hearings conducted by the Democratic convention's credentials committee, their hopes for acceptance by the convention were soon dashed. Lyndon Johnson, fearful of losing the Democratic South to his Republican opponent, intentionally preempted Hamer's moving testimony before the credentials committee by suddenly appearing on television himself. Later, under orders from Johnson, the convention offered only two at-large seats to the Freedom party delegation. Summing up the Freedom party delegates' reaction, Hamer declared that they "didn't come all this way for no two seats!"[7] The Freedom party's experience at the Democratic convention proved a bitter experience for many involved in SNCC/COFO organizing in Mississippi. As you read the sources that follow, consider what they reveal about the tensions created by Freedom Summer and the lessons some black activists drew from this experience. What do they reveal about the reasons that such SNCC activists as Stokely Carmichael became advocates of "black power" later in the 1960s? Did such a position represent a radical change for SNCC?

10 Jane Stembridge, a student at the Union Theological Seminary, worked as the "office secretary" for the SNCC executive committee starting in 1960. In that capacity, she was privy to many discussions held by the organization's leaders. Stembridge was interviewed by Emily Stoper, a graduate student at Harvard University, in 1966.

An "Insider" Recalls the Divisions in SNCC (1966)

JS: I don't think SNCC people, even in the early days, were interested in brotherhood, in reconciliation, in integration. SNCC has not changed radically, taking the position of Black Power. I think SNCC wanted desegregation, they wanted Negro rights, they wanted to go to Woolworth's and eat, but they simply didn't say the same things that Dr. King has said and I don't think they wanted the same things that he seems to want. They also were in a bigger hurry than SCLC. They were also alienated by SCLC's big office and office staff and all the red tape and the same old kind of organization, bureaucracy thing, that stayed in Atlanta and really didn't have much contact with the grass roots, or so it seemed then and still does, really. That this is just another Negro organization, is what they would say. Very cynical about it and just really didn't want to have anything to do with it. . . .

ES: What effect did the summer of '64 have on SNCC?

JS: Well, it did focus some attention on the state of Mississippi. People did get killed. It did reinforce the old ideas. It did put the cap on the development of local leadership to some extent. This varied from project to project, depending on what kind of white kids had come in there and what kind of local people were there to begin with. Most of the white kids tried to be sensitive to this kind of thing; some of them were not sensitive to it. But it did impede that. I think the biggest lesson SNCC learned from it was that you can't bring in white kids to help develop Negro leadership. It's an impossibility. I think that's true, too. And it was after the summer project that I learned that I could not help develop Negro leadership because I was white. . . .

ES: Was their presence one of the reasons that other people were upset?. . .

JS: Well, their presence made some of the Negro people angry. I mean there were some Southern Negro kids who were on the SNCC staff who were just as insecure as local Negroes and the fact that a white kid came in and could do this or that, the other, made them mad as hell. Again, you talk about black power and black this and black the other, which is not what Stokely's saying or why Stokely's saying what he's saying, but there was some personal antagonism towards them. The more whites that came in, the greater this antagonism. "This is our organization. This is our identity. Why the hell does this kid have to come and join it," kind of thing. The more that came in, naturally, the madder they got.

Source: Emily Stoper, *The Student Nonviolent Coordinating Committee: The Growth of Radicalism in a Civil Rights Organization* (Brooklyn: Carlson Publishing Inc., 1989). Reprinted with the permission by the author.

In her autobiography, Fannie Lou Hamer discussed what she learned from her experiences at the Democratic National Convention in 1964.

Fannie Lou Hamer on the Lessons of 1964 (1967)

In 1964 we registered 63,000 black people from Mississippi into the Freedom Democratic Party. We formed our own party because the whites wouldn't even let us register. We decided to challenge the white Mississippi Democratic Party at the National Convention. We followed all the laws that the white people themselves made. We tried to attend the precinct meetings and they locked the doors on us or moved the meetings and that's against the laws they made for their ownselves. So we were the ones that held the real precinct meetings. At all these meetings across the state we elected our representatives to go to the National Democratic Convention in Atlantic City. But we learned the hard way that even though we had all the law and all the righteousness on our side—that white man is not going to give up his power to us.

We have to build our own power. We have to win every single political office we can, where we have a majority of black people. . . .

. . . The question for black people is not, when is the white man going to give us our rights, or when is he going to give us good education for our children, or when is he going to give us jobs—if the white man gives you anything—just remember when he gets ready he will take it right back. We have to take for ourselves.

Source: From Clayborne Carson et al., *The Eyes on the Prize Civil Rights Reader: Documents, Speeches, and Firsthand Accounts from the Black Freedom Struggle, 1954–1990* (Viking Press, 1991), pp. 178–179; Originally from *To Praise Our Bridges: An Autobiography of Mrs. Fanny* [sic] *Lou Homer* (Jackson: Kipo, 1967).

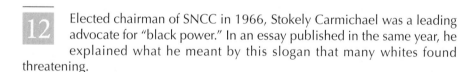

Elected chairman of SNCC in 1966, Stokely Carmichael was a leading advocate for "black power." In an essay published in the same year, he explained what he meant by this slogan that many whites found threatening.

"What We Want" (1966)
STOKELY CARMICHAEL

One of the tragedies of the struggle against racism is that up to now there has been no national organization which could speak to the growing

Source: "What We Want" by Stokely Carmichael, as seen in Clayborne Carson et al., The Eyes on the Prize Civil Rights Reader: Documents, Speeches, and Firsthand Accounts from the Black Freedom Struggle, 1954–1990.

militancy of young black people in the urban ghetto. There has been only a civil rights movement, whose tone of voice was adapted to an audience of liberal whites. It served as a sort of buffer zone between them and angry young blacks. None of its so-called leaders could go into a rioting community and be listened to. In a sense, I blame ourselves—together with the mass media—for what has happened in Watts, Harlem, Chicago, Cleveland, Omaha. Each time the people in those cities saw Martin Luther King get slapped, they became angry; when they saw four little black girls bombed to death, they were angrier; and when nothing happened, they were steaming. We had nothing to offer that they could see, except to go out and be beaten again. We helped to build their frustration. . . .

An organization which claims to be working for the needs of a community—as SNCC does—must work to provide that community with a position of strength from which to make its voice heard. This is the significance of black power beyond the slogan.

Black power can be clearly defined for those who do not attach the fears of white America to their questions about it. We should begin with the basic fact that black Americans have two problems: they are poor and they are black. All other problems arise from this two-sided reality: lack of education, the so-called apathy of black men. Any program to end racism must address itself to that double reality. . . .

The concept of "black power" is not a recent or isolated phenomenon: It has grown out of the ferment of agitation and activity by different people and organizations in many black communities over the years. Our last year of work in Alabama added a new concrete possibility. In Lowndes County, for example, black power will mean that if a Negro is elected sheriff, he can end police brutality. If a black man is elected tax assessor, he can collect and channel funds for the building of better roads and schools serving black people—thus advancing the move from political power into the economic arena. In such areas as Lowndes, where black men have a majority, they will attempt to use it to exercise control. This is what they seek: control. Where Negroes lack a majority, black power means proper representation and sharing of control. It means the creation of power bases from which black people can work to change statewide or nationwide patterns of oppression through pressure from strength—instead of weakness. Politically, black power means what it has always meant to SNCC: the coming-together of black people to elect representatives and *to force those representatives to speak to their needs*. It does not mean merely putting black faces into office. A man or woman who is black and from the slums cannot be automatically expected to speak to the needs of black people. Most of the black politicians we see around the country today are not what SNCC means by black power. The power must be that of a community, and emanate from there. . . .

Ultimately, the economic foundations of this country must be shaken if black people are to control their lives. The colonies of the United States—and this includes the black ghettoes within its borders, north and south—must be liberated. For a century, this nation has been like an octopus of exploitation, its tentacles stretching from Mississippi and Harlem to South America, the Middle East, southern Africa, and Vietnam; the form of exploitation varies from area to area but the essential result has been the same—a powerful few have been maintained and enriched at the expense of the poor and voiceless colored masses. This pattern must be broken. As its grip loosens here and there around the world, the hopes of black Americans become more realistic. For racism to die, a totally different America must be born. . . .

But our vision is not merely of a society in which all black men have enough to buy the good things of life. When we urge that black money go into black pockets, we mean the communal pocket. We want to see money go back into the community and used to benefit it. We want to see the cooperative concept applied in business and banking. We want to see black ghetto residents demand that an exploiting store keeper sell them, at minimal cost, a building or a shop that they will own and improve cooperatively; they can back their demand with a rent strike, or a boycott, and a community so unified behind them that no one else will move into the building or buy at the store. The society we seek to build among black people, then, is not a capitalist one. It is a society in which the spirit of community and humanistic love prevail. . . .

CONCLUSION

As we saw in Chapter 9, even popular culture in the postwar era was not immune from the influences of anticommunist hysteria. This chapter reminds us that our view of the past is not immune from the influence of popular culture itself. Few episodes in recent American history illustrate better than the civil rights struggle how perceptions of the past have been shaped by images embedded in our culture. Because this struggle ultimately received extensive media coverage, popular memories of it have been shaped, as historian Charles Payne pointed out, by a few "Big Events" highlighted by the media. Payne's point reminds us once again that the way we frame our view of the past—the process by which events are selected, emphasized, and presented—is never objective. Because these "Big Events" often put a handful of prominent leaders in the spotlight, Payne's point also illustrates the lessons of Chapters 7 and 8, that is, whether we choose to look at history from the "top down" or the "bottom up" will determine the past that we see. Finally, examining the civil rights struggle also reminds us that such questions matter. As Payne observes—and as we shall see when we turn to the Vietnam War in Chapter 11—the way we view the past determines the lessons that we draw from it.

FURTHER READING

Clayborne Carson, *In Struggle: SNCC and the Black Awakening of the 1960s* (Cambridge, Mass.: Harvard University Press, 1981).

John Dittmer, *Local People: The Struggle for Civil Rights in Mississippi* (Urbana: University of Illinois Press, 1994).

Cheryl Lynn Greenberg, ed., *A Circle of Trust: Remembering SNCC* (New Brunswick, N.J.: Rutgers University Press, 1998).

Henry Hampton and Steve Fayer, eds., *Voices of Freedom: An Oral History of the Civil Rights Movement from the 1950s through the 1980s* (New York: Bantam Books, 1990).

Peniel E. Joseph, *Waiting 'Til the Midnight Hour: A Narrative History of Black Power in America* (New York: Henry Holt and Co., 2006).

Nicholaus Mills, *Like a Holy Crusade: Mississippi 1964—The Turning of the Civil Rights Movement in America* (Chicago: Ivan R. Dee, 1992).

Patricia Sullivan, *Lift Every Voice: The NAACP and the Making of the Civil Rights Movement* (New York: New Press, 2009).

Robert Weisbrot, *Freedom Bound: A History of America's Civil Rights Movement* (New York: W. W. Norton & Company, 1990).

NOTES

1. Quoted in Nicholaus Mills, *Like a Holy Crusade: Mississippi 1964—The Turning of the Civil Rights Movement in America* (Chicago: Ivan R. Dee, 1992), p. 28.
2. Quoted in ibid., pp. 28–29.
3. Quoted in Robert Weisbrot, *Freedom Bound: A History of America's Civil Rights Movement* (New York: W. W. Norton & Company, 1990), p. 82.
4. Quoted in Fred Powledge, *Free at Last? The Civil Rights Movement and the People Who Made It* (Boston: Little, Brown and Company, 1990), p. xix.
5. Clayborne Carson, "Civil Rights Reform and the Black Freedom Struggle," in Charles W. Eagles, ed., *The Civil Rights Movement in America* (Jackson: University Press of Mississippi, 1986), p. 27.
6. Ibid., p. 23.
7. Quoted in Weisbrot, *Freedom Bound*, p. 122.

Chapter

11

Causation and the Lessons of History: Explaining America's Longest War

This chapter presents two secondary sources and several primary sources dealing with America's involvement in the Vietnam War.

Secondary Sources

1. Fighting in "Cold Blood": LBJ's Conduct of Limited War in Vietnam (1994), **GEORGE HERRING**

2. God's Country and American Know-How (1986), **LOREN BARITZ**

Primary Sources

3. LBJ Expresses Doubts About Vietnam (1965)
4. LBJ Recalls His Decision to Escalate (1971)
5. The Central Intelligence Agency Reports on the War (1967)
6. McNamara Recalls the Decision to Escalate (1995)
7. Fighting a Technological War of Attrition (1977)
8. A Medical Corpsman Recalls the Vietnamese People (1981)
9. A Marine Remembers His Shock (1987)
10. A Foreign Service Officer Acknowledges American Ignorance (1987)

*T*he end of the Vietnam War came suddenly in 1975. For eighteen hours on April 29, marine and air force helicopters hovered over landing pads on the roofs of a few of Saigon's tallest buildings. As the Viet Cong and North Vietnamese troops advanced on the capital, the helicopters lifted more than 1,000 Americans and 5,000 South Vietnamese to waiting ships in the South China Sea. Meanwhile, the U.S. embassy was a scene of confusion. Thousands of South Vietnamese desperately looking for a way out of their country had come to the compound. When they tried to scale the walls, marine guards used their boots and rifle butts to force them back. One North Vietnamese commander said they were "fighting their way in, smashing doors, climbing walls, climbing each other's backs, tussling, brawling, and trampling each other as they sought to flee."[1]

At 5:00 A.M the next morning, the American ambassador, under orders from President Ford to get out "without a moment's delay," boarded a CH-46 helicopter. Then nine more CH-46s landed and took off with the remaining marines, who had to spray Mace to fend off the Vietnamese still trying to break into the compound. When the last helicopter lifted off, three years after the last American combat troops had gone home, American involvement in Vietnam was finally over. Within hours, so was the war that the United States had officially abandoned two years before. By the afternoon, communist troops rolled into the heart of Saigon, smashed their way into the presidential palace, and raised their single-starred flag in triumph.

A three-decade effort to prevent the spread of communism to Vietnam had failed. That commitment had led the United States to back Cold War–ally France as it fought to retain colonial control in Southeast Asia. As Communists took over the North after the French defeat in 1954, the United States backed a noncommunist government in the South. Already, President Dwight Eisenhower had justified American involvement in Vietnam with the domino theory. Nations could easily fall to communism in a chain reaction much like a row of falling dominos. As the region's first "domino," South Vietnam in time came to assume enormous strategic importance. Moreover, Democrats John Kennedy and Lyndon Johnson well remembered the Republican charges that the Truman administration had "lost" China in 1949. Fearful of political fallout from "losing" yet another Asian nation, John Kennedy and Lyndon Johnson escalated the American commitment to South Vietnam in the face of a rising communist insurgency backed by North Vietnam. By 1963, JFK had deployed 13,000 military advisers to South Vietnam. In 1965, LBJ initiated a bombing campaign against North Vietnam and later that year sent the first American ground troops into the South. By the end of 1968, they numbered 540,000.

By the time the United States finally ended military operations in Vietnam in 1973, it had expended an estimated $600 billion to defend South Vietnam. American planes dropped more than 10 million tons of bombs on the Southeast Asian country. About 2.7 million American soldiers fought there. Approximately 300,000 of them were wounded, and nearly 58,000 lost their lives. All of it had been done to prevent what happened in Saigon on April 30. Confronting failure, many Americans could only wonder what the effort had been for. "Now it's all gone down the drain and it hurts," said one Pennsylvanian who had lost a son in Vietnam. "What did he die for?"[2] In the four decades since the fall of South Vietnam, the sense of failure and personal loss has gradually lessened. Now, many historians study the Vietnam War to discover why the United States fought this war as it did. They also want to know why it turned out as it did and what it would have taken for it to end differently. In this chapter we turn to those questions about America's longest war and its biggest military loss.

SETTING

Four years before the fall of South Vietnam, Lyndon Johnson predicted that the debate about Vietnam would continue for a long time as historians made "judgments on the decisions made and the actions taken."[3] In fact, the historical debate about Vietnam started even before LBJ left the presidency. With the war still raging, many historians wanted to know how the United States had come to be involved in Vietnam in the first place. Contemporary answers to that question varied. Historians Patrick J. Hearden and Gabriel Kolko saw the war as the result of a rational assessment by American policymakers concerned about a capitalist economy's need for markets and resources. Other students of the war, including Arthur Schlesinger and David Halberstam, argued that successive administrations made a series of mistakes that gradually and unthinkingly led the United States into a quagmire. Still others disputed the notion that the United States ended up in Vietnam by accident. Daniel Ellsberg, the Defense Department analyst who leaked *The Pentagon Papers*—a secret history of the war—to the *New York Times*, argued that presidents from Truman to LBJ were concerned about losing Vietnam to communism. These presidents, Ellsberg argued, made clear-sighted decisions and had no illusions about the chances of long-run success. Other scholars have also argued against the unthinking nature of America's commitment to Vietnam. In a study of the foreign policy elite, for instance, John Donovan argued that American policymakers were guided by a belief in containing communist expansion and simply misapplied the policy to Vietnam.

After the fall of South Vietnam, the debates shifted focus. They now reflected the failure of America's commitment and an increasingly conservative national mood. By the late 1970s, such revisionists as Harry G. Summers, Jr., and Norman Podhoretz began to treat the American effort in Vietnam more sympathetically. Instead of asking why the United States fought there, they inquired how the war was fought and how it could have turned out differently. Their guiding assumption was that the United States could have won. Rejecting earlier assessments that saw Vietnam as a mistake, they also drew a different lesson from America's military experience there. Rather than accept the conclusion that the United States should "never again" become involved militarily in distant lands, revisionists pointed to the dangers of isolationism and "appeasement."

More recently, Loren Baritz, Gary Hess, Larry Berman, and other scholars have taken on the revisionists. These postrevisionists are critical of American intervention in Vietnam and argue that the United States could not have won the war for many reasons, including the American ignorance about Vietnamese culture and society. Some of them are also more sympathetic to Lyndon Johnson, who was responsible for the rapid American military escalation in the late 1960s. Far from the blundering and thoughtless hawk of many earlier accounts, they view LBJ as a cautious leader who understood the difficulty of military success in Vietnam and actually expressed doubts about escalation. Many postrevisionists argue that the way America fought the war was determined by domestic political considerations. LBJ chose to escalate the war in a limited way to save his Great Society domestic program. A masterful politician, Johnson simply miscalculated when it came to the war. Ironically, while pointing to LBJ's flawed judgment, these postrevisionists also demonstrate that he got one thing right about Vietnam: It will be a long time before this war loses its power to elicit deeply felt debate.

INVESTIGATION

In this chapter you have the opportunity to compare two historians' assessments of the war in Vietnam. Their discussions focus on the policies and conduct of the war by the Johnson administration. Your primary job is to compare and evaluate these two historians' conclusions about the reason for the American failure in Vietnam and about the lessons that they draw from it. Your analysis should address the following main questions:

1. **What assumptions guided the escalation of the war in Vietnam, according to historians George Herring and Loren Baritz in Source 1 and Source 2?** Why do the authors think these assumptions were flawed? How do the authors respond to the argument that the war could have turned out differently?

2. **What role do Herring and Baritz assign to Lyndon Johnson in explaining the American failure in Vietnam?** Do the authors agree about the role of Johnson's personality and beliefs in determining American war policy?

3. **Are the historians' arguments in the essays supported by the evidence in the primary sources?** Do the primary sources suggest that the main reason for the American failure in Vietnam was the inherent difficulty of fighting a limited war, false assumptions rooted in American culture, or some other factor?

Before you begin, read the sections about Vietnam in your textbook, especially those dealing with the escalation of the war during the Johnson administration.

SECONDARY SOURCES

1 In this selection, historian George Herring offers an explanation for the way the United States fought in Vietnam. It focuses on the Johnson administration's decision to fight a limited war: one that would not arouse the passions of Americans, but rather could be fought in "cold blood." Note Herring's explanation for the American leaders' lack of an overall strategy for fighting the war and the extent to which Johnson's personality shaped American war policy. Does Herring explain why the Johnson administration failed to wage limited war successfully?

Fighting in "Cold Blood": LBJ's Conduct of Limited War in Vietnam (1994)

GEORGE HERRING

Of the two great questions concerning involvement in Vietnam—why did the United States intervene and why did it fail—the latter has provoked the most emotional controversy. Historically, as a nation, America has been uniquely successful, so much so that its people have come to take success for granted. When failure occurs, scapegoats are sought and myths concocted to explain what is otherwise inexplicable. In the case of Vietnam, many critics of America's conduct of the war have thus insisted that a different approach would have produced the "proper" results. Such arguments can never be proven, of course, and they are suspect in method. As Wayne Cole observed many years ago of a strikingly similar debate in the aftermath of World War II, the "most heated controversies . . . do not center on those matters for which the facts and truth can be determined with greatest certainty. The interpretive controversies, on the contrary, rage over questions about which the historian is least able to determine the truth." . . .

The most glaring deficiency is that in an extraordinarily complex war there was no real strategy. President Johnson and Secretary of Defense Robert S. McNamara provided no firm strategic guidance to those military and civilian advisers who were running programs in the field. They set no clearcut limits on what could be done, what resources might be employed, and what funds expended. Without direction from the top, each service or agency did its own thing. Strategy emerged from the field on an improvised basis without careful calculation of the ends to be sought and the means used to attain them.

Perhaps equally important and less generally recognized, despite widespread and steadily growing dissatisfaction among the president's top advisers with the way the war was being fought and the results that were being

Source: From *LBJ and Vietnam: A Different Kind of War* by George C. Herring, Copyright © 1994. By permission of the University of Texas Press.

obtained, there was no change of strategy or even systematic discussion of such a change. Not until the shock of the 1968 Tet offensive compelled it were the basic issues of how the war was being fought even raised. Even then, they were quickly dropped and left largely unresolved. Despite talk among the president's top advisers of borrowing a page from the communists' book and fighting while negotiating, the administration after Tet replaced one make-shift strategy with another, perpetuating and in some ways exacerbating the problems that had afflicted its management of the war from the beginning.

Closely related to and to some extent deriving from the absence of strat-egy was the lack of coordination of the numerous elements of what had become by 1966 a sprawling, multifarious war effort. Johnson steadfastly refused to assume overall direction of the war, and he would not create spe-cial machinery or designate someone else to run it. In Vietnam, therefore, each service or agency tended to go about its own business without much awareness of the impact of its actions in other areas or on other programs. The air war against North Vietnam operated separately from the ground war in South Vietnam (and the air war in Laos was run separately from both). . . .

It is more difficult to determine why these problems existed. In part, no doubt, institutional imperatives were at fault. The rule in bureaucracy . . . is that when an organization does not know what to do—or is not told what to do—it does what it knows how to do. Thus, in the absence of strong leader-ship from the top, the various services and agencies acted on the basis of their own standard operating procedures whether or not they were appropri-ate or compatible. CIA operative William Colby recalls warning McGeorge Bundy during the U.S. buildup in 1965 that the growing militarization of the war was diverting attention from the more urgent problems in the villages of South Vietnam. He pleaded with the presidential adviser to refocus the administration's attention toward the proper area. "You may be right, Bill," Colby remembered Bundy answering, "but the structure of the American government won't permit it." "What he meant," Colby concluded, "was that the Pentagon had to fight the only war it knew how to fight, and there was no American organization that could fight any other." This was most true of the army, air force, and navy, but it was also true of the civilian agencies.

Limited war theory also significantly influenced the way the war was fought. Korea and especially the Truman-MacArthur controversy stimulated a veritable cult of limited war in the 1950s and 1960s, the major conclusion of which was that in a nuclear age where total war was unthinkable limited war was essential. McNamara, William and McGeorge Bundy, Rusk,* and indeed Lyndon Johnson were deeply imbued with limited war theory, and it deter-mined in many crucial ways their handling of Vietnam. Coming of age in World War II, they were convinced of the essentiality of deterring aggression to avoid a major war. Veterans of the Cuban missile crisis, they lived with the awesome responsibility of preventing nuclear conflagration and they were thus committed to fighting in "cold blood" and maintaining tight operational

*William Bundy was assistant secretary of state for eastern affairs; McGeorge Bundy was a national security advisor; and Dean Rusk was secretary of state.

control over the military. They also operated under the mistaken assumption that limited war was more an exercise in crisis management than the application of strategy, and they were thus persuaded that gradual escalation would achieve their limited goals without provoking the larger war they so feared. Many of their notions, of course, turned out to be badly flawed.

To an even greater extent, Lyndon Johnson's own highly personalized style indelibly marked the conduct of the war and contributed to its peculiar frustrations. LBJ was a "kind of whirlwind," David Lilienthal has observed, a man of seemingly boundless energy who attempted to put his personal brand on everything he dealt with. He dominated the presidency as few others have. He sought to run the war as he ran his household and ranch, his office and *his* government, with scrupulous attention to the most minute detail. As with every other personal and political crisis he faced he worked tirelessly at the job of commander in chief of a nation at war. His approach was best typified by his oft-quoted and characteristically hyperbolic boast that U.S. airmen could not bomb an outhouse in North Vietnam without his approval. In the case of Vietnam, however, the result was the worst of both worlds, a strategic vacuum and massive intrusion at the tactical level, micromanagement without real control. Whether he would admit it or not, moreover, LBJ quickly found in Vietnam a situation that eluded his grasp and dissipated even *his* seemingly inexhaustible storehouse of energy.

In so many ways, the conduct of the war reflected Johnson's modus operandi. The reluctance to provide precise direction and define a mission and explicit limits, the highly politicized, for Johnson characteristically middle-of-the-road approach that gave everybody something and nobody what they wanted, that emphasized consensus and internal harmony over results on the battlefield or at the negotiating table, all these were products of a thoroughly political and profoundly insecure man, a man especially ill at ease among military issues and military people.

Johnson's intolerance for any form of intragovernmental dissent and his unwillingness to permit, much less order, a much-needed debate on strategic issues deserve special note. It was not, as his most severe critics have argued, the result of his determination to impose a hermetically sealed system or his preference for working with sycophants, the so-called Caligula syndrome. LBJ was a domineering individual, to be sure, and he did have a strong distaste for conflict in his official family. As David Barrett and others have pointed out, however, he eagerly sought out and indeed opened himself to a wide diversity of viewpoints. Whatever their faults, the people that worked with him were anything but sycophants.

The problem went much deeper than that. In part, it reflected the peculiar mix of personalities involved, the rigorous standards of loyalty of a Rusk or McNamara, Harriman's determination to retain influence at the cost of principle and candor. From Johnson's standpoint, it was largely a matter of control. "He wanted to control everything," Joe Califano* recalled. "His greatest

---

*W. Averell Harriman was an ambassador-at-large; Joseph Califano was a presidential aide.

outbursts of anger were triggered by people or situations that escaped his control." He therefore discouraged the sort of open exchange of ideas, free-wheeling discussion of alternatives, or ranging policy reviews that might in any way threaten his control. His admonition to McGeorge Bundy that his advisers must not "gang up" on him reflected his reluctance to permit them to engage in discussions except under his watchful eye. . . .

It would be a serious mistake to attribute America's failure in Vietnam solely or even largely to bureaucratic imperatives, the false dogmas of limited war theory, or the eccentricities of Johnson's leadership style. Had the United States looked all over the world in 1965 it might not have been able to find a more difficult place to fight. The climate and terrain were singularly inhospitable. More important, perhaps, was the formless, yet lethal, nature of warfare in Vietnam, a conflict without distinct battlelines or fixed objectives where traditional concepts of victory and defeat were blurred. And from the outset, the balance of forces was stacked against the United States in the form of a weak, divided, and far too dependent client lacking in political legitimacy and a fanatically determined and resilient enemy that early on seized and refused to relinquish the banner of Vietnamese nationalism.

American military leaders have left ample testimony of the complex and often baffling challenge they faced in Vietnam and on the home front. Speaking of the "fog of war" in December 1967, [General Earle] Wheeler observed that Vietnam was the "foggiest war" in his memory and the first where the fog was "thicker away from the scene of the conflict than on the battlefield." Marine Gen. Lewis Walt concurred. "Soon after I arrived in Vietnam," he later admitted, "it became obvious to me that I had neither a real understanding of the nature of the war nor any clear idea how to win it." Abysmal ignorance of Vietnam and the Vietnamese on the part of Lyndon Johnson, his advisers, and the nation as a whole thickened the fog of war, contributing to a mistaken decision to intervene, mismanagement of the conflict, and ultimate failure.

A considerable part of the problem also lay in the inherent difficulty of waging limited war. Limited wars, as Stephen Peter Rosen has noted, are by their very nature "*strange* wars." They combine political, military, and diplomatic dimensions in the most complicated way. Conducting them effectively requires rare intellectual ability, political acumen, and moral courage.

Johnson and his advisers went into the conflict confident—probably over-confident—that they knew how to wage limited war, and only when the strategy of escalation proved bankrupt and the American people unwilling or unable to fight in cold blood did they confront their tragic and costly failure. . . .

Nor is there any obvious solution to the dilemma of domestic opinion. Vietnam exposed the enormous difficulties of fighting in cold blood. Without arousing popular emotions and especially without measurable success on the battlefield it was impossible over a long period of time to sustain popular support. Frederick the Great's dictum that war could only be successful when people did not know about it could not possibly work in the age of instant communications and mass media, especially when, as in the case of Vietnam, the size of the U.S. commitment quickly outgrew the presumed parameters of limited war. On the other hand, trying to play down the war also caused major problems. The Johnson and Nixon administrations both went to considerable lengths to maintain the semblance of normality at home. Thus, as D. Michael Shafer has observed, "those fighting [in Vietnam] faced the bitter irony that back in 'The World' life went on as normal while they risked their lives in a war their government did not acknowledge and many fellow citizens considered unnecessary or even immoral."

Johnson's inability to wage war in cold blood produced what appears on the surface a great anomaly—one of the shrewdest politicians of the twentieth century committing a form of political suicide by taking the nation into a war he would have preferred not to fight. To some extent, of course, LBJ was the victim of his considerable political acumen. He took the nation to war so quietly, with such consummate skill (and without getting a popular mandate) that when things turned sour the anger was inevitably directed at him. His inability to manage effectively the war he got [in] so skillfully is typical of his leadership record. He was also much more effective in getting domestic programs through Congress than in managing them once enacted. In the final analysis, however, Johnson's failure reflects more than anything else the enormity of the problem and the inadequacy of the means chosen to address it.

Partial mobilization or a declaration of war provides at best debatable alternatives. George Bush's apparent success in mobilizing support for the Persian Gulf War in 1991 confirmed in the eyes of some critics the deficiencies of Johnson's leadership in Vietnam. In fact, the remarkable popular support for the Gulf War and especially for the troops was in a very real sense an expiation of lingering guilt for nonsupport in Vietnam. It also owed a great deal to perceptions of military success and the rapidity with which the war ended. In any event, Johnson's and Rusk's reservations about the dangers of a declaration of war in the Cold War international system were well taken, and congressional sanction in the War of 1812 and the Mexican War did nothing to stop rampant and at times crippling domestic opposition.

However much we might deplore the limitations of Johnson's leadership and the folly of limited war theory, they alone are not responsible for America's failure in Vietnam. That conflict posed uniquely complex challenges for U.S. war managers both in terms of the conditions within Vietnam itself and the international context in which it was fought. American policymakers thus took on in Vietnam a problem that was in all likelihood beyond their control.

In the new world order of the post–Cold War era, the conditions that appeared to make limited war essential and that made the Vietnam War especially difficult to fight will probably not be replicated, and the "lessons" of Vietnam will have at best limited relevance. There are many different kinds of limited war, however. Korea, Vietnam, the Persian Gulf War (which was, after all, limited in both ends and means) were as different from each other as each was from World War II. What they shared was the complexity in establishing ends and formulating means that is inherent in the institution of limited war itself. Even in this new era, therefore, it would be well for us to remember Vietnam and to recall Lady Bird Johnson's 1967 lament: "It is unbearably hard to fight a limited war."

---

2   In his study of the Vietnam War, historian Loren Baritz argues that American culture not only led the United States into Vietnam but also determined the way Americans fought the war. Note how Baritz explains the American failure in Vietnam and how the cause of failure manifested itself in the actions of the Johnson administration and American military personnel. How does Baritz account for the American determination to fight in "cold blood" and for the failure of the Johnson administration to formulate a war strategy? How does his explanation for failure in Vietnam differ from Herring's?

God's Country and American Know-How (1986)
LOREN BARITZ

America was involved in Vietnam for thirty years, but never understood the Vietnamese. We were frustrated by the incomprehensible behavior of our Vietnamese enemies and bewildered by the inexplicable behavior of our Vietnamese friends. For us, this corner of Asia was inscrutable. These Asians successfully masked their intentions in smiles, formal courtesies, and exotic rituals. The organic nature of Vietnamese society, the significance of village life, the meaning of ancestors, the relationship of the family to the state, the subordinate role of the individual, and the eternal quest for universal agreement, not consensus or majorities, were easily lost on the Americans.

Most of the Vietnamese were so poor, American GIs said that they lived like animals. Some said they were animals. They did not bathe, had no toilets, and ate food whose smell made some young Americans vomit. There was something about the very great age of Vietnamese culture that seemed to resist our best efforts to understand. . . . They were not part of our century and not part of our world.

When we did try to impose changes, for the better of course, the resistance of the people could seem like ingratitude or stupidity, as it did to a young GI, Steve Harper. The Vietnamese enraged him. "We were there to help but Vietnamese are so stupid they can't understand that a great people want to help a weak people." He said that "somebody had to show poor people better ways of livin'," like sewer disposal and sanitation and things like that." He once watched an American team enter a village to teach the

Source: From Loren Baritz, *Backfire: A History of How American Culture Led Us into Vietnam and Made Us Fight the Way We Did.* Copyright © 1985 by Loren Baritz. Originally published by William Morrow & Company, New York. Reprinted with the permission of Gerald McCauley Agency, Inc.

peasants sanitation while members of South Vietnam's army stood around laughing because they thought it was a pointless waste of energy. His worst experience was his R&R tour in Tokyo, "the greatest sin city":

> I would walk down the Ginza, their main street, and look at all the slant eyes and I swear I'd start to get sick. I was even tempted by some of the prostitutes but one look at their faces and I'd walk away in disgust. . . . I began to get angry at Asians and at my own country. Why couldn't they take care of their own problems?

Americans who were most responsible for our Vietnam policies often complained about how little they knew about the Vietnamese. They mistakenly thought they were especially uninformed about the northerners. For example, General Maxwell Taylor, America's ambassador to Saigon, admitted that "we knew very little about the Hanoi leaders . . . and virtually nothing about their individual or collective intentions.". . .

Our difficulties were not with the strangeness of the land or the inscrutability of its people. Modern, secular, well-educated people, such as we are, such as General Taylor and Dr. Kissinger* were, can learn about exotic people in distant places. Our difficulty was not with the peculiarities of the Vietnamese. The problem was us, not them. Our difficulty was that the foot soldier slogging through a rice paddy, the general in his Saigon office planning great troop movements, the official in the Pentagon, and the Presidents who made the war were all Americans. Peer de Silva, a CIA chief of station in Saigon, said, "The American official posted in Asia very often finds himself, whether he realizes it or not, standing solemnly before the Asians, his finger pointed skyward and the word 'repent' on his lips." We wanted the Vietnamese to repent for being Vietnamese. There was something about the condition of being an American that prevented us from understanding the "little people in black pajamas" who beat the strongest military force in the world.

In common with most Asians, the Vietnamese had one custom that American soldiers could not tolerate. The people of Vietnam hold hands with their friends. Two Vietnamese soldiers would walk down the street holding hands. An American marine from south Boston noticed this custom: "They all hold hands, see. I fucking hated that." The intensity of this marine's reaction was characteristic of America's fighting men. The custom proved to the GIs that South Vietnamese men were homosexuals, and this diagnosis explained why the Vietnamese were incompetent warriors, raising the question about why Americans had to die in defense of perverts. . . .

This could all be dismissed as just another example of American cultural ignorance except that it occasionally had hideous consequences. A marine's truck was stopped by South Vietnamese soldiers who wanted the Americans to take a wounded South Vietnamese soldier to a hospital. His leg had been shot off. One of the marines said, "Fuck him. Let him hop." But the commander of the truck told the wounded man to climb in. "The fucking little slope grabbed my leg." The truck commander said that he had been

*Henry Kissinger was a national security advisor and, later, secretary of state.

in Vietnam long enough "to know that most of them are queer. They hold hands and stuff." One of the Americans "whacked" the wounded soldier and told the driver to get going. They threw the wounded man out of the moving truck: "The poor fucking bastard was screaming and crying and begging us. 'Fuck you, you slope. Out you go.'"

The Americans did not see guerrillas or North Vietnamese strolling hand in hand down the street, or if they did they did not realize they were North Vietnamese. It was usual for grunts to respect the enemy more than the ally. As GIs watched our gunships pulverize an area, one said, "You couldn't believe that anyone would have the courage to deal with that night after night . . . and you cultivated a respect for the Viet Cong and NVA [North Vietnamese army]. . ." He also told of a lone sniper firing at a marine base from his hole in the ground. The marines fired everything they had at him, but he always reappeared to fire another round. Finally, napalm was dropped on his position and the entire area was burned to the ground. "When all of it cleared, the sniper popped up and fired off a single round, and the Marines in the trenches cheered. They called him Luke the Gook, and after that no one wanted anything to happen to him."

Thomas Bailey, an interrogation officer stationed in Saigon in the early seventies, believed that Americans did not understand themselves well enough to understand the Vietnamese. He became frustrated because "their civilization was so much older than ours, although we would characterize them as being uncivilized. I would have a difficult time defining the way in which they were more civilized than we were, but they were. It's my gut feeling." It was difficult for the young Americans who were sent to save the South Vietnamese both from themselves and from North Vietnam to encounter people who did not want to be saved in the way we intended. "Government is not important," a villager said, "rice is important." America corrupted the urban elites of South Vietnam by dangling riches in front of them. But it was the city dwellers, especially the Buddhists, who struggled hardest against the other corruption, the cultural pride and myopia of the Americans. They were as proud of their traditions and culture as we were of ours. . . .

Americans were ignorant about the Vietnamese not because we were stupid, but because we believe certain things about ourselves. Those things necessarily distorted our vision and confused our minds in ways that made learning extraordinarily difficult. To understand our failure we must think about what it means to be an American.

The necessary text for understanding the condition of being an American is a single sentence written by Herman Melville in his novel *White Jacket:* "And we Americans are the peculiar, chosen people—the Israel of our time; we bear the ark of the liberties of the world." This was not the last time this idea was expressed by Americans. It was at the center of thought of the men who brought us the Vietnam War. It was at the center of the most characteristic American myth. . . .

In countless ways Americans know in their gut—the only place myths can live—that we have been Chosen to lead the world in public morality and to instruct it in political virtue. We believe that our own domestic goodness results in strength adequate to destroy our opponents who, by definition, are enemies of virtue, freedom, and God. Over and over, the founding Puritans described their new settlement as a beacon in the darkness, a light whose radiance could keep Christian voyagers from crashing on the rocks, a light that could brighten the world. In his inaugural address John Kennedy said, "The energy, the faith, the devotion which we bring to this endeavor [defending freedom] will light our country and all who serve it—and the glow from that fire can truly light the world.". . .

In other words, we assumed that we had a superior moral claim to be in Vietnam, and because, despite their quite queer ways of doing things, the Vietnamese shared our values, they would applaud our intentions and embrace our physical presence. Thus, Vice-President Humphrey later acknowledged that all along we had been ignorant of Vietnam. He said that "to LBJ, the Mekong and the Pedernales were not that far apart." Our claim to virtue was based on the often announced purity of our intentions. It was said, perhaps thousands of times, that all we wanted was freedom for other people, not land, not resources, and not domination. . . .

Joining the American sense of its moral superiority with its technological superiority was a marriage made in heaven, at least for American nationalists. We told ourselves that each advantage explained the other, that the success of our standard of living was a result of our virtue, and our virtue was a result of our wealth. Our riches, our technology, provided the strength that had earlier been missing, that once had forced us to rely only on our virtue. Now, as Hiroshima demonstrated conclusively, we could think of ourselves not only as morally superior, but as the most powerful nation in history. The inevitable offspring of this marriage of an idea with a weapon was the conviction that the United States could not be beaten in war—not by any nation, and not by any combination of nations. For that moment we thought that we could fight where, when, and how we wished, without risking failure. For that moment we thought that we could impose our will on the recalcitrant of the earth. . . .

In Vietnam we had to find a technology to win without broadening the war. The nuclear stalemate reemphasized our need to find a more limited ground, to find, so to speak, a way to fight a domesticated war. We had to find a technology that would prevail locally, but not explode internationally. No assignment is too tough for the technological mentality. In fact, it was made to order for the technicians who were coming into their own throughout all of American life. This war gave them the opportunity to show what they could do. This was to be history's most technologically sophisticated war, most carefully analyzed and managed, using all of the latest wonders of managerial procedures and systems. It was made to order for bureaucracy. . . .

In summary, our national myth showed us that we were good, our technology made us strong, and our bureaucracy gave us standard operating procedures. It was not a winning combination. . . .

To make matters worse, President Johnson had a warm and giving nature. He genuinely believed that all the peoples of the earth were the same in their need for food, health, and education, as of course they are. He had no comprehension that different cultures search for the satisfaction of these essential needs in quite different ways. His understanding of the Vietnamese, North and South, was minimal. His textbook was his own experience in west Texas; his textbook was his own life. That is what Vice-President Humphrey meant when he said that for LBJ the Pedernales and the Mekong were not so far apart. That is why the President could even think of offering a massive flood-control project to the North Vietnamese if they would only please stop fighting. He could imagine trading an enormous TVA project in exchange for the ideology of the North. With typical enthusiasm, he said "We're going to turn the Mekong into a Tennessee Valley." North Vietnam responded that this was a "bribe.". . .

He believed that his was the voice of "the common people" because he thought he was one of them, and believed that he therefore understood their needs and dreams whether in America or Vietnam. While he was destroying the country with bombing, defoliation, and napalm, he could without cynicism speak of peace and progress. He believed that the destruction was unfortunately necessary before the construction could occur. That was Ho Chi Minh's fault. . . .

War is a product of culture. It is an expression of the way a culture thinks of itself and the world. Different cultures go to war for different reasons and fight in different ways. There is an American way of war. Our Vietnam War was started and fought in ways our culture required. . . .

American political culture—the self-righteousness of our nationalism—merged with the impulses of our technological culture—tell us what to do and we'll do it, no questions asked. President Kennedy's enthusiasm for counterinsurgency led the nation to assume that we could successfully intervene in Vietnamese politics in ways that were foreign to America's genius. Our managerial sophistication and technological superiority resulted in our trained incompetence in guerrilla warfare.

The conclusion is obvious: If this nation cannot use its managerial and technological strengths in international conflict, it would be wise to avoid engagement. If our expensive weapon systems will not contribute to victory, it would be wise not to pretend that we have other resources. . . .

The technician's mind is organized around the question *how*. He is motivated by a desire, sometimes a need, to solve problems. He is rational, practical, hardheaded, and believes that if an idea can be transformed into a solution that actually works, the idea was true. Most of the war's planners exhibited these traits. Three other attributes of the technological mentality had an even more direct impact on the war. The technician's language is amoral, dispassionate, and optimistic. For example, Secretary McNamara's perception of Vietnam as a limited war reveals all these habits of mind: "The greatest contribution Vietnam is making—right or wrong is beside the point—is that it is developing an ability in the United States to fight a limited war, to go to war without the necessity of arousing the public ire.". . .

North Vietnam finally won its war because it was willing to accept more death than we considered rational. That is why the bombing campaigns failed. It is not that our technology failed. Our cultural perceptions failed when so many intelligent men in high positions simply assumed that our enemy's culture was sufficiently like ours that he would quit at a point where we believed we would quit.

We lost the war because we were never clear about the guerrillas, their popular support, the North Vietnamese, or ourselves. Our marvelously clever technology did not help us to understand the war and, in fact, confused us even more because it created our unquestioning faith in our own power. Finally, the North's decision to continue fighting, and our decision to stop, were each consistent with the cultural imperatives of each nation. Because the army of South Vietnam was trained by us to fight in the American style, it was forever dependent on a supply of hardware and fuel. That army was incongruent with the culture it was trying to defend.

This is why the military's continuing claim that we could have won the war if it had been allowed to fight differently is pointless. We could not have fought it differently. The constraints on the tactics of the war, and the absence of a political goal to shape those tactics, were products of American culture at the time. It is meaningless to argue that "next time we'll do it differently and win." The only reasonable prediction about the cultural pressures surrounding a "next time" is that they will at least resemble those that existed in the 1960s and exist now.

PRIMARY SOURCES

The Vietnam War left historians with a wealth of primary sources. Many of them reveal the thinking of policymakers, including LBJ and his top advisers. Others reflect the experience of military personnel in Vietnam. Some of the primary sources in this chapter document the concerns of policymakers in the Johnson administration as they considered military options. Others demonstrate the nature of the Vietnam War, the consequences of the administration's war policies, and the attitudes of Americans about Vietnam. Together such sources can help historians understand, perhaps better than many of the participants themselves, why the United States fought the war the way it did and why the war ended as it did.

3   One month before Lyndon Johnson decided to send an additional 125,000 American combat troops to Vietnam, he told Secretary of Defense Robert McNamara what he foresaw there. Do the doubts LBJ expresses here help to explain the Johnson administration's later conduct of the war?

LBJ Expresses Doubts About Vietnam (1965)

I think that in time . . . it's going to be difficult for us to very long prosecute effectively a war that far away from home with the divisions that we have here and particularly the potential divisions. And it's really had me concerned for a month and I'm very depressed about it because I see no program from either Defense or State that gives me much hope of doing anything except just praying and grasping to hold on during [the] monsoon [season] and hope they'll quit. And I don't believe they're ever goin' to quit. And I don't see . . . that we have any . . . plan for victory militarily or diplomatically. . . . Russell* thinks we ought to take one of these [regime] changes to get out of there. I do not think we can get out of there with our treaty like it is and with what all we've said and I think it would just lose us face in the world and I just shudder to think what all of 'em would say.

*Richard B. Russell (D-Ga.), Johnson's old Senate mentor and powerful chairman of the Senate Armed Services Committee.

Source: From *In Retrospect: The Tragedy and Lessons of Vietnam* by Robert S. McNamara, copyright © 1995 by Robert S. McNamara. Used by permission of Times Books, a division of Random House, Inc.

4   Because they are often written to justify past actions and policies, memoirs must be evaluated very carefully, particularly when such sources deal with such a controversial subject as Vietnam. In his memoir, Johnson defended his decision to seek a middle course in Vietnam. Note how he justifies his decision in this excerpt. Were his assumptions well-founded? How does this statement compare to that in Source 3?

LBJ Recalls His Decision to Escalate (1971)

We continued our review of the military situation and the requirement for additional forces. Our military commanders had refined their estimates and indicated they could meet the immediate demand with 50,000 men. I called a meeting of the National Security Council two days later, on July 27. I asked McNamara at that time to summarize again the current need as he saw it.

Source: From Lyndon Johnson, *The Vantage Point: Perspectives of the Presidency, 1963–1969,* 1971, pp. 148–149.

McNamara noted that the Viet Cong had increased in size through local recruitment and replacements from the North. Regular North Vietnamese army units had increased in number and strength. Communist control of the countryside was growing. A dozen provincial capitals were virtually isolated from surrounding rural areas. The South Vietnamese army was growing, but not nearly fast enough to keep pace with the expanding enemy forces. Without additional armed strength, South Vietnam would inevitably fall to Hanoi. I told the NSC there were five possible choices available to us.

"We can bring the enemy to his knees by using our Strategic Air Command," I said, describing our first option. "Another group thinks we ought to pack up and go home."

"Third, we could stay there as we are—and suffer the consequences, continue to lose territory and take casualties. You wouldn't want your own boy to be out there crying for help and not get it."

"Then, we could go to Congress and ask for great sums of money; we could call up the reserves and increase the draft; go on a war footing; declare a state of emergency. There is a good deal of feeling that ought to be done. We have considered this. But if we go into that kind of land war, then North Vietnam would go to its friends, China and Russia, and ask them to give help. They would be forced into increasing aid. For that reason I don't want to be overly dramatic and cause tensions. I think we can get our people to support us without having to be too provocative and warlike."

"Finally, we can give our commanders in the field the men and supplies they say they need."

I had concluded that the last course was the right one. I had listened to and weighed all the arguments and counterarguments for each of the possible lines of action. I believed that we should do what was necessary to resist aggression but that we should not be provoked into a major war. We would get the required appropriation in the new budget, and we would not boast about what we were doing. We would not make threatening noises to the Chinese or the Russians by calling up reserves in large numbers. At the same time, we would press hard on the diplomatic front to try to find some path to a peaceful settlement.

I asked if anyone objected to the course of action I had spelled out. I questioned each man in turn. Did he agree? Each nodded his approval or said "yes."

---

5 In 1965, the Johnson administration initiated Rolling Thunder, a bombing campaign against North Vietnam. As you read this assessment, note the CIA's conclusion about the effects of that campaign and what this report reveals about the problems the United States confronted in waging a war in Vietnam using sophisticated technology.

The Central Intelligence Agency Reports on the War (1967)

Through the end of April 1967 the US air campaign against North Vietnam—Rolling Thunder—had significantly eroded the capacities of North Vietnam's limited industrial and military base. These losses, however, have not meaningfully degraded North Vietnam's material ability to continue the war in South Vietnam.

Total damage through April 1967 was over $233 million, of which 70 percent was accounted for by damage to economic targets. The greatest amount of damage was inflicted on the so-called logistics target system—transport equipment and lines of communication.

By the end of April 1967 the US air campaign had attacked 173 fixed targets, over 70 percent of the targets on the JCS [Joint Chiefs of Staff] list. This campaign included extensive attacks on almost every major target system in the country. The physical results have varied widely. . . .

North Vietnam's ability to recuperate from the air attacks has been of a high order. The major exception has been the electric power industry. . . .

The recuperability problem is not significant for the other target systems. The destroyed petroleum storage system has been replaced by an effective system of dispersed storage and distribution. The damaged military target systems—particularly barracks and storage depots—have simply been abandoned, and supplies and troops dispersed throughout the country. The inventories of transport and military equipment have been replaced by large infusions of military and economic aid from the USSR and Communist China. Damage to bridges and lines of communications is frequently repaired within a matter of days, if not hours, or the effects are countered by an elaborate system of multiple bypasses or pre-positioned spans.

Source: CIA Intelligence Memo, May 12, 1967, declassified document reprinted in Gareth Porter, ed., *Vietnam: The Definitive Documentation of Human Decisions* (Stanfordville, N.Y.: Earle M. Coleman, 1979), II: pp. 470–472.

 Twenty years after the fall of South Vietnam, Robert McNamara published his memoir. In this excerpt, he discusses LBJ's decision to commit combat troops to Vietnam. Note McNamara's explanation for LBJ's determination to downplay the escalation of the war and how his recollection of this decision differs from Johnson's. What accounts for the difference?

McNamara Recalls the Decision to Escalate (1995)

On January 27, 1965—just one week after the inauguration—Mac* and I gave President Johnson a short but explosive memorandum. Mac and I believed events were at a critical juncture. We told LBJ:

*National Security Advisor McGeorge Bundy.

Source: From *In Retrospect: The Tragedy and Lessons of Vietnam* by Robert S. McNamara, copyright © 1995 by Robert S. McNamara. Used by permission of Crown Publishers, a division of Random House, Inc.

The worst course of action is to continue in this essentially passive role which can only lead to eventual defeat and an invitation to get out in humiliating circumstances. We see two alternatives. The first is to use our military power in the Far East and to force a change in Communist policy. The second is to deploy all our resources along a track of negotiation, aimed at salvaging what little can be preserved with no major addition to our present military risks. [We] tend to favor the first course, but we believe that both should be carefully studied.

After months of uncertainty and indecision, we had reached the fork in the road.

The first six months of 1965 that followed our memo marked the most crucial phase of America's thirty-year involvement in Indochina. Between January 28 and July 28, 1965, President Johnson made the fateful choices that locked the United States onto a path of massive military intervention in Vietnam, an intervention that ultimately destroyed his presidency and polarized America like nothing since the Civil War.

During this fateful period, Johnson initiated bombing of North Vietnam and committed U.S. ground forces, raising the total U.S. troop strength from 23,000 to 175,000—with the likelihood of another 100,000 in 1966 and perhaps even more later. All of this occurred without adequate public disclosure or debate, planting the seeds of an eventually debilitating credibility gap. . . .

Why did President Johnson refuse to take the American people into his confidence? Some point to his innate secretiveness, but the answer is far more complex. One factor was his obsession with securing Congress's approval and financing of his Great Society agenda; he wanted nothing to divert attention and resources from his cherished domestic reforms. The other was his equally strong fear of hard-line pressure (from conservatives in both parties) for greater—and far riskier—military action that might trigger responses, especially nuclear, by China and/or the Soviet Union. The president coped with his dilemma by obscuring it—an unwise and ultimately self-defeating course. . . .

From the beginning of our involvement in Vietnam, the South Vietnamese forces had been giving us poor intelligence and inaccurate reports. Sometimes these inaccuracies were conscious attempts to mislead; at other times they were the product of too much optimism. And sometimes the inaccuracies merely reflected the difficulty of gauging progress accurately.

But I insisted we try to measure progress. Since my years at Harvard, I had gone by the rule that it is not enough to conceive of an objective and a plan to carry it out; you must monitor the plan to determine whether you are achieving the objective. If you discover you are not, you either revise the plan or change the objective. I was convinced that, while we might not be able to track a front line, we could find variables that would indicate our success or failure. So we measured the targets destroyed in the North, the traffic down the Ho Chi Minh Trail, the number of captives, the weapons seized, the enemy body count, and so on.

The body count was a measurement of the adversary's manpower losses; we undertook it because one of Westy's* objectives was to reach a so-called crossover point, at which the Vietcong and North Vietnamese casualties would be greater than they could sustain. Critics point to use of the body count as an example of my obsession with numbers. "This guy McNamara," they said, "he tries to quantify everything." Obviously, there are things you cannot quantify; honor and beauty, for example. But things you can count, you ought to count. Loss of life is one, when you are fighting a war of attrition. We tried to use body counts as a measurement to help us figure out what we should be doing in Vietnam to win the war while putting our troops at the least risk.

*General William Westmoreland.

American Personnel in Vietnam

Americans fought against the Vietnamese and alongside them in an unconventional war waged by an often unseen enemy. In oral histories, memoirs, and interviews, many of the soldiers expressed their thoughts about the war, the South Vietnamese, and the enemy. What do these sources reveal about American attitudes toward the Vietnamese and about the problems Americans encountered as they fought an unconventional war? What do they reveal about policymakers' assumptions regarding the war?

 Philip Caputo was a marine lieutenant in Vietnam in 1965. His memoir, *A Rumor of War*, describes his experiences there.

Fighting a Technological War of Attrition (1977)

Everything rotted and corroded quickly over there: bodies, boot leather, canvas, metal, morals. Scorched by the sun, wracked by the wind and rain of the monsoon, fighting in alien swamps and jungles, our humanity rubbed off of us as the protective bluing rubbed off the barrels of our rifles. We were fighting in the cruelest kind of conflict, a people's war. It was no orderly campaign, as in Europe, but a war for survival waged in a wilderness without rules or laws; a war in which each soldier fought for his own life and

Source: Excerpts from *A Rumor of War* by Philip Caputo (New York: Henry Holt and Company, Inc., 1977). By permission of The Aaron Priest Literary Agency.

the lives of the men beside him, not caring who he killed in that personal cause or how many or in what manner and feeling only contempt for those who sought to impose on his savage struggle the mincing distinctions of civilized warfare—that code of battlefield ethics that attempted to humanize an essentially inhuman war. According to those "rules of engagement," it was morally right to shoot an unarmed Vietnamese who was running, but wrong to shoot one who was standing or walking; it was wrong to shoot an enemy prisoner at close range, but right for a sniper at long range to kill an enemy soldier who was no more able than a prisoner to defend himself; it was wrong for infantrymen to destroy a village with white-phosphorus grenades, but right for a fighter pilot to drop napalm on it. Ethics seemed to be a matter of distance and technology. You could never go wrong if you killed people at long range with sophisticated weapons. And then there was that inspiring order issued by General Greene: kill VC.* In the patriotic fever of the Kennedy years, we had asked, "What can we do for our country?" and our country answered, "Kill VC." That was the strategy, the best our best military minds could come up with: organized butchery. But organized or not, butchery was butchery, so who was to speak of rules and ethics in a war that had none?

* Viet Cong

Medic David Ross, who served in Vietnam from 1965 until 1967, provided an oral history of his experience.

A Medical Corpsman Recalls the Vietnamese People (1981)

When Americans are talking about Vietnamese or people in India or somewhere similar, it's not like we're looking at them like they're our next-door neighbors. If someone came to our neighborhood and burned all of our houses and most of our possessions and put us in flying saucers which we'd never seen before and zipped us across the universe, setting us down somewhere in tent city in the middle of a sandbox with wire all around us, I guess we might not be too excited about it. Most of us were never able to see the Vietnamese as real people. I remember President Johnson in one of the psy-op [psychological warfare] flicks we saw saying that the communists weren't like us—they didn't have feelings. But I always remembered that old woman or remembered after a B-52 strike going into this area where there was a little girl with her leg . . . traumatic amputation . . . and . . . still alive. Her mother dead. The whole place turned upside down, a few people still screaming, some people wandering around with the look of the dead, a totally shocked daze. I wondered how people would feel in Pittsburgh if the Vietnamese came over in B-52s and bombed them. And while I feel some real sympathy for the POWs who were airmen, I pick Pittsburgh simply because it's a steel city and it has the image of the real hard-working honest American man. I'm trying to imagine a bunch of steelworkers after their wives, children, fiancées, parents, grandparents, have been blown up or are running around screaming in agony and some Vietnamese pilot comes swooping down in a parachute. I don't imagine they'd give him a very friendly reception. . . .

There was another thing I remember, too. We were going through a rice-paddy area in armored personnel carriers, and of course track vehicles going through a rice paddy isn't . . . The amount of labor they put into maintaining the rice and the paddy berms and the irrigation system and everything—it's all by hand. They don't have the equipment. It's all built a basket of dirt at a time and things have built up over generations. We're just ripping through there on the tracks, tearing the whole damn thing apart. This farmer out there is stomping on his hat and beating his hand against his head. I guess, really, the bottom line is that all his stocks and bonds and his future and his Mercedes and his dreams he hoped for his kids, we just drove through there and in three or four minutes made a helluva mess of it.

For eight months starting in the fall of 1968, Bobby Muller was in Vietnam as a Marine lieutenant. Paralyzed by a bullet through his spine, Muller later founded the Vietnam Veterans of America.

A Marine Remembers His Shock (1987)

Probably the first two months I was there, I spent out in the bush. Out there the war was easy in a way because there was no ambiguity. Anybody you met out there was hard core NVA* regular. No "good guy, bad guy" problem. Later, when we came back to work the coastal area where there were villages and refugees, that's when things started to go "wait a second." Cam Lo, which is one I remember very well, was a refugee village where people had been taken from another place called Gio Linh, ten or fifteen miles away. I didn't understand it then, but for Vietnamese, villagers, their rice paddy and their little ancestral burial ground defines their

*North Vietnamese Army.

Source: "Bobby Muller," from *The Bad War,* edited by Kim Willenson, copyright © 1987 by Newsweek, Inc. Used by permission of Dutton Signet, a division of Penguin Group (USA) Inc.

universe. You take them away as we did and you've totally disrupted what they relate to. And in Cam Lo what I experienced was just hatred in the eyes of people.

The Vietnamese did not like us and I remember I was shocked. I still naively thought of myself as a hero, as a liberator. And to see the Vietnamese look upon us with fear or hatred visible in their eyes was a shock. The only thing we were good for is to sell us something. And frankly every time we operated around Cam Lo we got fucked with. Any patrol, any operation, any convoy passing by would get a smack. So the people that I thought would regard us as heroes were the very people that we were fighting, and all of a sudden my black-and-white image of the world became real gray and confused.

Then I came into contact with the ARVN* and that was all the more absurd. First there were some joint operations and then I went with MACV† as an advisor and worked with three different ARVN battalions and that's when everything just went screwy in my head. Every night I slept with the battalion commander. We had personal bodyguards and the reason was that a good percentage of the guys in the ranks were VC or even North Vietnamese. The bodyguards were to protect us against getting blown away by the guys we were fighting with. We went out into the A Shau valley for what was supposed to be a ten-day operation and it wound up being ten weeks, and we lost a good number of guys not because of firefights but because they took as much rice as they could carry and they split. The A Shau was badlands. It was not a friendly place. And when you leave your unit out in the A Shau you ain't leaving to go bring in the crops back at the farm. You're leaving because you're joining the other side.

It was a joke. The enemy was a tough, hard, dedicated fucking guy, and the ARVN didn't want to hear about fighting. It was LaLa Land. Every, every, every, *every* firefight that we got into, the ARVN broke, the ARVN fucking ran. I was with three different battalions and the story never changed. I almost fell over laughing once. I had an Australian I was working with, and this NVA unit had just ambushed us. We had two companies of ARVN, and finally they got on line to counterattack, and the company commanders give the order to move and nobody moves. And they have to run up and down line with little sticks, beating these guys and kicking them in the fucking rear end to get them up out of their holes. And the Aussie and I look at each other, and we know then and there that this ain't going to work.

*Army of the Republic of Vietnam (South Vietnam).
†Military Assistance Command, Vietnam.

Gary Larsen was a foreign service officer in Vietnam from 1969 to 1973.

A Foreign Service Officer Acknowledges American Ignorance (1987)

The thing I remember most vividly is how little we knew about Vietnam. It was as though the people, their culture, their country existed in another dimension which [only] obliquely intersected with ours. To be sure, we made the obligatory gestures. We had our linguists, our culture specialists, our orientation studies. Yet for the vast majority of Americans the Vietnamese were puppets and their country a stage on which we pulled the strings and rearranged the props at our whim.

This is not surprising when you consider that we had no consideration of Vietnam as an ancient civilization. What was surprising was that our efforts to learn were so meager and so late. Very few people ever realized, for example, that the streets of Saigon were largely named for kings, heroes, and poets rather than for trees, flowers, and places. Or that Vietnam had a flourishing civilization when Washington, D.C., was only a swamp. Ironically, Vietnam's literary masterpiece, Kim Van Kieu, which occupies a place in Vietnam analogous to that held in the West by the masterpieces of Chaucer and Dante, never appeared in this country until 1973, the year we finally declared peace and withdrew.

Our ignorance was reinforced by our inability to communicate. There were, of course, some people who spoke the language, read the literature, and invested the time to pierce the veil. Unfortunately, they rarely made the decisions, and when their comments were at odds with accepted policy, they were dismissed as having "poor attitudes," or as having "gone native." In the absence of English-speaking counterparts, the only people [most of us] felt comfortable talking to were our interpreters, who often unknown to us, seized control of the dialogue and while our interest waned, put forth their own ideas—or ours as they understood them—and in the process promoted themselves.

We compounded this infidelity to competence by vacations, short tours, and our own enclaves. In fact life in Saigon was so complete, and the circle of office, PX, and clubs so secure, that one could go for extended periods of time meeting only Vietnamese who served as drivers, secretaries, maids, and bartenders. And when the occasional ceremony or meeting brought us into contact with other Vietnamese, we retreated into small talk, cliches, and drink, which isolated us from any deep awareness of where we were or what we were doing.

This ignorance nourished our arrogance. For if we were not aware of the consequences of our presence, we could proceed blissfully with actions based on our own one-dimensional view of the country and the people. And proceed we did, getting no smarter but simply overwhelmed. As somebody once said, "We did not have twenty years of experience. We had one year twenty times." In the end we made peace and withdrew with the same arrogant disregard for the people and their country which had characterized our whole involvement. And the lessons were buried under self-praise for a noble effort and guilt-expiating succor for tens of thousands of refugees. Fortunately, there is ample blame for all involved.

CONCLUSION

History is the collective memory that we use to guide us in the present. However, sometimes its lessons are not clear. Few wars have been as carefully scrutinized as the Vietnam War, but historians disagree about the lessons it yields. They have different explanations for the way Americans fought it and thus for the way it turned out.

Some historians locate the cause of America's defeat in its leaders' decisions about how to fight the war. These decisions, in turn, reflected such forces as personality or bureaucratic mentality. For these historians, the lesson of Vietnam is to avoid similar decisions in the future. Other historians see a deeper cause for defeat in certain American assumptions that made military disaster a virtual certainty. For these historians America's failure in Vietnam can be traced to a single powerful force: American culture.

Yet Vietnam may hold a lesson that has nothing to do with avoiding future military disasters. It involves the unintended consequences that wars have on societies fighting them. As we saw by examining white Indian reformers in Chapter 3 and the Cold War in Chapter 9, cultural assumptions can have powerful consequences. Yet culture is not static, as Vietnam's impact on Americans makes clear. The disillusionment fostered by this war helped crack a powerful Cold War culture. Ideas about gender made up one prominent strand woven into that culture. As we will see next, changing ideas about gender contributed to its unraveling in the 1960s and 1970s.

FURTHER READING

Larry Berman, *Lyndon Johnson's War: The Road to Stalemate in Vietnam* (New York: W. W. Norton and Company, 1989).

George Herring, *America's Longest War: The United States in Vietnam, 1950–1975*, rev. ed. (New York: McGraw-Hill, Inc., 1986).

Stanley Karnow, *Vietnam: A History* (New York: Penguin Books, 1991).

David Levy, *The Debate over Vietnam* (Baltimore: Johns Hopkins University Press, 1991).

Fredrik Logevall, *Choosing War: The Lost Chance for Peace and the Escalation of War in Vietnam* (Berkeley: University of California Press, 1999).

Al Santoli, *Everything We Had: An Oral History of the Vietnam War by Thirty-three American Soldiers Who Fought It* (New York: Ballantine Books, 1981).

Marilyn B. Young, *The Vietnam Wars, 1945–1990* (New York: HarperCollins, 1991).

NOTES

1. Quoted in "A North Vietnamese Commander Celebrates the 'Great Spring Victory,'" in *Major Problems in the History of the Vietnam War,* ed. Robert J. McMahon, 2nd ed. (Lexington, Mass.: D. C. Heath, 1995), p. 578.
2. Quoted in George C. Herring, *America's Longest War: The United States in Vietnam, 1950–1975* (New York: John Wiley, 1979), p. 264.
3. Lyndon B. Johnson, *The Vantage Point: Perspectives of the Presidency, 1963–1969* (New York: Holt, Rinehart, and Winston, 1971), p. x.

Chapter

12

Gender, Ideology, and Historical Change: Explaining the Women's Movement

The sources in this chapter relate to the rise of the women's movement in the 1960s and 1970s.

Secondary Sources

1. Cold War Ideology and the Rise of Feminism (1988), ELAINE TYLER MAY
2. Women's Liberation and Sixties Radicalism (2002), ALICE ECHOLS

Primary Sources

3. The Problem That Has No Name (1963), BETTY FRIEDAN
4. Civil Rights and the Rise of Feminism (1987), MARY KING
5. NOW's Statement of Purpose (1966)
6. Redstockings Manifesto (1969)
7. "What's Wrong with 'Equal Rights' for Women?" (1972), PHYLLIS SCHLAFLY
8. The Combahee River Collective Statement (1986)
9. On Women and Sex (1972), JOYCE MAYNARD
10. *Our Bodies, Ourselves* (1973)
11. The Politics of Housework (ca. 1970), PAT MAINARDI
12. Sex Ratios of High School and College Graduates in the United States, 1940–1990
13. Women's Labor Force Participation, by Marital Status, 1940–1990

*E*vidence of coming turmoil was everywhere in 1965. In the first week of June, *Newsweek* detailed several scenarios for the growing war in Vietnam. One of them read that the United States "steadily enlarges its ground combat commitment but its hopes are frustrated; there is no conclusion to the war in sight."[1] The same week, *U.S. News & World Report* covered an "uproar" in Chicago over segregated public schools, yet another sign that the civil rights movement had moved north by the mid-1960s. In the same issue, *U.S. News* reported on the growing campus demonstrations against U.S. foreign policy: "Speakers draw cheers with demands for American withdrawal from the war against the Communists in Vietnam."[2]

Far less obvious was the hint of looming trouble in *Time's* cover story the following week on the best-selling poet Phyllis McGinley, a suburban Connecticut housewife. McGinley proclaimed that women exercise their greatest influence in the home. She "finds herself the sturdiest exponent of the glory of housewifery," *Time* observed, "standing almost alone against a rising chorus of voices summoning women away from the hearth." The loudest voice in the chorus, the story also noted, belonged to Betty Friedan, whose best-selling "broadside," *The Feminine Mystique* (1963), proclaimed "that the college-educated woman who seeks fulfillment in domesticity will never find it. . . ." Given McGinley's nine books of poetry, two volumes of essays, fifteen children's books, and one Pulitzer Prize, *Time* could only conclude that Friedan's attitude was "tinged with envy."[3]

Values are often defended only when they are no longer taken for granted. *Time's* profile of McGinley exposed growing doubts by 1965 that women could find happiness only at home. Indeed, in the coming years, the rejection of domesticity fed a powerful women's movement that transformed the way homes, workplaces, churches, and the halls of government looked and functioned. Three decades after a suburban housewife like Phyllis McGinley could become a controversial figure, historians ask what gave rise to a women's movement that caught most Americans off guard in the 1960s. In this chapter, we consider some of their answers.

SETTING

By 1970, the growing women's protest had a name: the "women's liberation movement." Journalists, commentators, and women activists themselves had other labels for it as well. Some called it the "women's rights movement." Others labeled it "feminist protest," and later many settled on "the women's movement." The failure to pin one name on the women's revolt of the 1960s and 1970s reveals something about it. First, it was a movement only in the loosest sense. As *Newsweek* put it in 1970, "The women's liberation movement [is] a very loose designation for a multiplicity of small groups led by a multiplicity of women."[4] All of the participants might agree that women were subject to sexism and sexual discrimination, and thus did not enjoy full equality in American society. Yet not all women activists shared the same analysis of their problems. Nor did they agree on what to do about them. Liberation, they discovered, could mean many things.

Women's diverse backgrounds influenced their analysis of the gender problem. Social class, education, occupation, marital status, and even sexual orientation influenced women's views of equality. Thus, the women's movement had little appeal for many black, Hispanic, and working-class women, who often saw their inequality in economic or racial terms. On the other hand, it attracted many educated, middle-class women, for whom *The Feminine Mystique* struck a responsive chord. Friedan had asserted that education and employment outside the home was the solution for women's unhappiness and lack of self-esteem. When the National Organization for Women (NOW) was formed in 1966 with Friedan as its first president, its ranks were filled with professional women who faced discrimination in the job market and felt bridled by traditional attitudes about women's domestic duties. NOW denied hostility toward men, however. Rather, it called for "a fully equal partnership of the sexes," and pressed for an end to sexual discrimination through such measures as the Equal Rights Amendment.

By the late 1960s, younger women began to challenge NOW with different analyses of women's oppression and alternative responses to it. Often veterans of the civil rights and antiwar movements or New Left political organizations, these radical feminists dismissed NOW's efforts to end sexual discrimination through political action as "bourgeois" and insufficient. They also pointed out that gaining equality in the workplace, the political arena, the media, and elsewhere in the "public" sphere was not enough. With no equality in the "private" sphere of domestic relations, women would be expected to "do it all."

For radical feminists, NOW's legislative solutions were too narrow, and women could not be truly liberated without a radical restructuring of society. Some insisted that women's liberation could only be achieved with the rejection of capitalism. Yet most radical feminists advanced cultural rather than economic radicalism. They divided with moderates not on questions about the economic order but on the matters of marriage and family. Radicals like Kate Millett and Susan Brownmiller, for instance, argued that women could liberate themselves through communal living arrangements and even by ending women's function as childbearers. Others, such as the Radicalesbians, insisted that the problem lay in heterosexual relations. Rather than point to the barriers to access, radical feminists emphasized the oppressive nature of a male-dominated society and the need to view all relations between men and women in political terms.

The difference, said some feminists, was between the moderates' "egalitarian ethic" and the radicals' "liberation ethic." Yet it was not quite that simple.

Friedan and other moderates had advocated the liberation of women from an ideology of domesticity, and radicals were guided by the ideal of gender equality. In addition, both moderates and radicals proclaimed opposition to sexism. Moreover, by the mid-1970s there were thousands of feminist groups raising numerous issues supported by both sides, including legal abortion, domestic violence, women's health, and child care. Maybe the most accurate assessment of the growth of women's groups was offered by one feminist writer, who proclaimed, "It's not a movement, it's a State of Mind."[5]

By 1975, that "state of mind" had influenced public consciousness. The protests and lobbying of women's groups and a flood of books and articles by such feminists as Kate Millett, Gloria Steinem, and Robin Morgan had raised awareness of women's issues. Feminism had gained legitimacy, although not in the radical sense of eliminating gender differences. By the end of the 1970s, laws and court decisions embodied many demands of the women's movement. Although factionalized and under a conservative counterattack, women had succeeded in altering their status as a group and changing the lives of countless women and men.

INVESTIGATION

Like the antebellum women's rights movement, the feminist revolt of the 1960s and 1970s was led mostly by middle-class women. Also like the earlier movement, it rebelled against an ideology at the same time that it was divided by ideology. And like the pre–Civil War women's protest, it arose at a time of widespread unrest. To understand the rise of feminist protest in the 1960s and 1970s, historians must therefore study a number of influences on women. They must also consider the power of ideology to stimulate and define the limits of reform.

This chapter examines what led many women to become women's rights advocates seeking legal equality and equal treatment in the workplace, or even to become feminists seeking to completely redefine the meaning of gender. It presents two historians' contrasting views about the changes responsible for the rise of the women's movement. Your main assignment is to evaluate these arguments and develop an explanation for the rise of the women's movement in the 1960s and 1970s. Your analysis should explain the impact of economic, social, political, and cultural changes on women's views about their status. It should also address the following main questions:

1. **How do the explanations of historians Elaine Tyler May and Alice Echols for the rise of the women's movement differ?** Which one better explains its rise? Why? Are their explanations mutually exclusive?

2. **What do the primary sources reveal about the experiences that led many women to change their views about their status?** What did major cultural,

political, and economic trends, including the civil rights and antiwar movements and the sexual revolution, have to do with the rise of the women's movement?

3. **What do the sources reveal about the major goals of the women's movement and the most important factors limiting their attainment?** How do May's and Echols's explanations for the limits of the women's movement differ?

Before you begin, read the sections in your textbook on the status of women in postwar society and on the women's movement of the 1960s and 1970s. Note how your text accounts for the rise of this movement.

SECONDARY SOURCES

In this selection, historian Elaine Tyler May examines the impact of political changes on American families, specifically the relationship between the demise of a Cold War ideology and the ideal of domesticity in the 1960s. Pay attention to May's argument about the way a Cold War ideology "contained" women. Does she make a convincing case that a domestic ideology and Cold War militance rose and fell together? Do you think the postwar marriage and baby booms were the result of Cold War ideology or of other factors, such as the return of peace and prosperity? Also think about whether the idea of containment can be applied to family relations and if May shows that containment cut off pre–Cold War changes within families.

Cold War Ideology and the Rise of Feminism (1988)
ELAINE TYLER MAY

The politics of the cold war and the ideology and public policies that it spawned were crucial in shaping postwar family life and gender roles. . . .

With security as the common thread, the cold war ideology and the domestic revival reinforced each other. The powerful political consensus that supported cold war policies abroad and anticommunism at home fueled conformity to the suburban family ideal. In turn, the domestic ideology encouraged private solutions to social problems and further weakened the potential for challenges to the cold war consensus. Personal adaptation, rather than political resistance, characterized the era. But postwar domesticity never fully delivered on its promises. The baby-boom children who grew up in suburban homes abandoned the containment ethos when they came of

Source: From *Homeward Bound* by Elaine Tyler May. Copyright © 1988 by Elaine Tyler May. Reprinted by permission of Basic Books, a member of Perseus Books Group.

age. As young adults in the 1960s, they challenged both the imperatives of the cold war and the domestic ideology that came with it. At the same time, they forged new paths to pursue the unfulfilled dreams of their parents . . . .

. . . Among the first to criticize the status quo were postwar parents themselves. In 1963, Betty Friedan published her exposé of domesticity, *The Feminine Mystique*. Friedan gave a name to the "problem that has no name" for career homemakers. A postwar wife and mother herself, Friedan spoke directly to women . . . who had lived according to the domestic containment ideology. She urged them to break away from their domestic confines, go back to school, pursue careers, and revive the vision of female independence that had been alive before World War II. *The Feminine Mystique* became an immediate best-seller and created a national sensation. The book enabled discontented women across the country to find their voices. It was as if someone was finally willing to say that the emperor had no clothes; soon a chorus joined in support. Hundreds of readers wrote to Friedan, telling their stories. These personal testimonies reveal the stated and unstated messages that this generation of parents gave their children.

The letters to Friedan reveal widespread disenchantment among women who had struggled to conform to the prevailing familial norm. Some of the writers were children of activist parents who had fought for equal rights in the early part of the century. Nearly all expressed the hope that their children would avoid the domestic trap in which they found themselves. . . .

A Mount Holyoke graduate who joined the "stampede back to the nest" described her path into domesticity: "I entered graduate school at Yale, met a man, left school, and married in 1951. I have since then moved thirteen times, lived in eight states, had four miscarriages and produced two children." But she also struggled at home and alone to become a painter. *So* "finally, when I fill out the income tax now, it is occupation: Painter, not housewife." . . .

Friedan's book sparked readers to comment not only on the connection between women's and men's fate, but between domesticity and cold war politics. One woman believed that political activism was the only way to bring women out of "their cozy cocoons in America," but she also perceived that challenges to women's roles would be seen as un-American. Women would need to "make determined efforts to free themselves," she noted, "and they may expect hostility from conservative elements politically as well as from their fellow timid sisters and timid men. I am not advocating that women become Communist sympathizers, but I am expecting that progressive women will be so labelled." . . .

Many of the women who wrote to Friedan were those who could respond to her call for self-realization through education and careers. They were affluent. If married, they had husbands who provided an income that was adequate enough to allow them to develop outside interests for self-fulfillment. But there were others who found Friedan's message troubling. It was fine to have ambitions, but it was another matter to work out of necessity, face a sex-segregated job market, and do double duty at home as well.

One woman expressed her irritation at "the false emphasis that is placed on the entire matter of women fulfilling themselves through a career. The vast majority of working women don't have careers. We have jobs, just like men. We work for money to buy things that our families need. If we're lucky, we like our jobs, and find some satisfaction in doing them well, but it is hard to hold a commercial job, raise a family and keep a house." . . .

As these letters indicate, domestic containment was not going to die a quick or natural death. Yet it was clearly doomed from its own internal contradictions. Betty Friedan spoke for a generation whose children would later be credited with initiating a decade of political and social upheaval, but many of their parents had paved the way. Even those who thought that it was too late to change their own ways and routines knew it was not too late for their children. They encouraged their children—implicitly if not explicitly—to follow new paths. Frustrated women and exhausted men provided ambiguous role models for children hoping to avoid the discontent of their mothers and the pressure and ill health the stresses of the work place had inflicted on their fathers.

Still, change came slowly. In the early 1960s, it was not immediately obvious that a unique historical era was coming to an end. Signs that the postwar consensus was beginning to crack were hardly more visible than they had been in the fifties: a few voices of dissent from the intelligentsia, the growing popularity of counterculture heroes such as Elvis Presley and James Dean, and the spread of the civil rights movement from black activists in the South to northern whites. Oral contraceptives first became available in 1960, but they did not immediately bring about a change in behavior, even though years later, many would credit (or blame) "The Pill" for the "sexual revolution." Most cultural signs still pointed toward the cold war consensus at home and abroad, and the ideology of domesticity was still alive and well. . . .

On November 1, 1961, 50,000 American housewives walked out of their homes and jobs in a massive protest, "Women Strike for Peace." These activists were among the first postwar middle-class whites to organize against the social and political status quo. Several of the leaders of the strike were part of a small group of feminists who had worked on behalf of women's rights throughout the forties and the fifties. According to *Newsweek*, the strikers "were perfectly ordinary looking women. . . .They looked like the women you would see driving ranch wagons, or shopping at the village market, or attending PTA meetings . . . many [were] wheeling baby buggies or strollers." Within a year their numbers grew to several hundred thousand.

Anticommunists worried that Women Strike for Peace signaled that "the pro-Reds have moved in on our mothers and are using them for their own purposes," and the Federal Bureau of Investigation kept the group under surveillance from its inception in 1961. The following year, the leaders of

Women Strike for Peace were called before the House Un-American Activities Committee. Under questioning, these women spoke as mothers, claiming that saving American children from nuclear extinction was the essence of "Americanism," thereby turning the ideology of domesticity against the assumptions of the cold war. These women carried the banner of motherhood into politics, much like their reformist Victorian sisters in the last century. But their ability to attack the cold war with domesticity as their tool and make a mockery of the congressional hearings indicates that the familial–cold war consensus was beginning to lose its grip.

Increasing political pressure resulted in several important new public policies that challenged the status quo. In 1961, President Kennedy established the President's Commission on the Status of Women, chaired appropriately by an activist from the 1930s, Eleanor Roosevelt. Within the next three years, Congress passed the Equal Pay Act and Title VII of the Civil Rights Act (which prohibited discrimination on the basis of sex, as well as race, color, religion, and national origin), and the United States and the Soviet Union signed the first treaty banning the atmospheric testing of nuclear weapons.

While these policies were taking shape, Students for a Democratic Society (SDS), inspired largely by the civil rights movement, gained thousands of members in chapters across the country. Out of the student movement came the antiwar movement and the new feminism. By the late sixties, hundreds of thousands of young activists mobilized against the gender assumptions as well as the cold war policies that had prevailed since World War II.

The simultaneous attack on domestic containment and the cold war ideology also found expression in the popular culture. Within a few months of the publication of *The Feminine Mystique* came Stanley Kubrick's film, *Dr. Strangelove: Or, How I Learned to Stop Worrying and Love the Bomb*, a biting satire that equated the madness of the cold war with Americans' unresolved sexual neuroses. Such attacks against the sanctity of the postwar domestic ideology and the politics of the cold war would have been risky endeavors ten years earlier. The film probably would have been suppressed and its creators called before the House Un-American Activities Committee. By the early sixties, however, although the cold war was still in full force, and some viewers found the film offensive and un-American, critics as well as audiences were, for the most part, wildly enthusiastic.

By the end of the decade, the new feminist movement had pushed beyond Betty Friedan's call for self-realization into a full-fledged assault on sexism in all its forms, organized by younger women who emerged from their activism in the civil rights movement and the New Left with newly discovered skills and strengths. The new feminists demanded access to professional occupations and skilled jobs, protested low wages, and worked for pay equity. They formed consciousness-raising groups all over the country, challenged the gender division of labor in the home, and railed against the sexual double standard. In a 1970 survey of women entering an open-admission, tuition-free public university, most saw their future role as "married career woman with children"—a vast change from the 1950s when most women of all classes saw their future career as homemaker. . . .

Married or divorced, professional as well as nonprofessional wage-earning women continued to face inequalities at work and at home. Nevertheless, political activism opened up new opportunities for women to achieve autonomy that had been unavailable to their mothers. Women of the fifties, constrained by tremendous cultural and economic pressures to conform to domestic containment, gave up their independence and personal ambitions. Once they made the choice to embrace domesticity, they did their best to thrive within it and claimed that their sacrifices were ultimately worthwhile. Many of their daughters abandoned security and material comfort to follow a more autonomous path that brought them face to face with economic hardship and pervasive discrimination. Yet, like their mothers, many would say that the struggles were worth it. Their mothers paid a price for security and dependence; the daughters paid a price for autonomy and independence. In both cases, the lack of equal opportunity for women limited their options. Yet there is no question that the daughters had more opportunities than their mothers as a result of the hard-won political achievements of the sixties and seventies: they were no longer bound to the home.

Political goals were only partially achieved, however. Even before the end of the 1960s, the "silent majority" rose up against the noisy, youthful minority. In 1968, the quintessential fifties politician, Richard Nixon, was back in the White House, this time as president. The ideology of the cold war, although dealt a serious blow by the disastrous war in Vietnam, remained a powerful force in national politics—and it continued to be tied to the ideology of domesticity. Those who claimed that South Vietnam fell as a result of softness against communism also blamed feminism for what they perceived as the destruction of the family.

It is no accident that in the wake of feminism, the sexual revolution, and the peace movement of the 1960s, the New Right emerged in the 1970s and 1980s as a powerful political force with the dual aims of reviving the cold war and reasserting the ideology of domesticity. It should not be surprising that the most vigorous opponent of the Equal Rights Amendment, Phyllis Schlafly, began her career as an avid Cold Warrior. Proponents of the New Right gained strength by calling for militance in foreign policy, opposing the Equal Rights Amendment, and condemning student radicalism, the counterculture, feminism, and the sexual revolution. They went on to triumph in 1980, with the election of Ronald Reagan to the presidency.

Reagan, like Nixon, received his political groundings in the late 1940s and 1950s as an anticommunist crusader in California. Appropriately, his media image was that of the family man par excellence, as he promoted home-centered consumerism as host of the General Electric Theater. The all-electric home that Reagan advertised (and also inhabited) was virtually identical to the "model home" Nixon praised in Moscow in 1959. In the 1960s, Reagan carried his image into California politics, where he promised to crack down on student protestors. With Reagan in the White House in the 1980s, the rhetoric of containment returned, with its support for cold-war militance and calls for a strengthened "traditional" family. . . .

It is clear that in recent decades, the domestic ideology and cold war militance have risen and fallen together. Immediately after World War II, stable family life seemed necessary for national security, civil defense, and the struggle for supremacy over the Soviet Union. For a generation of young adults who grew up amid depression and war, domestic containment was a logical response to specific historical circumstances. It allowed them to pursue, in the midst of a tense and precarious world situation, the quest for a sexually fulfilling, consumer-oriented personal life that was free from hardship. But the circumstances were different for their children, who broke the consensus surrounding the cold war and domestic containment. Whether the baby-boom children will ultimately be more successful than their parents in achieving fulfilling lives and a more just and tolerant world remains to be seen. But one thing is certain: gender, family, and national politics are still intertwined in the ongoing saga of postwar cultural change.

---

2   In this selection, Alice Echols relates the rise of feminist consciousness in the 1960s to numerous changes in American society, especially the rise of other protest movements. What connection does she see between the women's liberation movement and the civil rights, antiwar, and student movements? Does Echols explain the rise of a women's rights movement, as symbolized by the National Organization for Women? How would you compare Echols's conclusion about the impact of the women's liberation movement to Elaine Tyler May's conclusion in Source 1 about the limited success of the women's movement?

Women's Liberation and Sixties Radicalism (2002)
ALICE ECHOLS

On September 7, 1968, the sixties came to that most apple-pie of American institutions, the Miss America Pageant. One hundred women's liberation activists descended upon Atlantic City to protest the pageant's promotion of physical attractiveness as the primary measure of women's worth. Carrying signs that read, "Miss America Is a Big Falsie," "Miss America Sells It," and "Up Against the Wall, Miss America," they formed a picket line on the boardwalk, sang anti–Miss America songs in three-part harmony, and performed guerrilla theater. Later that day, they crowned a live sheep Miss America and paraded it on the boardwalk to parody the way the contestants, and, by extension, all women, "are appraised and judged like animals at a county fair." They tried to convince women in the crowd that the tyranny of beauty was but one of the many ways that women's bodies were colonized. By announcing beforehand that they would not speak to male reporters (or to any man for that matter), the demonstrators challenged the sexual division of labor that consigned female reporters to the "soft" stories while reserving for male reporters the coveted "hard" news stories. Newspaper editors who wanted to cover the protest were thus forced to pull their women reporters from the society pages.

The protesters set up a "Freedom Trash Can" and filled it with various "instruments of torture"—high-heeled shoes, bras, girdles, hair curlers, false eyelashes, typing books, and representative copies of *Cosmopolitan*, *Playboy*, and *Ladies Home Journal*. They had wanted to burn the contents of the Freedom Trash Can, but they were thwarted by a city ordinance prohibiting bonfires on the boardwalk. However, word had been leaked to the press that the protest would include a symbolic bra-burning, and, as a consequence, reporters were everywhere. Although they burned no bras that day on the boardwalk, the image of the bra-burning, militant feminist remains part of our popular mythology about the women's liberation movement. . . .

In its wit, passion, and irreverence, not to mention its expansive formulation of politics (to include the politics of beauty, no less!), the Miss America protest resembled other sixties demonstrations. . . . Judging from their response, this new thing, "women's liberation," was about as popular as the antiwar movement. The protesters were jeered, harassed, and called "manhaters" and "commies." One man suggested that "it would be a lot more useful" if the demonstrators threw themselves, and not their bras, girdles, and make-up, into the trash can.

But nothing—not even the verbal abuse they encountered on the boardwalk—could diminish the euphoria women's liberationists felt as they started to mobilize around their own, rather than other people's, oppression. Ann Snitow speaks for many when she recalls that in contrast to her experience in the larger, male-dominated protest Movement,* where she had felt sort of "blank and peripheral," women's liberation was like "an ecstasy of discussion." Precisely because it was about one's own life, there was, she says, "nothing distant about it." Robin Morgan has claimed that the Miss America protest "announced our existence to the world." That is only a slight exaggeration, for as a consequence of the protest, women's liberation

---

*Echols uses the term "Movement" to refer primarily to the black, student, and antiwar protest movements of the 1960s. She refers to the women's liberation movement as the "movement."

achieved the status of a movement both to its participants and to the media; as such, the Miss America demonstration represents an important moment in the history of the sixties.

Although the women's liberation movement only began to take shape toward the end of the decade, it was a quintessentially sixties movement. It is not just that many early women's liberation activists had prior involvements in other sixties movements, although that was certainly true, as has been ably documented by Sara Evans. And it is not just that, of all the sixties movements, the women's liberation movement alone carried on and extended into the 1970s that decade's political radicalism and rethinking of fundamental social organization. Although that is true as well. Rather, it is that the larger, male-dominated protest Movement, despite its considerable sexism, provided much of the intellectual foundation and cultural orientation for the women's liberation movement, many of whose ideas and approaches—especially its concern with revitalizing democratic process and reformulating "politics" to include the personal—were refined and recast versions of those already present in the New Left and the black freedom movement. . . .

Women's discontent with their place in America in the 1960s was, of course, produced by a broad range of causes. Crucial in reigniting feminist consciousness in the 1960s was the unprecedented number of women (especially married white women) being drawn into the paid labor force, as the service sector of the economy expanded and rising consumer aspirations fueled the desire of many families for a second income. As Alice Kessler-Harris has pointed out, "homes and cars, refrigerators and washing machines, telephones and multiple televisions required higher incomes." So did providing a college education for one's children. These new patterns of consumption were made possible in large part through the emergence of the two-income family as wives increasingly "sought to aid their husbands in the quest for the good life." By 1960, 30.5 percent of all wives worked for wages. Women's growing labor force participation also reflected larger structural shifts in the U.S. economy. Sara Evans has argued that the "reestablishment of labor force segregation following World War II ironically reserved for women a large proportion of the new jobs created in the fifties due to the fact that the fastest growing sector of the economy was no longer industry but services." Women's increasing labor force participation was facilitated as well by the growing number of women graduating from college and the introduction of the birth control pill in 1960.

Despite the fact that women's "place" was increasingly in the paid work force (or perhaps because of it), ideas about women's proper role in American society were quite conventional throughout the fifties and the early sixties, held there by a resurgent ideology of domesticity—what Betty Friedan coined the "feminine mystique." But, as Jane De Hart-Mathews has observed, "the bad fit was there: the unfairness of unequal pay for the same work, the low value placed on jobs women performed, the double burden of housework and wage work." By the mid-sixties at least some American women felt that the contradiction between the realities of paid work and higher education on the one hand, and the still pervasive ideology of domesticity on the other hand, had become irreconcilable.

However, without the presence of other oppositional movements the women's liberation movement might not have developed at all as an organized force for social change. It certainly would have developed along vastly different lines. The climate of protest encouraged women, even those not directly involved in the black movement and the New Left, to question conventional gender arrangements. Moreover, as already noted, many of the women who helped form the women's liberation movement had been involved as well in the male-dominated Movement. If the larger Movement was typically indifferent, or worse, hostile, to women's liberation, it was nonetheless through their experiences in that Movement that the young and predominately white and middle-class women who initially formed the women's liberation movement became politicized. The relationship between women's liberation and the larger Movement was at its core paradoxical. The Movement was a site of sexism, but it also provided white women a space in which they could develop political skills and self-confidence, a space in which they could violate the injunction against female self-assertion. Most important, it gave them no small part of the intellectual ammunition—the language and the ideas—with which to fight their own oppression. . . .

. . . Women's liberationists shared new leftists' and black radicals' rejection of liberalism, and, as a consequence, they often went to great lengths to distinguish themselves from the liberal feminists of the National Organization for Women (NOW). (In fact, their disillusionment with liberalism was more thorough during the early stages of their movement-building than had been the case for either new leftists or civil rights activists because they had lived through the earlier betrayals around the War and civil rights. Male radicals' frequent denunciations of feminism as "bourgeois" also encouraged women's liberationists to distance themselves from NOW.) NOW had been formed in 1966 to push the federal government to enforce the provisions of the 1964 Civil Rights Act outlawing sex discrimination—a paradigmatic liberal agenda focused on public access and the prohibition of employment discrimination. To women's liberationists, NOW's integrationist, access-oriented approach ignored the racial and class inequalities that were the very foundation of the "mainstream" that the feminists of NOW were dedicated to integrating. In the introduction to the 1970 bestseller she edited, *Sisterhood Is Powerful,* Robin Morgan declared that "NOW is essentially an organization that wants reforms [in the] second-class citizenship of women—and this is where it differs drastically from the rest of the Women's Liberation Movement." In *The Dialectic of Sex* Shulamith Firestone described NOW's political stance as "untenable even in terms of immediate political gains" and deemed it "more a leftover of the old feminism rather than a model of the new." Radical feminist Ti-Grace Atkinson went even further, characterizing many in NOW as only wanting "women to have the same opportunity to be oppressors too."

Women's liberationists also took issue with liberal feminists' formulation of women's problem as their exclusion from the public sphere. Younger activists argued instead that women's exclusion from public life was inextricable from their subordination in the family, and would persist until this larger problem was addressed. For instance, Firestone claimed the solution to women's oppression wasn't inclusion in the mainstream, but the eradication of the biological family, which she argued was the "tapeworm of exploitation."

Of course, younger activists' alienation from NOW was often more than matched by NOW members' annoyance with them. Many liberal feminists were appalled (at least initially) by women's liberationists' politicization of personal life. NOW founder Betty Friedan frequently railed against women's liberationists for waging a "bedroom war" that diverted women from the real struggle of integrating the public sphere.

Women's liberationists believed that they had embarked upon a much more ambitious project—the virtual remaking of the world. Nothing short of radically transforming society was sufficient to deal with what they were discovering: that gender inequality was thoroughly embedded in everyday life. As Shulamith Firestone put it, "sex-class is so deep as to be invisible." The pervasiveness of sexism and gender's status as a naturalized category demonstrated to women's liberationists the inadequacy, the shallowness, of NOW's legislative and judicial remedies and the necessity of thoroughgoing social transformation. Thus, whereas liberal feminists talked of ending sex discrimination, women's liberationists called for nothing less than the destruction of patriarchy and capitalism. As defined by feminists, patriarchy, in contrast to sex discrimination, defied reform. . . .

The totalism of their vision would have been difficult to translate into a concrete reform package, even had they been interested in doing so. But electoral politics and the legislative and judicial reforms that engaged the energies of liberal feminists did little to animate most women's liberationists. Like other sixties radicals, they were instead taken with the idea of developing forms that would prefigure the utopian community of the imagined future. . . .

Sixties radicalism proved compelling to many precisely because it promised to transform life. Politics was not about the subordination of self to a larger political cause; instead it was the path to self-fulfillment. This ultimately was the power of sixties radicalism. . . . Thus the idea that "politics is how you live your life, not who you vote for," as Yippie leader Jerry Rubin put it, could and did lead to a subordination of politics to lifestyle. But if the idea led some to confuse personal liberation for political struggle, it led others to embrace an asceticism that sacrificed personal needs and desires to political imperatives. Some women's liberation activists followed this course, interpreting the idea that the personal is political to mean that one's personal life should conform to some abstract standard of political correctness. At first this tendency was mitigated by the founders' insistence that there were no personal solutions, only collective solutions, to women's oppression. However, over time one's self-presentation, marital status, and sexual preference frequently came to determine one's standing or ranking in the movement. The most notorious example of this involved the New York radical group, The Feminists, who established a quota to limit the number of married women in the group. Policies such as these prompted Barbara Ehrenreich to question "a feminism which talks about universal sisterhood, but is horrified by women who wear spiked heels or call their friends 'girls.' " At the same time, what was personally satisfying was sometimes upheld as politically correct. In the end, both the women's liberation movement and the larger protest Movement suffered, as the idea that the personal is political was often interpreted in ways that made questions of lifestyle absolutely central. . . .

To engender this sense of sisterhood or "we-ness," women's liberationists developed consciousness-raising, a practice involving "the political reinterpretation of personal life." According to its principal architects, its purpose was to "awaken the latent consciousness that . . . all women have about our oppression." In talking about their personal experiences, it was argued, women would come to understand that what they had believed were personal problems were, in fact, "social problems that must become social issues and fought together rather than with personal solutions."

New York women's liberationist Kathie Sarachild was reportedly the person who coined the term consciousness-raising. However, the technique originated in other social movements. As Sarachild noted in 1973, those who promoted consciousness-raising "were applying to women and to ourselves as women's liberation organizers the practice a number of us had learned in the civil rights movement in the South in the early 1960s." There they had seen that the sharing of personal problems, grievances, and aspirations— "telling it like it is"—could be a radicalizing experience. Moreover, for some women's liberationists consciousness-raising was a way to avoid the tendency of some in the movement to try to fit women into existing (and often Marxist) theoretical paradigms. By circumventing the "experts" on women and going to women themselves, they would be able not only to construct a theory of women's oppression but to formulate strategy as well. Thus women's liberationists struggled to find the commonalities in women's experiences in order to generate generalizations about women's oppression.

Consciousness-raising was enormously successful in exposing the insidiousness of sexism and in engendering a sense of identity and solidarity among the largely white, middle-class women who participated in "c-r" groups. By the early seventies even NOW, whose founder Betty Friedan had initially derided consciousness-raising as so much "navel-gazing," began sponsoring c-r groups. But the effort to transcend the particular was both the strength and weakness of consciousness-raising. If it encouraged women to locate the common denominators in their lives, it inhibited discussion of women's considerable differences. Despite the particularities of white, middle-class women's experiences, theirs became the basis for feminist theorizing about women's oppression. . . .

Accounts of sixties radicalism usually cite its role in bringing about the dismantling of Jim Crow and disfranchisement, the withdrawal of U.S. troops from Vietnam, and greater gender equality. However, equally important, if less frequently noted, was its challenge to politics as usual. Sixties radicals succeeded both in reformulating politics, even mainstream politics, to include personal life, and in challenging the notion that elites alone have the wisdom and expertise to control the political process. For a moment, people who by virtue of their color, age, and gender were far from the sites of formal power became politically engaged, became agents of change.

Given the internal contradictions and shortcomings of sixties radicalism, the repressiveness of the federal government in the late sixties and early seventies, and changing economic conditions in the United States, it is not surprising that the movements built by radicals in the sixties either no longer exist or do so only in attenuated form. Activists in the women's liberation movement, however, helped to bring about a fundamental realignment of gender roles in this country through outrageous protests, tough-minded polemics, and an "ecstasy of discussion." Indeed, those of us who came of age in the days before the resurgence of feminism know that the world today, while hardly a feminist utopia, is nonetheless a far different, and in many respects a far fairer, world than what we confronted in 1967.

PRIMARY SOURCES

The sources in this section will help you further analyze the two essays and thus formulate answers to the main questions in the Investigation section. These sources reflect a number of economic, cultural, political, and demographic influences on the women's movement. They also illustrate the varied ways women attempted to achieve equality and some of the obstacles they confronted.

---

3   Betty Friedan attacked the postwar domestic ideal in her best-selling book, *The Feminine Mystique*. As you read this excerpt, note what problem accompanied the widespread acceptance of the domestic ideal, according to Friedan. Why was the feminine mystique so powerful in the 1960s? Did its hold have more to do with demographic or with political factors?

The Problem That Has No Name (1963)

BETTY FRIEDAN

The problem lay buried, unspoken, for many years in the minds of American women. It was a strange stirring, a sense of dissatisfaction, a yearning that women suffered in the middle of the twentieth century in the United States. Each suburban wife struggled with it alone. As she made the beds, shopped for groceries, matched slipcover material, ate peanut butter sandwiches with her children, chauffeured Cub Scouts and Brownies, lay beside her husband at night—she was afraid to ask even of herself the silent question—"Is this all?"

For over fifteen years there was no word of this yearning in the millions of words written about women, for women, in all the columns, books and articles by experts telling women their role was to seek fulfillment as wives and mothers. Over and over women heard in voices of tradition and of Freudian sophistication that they could desire no greater destiny than to glory in their own femininity. Experts told them how to catch a man and keep him, how to breastfeed children and handle their toilet training, how to cope with sibling rivalry and adolescent rebellion; how to buy a dishwasher, bake bread, cook gourmet meals, and build a swimming pool with their own hands; how to dress, look, and act more feminine and make marriage more exciting; how to keep their husbands from dying young and their sons from growing into delinquents. They were taught to pity the neurotic, unfeminine, unhappy women who wanted to be poets or physicists or presidents. They learned that truly feminine women do not want careers, higher education, political rights—the independence and the opportunities that the old-fashioned feminists fought for. Some women, in their forties and fifties, still remembered painfully giving up those dreams, but most of the younger women no longer even thought about them. A thousand expert voices applauded their femininity, their adjustment, their new maturity. All they had to do was devote their lives from earliest girlhood to finding a husband and bearing children. . . .

The suburban housewife—she was the dream image of the young American women and the envy, it was said, of women all over the world. The American housewife—freed by science and labor-saving appliances from the drudgery, the dangers of childbirth and the illnesses of her grandmother. She was healthy, beautiful, educated, concerned only about her husband, her children, her home. She had found true feminine fulfillment. As a housewife and mother, she was respected as a full and equal partner to man in his world. She was free to choose automobiles, clothes, appliances, supermarkets; she had everything that women ever dreamed of.

In the fifteen years after World War II, this mystique of feminine fulfillment became the cherished and self-perpetuating core of contemporary American culture. Millions of women lived their lives in the image of those pretty pictures of the American suburban housewife, kissing their husbands goodbye in front of the picture window, depositing their station-wagonsful of children at school, and smiling as they ran the new electric waxer over the spotless kitchen floor. They baked their own bread, sewed their own and their children's clothes, kept their new washing machines and dryers running all day. They changed the sheets on the beds twice a week instead of once, took the rug-hooking class in adult education, and pitied their poor frustrated mothers, who had dreamed of having a career. Their only dream was to be perfect wives and mothers; their highest ambition to have five children and a beautiful house, their only fight to get and keep their husbands. They had no thought for the unfeminine problems of the world outside the home; they wanted the men to make the major decisions. They gloried in their role as women, and wrote proudly on the census blank "Occupation: housewife.". . .

If a woman had a problem in the 1950's and 1960's, she knew that something must be wrong with her marriage, or with herself. Other women were satisfied with their lives, she thought. What kind of a woman was she if she did not feel this mysterious fulfillment waxing the kitchen floor? She was so ashamed to admit her dissatisfaction that she never knew how many other women shared it. If she tried to tell her husband, he didn't understand what she was talking about. She did not really understand it herself. For over fifteen years women in America found it harder to talk about this problem than about sex.

---

4   Like pre–Civil War women's rights activists, many modern feminists were first involved in other reforms or protests before becoming committed to feminism. Mary King, the author of this selection, was a white civil rights worker involved in the Student Nonviolent Coordinating Committee, a civil rights organization founded in 1960 to coordinate efforts to desegregate the South. Many black and white college students were members of SNCC. What effect did involvement in the civil rights movement have on King as a woman?

Civil Rights and the Rise of Feminism (1987)
MARY KING

1. Staff was involved in crucial constitutional revisions at the Atlanta staff meeting in October. A large committee was appointed to present revisions to the staff. The committee was all men.

Source: From Mary E. King, *Freedom Song.* Copyright © 1987 by Mary Elizabeth King. Originally published by William Morrow & Company, New York. Reprinted with the permission of Gerard McCauley Agency, Inc.

2. Two organizers were working together to form a farmer's league. Without asking any questions, the male organizer immediately assigned the clerical work to the female organizer although both had had equal experience in organizing campaigns.

3. Although there are women in Mississippi project who have been working as long as some of the men, the leadership group in COFO is all men.

4. A woman in a field office wondered why she was held responsible for day to day decisions, only to find out later that she had been appointed project director but not told.

5. A fall 1964 personnel and resources report on Mississippi projects lists the number of people in each project. The section on Laurel however, lists not the number of persons, but "three girls."

6. One of SNCC's main administrative officers apologizes for appointment of a woman as interim project director in a key Mississippi project area.

7. A veteran of two years work for SNCC in two states spends her day typing and doing clerical work for other people in her project. . . .

Undoubtedly this list will seem strange to some, petty to others, laughable to most. The list could continue as far as there are women in the movement. Except that most women don't talk about these kinds of incidents, because the whole subject is not discussable—strange to some, petty to others, laughable to most. The average white person finds it difficult to understand why the Negro resents being called "boy," or being thought of as "musical" and "athletic," because the average white person doesn't realize that he assumes he is superior. And naturally he doesn't understand the problem of paternalism. So too the average SNCC worker finds it difficult to discuss the woman problem because of the assumption of male superiority. Assumptions of male superiority are as widespread and deep rooted and every much as crippling to the woman as the assumptions of white supremacy are to the Negro. Consider why it is in SNCC that women who are competent, qualified and experienced, are automatically assigned to the "female" kinds of jobs such as typing, desk work, telephone work, filing, library work, cooking and the assistant kind of administrative work but rarely the "executive" kind.

The woman in SNCC is often in the same position as that token Negro hired in a corporation. The management thinks that it has done its bit. Yet every day the Negro bears an atmosphere, attitudes and actions which are tinged with condescension and paternalism, the most telling of which are when he is not promoted as the equally or less skilled whites are. . . .

5   The National Organization for Women proclaimed its premises and goals at its first meeting in 1966. Note what NOW saw as the principal problems confronting women. Did its proposals to achieve equality

pertain to the "public" or the "private" sphere? How does this statement reflect the influence of other developments in American society by the 1960s?

NOW's Statement of Purpose (1966)

We, men and women who hereby constitute ourselves as the National Organization for Women, believe that the time has come for a new movement toward true equality for all women in America, and toward a fully equal partnership of the sexes, as part of the world-wide revolution of human rights now taking place within and beyond our national borders.

The purpose of NOW is to take action to bring women into full participation in the mainstream of American society now, exercising all the privileges and responsibilities thereof in truly equal partnership with men.

We believe the time has come to move beyond the abstract argument, discussion and symposia over the status and special nature of women which has raged in America in recent years: the time has come to confront, with concrete action, the conditions that now prevent women from enjoying the equality of opportunity and freedom of choice which is their right as individual Americans, and as human beings.

NOW is dedicated to the proposition that women first and foremost are human beings, who, like all other people in our society, must have the chance to develop their fullest human potential. We believe that women can achieve such equality only by accepting to the full the challenges and responsibilities they share with all other people in our society, as part of the decision-making mainstream of American political, economic and social life.

We organize to initiate or support action, nationally or in any part of this nation, by individuals or organizations, to break through the silken curtain of prejudice and discrimination against women in government, industry, the professions, the churches, the political parties, the judiciary, the labor unions, in education, science, medicine, law, religion and every other field of importance in American society. . . .

There is no civil rights movement to speak for women, as there has been for Negroes and other victims of discrimination. The National Organization for Women must therefore begin to speak.

WE BELIEVE that the power of American law, and the protection guaranteed by the U.S. Constitution to the civil rights of all individuals, must be effectively applied and enforced to isolate and remove patterns of sex discrimination, to ensure equality of opportunity in employment and education, and equality of civil and political rights and responsibilities on behalf of women, as well as for Negroes and other deprived groups. . . .

WE DO NOT ACCEPT the token appointment of a few women to high-level positions in government and industry as a substitute for a serious continuing effort to recruit and advance women according to their individual abilities. To this end, we urge American government and industry to mobilize the same resources of ingenuity and command with which they have solved problems of far greater difficulty than those now impeding the progress of women.

WE BELIEVE that this nation has a capacity at least as great as other nations, to innovate new social institutions which will enable women to enjoy true equality of opportunity and responsibility in society, without conflict with their responsibilities as mothers and homemakers. In such innovations, America does not lead the Western world, but lags by decades behind many European countries. We do not accept the traditional assumption that a woman has to choose between marriage and motherhood, on the one hand, and serious participation in industry or the professions on the other. We question the present expectation that all normal women will retire from job or profession for ten or fifteen years, to devote their full time to raising children, only to reenter the job market at a relatively minor level. . . .

WE REJECT the current assumptions that a man must carry the sole burden of supporting himself, his wife, and family, and that a woman is automatically entitled to lifelong support by a man upon her marriage, or that marriage, home and family are primarily woman's world and responsibility—hers, to dominate, his to support. We believe that a true partnership between the sexes demands a different concept of marriage, an equitable sharing of the responsibilities of home and children and of the economic burdens of their support. We believe that proper recognition should be given to the economic and social value of homemaking and child care. To these ends, we will seek to open a reexamination of laws and mores governing marriage and divorce, for we believe that the current state of "half-equality" between the sexes discriminates against both men and women, and is the cause of much unnecessary hostility between the sexes.

---

6 Redstockings was one of many radical feminist organizations that had sprung up by the late 1960s. How does this analysis of women's inequality differ from NOW's? Do Redstockings's analysis and rhetoric reveal the influence of other protest movements in the 1960s?

Redstockings Manifesto (1969)

I.   After centuries of individual and preliminary political struggle, women are uniting to achieve their final liberation from male supremacy. Redstockings is dedicated to building this unity and winning our freedom.

Source: Mary Beth Norton, *Major Problems in American Women's History* (Lexington, Mass.: D. C. Heath and Company, 1989), p. 400.

II. Women are an oppressed class. Our oppression is total, affecting every facet of our lives. We are exploited as sex objects, breeders, domestic servants, and cheap labor. We are considered inferior beings, whose only purpose is to enhance men's lives. Our humanity is denied. Our prescribed behavior is enforced by the threat of physical violence.

Because we have lived so intimately with our oppressors, in isolation from each other, we have been kept from seeing our personal suffering as a political condition. This creates the illusion that a woman's relationship with her man is a matter of interplay between two unique personalities, and can be worked out individually. In reality, every such relationship is a *class* relationship, and the conflicts between individual men and women are *political* conflicts that can only be solved collectively.

III. We identify the agents of our oppression as men. Male supremacy is the oldest, most basic form of domination. All other forms of exploitation and oppression (racism, capitalism, imperialism, etc.) are extensions of male supremacy: men dominate women, a few men dominate the rest. All power structures throughout history have been male-dominated and male-oriented. Men have controlled all political, economic and cultural institutions and backed up this control with physical force. They have used their power to keep women in an inferior position. *All men* receive economic, sexual, and psychological benefits from male supremacy. *All men* have oppressed women.

---

7 Phyllis Schlafly, the chairwoman of STOP ERA, was a leading critic of the Equal Rights Amendment. On what grounds does she argue against equal rights for women? What does this source reveal about important factors limiting the success of the women's movement?

"What's Wrong with 'Equal Rights' for Women?" (1972)
PHYLLIS SCHLAFLY

Of all the classes of people who ever lived, the American woman is the most privileged. We have the most rights and rewards, and the fewest duties. Our unique status is the result of a fortunate combination of circumstances.

1. We have the immense good fortune to live in a civilization which respects the family as the basic unit of society. This respect is part and parcel of our laws and our customs. It is based on the fact of life—which no legislation or agitation can erase—that women have babies and men don't.

Source: Reprinted with permission from The Phyllis Schlafly Report, February 1972.

If you don't like this fundamental difference, you will have to take up your complaint with God because He created us this way. The fact that women, not men, have babies is not the fault of selfish and domineering men, or of the establishment, or of any clique of conspirators who want to oppress women. It's simply the way God made us.

Our Judeo-Christian civilization has developed the law and custom that, since women must bear the physical consequences of the sex act, men must be required to bear the other consequences and pay in other ways. These laws and customs decree that a man must carry his share by physical protection and financial support of his children and of the woman who bears his children, and also by a code of behavior which benefits and protects both the woman and the children.

The Greatest Achievement of Women's Rights *motherhood*

This is accomplished by the institution of the family. *Our* respect for the family as the basic unit of society, which is ingrained in the laws and customs of our Judeo-Christian civilization, is the greatest single achievement in the entire history of women's rights. It assures a woman the most precious and important right of all—the right to keep her own baby and to be supported and protected in the enjoyment of watching her baby grow and develop.

The institution of the family is advantageous for women for many reasons. After all, what do we want out of life? To love and be loved? Mankind has not discovered a better nest for a lifetime of reciprocal love. A sense of achievement? A man may search 30 to 40 years for accomplishment in his profession. A woman can enjoy real achievement when she is young—by having a baby. She can have the satisfaction of doing a job well—and being recognized for it.

Do we want financial security? We are fortunate to have the great legacy of Moses, the Ten Commandments, especially this one: "Honor thy father and thy mother that thy days may be long upon the land." Children are a woman's best social security—her best guarantee of social benefits such as old age, pension, unemployment compensation, workman's compensation, and sick leave. The family gives a woman the physical, financial and emotional security of the home—for all her life.

The Financial Benefits of Chivalry

2. The second reason why American women are a privileged group is that we are the beneficiaries of a tradition of special respect for women which dates from the Christian Age of Chivalry. The honor and respect paid to Mary the Mother of Christ, resulted in all women, in effect, being put on a pedestal.

This respect for women is not just the lip service that politicians pay to "God, Motherhood, and the Flag." It is not—as some youthful agitators seem to think—just a matter of opening doors for women, seeing that they are seated first, carrying their bundles, and helping them in and out of automobiles. Such good manners are merely the superficial evidences of a total attitude toward women which expresses itself in many more tangible ways, such as money. . . .

The Real Liberation of Women

3. The third reason why American women are so well off is that the great American free enterprise system has produced remarkable inventors who have lifted the backbreaking women's work from our shoulders.

In other countries and in other eras, it was truly said that "Man may work from sun to sun, but woman's work is never done." Other women have labored every waking hour—preparing food on wood burning stoves, making flour, baking bread in stone ovens, spinning yarn, making clothes, making soap, doing the laundry by hand, heating irons, making candles for light and fires for warmth, and trying to nurse their babies through illnesses without medical care.

The real liberation of women from the backbreaking drudgery of centuries is the American free enterprise system which stimulated inventive geniuses to pursue their talents—and we all reap the profits. The great heroes of women's liberation are not the straggly-haired women on television talk shows and picket lines, but Thomas Edison who brought the miracle of electricity to our homes to give light and to run all those labor-saving devices—the equivalent, perhaps, of a half dozen household servants for every middle-class American woman. *Or* Elias Howe who gave us the sewing machine which resulted in such an abundance of ready made clothing. *Or* Clarence Birdseye who invented the process for freezing foods. *Or* Henry Ford, who mass-produced the automobile so that it is within the price-range of every American, man or woman. . . .

The Fraud of the Equal Rights Amendment

In the last couple of years, a noisy movement has sprung up agitating for "women's rights." Suddenly everywhere we are afflicted with aggressive females on television talk shows yapping about how mistreated American women are, suggesting that marriage has put us in some kind of "slavery," that housework is menial and degrading, and—perish the thought—that women are discriminated against. New "women's liberation" organizations are popping up, agitating and demonstrating, serving demands on public officials, getting wide press coverage always, and purporting to speak for some 100,000,000 American women.

It's time to set the record straight. The claim that American women are downtrodden and unfairly treated is the fraud of the century. The truth is that American women never had it so good. Why should we lower ourselves to "equal rights" when we already have the status of special privilege?

The proposed Equal Rights Amendment states: "Equality of rights under the law shall not be denied or abridged by the United States or by any state on account of sex." So what's wrong with that? Well, here are a few examples of what's wrong with it.

This amendment will absolutely and positively make women subject to the draft. Why any woman would support such a ridiculous and un-American proposal as this is beyond comprehension. Why any Congressman who had any regard for his wife, sister or daughter would support such a proposition is just as hard to understand. Foxholes are bad enough for men, but they certainly are not the place for women—and we should reject any proposal which would put them there in the name of equal rights. . . .

Another bad effect of the Equal Rights Amendment is that it will abolish women's right to child support and alimony, and substitute what the women's libbers think is a more "equal" policy, that "such decisions should be within the discretion of the court and should be made on the economic situation and need of the parties in the case."

Under present American laws, the man is *always* required to support his wife and each child he caused to be brought into the world. Why should women abandon these good laws—by trading them for something so nebulous and uncertain as the "discretion of the Court"?. . .

Women's Libbers Do NOT Speak for Us

The "women's lib" movement is not an honest effort to secure better jobs for women who want or need to work outside the home. This is just the superficial sweet-talk to win broad support for a radical "movement." "Women's lib" is a total assault on the role of the American woman as wife and mother, and on the family as the basic unit of society.

Women's libbers are trying to make wives and mothers unhappy with their career, make them feel that they are "second class citizens" and "abject slaves." Women's libbers are promoting free sex instead of the "slavery" of marriage. They are promoting "Federal" day care-centers for babies instead of homes. They are promoting abortions instead of families.

Why should we trade in our special privileges and honored status for the alleged advantage of working in an office or assembly line? Most women would rather cuddle a baby than a typewriter or factory machine. Most women find that it is easier to get along with a husband than a foreman or office manager. Offices and factories require many more menial and repetitious chores than washing dishes and ironing shirts.

Women's libbers do *not* speak for the majority of American women. American women do *not* want to be liberated from husbands and children. We do *not* want to trade our birthright of the special privilege of American women—for the mess of pottage called the Equal Rights Amendment. . . .

8
The Combahee River Collective was a black feminist group in Boston. Organized in 1974, the group took the name of an armed raid led by Harriet Tubman in South Carolina during the Civil War that brought freedom to greater than seven hundred slaves. According to this group, in what ways is the position of black women in American society unique?

The Combahee River Collective Statement (1986)

WE are a collective of Black feminists who have been meeting together since 1974. During that time we have been involved in the process of defining and clarifying our politics, while at the same time doing political work within our own group and in coalition with other progressive organizations and movements. The most general statement of our politics at the present time would be that we are actively committed to struggling against racial, sexual, heterosexual, and class oppression, and see as our particular task the development of integrated analysis and practice based upon the fact that the major systems of oppression are interlocking. The synthesis of these oppressions creates the conditions of our lives. As Black women we see Black feminism as the logical political movement to combat the manifold and simultaneous oppressions that all women of color face. . . .

A Black feminist presence has evolved most obviously in connection with the second wave of the American women's movement beginning in the late 1960s. Black, other Third World, and working women have been involved in the feminist movement from its start, but both outside reactionary forces and racism and elitism within the movement itself have served to obscure our participation. In 1973, Black feminists, primarily located in New York, felt the necessity of forming a separate Black feminist group. This became the National Black Feminist Organization (NBFO).

Black feminist politics also have an obvious connection to movements for Black liberation, particularly those of the 1960s and 1970s. Many of us were active in those movements (Civil Rights, Black nationalism, the Black Panthers), and all of our lives were greatly affected and changed by their ideologies, their goals, and the tactics used to achieve their goals. It was our experience and disillusionment within these liberation movements, as well as experience on the periphery of the white male left, that led to the need to develop a politics that was anti-racist, unlike those of white women, and anti-sexist, unlike those of Black and white men.

There is also undeniably a personal genesis for Black feminism, that is, the political realization that comes from the seemingly personal experiences of individual Black women's lives. Black feminists and many more Black women who do not define themselves as feminists have all experienced sexual oppression as a constant factor in our day-to-day existence. . . .

This focusing upon our own oppression is embodied in the concept of identity politics. We believe that the most profound and potentially most radical politics come directly out of our own identity, as opposed to working to end somebody else's oppression. In the case of Black women this is a particularly repugnant, dangerous, threatening, and therefore revolutionary concept because it is obvious from looking at all the political movements that have preceded us that anyone is more worthy of liberation than ourselves. We reject pedestals, queenhood, and walking ten paces behind. To be recognized as human, levelly human, is enough.

We believe that sexual politics under patriarchy is as pervasive in Black women's lives as are the politics of class and race. We also often find it difficult to separate race from class from sex oppression because in our lives they are most often experienced simultaneously. We know that there is such a thing as racial-sexual oppression which is neither solely racial nor solely sexual, e.g., the history of rape of Black women by white men as a weapon of political repression. . . .

One issue that is of major concern to us and that we have begun to publicly address is racism in the white women's movement. As Black feminists we are made constantly and painfully aware of how little effort white women have made to understand and combat their racism, which requires among other things that they have a more than superficial comprehension of race, color, and Black history and culture. Eliminating racism in the white women's movement is by definition work for white women to do, but we will continue to speak to and demand accountability on this issue.

The Sexual Revolution and the Women's Movement

The civil rights and antiwar movements brought important changes to American society in the 1960s. So, too, did a sexual revolution. As you read these selections, think about the relationship between a sexual revolution in the 1960s and the rise of the women's movement. How did a more liberated social climate bring both liberation and tyranny for women?

In this selection a writer looks at the effects of the sexual revolution.

On Women and Sex (1972)

JOYCE MAYNARD

For about three weeks of my freshman year at college I had two roommates instead of one—the girl in the bottom bunk and her friend, who made our quarters especially cramped because, in addition to being six feet tall with lots of luggage, he was male. We slept in shifts—they together, until I came back to the room at night, then he outside in the living room on the couch, until she got up, then he in her bed and I in mine, or I in hers and he in mine, because it was easier for me to get out from the bottom without waking him, and he needed his sleep. . . . We never made it a threesome, but the awkwardness was always there (those squeaking bedsprings. . .), as it was for many girls I knew, and many boys. Coming back to the room and announcing my presence loudly with a well-directed, well-projected cough or a casual murmur, "Hmmmm—I think I'll go to my room now," it occurred to me that it wasn't my roommate but I—the one who slept alone, the one whose only pills were vitamins and aspirin—I was the embarrassed one. How has it happened, what have we come to, that the scarlet letter these days isn't A, but V?. . .

The sexual revolution. It's a cliché, but it exists all right, and its pressures are everywhere. All the old excuses ("I might get pregnant," "I'm not that kind of girl") are gone. Safe and increasingly available contraceptives (for anyone brave and premeditative enough to get them) make premarital sex possible; changing moral standards, an increased naturalness, make it commonplace; elegant models of sexual freedom—Julie Christie, Catherine Deneuve—have made it fashionable. Consider a virgin in the movies. Is there a single pretty young heroine who doesn't hop unself-consciously into bed? (Who is there left for her to identify with—Doris Day?) Then there are magazines, filled with discussions of intricate sexual problems (the timing of orgasms. . . do I get one? do I give one?) while the virgin remains on a whole other level—her fears compounded. (Our old, junior high notion of sex was that it got done to you; the girl with the purple eyeshadow just let it happen. Today all kinds of problems in technique make the issue much more complicated for an inexperienced, media-blitzed girl: not just *will* I but *can I*.) The people who've been making nice, simple love for years now, while the virgin became more and more unique, have, quite understandably, gone on to other things. There is foreplay and afterplay and the 999 positions of the

Source: Joyce Maynard, *Looking Back* (New York: Doubleday, 1973). Reprinted by permission of the author.

Kamasutra. . . The train has left the station before the virgin's bought her ticket or even, maybe, packed her bags. . . .

This source is an excerpt from the preface to the first edition of a book that has had a long history and a wide influence.

Our Bodies, Ourselves (1973)

The history of this book, *Our Bodies, Ourselves*, is lengthy and satisfying.

It began in a small discussion group on "women and their bodies" which was part of a women's conference held in Boston in the spring of 1969, one of the first gatherings of women meeting specifically to talk with other women. For many of us it was the very first time we had joined together with other women to talk and think about our lives and what we could do about them. Before the conference was over, some of us decided to keep on meeting as a group to continue the discussion, and so we did.

In the beginning we called ourselves "the doctors group." We had all experienced similar feelings of frustration and anger toward specific doctors and the medical maze in general, and initially we wanted to do something about those doctors who were condescending, paternalistic, judgmental and non-informative. As we talked and shared our experiences with one another, we realized just how much we had to learn about our bodies. So we decided on a summer project—to research those topics which we felt were particularly pertinent to learning about our bodies, to discuss in the group what we had learned, then to write papers individually or in groups of two or three, and finally to present the results in the fall as a course for women on women and their bodies.

As we developed the course we realized more and more that we really *were* capable of collecting, understanding, and evaluating medical information. Together we evaluated our reading of books and journals, our talks with doctors and friends who were medical students. We found we could discuss, question and argue with each other in a new spirit of cooperation rather than competition. We were equally struck by how important it was for us to be able to open up with one another and share our feelings about our bodies. The process of talking was as crucial as the facts themselves. Over time the facts and feelings melted together in ways that touched us very deeply, and that is reflected in the changing titles of the course and then the book—from *Women and Their Bodies* to *Women and Our Bodies* to, finally, *Our Bodies, Ourselves*. . . .

Many, many other women have worked with us on the book. A group of gay women got together specifically to do the chapter on lesbianism. Other chapters were done still differently. For instance, the mother of one woman in the group volunteered to work on menopause with some of us who have not gone through that experience ourselves. . . .

From the very beginning of working together, first on the course that led to this book and then on the book itself, we have felt exhilarated and energized by our new knowledge. Finding out about our bodies and our bodies' needs, starting to take control over that area of our lives, has released for us an energy that has overflowed into our work, our friendships, our relationships with men and women, and for some of us, our marriages and our parenthood. . . .

A second important result of this kind of learning is that we are better prepared to evaluate the institutions that are supposed to meet our health needs—the hospitals, clinics, doctors, medical schools, nursing schools, public health departments, Medicaid bureaucracies and so on. For some of us it was the first time we had looked critically, and with strength, at the existing institutions serving us. The experience of learning just how little control we had over our lives and bodies, the coming together out of isolation to learn from each other in order to define what we needed, and the experience of supporting one another in demanding the changes that grew out of our developing critique—all were crucial and formative political experiences for us. We have felt our potential power as a force for political and social change.

The learning we have done while working on *Our Bodies, Ourselves* has been a good basis for growth in other areas of life for still another reason. For women throughout the centuries, ignorance about our bodies has had one major consequence—pregnancy. Until very recently pregnancies were all but inevitable, biology *was* our destiny—that is, because our bodies are designed to get pregnant and give birth and lactate that is what all or most of us did. . . . It was not until we researched carefully and learned more about birth-control methods and abortion, about laws governing birth control and abortion, and not until we put all this information together with what it meant to us to be female, that we began to feel we could truly set out to control whether and when we would have babies.

This knowledge has freed us to a certain extent from the constant, energy-draining anxiety about becoming pregnant. It has made our pregnancies better because they no longer happen to us, but we actively choose them and enthusiastically participate in them. It has made our parenthood better because it is our choice rather than our destiny. . . . This is why people in the women's movement have been so active in fighting against the inhumane legal restrictions, the imperfections of available contraceptives, the poor sex education, the highly priced and poorly administered health care that keep too many women from having this crucial control over their bodies.

There is a fourth reason why knowledge about our bodies has generated so much new energy. For us, body education is core education. Our bodies are the physical bases from which we move out into the world; ignorance, uncertainty—even, at worst, shame—about our physical selves create in us an alienation from ourselves that keeps us from being the whole people that we could be. Picture a woman trying to do work and to enter into equal and satisfying relationships with other people—when she feels physically weak because she has never tried to be strong; when she drains her energy trying to change her face, her figure, her hair, her smells, to match some ideal norm set by magazines, movies and TV; when she feels confused and ashamed of the menstrual blood that every month appears from some dark place in her body; when her internal body processes are a mystery to her and surface only to cause her trouble (an unplanned pregnancy, or cervical cancer); when she does not understand or enjoy sex and concentrates her sexual drives into aimless romantic fantasies, perverting and misusing a potential energy because she had been brought up to deny it. Learning to understand, accept, and be responsible for our physical selves, we are freed of some of these preoccupations and can start to use our untapped energies. Our image of ourselves is on a firmer base, we can be better friends and better lovers, better people, more self-confident, more autonomous, stronger and more whole.

---

11   *The Feminine Mystique* proclaimed that women would find fulfillment through work outside the home. Note how this essay illustrates some of the problems women faced as they began to reject domesticity. Does it help to explain why feminists began to put increasing emphasis on reform within the "private" sphere?

The Politics of Housework (ca. 1970)
PAT MAINARDI

Liberated women—very different from Women's Liberation! The first signals all kinds of goodies, to warm the hearts (not to mention other parts) of the most radical men. The other signals—HOUSEWORK. The first brings sex without marriage, sex before marriage, cozy housekeeping arrangements ("I'm living with this chick") and the self-content of knowing that you're not the kind of man who wants a doormat instead of a woman. That will come later. After all, who wants that old commodity anymore, the Standard American Housewife, all husband, home and kids. The New Commodity, the Liberated Woman, has sex a lot and has a Career, preferably something that can be fitted in with the household chores—like dancing, pottery, or painting.

On the other hand is Women's Liberation—and housework. What? You say this is all trivial? Wonderful! That's what I thought. It seemed perfectly

Source: From *Women's Liberation in the 20th Century* by Mary C. Lynn, ed. Copyright © 1975. This material is used by permission of John Wiley & Sons, Inc.

reasonable. We both had careers, both had to work a couple of days a week to earn enough to live on, so why shouldn't we share the housework? So I suggested it to my mate and he agreed—most men are too hip to turn you down flat. You're right, he said. It's only fair.

Then an interesting thing happened. I can only explain it by stating that we women have been brainwashed more than even we can imagine. Probably too many years of seeing television women in ecstasy over their shiny waxed floors or breaking down over their dirty shirt collars. Men have no such conditioning. They recognize the essential fact of housework right from the very beginning. Which is that it stinks.

Here's my list of dirty chores: buying groceries, carting them home and putting them away; cooking meals and washing dishes and pots; doing the laundry; digging out the place when things get out of control; washing floors. The list could go on but the sheer necessities are bad enough. All of us have to do these things, or get someone else to do them for us. The longer my husband contemplated these chores, the more repulsed he became, and so proceeded the change from the normally sweet considerate Dr. Jekyll into the crafty Mr. Hyde who would stop at nothing to avoid the horrors of—housework. As he felt himself backed into a corner laden with dirty dishes, brooms, mops and reeking garbage, his front teeth grew longer and pointier, his fingernails haggled and his eyes grew wild. Housework trivial? Not on your life! Just try to share the burden. . . .

Participatory democracy begins at home. If you are planning to implement your politics, there are certain things to remember:

1. He *is* feeling it more than you. He's losing some leisure and you're gaining it. The measure of your oppression is his resistance.
2. A great many American men are not accustomed to doing monotonous repetitive work which never issues in any lasting, let alone important, achievement. This is why they would rather repair a cabinet than wash dishes. If human endeavors are like a pyramid with man's highest achievements at the top, then keeping oneself alive is at the bottom. Men have always had servants (us) to take care of this bottom strata of life while they have confined their efforts to the rarefied upper regions. It is thus ironic when they ask of women—where are your great painters, statesmen, etc. Mme Matisse ran a millinery shop so he could paint. Mrs. Martin Luther King kept his house and raised his babies.
3. It is a traumatizing experience for someone who has always thought of himself as being against any oppression or exploitation of one human being by another to realize that in his daily life he has been accepting and implementing (and benefiting from) this exploitation; that his rationalization is little different from that of the racist who says "Black people don't feel pain" (women don't mind doing the shitwork); and that

the oldest form of oppression in history has been the oppression of 50% of the population by the other 50%. . . .

I was just finishing this when my husband came in and asked what I was doing. Writing a paper on housework. Housework? he said, *Housework*? Oh my god how trivial can you get. A paper on housework.

Women's Changing Education and Employment Experience

As it can for other population groups, statistical information can reveal important changes in women's lives. As you examine these charts, consider whether they reveal reasons why many women in the 1960s rejected domesticity and joined the women's movement. Do they also provide evidence for the impact of that movement?

Sex Ratios of High School and College Graduates in the United States, 1940–1990

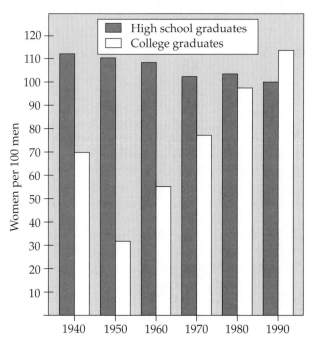

U.S. Bureau of the Census, *Historical Statistics of the United States, Colonial Times to 1970* (Washington, D.C.: GPO, 1975), pp. 379, 385–386; U.S. Bureau of the Census, *Statistical Abstract of the United States: 1988* (Washington, D.C.: GPO, 1987, 108th ed.), p. 140; Richard Sutch and Susan B. Carter, eds., *Historical Statistics of the United States: Earliest Times to the Present* (New York: Cambridge University Press, 2006), II, 422, 459–460.

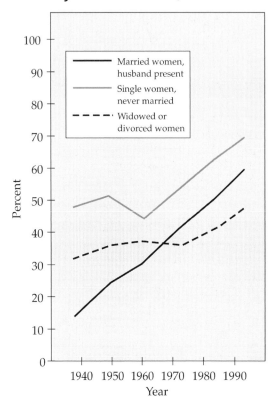

13 Women's Labor Force Participation, by Marital Status, 1940–1990

U.S. Bureau of the Census, *Historical Statistics of the United States, Colonial Times to 1970* (Washington, D.C.: GPO, 1975), p. 133; U.S. Bureau of the Census, *Statistical Abstract of the United States: 1988* (Washington, D.C.: GPO, 1987, 108th ed.), p. 373; Richard Sutch and Susan B. Carter, eds., *Historical Statistics of the United States: Earliest Times to the Present* (New York: Cambridge University Press, 2006), II, 80.

CONCLUSION

One month before *Time* magazine proclaimed 1975 "The Year of the Women" and a decade after it put Phyllis McGinley on its cover, *Newsweek* magazine ran a story on the exploding field of women's history. The timing of the stories was no coincidence. One of the most important consequences of the women's movement was the interest it stimulated in uncovering women's past. As we have already seen in this volume, our view of the past is shaped by the way people think about the present—and vice versa. As women began to think in new ways about their status in contemporary society, they also began to think differently about their place in the past. They found women mostly excluded from the pages of history, a reflection of their subordinate position in American society. Like African Americans, women began to recapture their past when they began to fight for equality.

The women's movement, which greatly stimulated the study of women's history, is now history itself. As this chapter's secondary sources demonstrate, women's historians do not write about it only to "raise consciousness," to prove past oppression, or to recount women's past contributions. More important, they are interested in placing women in the mainstream of the American past. They seek to understand the way women's experience influenced and in turn was influenced by American society and culture. Thus they illustrate important points about historical inquiry that we have seen repeatedly in this volume. For instance, to understand the rise of the women's movement, historians must consider the effects of many causal influences. To understand the motivations of feminists, moreover, those influences can rarely be considered apart from ideology. The study of the contemporary women's movement also reminds us that history happens to elites and non-elites alike. In fact, it is a double reminder of that message, because the voices of women in general and non-elite women in particular have usually not been heard in the past. By making connections between the "private" sphere of family life and the "public" sphere, the women's movement demonstrates why historians must be interested in more than the activities of statesmen and generals.

Finally, the modern women's movement illustrates the importance of historians' motivations. As we have seen in this chapter, historians are guided by contemporary concerns even as they seek to understand the past on its own terms. Although they may write history that serves to defend or attack contemporary policies, historians do not turn to the past merely to do that. That is a good lesson to keep in mind as we turn in Chapter 13 to the issue of immigration.

FURTHER READING

Lois Banner, *Women in Modern America: A Brief History* (San Diego: Harcourt Brace Jovanovich, 1984).

Nancy Cott, *The Grounding of Modern Feminism* (New Haven, Conn.: Yale University Press, 1987).

Sara Evans, *Personal Politics: The Roots of Women's Liberation in the Civil Rights Movement and the New Left* (New York: Vintage Books, 1979).

Betty Friedan, *The Feminine Mystique* (New York: W. W. Norton and Company, 1963).

Mary Thom, ed., *Letters to Ms., 1972–1987* (New York: Henry Holt and Company, 1987).

Winifred Wandersee, *On the Move: American Women in the 1970s* (Boston: Twayne Publishers, 1988).

NOTES

1. *Newsweek,* June 7, 1965, p. 55.
2. *U.S. News & World Report,* June 7, 1965, pp. 12, 53.
3. *Time,* June 18, 1965, pp. 75, 78.
4. *Newsweek,* March 23, 1970, pp. 71–72.
5. Quoted in Nancy Woloch, *Women and the American Experience* (New York: McGraw-Hill, 1984), p. 518.

Chapter

13

Why Historical Interpretation Matters: The Battle over Immigration

The sources in this chapter provide various perspectives on immigration's impact on American society in our time.

Secondary Sources

Primary Sources

Sometime before Sunday, September 14, 1998, Asuncion Hernandez Uriel crossed the border between the United States and Mexico. She entered the country in the desert of the Imperial Valley some hundred miles east of San Diego. She did not get far. Felled by the late-summer sun, she died of heat stress surrounded by companions who had entered the United States with her. Her body was found by the Border Patrol on Sunday. That weekend, two other bodies were discovered in the same area and a man who had been in a coma since August also died. After crossing the border, he collapsed in the desert when his body temperature soared to 108 degrees. This spate of deaths along one short section of the Mexican border was not particularly unusual. Between 1994 and 2004, roughly 2,000 migrants died along the entire length of that border.

These deaths in the Imperial Valley over one September weekend represent a small piece of the larger story of illegal entry into the United States. Likewise, illegal immigration is one part of the larger issue of immigration. In many ways it is also at the heart of the heated and often rancorous debate over that issue in contemporary America. In the last quarter-century, millions of immigrants sought entry into the United States. Most did so legally. But millions did not—and they could not have done so even if they had tried. American immigration laws made that virtually impossible. Those legal barriers, combined with the obvious and sometimes fatal attraction of millions of people around the world to the United States, have made immigration one of the most contentious issues of our time.

This chapter takes up that issue. It considers contemporary immigration from various perspectives. Because it is difficult to discuss one and not the other, it examines both legal and illegal immigration. Historians have entered the public discussion of the immigration issue and, like other Americans, they often disagree about it. Thus, this chapter looks at this debate from two different historical perspectives. It also considers the varied views of contemporary commentators and presents a few of the many stories that recent immigrants have to share.

SETTING

The oft-quoted words engraved at the base of the Statue of Liberty declare that the United States stands ready to take in the world's "huddled masses." To many Americans at the turn of our century, the nation seems to have more than lived up to that commitment in recent years. In the last decade of the twentieth century alone, more than nine million immigrants legally entered the United States—a stream that continues unabated in the first years of the new century. In fact, by 2002, more than 33 million Americans counted themselves immigrants, a record number. Those immigrants represented 11.5 percent of the total population, a portion not matched in the previous seven decades.

As with so many other topics, history provides a useful perspective in considering contemporary immigration. Against the broader sweep of American history, modern-day immigration in some ways does not seem that unusual. Through most of the nineteenth century and the first two decades of the twentieth century, for instance, immigrants as a percentage of the total population actually exceeded today's levels. Moreover, alarm about too many immigrants in American society is nothing new. Nativism, or anti-immigrant sentiment, appeared frequently in the past, especially when native-born Americans saw large numbers of newcomers in their midst. Not new either is the view of many native-born Americans that earlier immigrants were "better," more "virtuous," or more able to assimilate than those today.

At the same time, history reveals some important changes in contemporary immigration. During the nineteenth and early twentieth centuries, the over-whelming majority of newcomers came from Europe. Today, that is no longer true. In the last decade of the twentieth century, for instance, fewer than 1.4 million immigrants entered the country from Europe, while nearly 4.2 million came from Latin America and another 2.8 million from Asia. In fact, in the 1990s, almost a million more legal immigrants came from Mexico than from all of Europe. Because that trend shows no signs of abating, Americans of European descent will likely represent a minority of the population by the middle of our century.

These differences have helped shape many Americans' attitudes about immigration. Unlike those earlier in the twentieth century, the majority of immigrants today are non-white. Moreover, whereas many earlier immigrants were themselves divided by language, large numbers of them today share a common language—Spanish.

Other recent changes also play a role in making many Americans less recep-tive to immigration generally. Concern about loss of American jobs to workers overseas, for instance, has raised fears about competition with immigrant labor at home. At the same time, heightened environmental awareness has increased con-cerns about the impact of population growth on the nation's resources. Undoubt-edly most important in shaping contemporary American attitudes about this issue, however, is the rising number of illegal immigrants entering the country starting in the 1970s. During the last decade of the twentieth century alone, an estimated half-million illegal immigrants entered the country every year. Many more were apprehended at the border. In the first years of the 1990s, more than one million undocumented immigrants, mostly from Mexico, were arrested every year along the nation's southern border. Starting in 1995, that figure jumped to roughly 1.5 million every year as the Border Patrol stepped up its apprehension efforts.

The dramatic rise in undocumented entries has made immigration a hot topic in politics and the media. It has also heightened the focus on the nation's immigration laws. Much of the current legal debate begins with the Immigra-tion and Nationality Act of 1965, which abolished a national quota system favoring northern and western European nations. The new law replaced the national quotas that had been in place since the passage of the so-called National Origins Act of 1924. That act placed limits on European nationalities allowed to enter the United States each year. It also favored northern European nations while severely restricting emigration of southern and eastern Europeans who were overwhelmingly Roman Catholic, Orthodox, or Jewish and viewed as inferior "racial stocks" by many nativists. Under the 1965 act, on the other hand, immigration was guided by factors such as family reunification, the need to fill labor shortages in various occupations, and refugee status. Passed when a growing number of people from Latin America, Asia, and Africa wished to come to the United States, that law provided the foundation for a new wave of immigration—both legal and illegal. Though later adjusted, the annual immigration ceilings established under the 1965 law have been unable to accommodate all people who have sought to enter the country legally. Just two decades after its passage, the immigration visa waiting list stood at more than 1.75 million. As a result, millions of others have sought to enter illegally.

Meanwhile, massive legal and illegal immigration at the turn of our century have left Americans divided over a host of questions. Does the nation have too many immigrants of whatever legal standing? What are the costs and contributions of immigrants to American society? What should it do about the millions of illegal immigrants, many of whom have children born in the United States and are, therefore, American citizens? And what, if anything, should be done to secure the nation's borders, which remain porous even in the face of increasingly stringent measures to stem the tide of illegal immigration? These questions and others fuel an increasing divisive immigration debate that does not promise to end anytime soon.

INVESTIGATION

In this chapter, you will have the opportunity to assess the battle over immigration at the turn of our own century from various perspectives. Specifically, you will be able to consider two different views about the historical roots of the contemporary immigration phenomenon. The two secondary sources in this chapter emphasize very different historical factors to explain why so many legal and illegal immigrants have entered the country in recent years. They also offer two varying views regarding what should be done to address this situation. In other words, they make historical arguments to support their conclusions. After comparing their analyses of the causes of rising immigration, you will be able to consider evidence in the chapter's primary sources. They will provide additional perspectives on both legal and illegal immigration. When you are finished, you should be able to offer an explanation of the factors contributing to the present-day immigration situation. You should also be able to assess whether it is best understood as an alarming and uncontrolled invasion, a largely beneficial development related to long-term global trends, or a phenomenon with both positive and negative effects on American society.

Drawing from the chapter's sources, a good analysis will address the following questions:

1. **How would you compare the explanations in Source 1 and Source 2 for the current massive influx of immigrants into the United States?** What historical reasons does Otis Graham, Jr., offer in Source 1? How do they compare to those advanced by Alejandro Portes and Rubén G. Rumbaut in Source 2? How would you compare the explanations in these two sources regarding the failure of lawmakers in the United States to act on immigration?

2. **What evidence do the sources in this chapter offer regarding the impact of legal or illegal immigration on American society?** Do they support the conclusion that the overall impact has been positive or negative?

3. **What evidence do the sources provide about the factors attracting immigrants to the United States?** Overall, does the evidence seem to support the analysis offered in Source 1 or Source 2?

4. **What light does the evidence regarding the experience of immigrants in the United States shed on the issues of immigration and immigration restriction?** Do those experiences support the conclusions offered in either Source 1 or Source 2 regarding these issues?

Before you begin, make sure you have read the section in your textbook on immigration during the late twentieth century and its impact on American society. In particular, notice what it says about the causes of the immigration surge, the laws pertaining to immigration, and recent efforts to secure the nation's borders.

SECONDARY SOURCES

1   In this selection, historian Otis L. Graham, Jr., discusses the policies that have supported massive legal and illegal immigration in our time. Graham sees "mostly negative" effects in contemporary immigration. He also argues that it is necessary to turn to the past to understand contemporary immigration. According to Graham, how does history illuminate the immigration situation, in particular the lack of a response by lawmakers to what he calls majority views on this issue? What does he see as the risks inherent in current policies?

Unguarded Gates (2004)
OTIS L. GRAHAM, JR.

The American future is shaped by many complex forces. One of the most powerful—immigration—is, on balance, now taking America where it doesn't want to go—toward porous borders and uncontrolled entry, endless population growth, imported-worker competition with American labor, social fragmentation.

To understand how we have moved onto a road to a more troubled future we need to turn to our history.

This is so because our predicament finds us as a nation confused and misguided by our historical memories and myths, which tell us a flawed and misleading story, that immigration has always taken us where we wanted to go.

This is confusing because it is part of the truth, but only a part. Immigration of Europeans, Latin Americans, Asians, and others, as well as the forced immigration of many Africans, on balance and over the course of our colonial and national experience did advance economic development and nation-building, which was where we wanted to go. As a people we feel justifiably proud of this achievement (on the whole) and have long recognized that the Americans engaged in this nation-building were immensely aided by newcomers bringing renewed energy and their own cultural contributions.

On balance. The rest of the truth is that immigration's potential has a negative component, whose costs sometimes appear to exceed benefits. Immigration to the New World brought enormous injury to indigenous populations and the natural environment. In the nineteenth century immigration reached a scale and composition that brought or exacerbated substantial problems among Americans already here and seemed to many of them to actually threaten the unique national project of democratic nation-building. An extended period of such problematic immigration began in the decades before the Civil War, as a Great Wave of European immigration brought an unprecedented large number from Germany and Ireland. The flow of immigrants resumed after the war with source regions shifting to eastern and southern Europe. This era of mass immigration, substantial in numbers and also very different in cultural inheritances, generated in American political life a demand for control over this source of immense social change.

This [study] begins with the story of the process of moving from essentially an open-border policy and small-scale immigration to a new era in which the national government undertook to moderate and manage migrating human populations so that immigration would mesh with and promote our national purposes, rather than conflict with them. It then tells the modern story of how immigration, shaped by immigration policy, changed from bringing mostly positive to mostly negative contributions.

Regulation of immigration came slowly, because Americans always have been ambivalent about immigration. Between the 1880s and the 1920s a policy decision was finally reached. A system of national regulation of immigration was put in place, based on the national origins of the population of 1920 and aimed at greatly reduced numbers. With the help of external events such as world wars and economic depression worldwide, this system of regulation sharply lowered the incoming numbers and allowed the country to absorb and thus on the whole benefit by the large inflows of the First Great Wave.

Then in the 1960s a Second Great Wave began to surge across national borders, generated by global population growth, lowered transportation costs, and a widespread awareness of the wealth gap between developed and underdeveloped nations. Immigration policymakers, not recognizing this era of expanding immigration pressures, took a step toward expanding legal admissions. A reform of American immigration law and policy in 1965 was intended to bring important ethical improvements in the form of opening equal access to all nationalities, while having little practical effect. But the reforms of 1965 brought other, surprising effects of vast importance—a threefold expansion of legal immigrants, augmented by burgeoning numbers of illegal immigrants, and a radical shift in the source countries of American immigration. We are still sorting out the far-reaching impacts of this half-century (to date) experiment in porous borders between America and a world undergoing an unprecedented expansion of human population.

Today, after four decades of Second Great Wave immigration, legal and illegal, the American government's performance in the task of managing immigration is at the top of any list of government failures. This was true well before the deadly September 11, 2001, acts of terrorism by foreigners commandeering American airliners after residing and training in the United States under various mixtures of legal and illegal entry and extended illegal residency. Americans for decades have sensed that we are now in a phase of our national life in which immigration is on balance taking America where it doesn't want to go. All public-opinion polls since large-scale immigration resumed in the 1960s have reported pluralities (in the 1960s) and thereafter majorities (in all ethnic groups) in favor of reducing immigration. These polls are one form of expression of a sustained and tenacious vote of no confidence in the government's gate tending.

And with good reason. The numbers of legal immigrants has hovered around one million for two decades, augmented by illegal immigration, always estimated by official bodies as lower than subsequently found. An internal population of nine to ten million illegal immigrants is acknowledged by the early years of the twenty-first century. On the legal side, these new Americans are selected by a system placing primary emphasis on kinship, which means family ties to recent immigrants, rather than on national needs.

The costs of this new mass immigration collect across the ledger. They include labor market competition with native workers, rising social service costs, nurturing of illegal trade in drugs and indentured labor, the immigration contribution (70 percent at the end of the century, and rising) to population growth with all the costs that come attached to it in this era of global ecocrisis, an intensifying intersection of mounting human numbers with an era of erratic global warming and other stresses of a global eco-sphere mauled by more than six billion people in the process of expanding to or beyond ten billion. Other costs are more speculative, such as the concerns that the radical shift in immigrants' countries of origin from Europe to Latin America (especially Mexico),

Asia, and the Middle East may overwhelm the nation's capacity for assimilation. A century later, the national question is being asked again—is our fundamental national cohesion and coherence being lost?

Against this are weighed immigration's benefits—cheap labor for harvest agriculture and urban menial tasks, relatively cheap skilled labor in certain industries, a more culturally diversified cuisine and society, and scattered stories of urban revitalization.

Assessing this complex picture of immigration impacts in the mid-1990s, a national commission led by former congresswoman Barbara Jordan confirmed that immigration patterns were not aligned with the national interest and urged reforms. The numbers coming in legally should be reduced by almost half, and selected with more emphasis on the needs of the American economy. Illegal entry should be firmly combated. By this time that part of the nation's public policy elite knowledgeable about immigration had reversed an earlier complacency and begun to frequently express the alarm long felt by the public. The Brookings Institution in 2000 gathered a panel of historians and political scientists to reflect on the federal government's greatest achievements and failures since World War II, and it ranked controlling immigration as second among the top five failures. In a 2001 review of the literature on immigration's impacts, one of the nation's most respected social scientists, Harvard's Christopher Jencks, confirmed this overall negative assessment of the costs imposed by the four-decade run of mass immigration. Alarmed at the environmental and demographic effects from a likely doubling of the U.S. population to 500 million by 2050, a doubling attributable almost entirely to immigration, Jencks joined many other end-of-century writers in questioning whether such a "vast social experiment" had been authorized by the American people or was in their best interest. The nation's policy-studies elite had finally caught up with the American public, which had been expressing the same convictions to pollsters since the early 1970s. On the one occasion when voters were allowed a direct vote on the immigration status quo—at least, on the illegal part of it—Californians by a wide margin in 1992 endorsed Proposition 187, which withheld social services from illegal immigrants. A broadly negative perception of the American immigration policy regime faced no serious intellectual challenge at the end of the century. Apologists for the mass immigration status quo were few and fell back on historical analogy, arguing that similar waves of mass immigration of a century earlier had also been met by objections but the nation had nonetheless prospered.

Yet U.S. policymakers ignored this critical appraisal of the immigration regime, and in the first year of the twenty-first century drifted toward further dismantling of controls. President George W. Bush in 2001 proposed a virtual open border with Mexico, and, incredibly, congressional policymakers seemed receptive.

This presents us with an enormous puzzle. The vast social experiment in the form of mass immigration rushes on, entering its fifth decade. It is a product of policymaking in the world's foremost democracy, yet it has from the first been unpopular with the public and viewed with increasing skepticism by policy analysts. The costs of America's porous borders were piled to even more stunning heights on the morning of September 11, 2001. That day's terrorist attacks harshly illuminated a defect that had not formerly been high on the list of flaws in immigration policy, that our porous borders and governmental abandonment of virtually all interior immigration controls allowed terrorists to glide easily in and out of the country, illegally and legally, for periods of their choosing, as they contemptuously trained and prepared for mass murder in this affable and wide-open society. . . .

For understanding our situation we must follow history into the present, revisiting and rethinking the story of modern America's remarkable, turbulent, and unfinished encounter with that most emotional, difficult, and nation-changing of all public policy subjects—immigration. . . .

Historian David Reimers, in a chapter of *Unwelcome Strangers* (1998) titled "A Broken Immigration System," points out that while the 1965 law was responsible for a large increase in the numbers of legal immigrants, Congress, presidents, and courts continued for decades to turn up the volume. They did this with refugee and asylum "exceptions" on the legal side along with repeated amnesties, while they accepted the uncomfortable fact of porous borders to illegal immigration after the failed control effort of IRCA.* Thus the immigration flood that surged through the 1990s and into the twenty-first century was the work of years of policy "liberalization" against a background of global migration pressures. Immigration builds momentum if uninterrupted, and U.S. policymakers through all these years periodically augmented and extended the momentum. Because the public, when asked by pollsters, repeatedly favored smaller numbers, there was some complex political dynamic at work that produced counter-majoritarian results, decade after decade.

This was evident again in 1990, when Congress, apparently responding to pressure from ethnic lobbying groups, widened the gates another time. A law of that year expanded per country limits, readjusted preference categories while leaving kinship as the chief ground for admission, and granted Salvadoran "temporary" illegal entrants a longer stay. Showing no shame, Congress once again created an artificial "ceiling" by establishing a "flexible cap" (seven hundred thousand). . . . Yet, apparently uneasy with the one-sided changes it had just made, Congress added to the 1990 law a call for a commission on immigration reform—a title acknowledging a lack of confidence in the expansive and porous system national leaders had constructed and ineptly supervised.

---

*IRCA: The Immigration Reform and Control Act of 1986 proposed sanctions on employers of illegal aliens, extended amnesty for illegal aliens who had been in continuous residence in the United States since 1982, and created a program to legalize illegal agricultural workers.

The uneasiness was justified. Public frustration boiled over in the early 1990s. Grassroots citizens' organizations calling for immigration reform had been springing up in the most immigration-impacted states and cities, such as California, Florida, Texas, Miami, Los Angeles, [and] New York. A few organized with the support and encouragement of FAIR,* most independently. They increasingly made use of the new Internet e-mail capacities for quick communication. It was in California, caught in severe economic slump, where the new grassroots restrictionism became the most potent political force. Most of the complaints came from residents of border counties where the illegal traffic was daily visible, but as many as forty groups were formed from San Diego to Marin County, protesting rising crime rates, crowded schools, and other fiscal impacts of a growing population of low-income illegal immigrants. . . .

A group in Orange County, California, frustrated that writing letters to their representatives in Washington protesting illegal immigration produced no results, wrote Proposition 187, known as the Save Our State initiative to deny public services to illegal aliens. This popular idea was undercut for some by the proposition designers' decision to also deny public schooling to the children of illegal immigrants, who, if born in the United States, were American citizens. Controversy over the idea of state and local government engagement in immigration control was predictable, and the notion of schools as one enforcement point intensified it. Flawed as it was in design, Prop. 187 was increasingly seen by voters as the only option available to Californians to "send a signal" that they were angry at open borders and at America's policymakers who failed to control national borders. . . .

Prop. 187 passed by a resounding vote of 59 percent for and 41 percent against. Most Hispanic voters favored the measure in early polling, though only 31 percent voted for it after a long campaign in which Hispanic political leaders branded it as "anti-Hispanic." Geographer William Clark found that suburban Latinos joined all the state's ethnic and racial groups in favoring Prop. 187. . . .

The 1994 election also gave Republicans control of both houses of Congress, and the events in California suggested that the moment might have arrived for restrictionist reform. In March 1995, the Commission on Immigration Reform, chaired by African American former congresswoman Barbara Jordan, made its first report, and finished its work in 1997. Jordan set the tone. Testifying before Congress, she began with the usual praise of immigration in general ("the United States has been and should continue to be a nation of immigrants"), then confirmed that reform was the message: "Legal immigration, however, has costs as well as benefits," and "our current immigration system must undergo major reform to ensure that admissions continue to serve our national interests." The commission recommended a cut in overall legal immigration to 550,000, or 40 percent, a shift of selection

---

*FAIR, the Federation for American Immigration Reform, is a national organization that advocates reduced immigration.

criteria toward skills needed in the United States, and an end to family chain migration by eliminating the preferences for brothers and sisters and adult children of new immigrant citizens. As for "unlawful immigration," it "is unacceptable," as was the idea of a large-scale agricultural guest-worker program. . . .

Congress seemed to move in the reform direction in 1995 with a Republican task force report declaring that "IRCA had failed" to deter illegal aliens and demanding, among other things, an end to the grant of "birthright citizenship" to "anchor babies" born on American soil to illegal immigrants. Chairman of the Senate Immigration Subcommittee Alan Simpson declared that "the American people are so very fed up . . . with efforts to make them feel that Americans do not have that most fundamental right of any people: to decide who will join them here and help form the future country." He concluded that "it is time to slow down, to reassess." . . .

The first battle front was a welfare reform bill moving through the House. It would limit welfare benefits for recently arrived immigrants, including recent immigrants' elderly parents who had never worked in the United States. In general, sponsors of new immigrants would become more responsible for their care should they become a public charge. President Clinton objected to these new rules but eventually signed a larger welfare reform law in 1996.

Almost at once, courts and state welfare officials called the measures into question. Congress soon restored most of the cuts affecting immigrants. The likelihood of legal-immigration reform began to fade, as the Republican Party's leadership as well as President Clinton began to respond to aggressive lobbying by business and ethnic forces (in Clinton's case, mostly to one wealthy Democratic donor, John Huang, claiming to represent Asian Americans). Thus the Illegal Immigration Reform and Immigrant Responsibility Act of 1996 was stripped of all but minor changes, and one of these, pilot programs for testing electronic employment-verification systems, was never implemented. . . .

When the new century arrived, the Census Bureau's data gave a startling picture.

The U.S. population in the 1990s had grown by 32.7 million (to 281 million), the largest gain in history and the equivalent of adding the entire population of Canada. Immigrants were 13 to 14 million of that and, if one added the children born to them once in the country, the immigration-added total was 20 to 21 million, or two-thirds of the growth (in California, 96 percent). Since 1980, the United States had added 55 million people, or the equivalent of the population of France. The United States in 2001 contained more foreign-born residents than ever before (10.4 percent of the total population), and one in five Americans was either born abroad or to parents born abroad. Estimates of the illegal population ranged between 7 and 11 million. . . .

Both major parties' political leadership . . . quietly concluded that talk of immigration reform was a political loser, in view of the dynamic growth of the Spanish-speaking population in the United States and the imagined hostility of that "voting block" toward enforcement of immigration law. A formidable if bizarre lobbying coalition in favor of open borders had somehow come together under the same tent—business groups, most visibly Silicon Valley–type high-technology industrialists; organized labor; religious groups; immigration lawyers; and organizations representing immigrants' rights. The essential backdrop was a booming economy, labor shortages everywhere, and a general euphoria that dulled the edge of public concern about much of anything, including mass immigration. Whatever America was doing should be continued. . . .

The costs of America's porous borders were stunningly piled even higher on the morning of September 11, 2001. While Mexican President [Vicente] Fox traveled northward to Washington on his mission to open America's southern border to his surplus population, Islamic terrorists commandeered jetliners and struck the World Trade Center in New York and the Pentagon, killing nearly three thousand persons. . . .

That day's terrorist attacks harshly illuminated a defect that had not formerly been high on the list of flaws in American immigration policy, that our porous borders and governmental abandonment of virtually all interior immigration controls allowed terrorists to move at will into, around, and out of the country, legally and illegally. A study of the immigration history of the forty-eight terrorists convicted of (or admitting to) acts of terrorism against the United States since 1993 found that they had readily exploited every possible means of entry into the United States. "They came as students, tourists, and business visitors," found Center for Immigration Studies research director Steven Camarota, and seventeen had worked the system to enter and stay despite their terrorist occupations, becoming lawful permanent residents and even naturalized citizens of the country they hated. Some reached this permanent status by making fraudulent marriages or applying for asylum. Twelve were illegal aliens when they attacked, and twenty-one had been in illegal status at some point in the last ten years. Several gave officials false information on entry. Joel Mowbray of *National Review* obtained access to the visa applications of fifteen of the nineteen September 11 terrorists and expert analysis found so many elementary flaws that "all the applicants among the fifteen reviewed should have been denied visas." Forty-one of the larger group of forty-eight terrorists studied by Center for Immigration Studies had gone to U.S. consulates abroad and received visas, despite their backgrounds. Judging from the experience of these forty-eight murderers who were Middle Eastern young males with terrorist pasts, there are many ways for terrorists to get into America, legally or illegally, and many ways to stay there, some lawful and some not. It is an easy country to attack, from within.

2 Alejandro Portes and Rubén G. Rumbaut agree with Otis Graham that an understanding of history is important when confronting the issue of contemporary immigration. Yet these two scholars emphasize different parts of the past in their analysis of this topic. What developments in the last decades of the twentieth century do they see as particularly important in understanding immigration in contemporary American society? How does their reading of the past influence their conclusions about immigrants and immigration policy?

Immigrant America (2006)
ALEJANDRO PORTES AND RUBÉN G. RUMBAUT

The general perception of the foreign population among the native-born is not grounded in an understanding of the historical linkages between the United States and the countries of origin or by knowledge of the economic and social forces driving the phenomenon. The public view is guided instead by surface impressions. When foreign accents and faces are few, they are ignored. However, when they grow in number and concentrate in visible spaces, they trigger increasing apprehension. Natives are put on the defensive, fearing that their way of life and their control of the levers of political and economic power will be lost to the newcomers. The sentiment is expressed in familiar outcries such as "the end of white America," the "mongrelization of the race," "the rise of 'Mexifornia,'" and "the Hispanic challenge."

Policies stemming from these fears have followed two basic paths: to exclude the newcomers or to Americanize them as fast as possible. These two positions define the two great ideologies toward immigration among the general public. They have in common that, since neither is rooted in an understanding of the real forces at play, their transformation into policy leads to consequences that are commonly the opposite of those intended. The first ideology, which may be labeled *intransigent nativism*, seeks to stop all or most immigration, expel unauthorized immigrants, and put remaining immigrants on notice that they occupy an inferior position, ineligible for the privileges of citizens.

Supporters of this ideology look mainly to the present. They do not know or care to know about the factors underlying immigration or the history of the process. They give expression instead to the immediate concerns, discomfort, and anxieties of the native population. Accordingly, they lash out not against the true sources of migration but against the migrants themselves. Success for this position consists in rendering the foreign element

Source: From Alejandro Portes and Rubén G. Rumbaut, *Immigrant America: A Portrait*, pp. 346–350, 351–352, 353–356, 371–372. Copyright © 2006 Regents of the University of California. Reprinted by permission of the publisher, the University of California Press.

invisible once again. Intransigent nativism finds expression at a number of levels, ranging from elite intellectuals to xenophobic politicians, such as current Congressmen Tom Tancredo (R-Colorado) and James Sensenbrenner (R-Wisconsin), all the way to radio and television commentators, such as Lou Dobbs.

This ideology has registered some notable successes, such as the passage in 1994 of Proposition 187, the "Save Our State" (SOS) proposal in California (although it was struck down as unconstitutional by the federal courts three years later); the passage in 2004 of Proposition 200 in Arizona, a kindred measure dubbed "Protect Arizona Now" (PAN); the Illegal Immigration Reform and Immigrant Responsibility Act of 1996 (IIRAIRA); and the anti-immigrant provisions attached to the 1996 federal welfare reform bill (the Personal Responsibility and Work Opportunity Reconciliation Act, or PRWORA), which barred immigrants from access to a number of public assistance programs. . . .

Ronald Unz, the Jewish American millionaire who spearheaded Proposition 227, a California initiative dubbed "English for the Children" in 1998, explained his support for the measure as follows:

> As a strong believer in American assimilationism, I had a long interest in bilingual education. Inspired in part by the example of my own mother who was born in Los Angeles into a Yiddish-speaking immigrant home but had quickly and easily learned English as a young child, I had never understood why children were being kept for years in native-language classes, or why such programs had continued to exist or even expand after decades of obvious failure.

The second mainstream ideology is less irrational than the first. Forced assimilationism does look at the past, but less to find the origins of contemporary immigration than to search for ways in which prior flows were separated from their cultures and integrated into the American mainstream. The nation's success in absorbing so many foreigners in the past is attributed to its relentless hostility to the perpetuation of cultural enclaves and the immersion of foreign children into an English-only environment that made Americans out of them in the course of a single generation. . . . [T]he United States is indeed a veritable "cemetery of languages" in which the most varied linguistic backgrounds—from German to Italian; from Chinese to Spanish—have disappeared into a monolingual world in the course of two or three generations.

Assimilationists want the future to mirror this past as a proven way to restore unity and peace. Just as Yiddish-speaking mothers had to leave their culture and language behind, so should Mexican immigrants and Vietnamese refugees today. Though less traumatic than the effects of nativist exclusionary campaigns, forced assimilationism also has important consequences, and they are mostly negative. Policies derived from this ideology delegitimize the culture and language of immigrant parents, thus encouraging the phenomenon described . . . as dissonant acculturation. By instilling in second-generation youths the sense that their linguistic heritage is inferior and should be abandoned, this ideology drives a wedge across generations, weakening parental authority and efforts of parents to protect children against the dangers confronting them in schools and in the streets. . . .

A second consideration is the changing position of the United States in the world economy. By remaining fixed in the past, assimilationists neglect the changes that have been happening all around them in the last half century. One hundred years ago, immigrants came from remote lands to fill the labor needs of a rapidly industrializing country. Few other ties linked sending nations to the United States. At present, sending countries are increasingly part of a single global web, in which the United States plays a central role. In this new world order, in which economic, political, and cultural ties bind nations ever closer, it is not clear that the rapid extinction of foreign languages in America is in the interest of individual citizens or of the country as a whole. The urgent search for fluent Arabic speakers to staff government intelligence services in the wake of the 2001 terrorist attacks stand as the latest example of a commonly repeated saga in which the global communications needs of the United States are sorely served by a uniformly monolingual population.

In an increasingly interdependent global system, the existence of pools of American citizens able to communicate fluently in English plus another language represents not a threat to cultural integration but a resource and a source of enlightenment for individuals and communities alike. Despite being grounded in reflection on the country's past, forced assimilationist policies, such as that championed by Ronald Unz, are ultimately reactionary. They reflect a wish to restore America to its state at the beginning of the last century, not as it must be in the new millennium, after it emerged as the core of the global system. In the process, old-line assimilationism undermines the very forces of parental authority and ambition that can make the difference in guiding the second generation around major obstacles to successful adaptation and productive citizenship. . . .

The alternative path . . . under the label selective acculturation offers a much more viable way [than exclusion or forced assimilation] for successful integration of immigrant minorities and for the utilization of their capabilities. Selective acculturation must not be confused with multiculturalism, a pattern leading to the perpetuation of isolated ethnic enclaves. Instead, it means the acquisition of English fluency and American cultural ways *along with* preservation of certain key elements of the immigrant culture, of which language is paramount.

This pattern contributes to maintaining channels of communication open across generations, keeping youths linked to their community and the material and moral resources that it can provide, and providing a cognitive reference point to guide their successful integration. It is difficult to know where one is going without knowing where one came from. . . .

Underneath the debates about immigrant exclusion and assimilation, there is the hard reality of economic interests and economic survival. There are also real concerns about the growth prospects of the nation, dependent as always on its labor supply. In the postindustrial era, the American labor market has become increasingly bifurcated into an upper tier of professional and technical occupations, requiring advanced educational credentials, and a lower tier of manual occupations, requiring physical strength and few skills in sectors such as agriculture, construction, the food industry, and personal services. . . .

Labor immigration provides the answer to these needs. By reason of size, geographic proximity, and history, Mexico has become the real labor reservoir for the American economy. This huge economy, surpassing at present $12 trillion, more than the fifteen largest European economies combined, generates a huge labor demand at both ends of the labor market. Mexico is not really a poor but a middle-income nation, yet its proximity to the United States and the approximate seven-to-one wage gap for manual labor create a continuing incentive for peasants and workers to seek to join their conationals already working in the United States. As will be shown next, it is not individualistic calculations of gain, however, but forces buried deep in the history of the relationships between both nations that actually drive the process. . . .

The present system of international migration registers a close association between the history of prior contact, colonization, and influence of powerful nations over weaker "peripheral" ones and the onset of migratory movements out of the latter. The history of contact between the United States and the Latin American countries that supply the major contingents giving rise to today's "Hispanic" communities in the United States provides a suitable example. All of these countries—Mexico, Puerto Rico, and Cuba—were, each in its time, targets of a North American expansionist pattern that remolded their internal economic and social structures to the point that would-be migrants were already presocialized in American ways even before starting their journey. . . .

The Mexican framework of economic and political life constructed under Spanish colonial rule was severely undermined by contact with its more powerful North American neighbor. The Mexican-American War in the 1840s reduced Mexico's territory by almost half and, as Mexican American scholars are wont to repeat, converted a good part of the country's inhabitants into foreigners in their own land. North American expansion did not stop at military conquest, however, because rapid economic growth in what had been the northern provinces of Mexico reclaimed labor from the portion of the country left south of the Rio Grande.

In a pattern typical of the beginning of sizable labor flows elsewhere, Southwest growers and railroad companies started an active recruitment program where paid agents were sent into the interior of Mexico to offer free rail travel and cash advances as incentives for local peasants to come north. The result was to trigger a sizable rural labor outflow that, over time, became self-sustaining. At the time of the early recruitment waves in the nineteenth and early twentieth centuries, the southwestern U.S. border was scarcely enforced. As original settlers of the land, Mexicans came with the territory, and the arrival of new contract laborers and the movement back and forth across the Rio Grande met with little official resistance. Mexicans were thus an integral part of the Southwest population before they became immigrants and long before they became "illegal" immigrants.

Hence, contrary to today's portrayal of Mexican immigration as a movement initiated by individual calculations of gain, the process had its historical origins in U.S. geopolitical and economic expansion that first remolded the neighboring nation and then proceeded to organize dependable labor flows out of it. Such movements across the border of the reduced Mexican republic were a well-established routine in the Southwest before they became redefined as "illegal" immigration.

The process of structural imbalancing of peripheral areas of the world economy, followed by sustained immigration, has taken successive forms during the history of capitalism. Deliberate labor recruitment, such as the employer initiatives that gave rise to U.S.-bound Mexican migration, represents an intermediate form of a historical process that has ranged from coerced labor extraction (slavery) beginning in the sixteenth century to the present self-initiated labor flows. Migrant labor recruitment saw its height during the second half of the nineteenth century and the first two decades of the twentieth, when it was responsible for the onset of Italian and Polish as well as Mexican labor migrations to the United States and for the growth of sizable Italian and Asian populations in other countries of the Western Hemisphere such as Brazil and Argentina.

Self-initiated migrations are a product of the twentieth century, in which external imbalancing of peripheral societies does not take the form of organized coercion or deliberate recruitment. Instead, mass diffusion of new consumption expectations and the electronic transmission of information about life standards in the developed world suffice to encourage emigration. The gap between modern consumption standards and the economic realities of backward countries, plus increasing information about work opportunities abroad, provides enough incentives to generate an almost limitless supply of would-be migrants.

A key social effect of capitalist globalization is the rise of massive relative deprivation among citizens of nations fully exposed to modern goods and modern consumption but unable to afford them. The dominance of Western culture and consumption patterns thus places the advanced countries in the role of regulators of an inexhaustible flow of foreign workers who are willing to pay their transportation costs and assume all the risks of the journey. . . .

Despite pervasive absolute and relative deprivation in the global South, the specific historical ties between receiving and sending countries—primarily the impact on the latter of colonial and neocolonial episodes—continue to be clearly reflected in the major immigrant flows today. In the 1980s and 1990s, the top five countries sending legal immigrants to the United States were Mexico, the Philippines, China/Taiwan, South Korea, and Vietnam; the top two sending unauthorized immigrants were Mexico and El Salvador; and the four principal sources of refugees were Vietnam, Laos, Cambodia, and Cuba. A moment's reflection will bring to light the close historical ties between each of these countries and the United States, forged during successive North American interventions—from the Mexican and Spanish-American wars in the nineteenth century to successive anti-Communist struggles after World War II. . . .

A recent book by a well-known scholar of immigration, an immigrant himself, begins with a moving retrospective into the travails of his family as it struggled with poverty and the challenges of an unfamiliar culture and language. Like millions of immigrant families before them, the parents managed to cope and move ahead economically, paving the way for the author's college education, a doctorate from a major university, and a subsequent distinguished career. In a remarkable non sequitur, the book proceeds to attack contemporary immigration, arguing that its "quality" has declined and that it poses an increasing burden on the host society.

NIMBY is the acronym coined to refer to those who support construction of public facilities but "not in my backyard." In parallel fashion, we may coin PULLAM to refer to those who, having succeeded in America, wish to "pull the ladder after me." The book just mentioned is a notorious academic version of this syndrome, common among descendants of immigrants. . . .

But PULLAM and the policies that follow from it are counterproductive in ensuring the continuation of the process in the future. . . . [S]uccessful integration has never proceeded through pressure, for immigrants are incapable of turning themselves into instant Americans. Instead, with the aid of religious and ethnic institutions, they have carved niches for themselves, preserving their values, language, and customs and using them as platforms to find their way into their new social environment. It is this creative combination of the old and the new that accounts for the success story that immigration to America has been. In its extension to the second generation, what we have called selective acculturation, the nation will find the means to fend off the danger of downward assimilation and ensure the well-being and the productivity of this fast-rising population.

Nativists and forced assimilationists, including PULLAM advocates who extol their own past while attacking those who came after them, will undoubtedly continue to appear. Indeed, they proliferate today, making political hay out of the disconnect between the needs of the economy and the fears of the native population. These fearmongers will be discredited. Immigrants and refugees will continue to give rise to viable communities, infusing new blood in local labor markets, filling positions at different levels of the economy, and adding to the diversity of sounds, sights, and tastes of American cities. The history of this "nation of nations" is, to a large extent, the history of the arrival, struggles, and absorption of its immigrants. Despite the rising chorus of xenophobia and restrictionism as we pen these lines, the evidence points to a future that will mirror this past.

PRIMARY SOURCES

This section contains sources related to modern-day immigration and the experiences of contemporary immigrants. They reflect a variety of viewpoints and do not support a single conclusion. The first five sources present arguments about immigration and its various impacts. The second four offer evidence regarding individual immigrants and their experiences in the United States. In all these sources, look for evidence that supports the arguments of Graham in Source 1 or Portes and Rumbaut in Source 2. In particular, look for evidence regarding the positive or negative impact of immigration on American society and the reasons for the high levels of immigration into the nation.

Sources 3–7

Many contemporary commentators from varied backgrounds have weighed in on the immigration issue since the mid-1970s. What arguments do these sources offer for ending immigration or for supporting a more open or tolerant policy toward immigration and immigrants? What do their authors see as the most important effects of immigration on American society?

3 This article from the widely read *BusinessWeek* magazine addressed the gains and losses to the American economy brought by illegal immigration. Note the costs and benefits that are included and excluded in this calculation.

"Illegal Immigrants: The U.S. May Gain More Than It Loses" (1984)

Unquestionably, there are social and economic costs to illegal immigration. But new economic evidence suggests that, on balance, the nation benefits more from the increased economic growth and lower inflation stemming from illegal immigration than it loses in jobs, lower wages, and welfare costs.

Hard data on illegals are, of course, difficult to come by. Based on the recent surge in arrests of aliens, however, their numbers are growing. The Census Bureau estimates that there are now 5 million to 7.5 million illegal residents, who may be holding between 4 million and 6 million jobs.

While this seems like a huge number, many are jobs for which Americans do not compete. Some illegals are employed in agriculture, picking strawberries and tomatoes in 100° heat. Others hold such urban jobs as dishwashers, busboys, maids, and sewing-machine operators—unattractive to many Americans and therefore difficult for employers to fill. Michael J. Piore of the Massachusetts Institute of Technology argues that there is in effect a "two-tier" labor market in which low-skilled immigrants take unwanted jobs so that little displacement of American workers occurs.

Most experts, however, agree that illegals compete for some jobs that Americans want. The Immigration & Naturalization Service has found illegal aliens working in the garment and food-processing industries in California, casinos in Atlantic City, and electronics companies in Silicon Valley. Indeed, a 1979 government study estimated that one in five jobs held by an alien—in total, as many as 1.2 million jobs—could be filled by unemployed Americans. Those who are especially hurt by competition from illegals are low-skilled workers, primarily minorities and young people.

However, even 1.2 million jobs represents less than 1% of the total number in the economy. Moreover, that figure is calculated by looking only at the kinds of jobs where immigrants and Americans are most likely to compete. It fails to consider the spur to economic growth that immigration has generated over a long period of time. Illegal immigration, say most economists, has added to the nation's output. This increase in goods and services has created other jobs that have in good part offset the job loss to Americans from direct competition with illegals.

Indeed, many economists view immigration as they do international trade. While the nation as a whole benefits from free trade, uncompetitive industries and their employees can be hurt. Similarly, says Morgan O. Reynolds of Texas A&M University, "open immigration provides net gains for the economy by expanding output and lowering prices, but some people lose."

At the current pace of illegal immigration, which the Census Bureau estimates adds 500,000 people per year, the impact on future unemployment is likely to be quite small. Even if all of those are workers, Data Resources Inc. calculates that it would add only one-tenth of a percentage point to the unemployment rate. The impact on specific regions, such as the Southwest and Florida, would also be modest, says senior economist Elisabeth Allison. The DRI regional models show that higher immigration in these regions will drive up the unemployment rate, but only briefly. Allison explains that people in other states respond to increased immigration by deciding not to move there. This limits the labor force and curbs unemployment.

Such findings do not refute the contention that illegal immigrants drive down wages. Many illegals, for example, are paid less than the minimum: Sheldon L. Maram of California State University found that 21.8% of the illegal restaurant workers he studied were paid less than the minimum wage; compared with 8.4% of the legal workers. Since employers can threaten to report illegals to the authorities, illegals are more likely than others to work for less than the legal minimum wage and put up with sweatshop conditions.

Yet a study by Barton A. Smith of the University of Houston and Robert Newman of the University of British Columbia shows that the effect of lower wages paid to illegals may not be as severe as it seems at first, at least in certain areas. Smith and Newman compared the wages in towns in Texas near the Mexican border, where many illegals live, with towns farther from the border. The average wages in the border cities were 30% to 40% lower than in the more distant areas. But Smith and Newman found that real wages—wages adjusted for the cost of living in each area—were at most only 8% lower. Says Smith: "From the worker's point of view, what he's concerned about is the real wage." Smith believes that lower wages explain part, but not all, of the lower cost of living in the border areas.

Lower wage costs can have other beneficial effects. For one thing, they tend to keep overall prices low. Lower-paid illegal aliens in agriculture help hold down the prices of fresh fruits and vegetables. More important, low wages allow industries facing severe foreign competition to survive. Without lower wages, some industries—such as the garment industry and consumer electronics—would have to go overseas to compete. Says Yale economist Jennifer Roback: "As long as we have international trade, American industry will compete with low-wage workers. It may be better to employ them here than overseas." Despite the benefits of lower prices and the bolstering of otherwise endangered domestic industries, lower wages may lower U.S. productivity. Dale W. Jorgenson of Harvard believes that low-wage labor slows down the growth of capital spending and thus dampens productivity growth. More cheap labor from Latin America "could undermine to a certain extent the capital spending boom we anticipate in the 1980s," he says. Jorgenson points to a similar slowdown in productivity in the 1970s, which he attributes in part to the swollen labor force that reflected the baby boom and new female workers. Indeed, former Labor Secretary Ray Marshall notes that when child labor was abolished in the late 19th century, the garment industry invested in labor-saving equipment. This ultimately increased productivity in the industry and lowered prices. And Philip L. Martin of the University of California at Davis contends that the use of aliens in agriculture is holding back important mechanization.

To some extent, however, the substitution of cheap labor for capital will also be moderated by an expanding economy. Michael L. Wachter of the University of Pennsylvania notes that low-skilled workers may be substitutes for capital, but the increased output they produce also spurs capital investment.

4 Richard Lamm, a three-term governor of Colorado, and co-author Gary Imhoff expressed their opposition to large-scale immigration in their book *The Immigration Time Bomb*, from which the following selection is taken. Pay particular attention to the historical argument they make regarding immigrants as a threat to American culture and society.

Immigration as a Threat to Social Cohesion (1985)
RICHARD LAMM AND GARY IMHOFF

I believe that America's culture and national identity are threatened by massive levels of legal and illegal immigration. Admittedly, there are good historical reasons that some people remain complacent in the face of massive migration. After all, there were adjustment difficulties in earlier periods of peak migration, but the fears of Americans that migrants would permanently change the basis of American culture were unjustified, as were their fears that migrants and their children would not assimilate. And the yearly inflow of immigrants to the United States composes a lower percentage of our total population today than it did in the 1910s. Therefore, it is easy to assume that we're unjustified if we worry about the social effects of large-scale migration today.

I know that earlier large waves of immigrants didn't "overturn" America, but there are at least five reasons not to be complacent, reasons to believe that today's migration is different from earlier flows. First, the yearly inflow of immigrants is a small portion of our society's total population, but immigrants are not evenly dispersed throughout the country. They settle in a few big cities, and they constitute large proportions of those cities. The culture of Kansas and Nebraska is not much affected by the small influxes of migrants they receive, but the cultures of Miami, Florida; Los Angeles, California; and Washington, D.C., have been and are increasingly affected, visibly and markedly.

Second, the peak migration years of the 1910s were ended in 1921 by a new immigration law that set annual ceilings on migration levels. The peak immigration years of the 1970s and 1980s are continuing—and there is not now any plan that promises to end them. The migration stream of the 1910s would not have been assimilated had it continued unabated, had it been augmented by decades of followers.

Third, earlier flows of immigrants were well mixed by language groups, and no single group predominated. As Michael Teitelbaum pointed out in an influential article: "While there were substantial concentrations of a particular language group in past decades (e.g., 28 percent German-speaking in 1881–90 and 23 percent Italian-speaking in 1901–10), previous immigration flows generally were characterized by a broad diversity of linguistic groups ranging from

Chinese to Polish to Spanish to Swedish. Furthermore, those concentrations that did occur proved to be short-lived." But, Teitelbaum points out, today's migration stream is quite different: "The INS reports that, in the period 1968–77, approximately 35 percent of all legal immigrants to the United States were Spanish-speaking. If one adds to this figure plausible estimates of Spanish-speaking illegal immigrants, it becomes clear that over the past decade perhaps 50 percent or more of legal and illegal immigrants to the United States have been from a single foreign-language group." And this concentration shows no sign of changing in and of itself at any time in the near future.

Fourth, today's migrants come after the impact of the ethnic pride movements in America, after the death (or at least during the long critical illness) of the melting pot ideal. During the last peak of immigration to the United States, our society insisted on immigrants' assimilation. If adult migrants who settled with others of their own nationality were not required to learn English by the circumstances of their lives, at least their children who entered public schools were certainly expected—by their parents as well as by society—to make English their primary language. Today, with ever-growing language group subcultures, assimilation is controversial, and pressures within immigrant communities countervail against the attractions of assimilation.

Fifth, the argument that we need not worry about the assimilation of massive migrant groups ignores our actual experiences with immigration over the past decade. In fact, there have been numerous and profound problems in cities where recent large movements have settled. There has been a recent and threatening history of cultural clash and conflict, a record of widening community rifts, a new splintering of our society that results directly from large and continuing immigration—legal and illegal.

---

5 Writing for the Immigration Law Enforcement Monitoring Project in Houston, Texas, the author of this source argues that migrant immigrant workers should be viewed as part of a global labor force. Note the historical trends that she cites to support her argument.

Undocumented Workers as International Workers (1997)
MARIA JIMÉNEZ

Immigrants and immigration are buzz words in the U.S. public debates that stir emotions, polarize relations between ethnic and racial groups, and evoke hostility toward anyone foreign-born. Ironically, the process of globalization, economic integration and economic restructuring give rise to an increasing

Source: From "Enforcement: A Tool to Control the Flow of Labor at the U.S.-Mexico Border," by Maria Jiménez, *Fact Sheets,* Spring 1997, pp. 1–3. This article initially appeared in *Network News,* published by the National Network for Immigrant and Refugee Rights, Spring 1997. Reprinted by permission.

movement of persons across international boundaries. "International labor migrant" is a more precise term to describe those who move in the complex web of a global economic system. Since the 1960s, economic migrants from developing countries to industrialized nations have quadrupled, reaching about 940,000 per year.

Worldwide, immigration policies have made it possible for a small group of people to become more and more mobile by providing the legal flexibility for the exit and entrance of business owners, executives, administrators and support technical labor. However, physical and other barriers to the movement of poor people have proliferated. The inequality of mobility is a part of the maintenance of the larger socio-economic and political inequalities on a national and international scale.

The movement to industrialized countries is not a movement seeking a "transition to prosperity" but rather a response to the politics of economic integration created and imposed by global economic elites. Migration cannot be separated from the policies of debt collection by multi-lateral agencies like the World Bank and International Monetary Fund in acquiescence with domestic elites and national governments. Such policies have caused untold human suffering and widespread environmental destruction, rendering these countries with few resources to invest in economic and human recovery.

Border control is sought as a policy decision not so much to stop unauthorized migration, but to frame the conditions in which international labor participates in economic, social and political spheres. No other border control policies better illustrate this complex facet of global integration and the inequality of the movement of persons than those of the United States with respect to its border with Mexico.

These nations share the most integrated relationship between a rich and poor nation, in terms of debt, trade and migration. Mexico's debt to U.S. banks totals about 150 billion dollars. From 1965 to 1990, some 1.9 million Mexicans were admitted as legal permanent residents. During the same time period, there were more than 36 million undocumented entries from Mexico and more than 31 million departures. The process of social capital formation, human capital accumulation and market integration between the two countries is so far advanced in over 100 years of continuous migratory flows that stopping the flow of migration is impossible.

Increasing the INS budget by 75% to enhance border enforcement reflects more of a rejection of the presence of working poor, Spanish-speaking immigrants than policy decisions based on fact. Traditionally, concern for "borders out of control" has always been about the 2,000 miles of the U.S.-Mexico border and never the 4,000 miles of the U.S.-Canadian border. According to the Urban Institute, only four out of ten individuals who are illegally in the country entered by crossing the southern border; the other six entered with legal visas that later expired. Yet 85% of all the resources of the Immigration and Naturalization Service, including the Border Patrol, are located in southern border communities.

Walls, more agents and military support as tougher border enforcement measures only redirect the flows of undocumented immigrants to other parts of the border, delaying entry and increasing the risks to immigrants as they move toward more dangerous and remote areas of the border. A recent University of Houston study estimated that 190 to 300 persons died annually attempting to cross the Texas border; countless more die crossing the deserts of Arizona and mountains and highways of California.

At the same time, enforcement of immigration laws is selectively applied to persons of Mexican origin and/or descent. Mexican nationals represent 39% of the undocumented immigrants in the U.S., but they are 90 percent of those arrested for illegal entry by the Immigration and Naturalization Service. The Mexican-origin population bears the burden of civil and human rights violations. Deaths, beatings, sexual assaults, illegal arrests and other cases of abuse of authority are often reported by those confronting immigration authorities. In a recent study by the University of Arizona, 18 percent of 200 randomly surveyed persons in South Tucson indicated that they had been mistreated by immigration officials. Of these, 60% were citizens born in the United States. . . .

U.S. immigration policy is an artificial and misdirected effort to intervene in economic transactions between willing sellers of labor and willing buyers by interposing armed force both at the border and at worksites. It is the only aspect of employee and employer relations that is enforced through the use of guns. Ultimately, dependence of many U.S. industries on undocumented labor encourages contempt for the law, fosters contraband in human beings and the widespread falsification of identity documents. The international labor workforce is placed in a position of illegality, vulnerability, exploitation and socio-political marginalization.

In a historical continuum, this is nothing new for Mexican-origin populations in the United States. Racism, exclusion and segregation are all too familiar. The only change currently is that this fervor takes place in the context of the inequalities produced by a global economic system. In the short run, a realistic approach to border control on the U.S.-Mexico border is to recognize the movement of labor as an inevitable consequence of the ongoing processes of the market integration presently occurring and formally recognized by NAFTA.* Binational agreements on migratory flows within both countries must move toward developing a flexible legal framework for the movement of labor in both directions, guaranteeing equity and respect for the human rights and dignity of all human beings. In the long run, the construction of immigration control policies must evolve as a product of mutual agreement and acknowledgment between the people of both countries, that together work to construct a world of economic equity, social acceptance and peace.

*The North American Free Trade Agreement, approved in 1993, eliminated trade barriers among Canada, Mexico, and the United States.

6   Economists and other researchers have studied the impact of immigration on economic growth. The source below summarizes the work of one researcher who focused on the role of immigrants in the success of California's "Silicon Valley." What does this source suggest about the links between immigration and a global economy?

"The Secret of Success" (2002)

University of California professor AnnaLee Saxenian began to uncover the "wealth" of Silicon Valley while doing research for her book in 1994. In a seminal work called *Regional Advantage,* Saxenian examined the factors that contributed to the technology boom in Silicon Valley as opposed to Boston. Her findings discovered that one of the most important components in the success of Silicon Valley was the availability of immigrant labor and foreign capital in the Bay Area.

In 1999, the Public Policy Institute of California (PPIC) commissioned Saxenian to pursue her theory that the tremendous growth in Silicon Valley was directly linked to the circulation of high-skilled immigrant labor. In just five years, Saxenian found that Chinese or Indian Immigrants led 24 percent of all Silicon Valley firms and that foreign-owned firms accounted for approximately 14 percent of the region's total employment. The level of foreign ownership shocked many observers and dispelled the notion of California immigrants as low-skill workers.

Last year, the PPIC once again commissioned professor Saxenian to investigate the importance of immigrant networks as foreign professionals migrate in and out of the high-tech marketplace. Due to the tremendous presence of Asian-owned technology firms in Silicon Valley, Saxenian chose to look at immigrants whose country of origin was China, India or Taiwan. . . .

According to Saxenian, first-generation immigrants to Silicon Valley appear to be active entrepreneurs. Although most of the respondents were relatively recent arrivals in the U.S., 52 percent of immigrant scientists and engineers have been involved in either founding or running a start-up company.

Further findings showed that 60 percent of all Indian respondents reported being involved in starting companies—almost the same rate as their native-born counterparts. Fifty-one percent of Taiwan-born and 32 percent of Chinese respondents also confirmed they had participated in some start-ups. Saxenian's data found that age, gender (male), education and country of origin were all directly correlated to the degree of involvement an individual had in their start-up experience. . . .

Source: From "The Secret of Success: Immigrant Networks Keep Silicon Valley on Top," Immigration Policy Center Policy Brief, May 2002. This material was originally produced by the Immigration Policy Center at the American Immigration Council.

Although Saxenian administered her survey during one of the most volatile times for high-tech industries in Silicon Valley, 62 percent of immigrant respondents said they are considering starting their own company. This rate was significantly higher than the 46 percent of U.S. respondents who planned to begin a start-up. In fact, only 7 percent of foreign respondents said they would never open their own business, compared to 13 percent of natives.

Seventy-four percent of Indians surveyed said they would like to run their own business someday. A large consensus such as this hints that not only do foreign-born respondents tend to be more entrepreneurial than natives, but they also tend [to] be more inclined to convert their future businesses into transnational organizations.

Professor Saxenian notes that although many foreign-born entrepreneurs intend to establish commerce in their native countries, few countries provide the economic freedom required for new businesses to thrive. In countries such as China and Taiwan the government gives little if any financial incentive to entrepreneurs and access to capital is limited.

The PPIC survey presents substantial evidence that the "brain drain" from developing countries such as China and India no longer exists. The informal networks of immigrants in Silicon Valley allow a more complex phenomenon of "brain circulation" to prevail. The links between California and distant regional economies are developing quickly.

Saxenian found that many first-generation immigrants exchange information, jobs, and business opportunities with friends and colleagues back home. Her research suggests that local institutions and social networks within ethnic communities play a larger role towards business behavior than do national or personal interests.

---

7   The Federation for American Immigration Reform (FAIR) supports a large reduction in annual immigration to the United States. Note the argument in this FAIR *Issue Brief* about the relationship between immigration and economic growth. How does its conclusion compare to those in Source 3 and Source 6?

"Low Immigration and Economic Growth" (2007)

- America's experience with a low level of immigration provides a useful test of how that affects the nation's economic performance.
- Between 1925 and 1965 immigrant admissions averaged less than 180,000 persons per year.
- During that period, the share of women in the workforce nearly doubled and minorities gained access to new job opportunities.
- Over those decades, the economy not only grew significantly, it grew more rapidly than it has since mass immigration was again unleashed by legislation enacted in 1965.

One of the arguments currently made for increasing the intake of immigrants and guest workers is that it is vital to the health of the nation's economy. If this were true, a tough choice would have to be made between economic stagnation and the social and environmental impact of adding further population growth on top of what is already too much.

Fortunately, there is no real dilemma. The economy can grow in a healthy fashion with a low level of immigration. How do we know this? Our economic history demonstrates this fact. We had a level of immigration between 1925 and 1965 that averaged less than 180,000 admissions per year. Illegal immigration during that period was not the serious problem that it is today.

During that period of restricted immigration curtailed in part because of World War II and the Depression the overall trend in economic growth was impressive. It was a time of rapid industrialization and mechanization, a major move from rural America and work in agriculture to the cities and industrial jobs. Women entered the workforce in large numbers. In 1920, according to the Census, 23.7 percent of women were in the workforce. By 1970, before the effects of the 1965 change in the immigration law had significantly expanded immigrant admissions, the share of women in the workforce had grown to 43.3 percent.

The best indicator of how the U.S. economy responded to the period of low immigration between 1925 and 1966 may be seen in data that recorded the gross domestic product (GDP) per capita over that period. The following chart shows that trend in constant, inflation-adjusted dollars.

GDP per Capita 1925–2005

What is readily apparent for the pre-1966 period is the fact that, apart from a rapid jump in per capita GDP during WWII and a drop back following it, the overall trend is rising national product, i.e., economic development. It may also be seen that the increase in per capita GDP has continued since the 1965 Immigration Act unleashed rapid immigration growth. But, the rate of increase since 1966 is not as great as it was during the period of low immigration.

From 1925–1966 GDP per capita increased by 168.4 percent. That is an average annual increase of 4.0 percent. During the period since then (1966–2005) the increase in GDP per capita has been 114.2 percent. That is an annual average increase of 2.9 percent.

Of course, immigration is not the only factor influencing economic change. The role of labor unions, laws, trade, transportation, communication, and technology all play major roles in economic change. As the United States has become more enmeshed in international commerce and other countries have developed economically, greater competition exists for our produce.

It is tempting to look at the greater per annum GDP per capita growth during our earlier low immigration and conclude that a return to low immigration would result in a new surge in per capita growth. A slowing in the availability of low-wage labor, according to economic theory, should have the effect of causing wages to rise to attract more U.S. workers back into those occupations. If the nation's output continued to grow during a period of slowing growth in population, this would contribute to the growth in GDP per capita. However, because there are other economic forces at play in shaping the national product, that is not a clear-cut prospect. Nevertheless, the nation's history with low-level immigration and the economic growth during that period provides evidence that it is wrong to suggest that our economy will suffer if immigration and guest worker programs are not increased as business interests are currently asserting and it suggests, on the contrary, that the economy would continue to be healthy if immigration were significantly reduced.

Sources 8–11

The sources in this section are excerpts from the oral histories of immigrants. They present a variety of immigrant backgrounds and experiences. As you read them, keep in mind the arguments in the two secondary sources regarding the reasons for massive immigration and its costs and benefits. Varied as they are, do these immigrants' stories reveal patterns that shed light on the arguments made in the previous sources? Are the attitudes or hopes of these immigrants similar to one another or different?

8   In 1984, Rosa María Urbina, a widow with three children, began crossing the Rio Grande River from Juárez, Mexico, to find work in El Paso. Each night she would return home to her children. On one of those trips back to Juárez she met José Luis, a twenty-six-year-old farm worker. Once married, they decided to make their home in the United States.

Two Illegal Immigrants Tell Their Story (1988)

JOSÉ: The majority of the people in our apartment building have the same problem as my family. All of us are in El Paso without legal papers. I have been living here since 1981.

ROSA: I came in 1984, to find work. After José and I were married and we found a place to live, I brought my children from a previous marriage. We lived across the river, in Juárez. But I was born further south, in Zacatecas.

JOSÉ: My hometown is Juárez. Since I was nine years old, I've been coming to El Paso to work. At first I did gardening in people's yards, but I have stayed in El Paso constantly since 1981, going out to the fields to do farm work. I used to go to Juárez to visit my relatives at least one day each month. But in the last year. I haven't gone, because of the new immigration law. To visit Juárez I have to swim across the river. I can't cross the bridge or the *"migra"* [Border Patrol officers] can catch me right there.

During the past few months, the river has been very high and fast. That's one reason why not so many people have been crossing lately. I am not working now, because it isn't the growing or harvesting season on the big farms. On February 15, we usually begin to plant onions. That is when the main agricultural season begins. But during a three-month period between planting and harvesting, there is no work.

We haven't paid our rent since December. If we're lucky, I can find some part-time work to pay for food. Our baby, José Luis, is two months old. Because he was born in El Paso, he is an American citizen. We can only get food assistance for him. Once in a while, I find a job as a construction laborer, house painter, whatever is available. We use the money to buy food for the baby and the other three children first.

ROSA: I haven't been able to work lately, because the baby is so small. My other children are all in school. Lorenzo is twelve years old, José Rubén is ten, and Miriam is seven. From the time I came to El Paso, I have worked as a housekeeper and minding homes for people. I am not used to staying

Source: "Mojados (Wetbacks)," from *New Americans: An Oral History* by Al Santoli, copyright © 1988 by Al Santoli. Used by permission of Viking Penguin, a division of Penguin Group (USA) Inc., and the author.

in the apartment every day, but I have no other choice, because of my small baby.

I have known many changes in my life. I moved to Juárez from a farm in Zacatecas when I was seven years old. My mother and father were split up. After mother remarried, my stepfather took us to Juárez. We lived in an adobe house in the *colonias* [ramshackle housing projects] up in the hills.

When I was a teenager, I worked as a hairdresser in a beauty salon, cutting hair. My first husband was a mechanic, fixing cars. We made a good living. But my husband spent the money he made drinking in the *cantinas*. And after a while, he wouldn't let me work, because I had young children to take care of. When he died in 1984, he left me nothing at all. He drank too much and died from cirrhosis of his liver. I had no money . . . nothing. My children were nine, seven, and three years old. I had to find a way to pay rent and feed them.

At that time, the economy in Mexico had become horrible. Inflation was going crazy. The peso jumped to 500 per dollar. Today it is still climbing at 1,000 per dollar. I found a job working on an assembly line at a factory. We produced rubber gloves for hospitals and medical supplies like little caps for syringes. I would go into work at 4:30 in the afternoon and stay until 2:00 A.M. I was paid only 7,000 pesos [$14] each week. That was not enough to feed my kids. And I didn't have any relatives or friends to watch the kids while I worked. So I had no other choice but to put them in a special institution, like an orphanage, for children without parents. This upset me very much. But with my husband dead, and no other form of support, there was nothing I could do.

My only hope was to cross the river to the United States. If I could find a job that paid enough money, my children could join me. I wanted them to have an education and a proper life . . . to be someone.

After I made up my mind to cross the river, I met José Luis. It was like fate—we just found each other. You could say it was love at first sight. [Laughs] I had two young boys who needed a good man to learn from. When he asked me to live with him, I said yes.

JOSÉ: Before I met Rosa, I lived with my grandmother in Juárez. I would go back and forth across the river to work in El Paso or the farms in New Mexico. After Rosa and I fell in love, we decided to rent this apartment in El Paso and live together. . . .

ROSA: The majority of the people in the *colonia* where I lived in Juárez worked in El Paso, mostly as housekeepers, construction workers, or helpers in the fields. In the United States there is a lot of work, but in Mexico we have nothing.

JOSÉ: The men, like myself, who work in the fields come across the river at around 2:30 A.M. to meet the buses that take us to the fields from

El Paso. The transportation is owned by the *padrone* of the farms or by the labor-crew chiefs who hire and pay the workers. In the evenings, we ride the buses back to the river. Sometimes I work twelve hours in a day and earn $20. I've learned to check around to see which farms pay the best. Some pay up to $35 a day.

Farm-labor jobs are not very steady. We just grab whatever is open at the moment. I accept anything, any time, as long as it is work. But suppose I take a job that only pays me $12 a day. It would only be enough to cover my transportation and meals in the field. I must find jobs that pay enough to feed my family.

In order to make $25, I must pick seventy-two buckets of chili peppers. That could take me four or five hours, it depends on how fast my hands are. The total amount of buckets we pick depends upon the amount contracted by the big companies in California. For a big contract, we work as long as necessary to complete the order. But the most I can earn in a day is $35.

During the summer, it gets very hot in the fields, up to 110 degrees. We work for eight hours with a half-hour break for lunch. To save money, I bring my lunch from home. The companies usually provide us with a thermos bottle of cold water. The farthest we travel from El Paso is to Lordsburg, New Mexico. That is around three and a half hours by bus. We leave El Paso at 3:00 A.M. For Las Cruces we leave at 5:00 or 5:30 A.M. . . .

The landlord who owns this building is very generous. He lets us owe him rent for the months that I am not working. He understands how tough our life is. We pay whatever we can, even if it's only $50. And he knows that, if the day comes where we are raided by immigration officers, we will run.

The rent for this apartment is $125 a month plus electricity. We all live and sleep in this one room. The two boys sleep on the couch. Our daughter, Miriam, sleeps with us on the bed. And the baby sleeps in a crib next to our bed. Fortunately, we have a kitchen, and a closet in this room. Living conditions in Juárez were better, but there was no work at all.

If it is possible, Rosa and I would like to become American citizens. I would have my documents, and the government wouldn't be after us. All we want is to be able to work in peace.

Our dream is to be able to give the children the best of everything. We know that, for them to have a better future and purpose in life, they need a good education. Of the three children in school now, Miriam is the fastest learner. She received an award for being an honor student, the best in her classroom.

We hope the children can finish high school and have the career of their choice. We are going to sacrifice for them, so that they can have the profession that they desire.

9   Celia Noup came to the United States as a refugee from Cambodia in 1979. A widow whose husband was killed by the Communist Khmer Rouge, she fled to the United States after it began a resettlement program for Cambodians. That program started because many Cambodians who had been associated with the United States during the war in Southeast Asia were suffering at the hands of Communist forces. Noup first settled in Washington, D.C., before moving to California.

A Cambodian Immigrant's American Dream (1988)

I started this business from almost nothing at all. I named it House of Donuts, my own franchise. I spend most of my time in this shop, seven days a week. Why did a woman my age choose this kind of business? I know it's crazy. My children were already living in southern California. And my second daughter, Monie, was getting married here. That's why I moved from Washington, D.C., in 1983.

I get to the shop at 5:00 in the morning to open for breakfast, and I usually leave around 7:00 P.M. I work behind the counter, serving customers, and do the cleaning and sweeping. I work by myself most of the time. My youngest daughter, Parika, just began college, but she comes with me at 5:00 A.M. to help. At 10:00 A.M., she goes home to study, before she attends afternoon and evening classes at El Camino College. She works another part-time job, at May Company, in the children's department. She wants to buy a car.

At first I didn't want to come to California. When my daughters and I came to the United States in 1979, we were brought to Virginia, just outside of Washington, by my sister-in-law. But my first daughter, Mealy [pronounced "May Lee"], who was twenty-three years old, had a friend in southern California. She phoned our house and said, "Mealy, if you cannot find a job in Virginia, why don't you come here? I'll help you find a job."

So Mealy came to me and said, "Mom, the work situation here is very bad. It's very frustrating for me. Even during the bad times in Cambodia under the Khmer Rouge, I worked with my muscles to earn a bowl of rice. Why can't I find a job here? Let me go. I don't want to be on public assistance."

We never wanted to take money from the social services. I cried the day they interviewed me. And I also cried when they asked, "Are you married? Single? Widow?" I said, "I'm married." I cannot say that I'm a widow. My husband's death was never confirmed. That's why my American citizenship papers say that I am married.

I am pursuing the American dream—to have a house of my own, for my family. I try to make my children understand: "You have to help me in the shop, so that I can save and buy a small house." But they have their own lives, their own families, other jobs. The money they earn is not that much. So they still need me as much as I need them.

When I became an American citizen a few months ago, it was very emotional for me. I was happy that I could be part of my new country. I do feel loyalty to the United States. I think of myself as both Cambodian and an American citizen. I cannot forget where I came from.

My maiden name was Thann Meng Vann. When I became an American citizen, I took an American name, Celia, and my husband's family name, Noup, because I hope that he will some day return. I lost contact with him as our country was falling in April 1975. The outpost he commanded was surrounded by the Khmer Rouge. I have never found out what happened to him after he was captured. Sometimes I have seen him in my dreams, but he never talks to me. . . .

I've found that America is a country where people have come from all over the world. You do your job, you get paid like anybody else, and you're accepted. But Cambodians I know in France, like my sister, feel differently. People are not accepted if they are not French. But in America, you're part of the melting pot. . . .

For young and old refugees in this country, life is tough. If you don't earn money, you cannot live. The more we work, the more we earn, and life gets better. That's why I don't mind putting so many hours into my store. Other Cambodians feel the same way. We appreciate that we do get something in return. Not like under the Communists—we worked for nothing. We couldn't even satisfy our hunger.

Another reason that I work and try to save money is to be able to sponsor my cousin and her family from Cambodia. She is just like my sister. We were raised together by my mom. Until someone told my cousin that I was here, she thought that my daughters and I were killed on our way to Thailand. She's living with her husband and seven children in my mom's house in Phnom Penh. We try to write to each other. But I don't have much time, because I'm always working. Sometimes I send her small packages. They are so happy to receive them.

I would like for them to be here with us. But now the American program for Cambodian refugees is being closed. Even people who escape to the border camps in Thailand are no longer allowed to come to the United States. But they don't understand. They say "Sister, we are waiting for you. Hurry. Bring us out."

I know that things are getting more and more difficult in Cambodia under the Communists. I wrote them, "It's your risk. You are not a small family. Nine people cannot pass through the forest to Thailand unnoticed. It's very dangerous. But if you want to take your risk. . . ."

I would sponsor them here as immigrants from the refugee camp. I would tell the American government that I have some income ready for them. They have a place to work in my shop. They don't have to go on public assistance.

That's one of the main reasons I want to have this donut shop and try to keep it open. There're three reasons: for my children, for my cousin's family, and for the little house that I dream of. . . .

I want the house not only for myself—for everybody to live in. My daughters, my relatives from Phnom Penh—they could live in the garage if we fix it up nice. We wouldn't have to pay rent and be bothered all the time. It's my American dream to have that little house.

---

10   In 1993, Chinese garment workers in Oakland, California, organized to protest their treatment. As the result of a prior labor dispute, twelve women at the Lucky Sewing Company had been laid off. Lucky owed them $15,000 in back wages, but the company refused to pay them because it had gone bankrupt when the clothing manufacturer Jessica McClintock, Inc. ended its contract with Lucky. When Jessica McClintock claimed it was not responsible for the workers' loss, they decided to rally against it. Fu Lee, a Chinese immigrant, was one of the twelve women. She was also one of the speakers at a protest against Jessica McClintock that May.

A Chinese Immigrant Battles Jessica McClintock (1993)

Hello, my name is Fu Lee. I am forty-one years old, married, and I have a nine-year old daughter. I have been living in Oakland Chinatown since I left Hong Kong twelve years ago.

I want to tell you about the kind of exploitative working conditions I have had to endure in the sweatshops. I also want to tell you why me and my co-workers felt we had to stand up against the manufacturers to take responsibility for our loss of jobs and pay.

I worked as a seamstress at Lucky Sewing Company for two years. Before that, I worked as a seamstress at other similar sweatshops. All of the workers worked long hours, ten to twelve hours a day and six to seven days a week. We were paid by the piece, which sometimes was below the minimum wage. Overtime pay was unheard of. You may think sewing is an easy job. But it requires a lot of skill. For fancy dresses with laces, tiny buttons, and tricky fabric patterns, you really have to concentrate so you do not make any mistakes. My wage was never enough money for our family to live on. We always worried about our daughter getting sick because we had no health insurance.

My eyes hurt from straining under poor lighting; my throat hurt because of the chemical fumes from the fabric dye. Sometimes, I wore surgical masks so I would not have to breathe in all the dust from the fabric. My back never stopped hurting from bending over the sewing machine all day. Our boss

Source: From Judy Ying, Gordon H. Chang, and Him Mark Lai, eds., *Chinese American Voices: From the Gold Rush to the Present*, pp. 359, 361–362. Copyright © 2006 Regents of the University of California. Reprinted by permission of the publisher, the University of California Press.

was like a dictator. He was always pushing us to work faster. There was a sign in the shop that said, "No loud talking. You cannot go to the bathroom." When we did talk loudly or laugh during work, he would throw empty boxes at us and tell us to go back to work. When there was a rush order, we had to eat lunch at our work station.

Last year, my employer closed his shop and left us holding bad paychecks. We found out that he had filed for bankruptcy and had no intention of paying us our meager wages. The twelve Chinese seamstresses including myself were so mad. After working so hard under such horrendous working conditions, we should at least get our pay.

With the help of Asian Immigrant Women Advocates, we began searching for ways to get our pay. We were shocked to find out that the dresses we sewed were selling for $175 at an exclusive Jessica McClintock boutique in San Francisco. Our boss would receive only $10 for these dresses from Jessica McClintock, the manufacturer, and we seamstresses would be paid less than $5 for each of these dresses. And in our case, we got nothing! We also discovered that the main reason why our employer went out of business was because Jessica McClintock Inc. had terminated its contract with my employer, after ten years of exclusive dealings. We felt that since Jessica McClintock made the most profit from the dresses we sewed, she should pay us for our work when our boss cannot. So we asked Jessica McClintock Inc. to pay us our back wages.

When Jessica McClintock said no, we held public rallies in front of her stores. We had gone out to rallies wearing masks because we were still afraid of being blacklisted in our community. We would be called troublemakers and have a difficult time finding a job. You see, because we do not speak English and the American society does not recognize our skills, we have no choice but to go back to these dead-end jobs. But instead of listening to our demands, Jessica McClintock called our public rallies "a blatant shakedown" and "intimidation."

Our story is not unique. The San Francisco Bay Area's garment industry is the third largest in this country. There are over twenty-five thousand garment workers in the Bay Area. Eighty percent are women, most of whom are immigrant women like myself. For over a century, immigrant women have been the backbone of America's garment industry. Manufacturers use immigrant women's labor because it is cheap and no one speaks against the awful working conditions. To me this is terrible discrimination against immigrant women like me and my friends. Why else do you think the working conditions of sweatshops have been tolerated over a century? I also heard that attempts to pass reform legislation have been killed by powerful corporate lobbyists and unsympathetic politicians.

These are some realities, violations of immigrant women, which exist in the garment industry that sells fantasy to the public. I never dreamed I would be living this kind of life when I came to America. I hope you can help women like me so the next generation of immigrant women do not have to experience the things that me and my friends do now. Thank you.

---

11 Manuel Ortiz worked as a farm laborer in Texas and, for a time, lived inside an unlocked tomb of a cemetery. Later he did farm work in California. Like many immigrants from Mexico, he maintains close contacts with his native land, despite his feelings about the United States.

An Illegal Immigrant Contemplates Citizenship (2004)

I came to San Juan Batista [in California] and worked for Hanson Farms for twelve years. I started making two dollars an hour. And when the company closed their door, I was making over eight. That was good for someone with an eighth-grade education.

My father crossed the border as a "wetback," too. He didn't have papers. And he worked in Salinas with this farmer, and the guy helped him fix his papers. My father went back and started fixing papers for the rest of the family.

I have family in Mexico and some of my brothers are working here. Everybody has houses and cows in Mexico, and most of them come here temporarily.

My wife's family went to Chicago, and she was born in Chicago. When the parents returned to Mexico, they had a big dance, and that's where I met her. I also told her that I was coming to work in the United States. Then we went to several dances together, and then we broke up.

The reason that she decided to leave me in the beginning was because I was poor, and the house belonged to my parents, and I had nothing. Then I said to her, "If we get married, we would start saving money and get a home of our own." She believed me this time, and that's why she decided to do it.

Now I own land in Mexico. I have built a home for each one of my kids. I say, "I'm not rich, and I'm not poor, but I'm in between. I have my own home in Mexico. That's why my six kids believe in me." I have bettered myself because I have worked here real hard and made good money.

My wife stays home in Hollister and watches our six kids. My kids were all born and raised here, and they have their friends nearby, and that's why I consider them Americanos, and mostly because they speak English. They feel that they know that their parents and great-grandparents are from Mexico, and that they need to know their ways of living, too. When I go over there, I bring them back videos of the family and show them, and I tell them

Source: From Ellen Alexander Conley, *The Chosen Shore: Stories of Immigrants*, pp. 242–244. Copyright © 2004 Regents of the University of California. Reprinted by permission of the publisher, the University of California Press.

the way I was raised, and they feel that here in the United States education is better than in Mexico.

Everybody, American guys, are friendly and that is fine for me. All the time, "Hi, what's your name?"

"Oh, my name is Manuel, or my name is Williams or something." The Americans are good people to me. My children in school have no problem. Well, some problems from the Mexican guys, but not from the Americano guys.

I taught my kids, you want to meet friends, you look around for an American guy. For me, they're good people. In the school, the guys that got problems are the Mexican guys.

For one thing, my kids, they say, "Oh one guy fought me for a blue jacket." Mexicans that work here are the problem. All the time, I'm telling my kids, "Hey, I don't like for you all the time to be with Mexicans. You tell the friends, 'Hi,' or 'Good Morning,' but do not look for problems."

They said, "Okay."

I ask the teacher, "Hey, my kids are okay?"

"Oh yeah, the kids are all right; your kids are okay."

The first kid went to grade school here and then high school and now to the university in Mexico. He's studying to be a veterinarian.

And the little one maybe will go to the university. The next is a girl, maybe one day she marries. My kids all the time ask me, "One day will you go back to Mexico?"

I say, "Maybe." I don't have money for doing a business here, no house, no business, no land. All the time I pay rent. That is okay for a working man. Over there I've got this house. Nobody pays rent. I've got the small ranch, maybe sixteen acres.

My brother watches the ranch over there. Now I plant alfalfa, corn, and onions over there. It's a good business. Here I work for six dollars an hour, but I like to stay here. I stay here to put my children in school. I tell my wife, every kid speaks English fine.

I prefer the United States because the poor person here lives like a rich person in Mexico. So that's why I like it here. Over there, the poorest people work every day and eat beef one time a week. One family, they've got six kids. They don't have money to buy things. Here, everyday you want to drink a beer or eat beef, you're able to do it, but over there, no. One guy works all day for twenty pesos over there.

I put in the application for citizenship. Immigration says they're going to give me another chance. They sent me an application for U.S. citizenship, and I lost it, so they're going to send me another one to reapply.

My heart is in the United States. There are more benefits for us here than over there. I feel bad saying that, but I feel that the United States has done more for me than my mother country. It is embarrassing for me to say this, but I feel more Americanized.

CONCLUSION

Perhaps you have come to the conclusion that the impact of modern-day immigration is not easy to assess. It is certain that contemporary commentators and historians do not agree about this issue. Likewise, you may also have discovered that other students do not necessarily share your conclusions about it. One reason that ready answers may not be easy to come by, ironically, is our own close proximity to the problem. As time passes, it will be easier to evaluate the impact of late twentieth- and early twenty-first-century immigration on American society. With their own society as a reference point, future historians will be able to trace the long-term influences of contemporary immigration that are as yet unclear to us.

Even the passage of time, though, will not solve another problem regarding any assessments of immigration or its impact on our society. The final impartial judgment on immigration or anything else of historical importance is like a desert mirage: The closer we seem to get, the further it recedes from us. First, as we have seen repeatedly in this volume, historians' views of the past are shaped by their own times. As circumstances change, so, too, do their interpretations. Thus, just as the attacks on September 11, 2001, changed the perceptions of many people about immigration, so future events or trends will no doubt affect views as well. Moreover, much like your own conclusions about immigration, historical evaluation inevitably reflects the values of the historian. Furthermore, as we have seen, history is shaped by the historian's assumptions about historical inquiry itself. Whether expressed or not, all historians' work reflects views about the role of ideology in history, whether history is better written from the "bottom up" or "top down," and the relative importance of economic, political, social, or other factors in shaping the past. Thus, no matter how many years have passed, there will never be a last word on contemporary immigration's impact on American society.

As this chapter clearly demonstrates, however, this does not mean that our historical interpretations do not matter. Conflicts over immigration and the assimilation of people from different cultures are as old as the American republic itself. These issues are obviously still with us. And because they affect us all, we all have a vested interest in how they are resolved. As this chapter also reminds us, debates about these issues often turn on our understanding of the past. Thus, the immigration issue illustrates how those who interpret the past have the power to influence policies today. Whatever future historians conclude about the impact of immigration in our time, then, one thing is certain: None of them will likely deny that the conflicts over it in the late twentieth and early twenty-first centuries stand as a powerful reminder about the importance of historical interpretation.

FURTHER READING

Aviva Chomsky, *They Take Our Jobs! And 20 Other Myths About Immigration* (Boston: Beacon Press, 2007).

Ruben Martinez, *The New Americans* (New York: The New Press, 2004).

Joseph Nevins, *Operation Gatekeeper: The Rise of the "Illegal Alien" and the Making of the U.S.–Mexico Boundary* (New York: Routledge, 2002).

Mae Ngai, *Impossible Subjects: Illegal Aliens and the Making of Modern America* (Princeton: University of Princeton Press, 2004).

Juan F. Perea, ed., *Immigrants Out!: The New Nativism and the Anti-Immigrant Impulse in the United States* (New York: New York University Press, 1997).

Jorge Ramos, *Dying to Cross: The Worst Immigrant Tragedy in American History* (New York: HarperCollins Publishers Inc., 2005).

David M. Reimers, *Other Immigrants: The Global Origins of the American People* (New York: New York University Press, 2005).

_____, *Unwelcome Strangers: American Identity and the Turn Against Immigration* (New York: Columbia University Press, 1998).